Teaching Science in the Elementary School

Teaching Science in the Elementary School
Second Edition

John W. Renner
>University of Oklahoma

Don G. Stafford
>East Central State College and University of Oklahoma

William B. Ragan
>University of Oklahoma

Harper & Row, Publishers
New York, Evanston, San Francisco, London

To All Those Elementary School Teachers Who
Have Allowed the Authors to Participate in Their Classrooms

Teaching Science in the Elementary School, Second Edition
Copyright © 1973 by John W. Renner, Don G. Stafford, and William B. Ragan

Standard Book Number: 06-045384-2

LIBRARY OF CONGRESS CATALOG CARD NUMBER: 72-86368

Contents

Preface   *vii*

1 | *The Dimensions of Science*   1
2 | *Science and the Ability to Think*   35
3 | *The Child*   55
4 | *The Elements of Inquiry*   105
5 | *Essential Science Experiences: Observation, Measurement, and Experimentation*   136
6 | *Essential Experiences: Data Interpretation, Model Building, and Prediction*   173
7 | *Teacher Responsibilities in an Inquiry-Centered Science Program*   204
8 | *The Inquiry-Centered Classroom Environment*   234
9 | *Curriculum Models*   251
10 | *Evaluation in Science Education*   292
11 | *The Future*   323

Appendixes

Appendix A | *Research in Formal Operations*   341
Appendix B | *Overview of Concepts Found in Science—A Process Approach*   350
Appendix C | *Selected Readings*   364
Inquiry, Children, and Teachers   364
Teaching and Expanding Knowledge   370
The First-Grade Scientist   374
The Central Purpose of American Education   379
Piaget Is Practical   394

Index   403

Preface to the Second Edition

Since the appearance of the first edition of this book in 1968 many changes have taken place in elementary school science, and this edition reflects those changes.

Various elementary school science curriculum projects have been completed or discontinued; the Science Curriculum Improvement Study (SCIS), the Elementary Science Study (ESS), and SAPA (Science—A Process Approach) are among those projects that have been completed. These projects have provided three distinct curriculum models that are beginning to make their influence felt in schools around this country and in many foreign countries. All three are aimed at a common purpose—to lead the child to develop intellectually. SCIS, ESS, and SAPA have influenced publishers and other producers of elementary school science materials, but most important, they have had a tremendous impact upon the type of science education courses that future teachers take. This book has been developed for such courses.

A second influence felt since 1968 in education is that of Jean Piaget. Piaget's basic theses about intellectual development and of how learning takes place have been available for a long while. American education, however, chose to turn a deaf ear to those from Geneva, not unlike the way many earlier had turned deaf ears to John Dewey. Within the last few years, however, the findings and hypotheses of Piaget have been listened to by a wider and wider circle. The SCIS group, for example, used Piaget's intellectual development model as a guide when preparing that curriculum. Piaget's concept of conservation reasoning is being investigated for its possible utility in such areas as reading and social science. The educational population in this country, in particular, has awakened to the uses to which Piaget's concepts can be put.

The role of the teacher in the classroom, the broadening acceptance that schools do not exist just to transmit information to learners, and the changing role that evaluation occupies are among those topics that, we believe, have changed since the first edition of this book was published. We have given special attention to all these changes on the educational scene. The book, consequently, has undergone a *major* revision. We hope you approve.

We are grateful to all those publishers and authors who have permitted us to reproduce their materials. Thanks are also due to Oklahoma City and Norman, Oklahoma, public schools and the Science Curriculum Improvement Study for permitting us to use their illustrations. Thanks are also extended to our students and others who offered constructive criticism to the first edition.

You will note that throughout the book you are occasionally asked to respond in writing to a special situation. Please do this. The only opportunity authors have to teach by inquiry from the printed page is for the reader to get involved by responding to particular situations. Have a pleasant, profitable set of inquiries.

John W. Renner
Don G. Stafford
William B. Ragan

1 | The Dimensions of Science

As a teacher you assume the responsibility of leading children to those learnings that will enable them to become intelligent, happy, productive people. The tools the society and the school have provided you to accomplish that task are curricula. You must, therefore, examine every element of the curricula from the frame of reference of its usefulness in assisting you to discharge your responsibilities.

Science is certainly no exception to the foregoing. But before any discipline within the curricula can be so clinically evaluated, the evaluator must understand what that discipline really is. Then, and only then, can he make judgments about that discipline's usefulness in a classroom. Attempts are not made, for example, to teach computer design in the first grade because such subject matter is not suitable or usable at that educational level. But what from the several disciplines can be used to educate children at various educational levels? Or more particularly, what can science contribute to the education of children? Before that question can be answered, another must be asked and answered. What is science? Is it the facts and generalizations about the physical world and all the organisms in it? Is it knowing what gravity and DNA are? Is it being able to apply mathematics to a series of data from an experiment and arrive at the answer? Or is science the *solving* of a problem to arrive at *an* answer? Is science answers or is it questions? Or, is it both?

What Is Science?

Science, broadly defined, is what those who are generally recognized as scientists and those who study scientists say it is; and, it is what those scientists do when they practice their profession. Using this frame of reference, consider some definitions of science:

Science deals with the collection of information about natural phenomena. (Courtesy Science Curriculum Improvement Study, University of California, Berkeley.)

1. "The object of all science is to coordinate our experiences and bring them into a logical system."—Scientist, Albert Einstein[1]
2. "The task of science is both to extend the range of our experience and reduce it to order."—Scientist, Niels Bohr[2]
3. ". . . science . . . teaches the value of rational thought, as well as the importance of freedom of thought; the positive results that come from doubting that the lessons are all true."—Scientist, Richard P. Feynman[3]
4. "Science is man's attempt to explain natural phenomena." —Historian of science, Duane Roller[4]
5. "Science is the investigation and interpretation of events in the natural physical environment and within our bodies."—Science educator, Willard Jacobson[5]

[1] Verne H. Booth, *Physical Science* (New York: Macmillan, 1962), p. 151.
[2] Ibid.
[3] Richard P. Feynman, "What Is Science," *The Physics Teacher*, 7 (September 1969), 313–320.
[4] From a lecture, Historical Patterns in Science, given by Dr. Duane Roller, University of Oklahoma.
[5] Willard Jacobson, *The New Elementary School Science* (New York: Van Nostrand Reinhold, 1970), p. 6.

6. "Scientists are primarily discoverers and interpreters of information about nature."—Science-oriented organization, National Society of Professional Engineers[6]
7. "A scientist is a person who must have the primary goal of understanding nature and enlarging knowledge without regard for any immediate practical use."—Science-oriented organization, American Society of Civil Engineers[7]

Although each of the seven definitions is somewhat unique and contains elements and shades of meaning not found in all, there is also a discernable pattern of ideas common to all. Some of these ideas expressed or implied are:

Science has to do with *direct experience* (investigation and/or observation) with natural phenomena and *collection of information.*
Science has to do with *organization,* and *interpretation of information* collected by logical means.
Science has *creative* aspects since it attempts to *explain* and extend experience beyond the direct sensory and to *understand* nature or all phases of the environment.

The foregoing definitions of science also contain certain implications concerning the nature of science. Those implications are:

Science Has a Dual Nature. On the one hand science is a dynamic reservoir of explanations of natural phenomena contributed by scientists and generally accepted by the scientific community as "best yet" or "reasonable" explanations or "models" of nature. On the other hand, science is the testing, refinement, and exploration of generally accepted models of nature and the search for new models or explanations.

Science Has a Cumulative Nature Individual scientists do not usually begin anew in each effort to gain an understanding of natural phenomena; rather, they build on or attempt to reconstruct existing knowledge.

Science Has an Aesthetic Nature. This was beautifully stated by the French scientist Poincaré:

The scientist does not study nature because it is useful; he studies it because he delights in it because it is beautiful—of course, I do not speak of that beauty which strikes the senses, the beauty of quality and appearances; not that I undervalue such beauty, far from it, but it has

[6] *The Function of the Engineer and the Scientist* (Washington, D.C.: National Society of Professional Engineers, November 1962), p. 1.
[7] Ibid., p. 5.

nothing to do with science; I mean that profounder beauty which comes from the harmonious order of the parts and which a pure intelligence can grasp—intellectual beauty is sufficient unto itself, and it is for the future good of humanity, that the Scientist devotes himself to long and difficult labor.[8]

So science has many natures. But how are all of those natures wound together by practicing scientists? Furthermore, how does what practicing scientists do relate to what the practicing teacher does in the process of teaching children? In science, data are needed to answer questions, and the data needed here can be found only by examining how scientists actually work. The works of three outstanding contributors to science have been selected for examination.

Before inquiring into what science really is by examining the work of scientists, stop and consider what you think science is. Make a careful, written outline of your thoughts.

Case study number one

In the year 1854 the University of Lille in the northern part of France employed a 32-year-old man as dean of sciences and professor of chemistry. This might seem to be an excessive amount of responsibility for a man of this age, but this was no ordinary young man. At age 25, while working for his doctoral degree, he had found a solution to a problem in the field of crystal structure which had escaped some of the finest scientific minds of the day. His name was Louis Pasteur.

Until his acceptance of the position at Lille, Pasteur had been a "pure" scientist, that is, he had not been concerned with the practical applications of his findings. Many people believed that the type of mind which functioned successfully in the field of pure science could not perform successfully or happily in the field of applied science. Not so, said Louis Pasteur, "There are not two different kinds of science; there is science and there are the applications of science."[9] Shortly after his arrival in Lille Pasteur set out to prove his hypothesis.

To explain why Pasteur approached the problem in Lille we must go back seven years, to 1847, when Pasteur was but 25 years old. He had just begun thinking about the research work that would be neces-

[8] Jules Henri Poincaré, *Foundation of Science* (New York: Science Press, 1929), p. 18.
[9] René Dubos, *Pasteur and Modern Science* (Garden City, N.Y.: Doubleday Anchor Books, 1969), p. 41.

sary to the completion of his doctoral degree in chemistry at the École Normale Supérieure in France when he heard a lecture describing the work of a German chemist, Mitscherlich, on the characteristics of certain crystals.

After long and critical study of the crystals[10] (call them crystals A and B) that were formed during the process of wine fermentation, the German had announced that those crystals were alike in every way which he as a chemist could examine them except in the way they treated polarized light[11] that passed through them. Mitscherlich's work showed that crystal A rotated[12] the polarized light (turned it from the path it was following when it entered the crystal) and that crystal B did not.

These statements by an established chemist bothered the young Pasteur, and caused him to demonstrate what is probably the most basic characteristic of a scientist—curiousity. How, he probably asked himself, could two crystals be exactly alike in every chemical property and yet not treat polarized light in the same way? This was not logical; Pasteur was sure that there had to be some chemical differences between these crystals.

Pasteur had just performed two tasks that any scientist must perform at some time during his work; he had provided himself with a well-defined problem (why do crystals A and B treat polarized light differently when they seem to be chemically identical?), and he had advanced a probable answer—an hypothesis—to the problem. (These two crystals must have some basic structural differences because it is not logical to think that two chemicals can be alike in every way except the way in which they treat polarized light passing through them. The difference in the interaction between the crystals and polarized light must come from some basic chemical difference.)

---

10 These were the crystals of tartaric and paratartaric acid.

11 Light from any source, say, a light bulb, moves out from it in all directions. There are, however, certain kinds of materials which will let light move in only one direction, e.g., up and down; when this happens the light is said to be *plane polarized*. Polarized light is very useful in many experiments because it lets the experimenter have definite control of it.

12 When light is plane polarized, we can think of it as moving like this:

Direction the light wave is vibrating ⟶ Direction the light wave is moving

Notice that the light vibrates at a right angle (90°) to the direction the entire wave is moving. When the plane-polarized light is rotated, the angle between the direction the light *wave* is moving and the direction the light is vibrating is less than 90°.

Notice that Pasteur had a reason for his hypothesis; it was not just a blind guess.

The young scientist decided that he would investigate this problem and see whether his beliefs and the data he would collect were better than Professor Mitscherlich's generalizations. Now you must remember that Mitscherlich had devoted a great deal of time and hard work to the study of crystals and this particular problem. He undoubtedly possessed much more factual material about the crystals than Pasteur did. In fact, at this point, Pasteur knew nothing about these particular crystals. He did not have at his command many of the facts about the problem he was undertaking that other chemists in Europe had at their fingertips. In other words, experts in the field of study would have said Pasteur's "knowledge" of this field was so limited that he would not be able to contribute to it.

This latter point often makes elementary school teachers reluctant to teach science in their classrooms; they do not believe they "know enough" science to teach it to children. What these teachers are really saying is that they don't know enough of the formalized facts of science to be able to communicate them to children in encyclopedic fashion. These teachers have selected as their primary reason for teaching science the acquainting of children with the facts of science. There can be no doubt that the facts of science are important, but is the acquisition of those facts the most important reason for its study? Are the facts of such importance that a classroom teacher should build his students' entire educational experience around them? Had Pasteur confined his work to those areas where he possessed adequate factual information, his problem would never have been solved.

When a scientific problem is to be solved, the investigator must first know what the problem is. Pasteur had already defined his problem. He knew precisely what it was he wanted to investigate. His next task was to isolate all the specifics he could about the problem. He already knew of the work of Mitscherlich; that was the basis for the hypothesis he had advanced. So this left him with only one other source of information—the crystals themselves.

Pasteur was a skilled laboratory chemist and had already acquired through his previous inquiries a great deal of information about the field of chemistry. This is one aspect of the cumulative nature of science. Knowledge gained through previous exploration which is applicable to the current problem can and should be used. Using the information and his skills Pasteur prepared nineteen samples of the two crystals. These had to be his only sources of information—no one else could help him, he was on his own! What did he do? He observed! He spent many hours studying the two types of crystals under his microscope and his hours were fruitful. He discovered "a fact which had escaped the attention of other observers."[13]

When you look at a crystal—a diamond, for example—you notice that it has many small, plane surfaces. These surfaces are called "facets." Pasteur observed that on the A crystals all the facets were in the same position. Upon study of the B crystals he found that on some the facets were oriented just like the facets on the A crystals. But he also found that on many B crystals the facets were placed in exactly the *opposite* position to the facets on the A crystals. Here then was a basic, fundamental difference in the two types of crystals which Pasteur's logic told him should be there, one that had not been detected in all study by others. Pasteur had found it in a relatively short period of intensive study. The men who had studied similar crystals before Pasteur had as much, and no doubt more, experience with them as he. We cannot, then, attribute this basic "find" of Pasteur's to the fact that he "knew more," that is, possessed more encyclopedic factual knowledge, about basic crystal structure than had his predecessors. The young scientist had acquired the abilities of critical observation, comparison, and classification and these were among the talents he brought to his crystal study that made it possible for him to find what others had not found. In addition, he looked at the particular problem in a way that other investigators had not. He examined the crystals with regard to his hypothesis that a structural difference existed in them.

This discovery of the different orientation of facets on the crystals had given Pasteur a specific point to investigate. He had already found a fundamental difference in his crystals, and he had not as yet used what Mitscherlich had stated as the only fundamental difference between crystals A and B, that is, what happened to polarized light as it passed through them. When Pasteur passed polarized light through an A crystal, it rotated the light in one direction (let's say to the right), and when this light was passed through a B crystal whose facets were on one side (say, the right), it rotated light in exactly the same way as had crystal A. When light was passed through a B crystal whose facets were on the other side (say, the left), it rotated the plane of polarized light in that direction. This direction was, of course, exactly opposite to the direction in which the B crystal, whose facets were on the right, had rotated the light. Next Pasteur mixed all the right and left crystals of B and let polarized light pass through

[13] Dubos, op. cit., p. 26.

Working with the whirlybird from the SCIS unit Subsystems and Variables *is exciting and provides motivation for further exploration. (Photo courtesy Science Curriculum Improvement Study, University of California, Berkeley.)*

the crystalline mixture. If light first went through a crystal which bent it to the left and then one which bent it to the right, it finally emerged from the crystals without being bent at all. This is what Pasteur found. He then could sum up his work by saying that the German chemist Mitscherlich was not correct when he stated there were no fundamental differences between crystals A and B except the manner in which they treated polarized light.

But Pasteur's goal was not to prove that Mitscherlich was right or wrong. It was to solve a particular problem and in so doing he made a discovery. This discovery was thrilling to Pasteur; he met an associate of his in the hall and said, "I have just made a great discovery. . . . I am so happy I am shaking all over. . . ."[14] Motivated as he was, the 25-year-old Pasteur at that moment would have probably tackled any problem in science which he even vaguely understood.

If pupils in the elementary school could be provided the kind of motivation Pasteur had, they would see that learning is fun! You probably think that children cannot be expected to discover anything that is new, different, or original—and you are right. But think of the world that surrounds a child which is known to his teachers but not

14 Ibid., p. 28.

to him. If we lead him to discover this world, *what he discovers will not be original or new to us, his teachers, but it will be new and original to him.* Think also of the fun he will have in discovering his world and of the mental abilities he will use in his discoveries. Like Pasteur, your pupils will have to utilize the process of observation to carefully compare and classify basic information about the world around them in order to synthesize a satisfactory explanation for what they find, just as he compared and classified basic information about crystals in order to explain why crystal B did not rotate plane-polarized light.

Why is the example of Pasteur's discovery about these crystals important to you as a teacher of elementary school children? Most assuredly this example does *not* represent content that you are expected to teach children! The example of Pasteur's discovery is of importance to those of us interested in the educative process because of what it demonstrates. Let us look critically at what Pasteur did.

1. He identified his problem.
2. He stated his hypothesis; but note he had a *good reason* for stating the hypothesis—it was *not* a blind guess.
3. He observed the objects in which he was interested to obtain data he could classify and compare. He then searched for a pattern among those data which would let him synthesize an answer to his problem. This was really a time when he refined his general hypothesis to one that was specific enough to subject to rigorous tests.
4. He then submitted his refined hypothesis to the most rigorous of tests; he tested his own laboratory findings. We stated that he mixed the crystals to see if those which rotated polarized light to the left and the right would, when mixed, let light pass straight through unrotated.
5. From all of these data, he arrived at his generalization which made him so happy he was "shaking all over."

These are the processes that Pasteur used to make his first discovery, and that we would use to provide children meaningful learning experiences. But if we generalized from one case (one piece of data) that educational activity based on these processes would be good for children, we would be acting in a very *unscientific* manner. Let's investigate the solutions of other scientific problems.

Early in this chapter, we stated that Pasteur had been confronted with his first opportunity to apply the practices of the pure scientific laboratory to practical problems when he arrived at the University of Lille. One of the principal industries in Lille was the production of alcoholic beverages and, shortly after his arrival, Pasteur was called upon by Monsieur Bigo, who produced alcohol by the fermentation of beet juice. Bigo told Pasteur that in the process of producing alcohol there were many times when it became contaminated with unknown substances. According to Bigo, there was no satisfactory explanation for this contamination; the process of manufacture had been carried out in essentially the same manner each time, but nevertheless, in many cases, the alcohol became so contaminated it could not be sold.

Pasteur had spent his prior years in the study of basic chemistry, and particularly in the study of crystals. He had absolutely no understanding about the process of alcoholic fermentation. He did have, however, the curiosity that distinguishes a scientist, and the problem that Monsieur Bigo presented him with was an intriguing one.

The fact that Pasteur did not know anything about the problem he was undertaking points out very clearly where the practice of hypothesis formation fits into the scientific process. Notice that we have not said that Pasteur stated an hypothesis to the problem; it would have been imprudent for him to have done so because he did not as yet know anything about it. Many times teachers of science urge pupils to formulate an hypothesis before they know anything about the problem. This is an extremely unwise educational procedure because it encourages wild guessing, and it is most certainly unscientific. Science has seen people who could look at a particular situation and immediately see the exact problem and a solution to it. Such "intuitive leaps" are rare in science and are reserved for the Newtons, the Boyles, and the Einsteins.

Most progress is made in solving problems in science *or any field* not by giant strides but rather by inching from one known fact to the next. After enough information has been gathered about the problem, the data are inspected to see whether or not a pattern of results can be seen. This pattern of results is the basis for the formulation of an hypothesis. A clearly stated hypothesis can and must be verified (or denied) by subjecting it to rigorous tests under conditions that are like those surrounding the problem being investigated. Pasteur did not form an hypothesis to the problem with which he was presented because any hypothesis at this point would have been a *pure guess*. In the previous example, Pasteur did state a general hypothesis immediately on hearing the problem because he had a reason based on his experience as a chemist. Hypotheses are always based on experience with a problem; without such experience an hypothesis cannot be stated. Hypotheses are creative leaps of the mind as it "sees" a pat-

tern emerging from the mass of factual data and an underlying structure in nature which produces this pattern.

When Pasteur was working with crystals A and B, his original
hypothesis was that two crystals that were chemically identical could
not treat polarized light differently. As he worked with this problem,
he refined that hypothesis to state that the differences in the way
crystals A and B treated polarized light were due to the way their
facets were oriented. Such is the mental process of hypothesis formation—information about the problem must be available before a logical hypothesis regarding the problem's solution can be formulated.
Many times, scientific articles give a completely erroneous impression
about when the hypothesis to the problem emerged because it is one
of the first statements made in the article. The scientific investigator
did not, in all probability, state his hypothesis first. He probably
worked for some time before he was in a position to state the hypothesis that appears so prominently at the first of his paper. Why then
does he place it there? Probably to show other skilled scientists immediately the synthesized results of his work. When teaching children,
however, we must remember that they are not skilled scientists and
do not think as such. Rather, pupils in the elementary schools are
there to learn *how* to formulate possible solutions (hypotheses) to
problems, and this will be done *only* if the teacher leads them to
develop correct procedures in hypothesis formation. Pasteur did not
form a discrete hypothesis to the alcohol fermentation problem for
almost three years. But let us return from the elementary school class
room to the problem that Monsieur Bigo had given Pasteur and see if
the procedural pattern Pasteur had followed in his crystals problem
will be repeated here.

Since Pasteur knew little about the problem, he had to go to the
source of it, the alcohol factory, and learn. He spent a great deal of
time at the factory and observed everything he could, but he was
specifically interested in the product—fermenting beet juice. He took
samples of the product back to his laboratory and continued his
observations with his microscope, collecting all the data he could by
carefully describing and drawing diagrams of what he saw. As
Pasteur studied the fermenting beet juice under the microscope he
saw particles of yeast, but this was not unusual because these had been
seen by investigators before him. At this particular time such noted
chemists as the German Justus von Liebig and J. J. Berzelius of
Sweden were convinced that yeast was just a very intricate chemical
material that was present for the sole purpose of bringing about the
conversion of sugar into alcohol without taking part in the reaction

itself.[15] But in addition to the yeast particles, Pasteur also saw some other structures that did not look like yeast. These puzzled him because he had no idea what they were. The young investigator had acquired enough information to make it necessary to ask some questions but not enough as yet to form an hypothesis.

One of the most trusted axioms of learning is that we learn in terms of what we already know and understand. What a person "sees" is probably influenced by the way he looks at something, that is, his frame of reference and probably the degree to which his language system is developed. His frame of reference, however, is a result of previous experiences and understandings. This can also be said of a person's problem-solving approach. The approach proved successful in the past will very likely be used again. In teaching children science, this must never be forgotten. An idea is born, an hypothesis is advanced, or a problem is identified and framed in terms that the child (or the investigator) understands. Pasteur was no exception to this axiom. He had achieved great success in his work with crystals by studying their treatment of plane-polarized light. He put samples of the fermenting beet juice in his polarimeter (the instrument used to study the interaction between polarized light and a crystal) and found that the juice was optically active.[16] Earlier in his career as a chemist studying optical activity Pasteur had investigated whether or not all organic compounds were optically active. Perhaps you know that "organic" refers to living organisms; the dictionary defines "organic" as "of, relating to, or derived from living organisms."[17] For many years chemists thought that all organic compounds were from living organisms. Then, in 1824, the German chemist Friedrick Wohler artificially prepared the compound urea $CO(NH_2)_2$.

Following this discovery by Wohler, chemists became interested in the synthesis of organic compounds, a problem that because of the prevailing paradigm[18] in biology—that organic compounds were produced only by living organisms—had been considered absurd. Since that time thousands of organic compounds have been synthesized.

[15] Whenever a substance is responsible for promoting or bringing about a chemical reaction but does not take part in the reaction, that substance is said to be a "catalyst." This is exactly what the chemist of the mid-nineteenth century thought yeast was.

[16] A material is "optically active" when it rotates the plane of polarized light.

[17] *Webster's Seventh New Collegiate Dictionary* (Springfield, Mass.: Merriam-Webster, 1963), p. 594.

[18] Thomas S. Kuhn, *The Structure of Scientific Revolutions* (Chicago: University of Chicago Press, 1962), p. 23.

From his investigations, Pasteur observed a pattern—organic compounds that were optically active came from living things.

Here, then, was the basis for an hypothesis. Pasteur had found that the fermenting beet juice was optically active and that the alcohol he isolated from the ferment was also optically active.[19] He believed that optically active organic compounds came only from living organisms and inferred that yeast was responsible for the production of alcohol in the fermentation process. What then could he hypothesize? Yeast found during the alcoholic fermentation process and all the other organic substances found during this process (such as the structures he found under his microscope with the yeast) were not lifeless, intricate chemicals that just brought about chemical reactions. Rather, said Pasteur, yeast and the other materials found in fermentation are living things. The sugar is turned into alcohol because it serves as food for these living things, and alcohol is the product given off during the metabolic processes of these living organisms (the yeast).

Here indeed was a revolutionary hypothesis! But notice that Pasteur was careful to have adequate reasons for advancing it. He did not say, "I believe. . . ." Rather, he said, "I believe . . . because. . . ." Pasteur's challenge of such scientific giants as Berzelius and Liebig was at that time about as acceptable as would be a challenge today of Einstein's famous $E = mc^2$ by a completely unknown scientist. For, not only is challenging a highly regarded person in science difficult, challenging a widely accepted model or theory—one that has paradigm status—is also difficult. Such paradigms as the theory of universal gravitation, the Bohr model of the atom, and the theory of evolution are so widely accepted and have become so engrained in scientists' thinking (and teaching) that explorations of nature using those models as guiding principles are considered *normal* science. A solution to a problem that cannot be explained within the prevailing paradigm is frequently rejected by scientists as no solution at all. This respect for established authority in science plays an important role. It is responsible for causing an investigator who would propose a new explanation of phenomena to investigate the problem thoroughly in order to give as much evidence as possible in support of his proposed explanation.

Pasteur had yet to verify his hypothesis and then find ways to solve Monsieur Bigo's problem. But the problem of undesirable wine fermentation would not even have had an hypothesis proposed as its solution had not Pasteur been willing to push out into areas where his

---

[19] The alcohol he isolated was amyl alcohol.

factual knowledge was nonexistent using the same methods of problem solving which had been previously successful for him. Now, however, in order to make his hypothesis acceptable to the scientific community, it must be verified. *Verification*, then, is an important part of the process of science, but it is only a part. It is that part during which the hypothesis, which is based on the facts collected, is rigorously tested with respect to whether or not it really can represent a solution to the problem. During the verification phase of science a particular answer is anticipated. The investigator does experiments, makes measurements, or observes phenomena that will provide him with information to formulate the answer he anticipates. Much science teaching in today's schools resembles the description just given of verification. The experiences the children have consist of studying the already known facts and then doing some type of an "experiment" to verify that what they have "learned" is true. That procedure is a part of the total picture of science, but *only a part*. The importance of verification to the progress of science can be seen by considering the hypothesis of Monsieur Pasteur that fermentation is a process caused and carried on by living things.

One thing on which scientists generally agreed at the time Pasteur proposed his hypothesis was that there are certain characteristics that distinguish living things from nonliving. Two of these characteristics were that living things can be made to grow by properly feeding them and can be moved from place to place. If fermentation is caused by living things, these two criteria must be satisfied. Pasteur knew this and began to search for evidence that would satisfy himself as well as the critics. He needed a source of material which was readily available and in which fermentation takes place rapidly. Milk is such a material. Pasteur knew that milk soured (fermented) rapidly if left at room temperature for a period of time. In addition to being a material in which fermentation occurred rather rapidly, milk was readily available for experimentation. Pasteur also knew that the sugar in the milk was converted to lactic acid during the fermentation process, producing the characteristic sour taste of acids. Pasteur showed that the lactic acid ferment in the sour milk consisted of a great many microscopic organisms that looked alike. He also showed that by feeding these organisms milk sugar they increased in number and that, if he moved the organisms to a new sugar solution, lactic acid was produced very rapidly. He had, therefore, demonstrated that the two criteria had been satisfied—the organisms increased by feeding them, and they could be moved to a new place and demonstrate their metabolic process in their new environment.

There is, however, another point that must be raised here. A fire, which is a chemical reaction, will also satisfy the criteria in question. Once a fire is burning it will keep burning if it is fed. Furthermore, fire can be moved from place to place and continue to burn if the environment is right. We cannot know whether or not Pasteur and/or his critics concerned themselves with our fire example, but they did concern themselves with two other questions. They asked, "Where do these microorganisms come from?" and "If the microorganisms are living things, why can't they be killed?" What then had Pasteur accomplished by working with sour milk? Only this—that his microorganisms were found in places other than in fermenting mixtures which produced alcohol. He also established that the undesirable effects in fermenting beet juice were caused by organisms other than yeast, because yeast globules were always found in connection with fermentation which produced "healthy" alcohol, and the unknown organisms were found only when the fermenting beet juice had become contaminated. Pasteur also found unknown microorganisms in fermenting milk. From his evidence Pasteur concluded that yeast was a living plant that produced alcohol, and the other, unknown life was the "culprit" that must be eradicated. Still to be faced, however, was the problem of where this undesirable form of life came from and how it could be killed.

Pasteur figured he had learned enough about the fermentation process to establish firmly that it was not a chemical process as all the scientific giants of his time thought but was, instead, a biological process. In 1857 he published his results. Just slightly more than two years had passed since he began working on a problem about which he had absolutely no knowledge, and in a field (fermentation) in which the authorities had concluded that the problems had a definite explanation. Most certainly, then, the conclusion can be drawn that Pasteur was a success in his studies of fermentation not because of his encyclopedic knowledge of the field. Something else, then, was responsible for his success. It was Pasteur's ability to isolate a problem, gather information about it, state an hypothesis, and then verify it. Let us see how Pasteur verified his hypothesis that fermentation is caused by living things by answering the questions relative to what the microorganisms came from and how they could be killed.

In 1857 Pasteur returned to the institution that had granted him his doctorate, the École Normale Supérieure in Paris, and there is where he finally solved Monsieur Bigo's problem. In the summer of 1858 Pasteur was vacationing in that part of France in which he had grown up (Arbois), where he had many friends who had well-stocked wine cellars. He studied many different kinds of wines (Bordeaux, Champagne, Burgundy, etc.) and without exception he found that in the good wines there were only yeast cells, whereas in the defective wines there were other microscopic cells mixed with the yeast cells. These were exactly the findings he had made when he had examined the fermenting beet juice, and finally the alcohol, from Bigo's distilling plant.

Pasteur was not content with confining his attention to wine; he knew that beer and vinegar were closely related to wine, so he studied them also. If his hypothesis was valid, the microscopic cells should be found in them too. This illustrates another facet of Pasteur's problem-solving techniques and one that is common to scientists. He looked around for similar situations in which his hypothesis could be disproved. Here is a characteristic that has been completely missing from science teaching in the elementary schools. We have not given pupils the opportunity to state hypotheses and then see if they could disprove them. We have been so concerned with making sure the pupil "got the right answer," that we have not given him the opportunity to have the learning experience of disproving (or proving) an hypothesis. The learning activities that the child has been permitted to have, have been aimed at "doing" the problem, not "solving" it. Any time a pupil advances an hypothesis which to him explains a problem he should be immediately asked, "Can you disprove your hypothesis?" This procedure will show whether the pupil has obtained a functional understanding of the concepts he is using to solve the problem, or if he has just memorized a lot of miscellaneous information about it which he can mentally spew forth at any time. "Fact-spewing" science courses do not provide a child with the kinds of learning experiences he must have to be able to state and then prove or disprove hypotheses. In fact, they give him only one kind of experience—memorization; and as important as memorization is to the education of a child in science, it is *secondary* to the learning that results from actual hypothesis formulation and testing. Through this activity the child learns how much his understanding of a problem really advances if his hypothesis is a correct one, and how rapidly he will be able to discover his misunderstandings if his hypothesis is incorrect.

The value of disproof must not be overlooked in teaching children. They must always ask, "Can you be shown to be wrong?" and we, as teachers, must learn to accept wrong answers from children not as something to be frowned on but as something to be used to redirect the child's attention toward the objectives of the learning experience.

Children *must* be convinced that teachers are not always looking for what they feel is the correct answer to a question or problem. The learner must be made to feel that we want his contribution to the problem being investigated. We will examine classroom methodology for doing this in Chapter 7.

Pasteur was asking himself whether or not his hypothesis that the spoiling of wine was due to the microorganisms he found with yeast was correct when he investigated beer and vinegar. He was asking a question which if answered No (i.e., the spoiled beer and vinegar did not have the small microorganisms appearing in them) would disintegrate his whole theory concerning the functioning of these microorganisms and render useless all of the work he had done. Here indeed is demonstrated the intensity with which a scientist feels the value of disproof. Pasteur had, with his fermentation experiments, entered a field in which his factual knowledge was virtually nonexistent. Many men in Europe had devoted their lives to studying what Pasteur had undertaken. But in a few short years he had made more progress than they. Why? Dr. John R. Platt summed up why Pasteur succeeded when he wrote: "We praise the 'lifetime of study' but in dozens of cases, in every field, what was needed was not a lifetime of study but rather a few short months or weeks of analytical inductive inference."[20] What Dr. Platt is saying is that problems in science are not to be solved by what he calls "encyclopedism" but rather by trying to disprove the hypotheses in advance with crucial experiments. We must not be afraid to be wrong and we must teach our pupils the value of being wrong. Let's see what Pasteur gained by submitting his hypothesis to the arena of testing.

Imagine the joy the scientist felt when he looked through his microscope at spoiled beer and vinegar and actually saw his newly found microorganisms just as they had appeared in spoiled wine. Here indeed is a great reward for the self-discipline which must be imposed if an idea (i.e., optically active compounds come only from living things) is to be turned into an hypothesis (i.e., the spoiled wine was caused by living things) and finally verified when subjected to the rigor of possible disproof. *This same joy of discovery will be felt by the pupils if they are allowed to discover the facts, principles, and generalizations of science for themselves and are not fed these interesting and important concepts by the teacher.* Remember that the discoveries that pupils make are not meant to be original discoveries. Teachers should not be nearly as interested in what the child learns

[20] John R. Platt, "Strong Inference," *Science* (October 16, 1964), 351.

as we are in *how* he learns it. Even with his joy of discovery, however, Pasteur now faced an even bigger problem than he had faced before—how could he rid the wine of these microorganisms?

The many marvelous applications of exploration and identification of the problem, statement of hypotheses, design of experiments to gather information to exclude some of the hypotheses, selection of a tentative solution to the problem, and subjection of that tentative solution (really a refined hypothesis) to the rigor of disproof which Pasteur made will not be discussed in detail. He did find that when wort (a mixture of sugars often used as the basis for starting beer), which contained the microorganisms, was heated, pure yeast added, and the entire mixture protected from the air, the resulting beer was free of spoilage. This told Pasteur two things—*where* those microorganisms come from, and *how* to get rid of them. From these experiments the process of pasteurization was developed and was applied not only to alcoholic beverages but also to milk. Pasteurization of milk has saved untold lives and human suffering; this was a "bonus" to the principal problem he began to solve.

Pasteur's statement that the microorganisms came from the air attacked one of the basic beliefs of the day which many scientific experts thoroughly and completely embraced; that is, spontaneous generation. The theory of spontaneous generation states that living microorganisms can arise without parents in such materials as the fermenting beet juice Pasteur encountered in Monsieur Bigo's alcohol factory. We shall not devote the time or space to exploring how Pasteur disposed of this belief, but his work in this field is the epitome of problem identification, experimentation, hypothesis formation, and submission of findings to the possibility of disproof.

The experimenter we have been studying for the past few pages had indeed devised a method of problem solution which surpassed that of any scientist of his day and of most since. Or as John Platt describes him,

> Every 2 or 3 years he moved to one biological problem after another, from optical activity to the fermentation of beet sugar, to the "diseases" of wine and beer, to the diseases of silkworms, to the problem of "spontaneous generation," to the anthrax disease of sheep, to rabies. In each of these fields there were experts in Europe who knew a hundred times as much as Pasteur, yet each time he solved problems in a few months that they had not been able to solve. Obviously it was not encyclopedic knowledge that produced his success, and obviously it was not simple luck, when it was repeated over and over again; it can only have been the systematic power of a special method of exploration.[21]

21 Ibid., p. 351.

This "special method of exploration," then, is what Pasteur would say represents the dimensions of science—those mental processes by which a problem is analyzed; an experiment is imagined; an hypothesis is synthesized; experimental results are classified, compared, analyzed, and evaluated; generalizations are formed; and future results are inferred represent what is truly the heart or core of science. Science, according to Pasteur, is a process that uses *products* (facts) and *produces* more products as it progresses. Perhaps here are indications of what science in the elementary school should concentrate on if the pupils are to really *learn* it.

So far the work of only one scientist has been examined, but perhaps this is a good time to pause for reflection and comparison.

Compare the ideas you listed previously with how the working procedures of Pasteur described his understanding of what science is. Be sure to list any points we have expressed with which you disagree.

Case study number two

Henri Antoine Becquerel was an unusual man with an unusual heritage; his father, Alexandre Edmond Becquerel, and his grandfather, Antoine César Becquerel, both had been famous scientists. But neither his grandfather nor his father distinguished himself in the field of science as Henri did. Henri was particularly interested in luminescence—the property some materials have which allows them to shine brightly when they are exposed to light.[22] During the last few years of the nineteenth century, Becquerel had been experimenting with some uranium compounds and had noted that they had the property of luminescence. About this same time a German scientist named Wilhelm Röntgen discovered x-rays and stated that he believed they came from a luminescent spot on the wall of a cathode tube.[23] Immediately Becquerel thought that if x-rays came from the luminescent wall of a cathode tube, they could come from the luminescent uranium compounds he had been studying. He knew that x-rays exposed a photographic plate which "was wrapped with two sheets of black paper, so thick that the plate was not clouded by

[22] If a material continues to give off light after the source of light has been turned off, the material is said to have the property of "phosphorescence."

[23] We shall not pursue Professor Röntgen's researches, but those accounts are fascinating examples of how a true scientist works. The cathode tube which Röntgen was using was called a "Crookes tube" after its inventor, William Crookes. If you are interested in the functions and/or construction of a Crookes tube and why and how Röntgen became interested in it, see J. G. Feinberg, *The Story of Atomic Theory and Atomic Energy* (New York: Dover, 1960), chaps. 7 and 8.

exposure to the sun for a whole day."[24] Becquerel then set a piece of the uranium compound upon the carefully wrapped plate and placed them both in the sun. After a short time he took the plate and the uranium indoors and left the uranium on the wrapped plate for a short while. Within the same day, he carried the plate into the darkroom, unwrapped it and developed it. Becquerel was delighted when he found the outline of the piece of the uranium compound upon the plate. He knew that light could not penetrate paper and expose the plate. He reasoned that the sun caused the uranium to give off x-rays and expose the photographic plate. Becquerel hypothesized that he had discovered a real, plentiful, and easily obtained source of x-rays.

But scientists do not change hypotheses into generalizations until they have sufficient data to allow a pattern of results to form. Becquerel needed more data. In late February 1896 he prepared another plate and was going to place it in the sun when he discovered it was a very dark, sunless day. Becquerel carefully placed the plate in a drawer and set the chunk of uranium on top of it. After several days Becquerel decided to develop the plate to determine if the compound held any of the luminescence it showed in the sun. He was quite expecting a faint outline of the chunk of uranium to appear on the plate, but imagine his surprise when he found a very excellent silhouette of the uranium! This awareness of an *anomaly*, an outcome contrary to what the investigator expected or to what the prevailing theory of the day predicts, is frequently the prelude to discovery.[25] Perhaps, thought Becquerel, the rays did not come from the sun at all! Perhaps the rays that exposed the photographic plate came from the uranium itself.

To test that hypothesis Becquerel placed a crystal on a photographic plate and put them both in a darkened room. After the plate was developed, the image of the uranium sample was clearly visible. From all available data, Becquerel concluded that the rays which exposed the photographic plate were given off by the uranium completely independent of the idea of luminescence. Becquerel had to conclude that the energy which exposed the photographic plate must come from the material itself. What an idea! Imagine a piece of material that could give off energy without any apparent reason for doing so! This was a discovery that would revolutionize the thinking of the scientific world. We shall investigate immediately how this

[24] Morris H. Shamos, ed., *Great Experiments in Physics* (New York: Holt, Rinehart and Winston, 1959), p. 212.
[25] Kuhn, op. cit., p. 52.

would take place, but first let us see what Becquerel did which might give us deeper insight into the nature of science.

Becquerel compared his work with the work of another (Röntgen) and from this comparison he found a similarity. This similarity caused him to state an hypothesis that not only could x-rays be developed the way Röntgen had developed them but that they were also given off by the luminescent materials he had been studying. Becquerel had a firm reason for stating his hypothesis. His statement was not a guess; rather, it was a logical, reasoned summary of the data from his own experiments and those of Röntgen. This summary had one quality that is unique to hypotheses—it was open to investigation. Further, notice that Becquerel's investigations caused him to consider a second hypothesis. In other words, Becquerel had a multiple hypothesis approach to his problem. Having more than one hypothesis for a problem has certain advantages. T. C. Chamberlin states that working from a single hypothesis "becomes a controlling idea."[26] To avoid becoming controlled by a single idea, "the method of multiple working hypotheses is urged." Chamberlin explained why his method of multiple hypotheses is superior to a single hypothesis this way:

> The investigator at the outset puts himself in cordial sympathy and in parental relation (of adoption, if not by authorship) with every hypothesis that is at all applicable to the case under investigation. Having thus neutralized the partialities of his emotional nature, he proceeds with a certain natural and enforced erectness of mental attitude to the investigation, knowing well that some of his intellectual children will die before maturity, yet feeling that several of them will survive the results of final investigation, since it is the outcome of inquiry that several causes are found to be involved instead of a single one.[27]

So far our study of Becquerel has shown that he considered science to be problem location, hypothesis formation, investigation, and interpretation of the results. Dr. John R. Platt states that the solution of problems in science consists of

> . . . applying the following steps to every problem in science, formally and explicitly and regularly:
> 1. Devising alternate hypotheses;
> 2. Devising a crucial experiment (or several of them), with alternative possible outcomes, each of which will, as nearly as possible, exclude one or more of the hypotheses;

[26] T. C. Chamberlin, "The Method of Multiple Working Hypotheses," *Science*, 148 (May 7, 1965), 756. (Originally published in the February 7, 1890, issue of *Science*.)
[27] Ibid.

3. Carrying out the experiment so as to get a clear result; I') recycling the procedure, making subhypotheses or sequential hypotheses to refine the possibilities that remain; and so on.[28]

Science as practiced by two research experts, and summarized by a third begins to take definite shape as primarily a mental process-centered discipline. Learning science in the elementary school is learning the processes by which the scientist accumulates, organizes, and interprets information, much more so than learning the patterns or generalizations already found or explanations already given (products) by other scientsts.

The facts used by the scientists in our discussion so far were used in the process as a means of moving from one portion of the unsolved problem to another. These facts were not the end point; the scientists did not want to know the fact for the sheer joy of knowing it (although there is a great deal of personal pleasure in the sheer joy of knowing), but because knowing it helped them in the solution of a problem. But in order to have a complete and accurate description of how scientists use facts, we must have more information about that subject. Let us then look at an example of another scientist at work to ascertain whether or not the process-centered approach we have seen in the examples thus far considered continues to be evident, and to see whether or not there is a pattern in the way facts are found, used, and discarded.

Case study number three

The work of Becquerel attracted the attention of a Polish chemist who was working in Paris with her French husband. Her name was Marie Sklodovska Curie. At this time in her illustrious career (1897), she was studying for her doctorate and was seeking a problem which she could submit as the research requirement for the degree. As she tells the story,

> My attention had been drawn to the interesting experiments of Henri Becquerel on the salts of the rare metal uranium. Becquerel had shown that by placing some uranium salt on a photographic plate, covered with black paper, the plate would be affected as if light had fallen on it. . . . My husband and I were much excited by this new phenomenon, and I resolved to undertake the special study of it.[29]

[28] Platt, op. cit., p. 347.
[29] Arthur Beiser, ed., *The World of Physics* (New York: McGraw-Hill, 1960), p. 1450.

Becquerel had shown that the rays coming from the uranium crystal could neutralize something which was electrically charged. This was the point at which Marie Curie began her research. She, too, found that the radiation could neutralize electrical charge. Using this fact and combining it with the recently proposed idea that the atom was concerned with electrical charge, Marie Curie began to synthesize an hypothesis that the energy which radiated from the uranium compound came from the atoms of one of the elements of that compound. The hypothesis was a daring one because at that time atoms were thought to be tiny, hard, indivisible spheres. If an atom gave off energy, there would seem to be doubt that these atomic spheres were indivisible.

Here we see one of the supremely important qualities that a scientist must have—the ability to formulate an hypothesis based on the logic of the data he has available. In other words, to state what he believes is not enough for a scientist; he must be able to justify what he believes is a logical conclusion from the data. If you will carefully think through the qualities that are desirable in an excellent citizen, you will immediately conclude that he, too, must know why he believes as he does. If he is going to be able to decide how his vote should be cast and then be happy with his decision (whether he wins or loses), a citizen must not only hold beliefs but also know why he holds those beliefs. The field of science offers children excellent opportunities to gain experience in stating hypotheses based upon what they are able to find out about a problem, but they must be allowed to have such experiences before they can profit from them. The Educational Policies Commission states that science does indeed represent a curriculum area which can influence the social development of a learner, since the spread of science promotes respect for the role of reason in human affairs by demonstrating the power of the mind when used in accordance with the spirit of science. There is a tendency to be suspicious of absolutes, a respect for tentativeness, a kind of working skepticism.[30]

Marie Curie had stated an hypothesis—the radiation coming from the uranium compound was coming directly from one or more of the atoms in that compound. But the question was, which one? Using her talent as a chemist she found that the uranium atoms were the ones which were giving off the radiation. As Madame Curie put it, "Any

---

[30] Educational Policies Commission, *Education and the Spirit of Science* (Washington, D.C.: NEA, 1966), p. 4. EPC defines the spirit of science as the "spirit of rational inquiry." Ibid., p. 1.

substance containing uranium is as much more active in emitting rays, as it contains more of this element."[31]

This was a unique property of an element. Since it had happened in one element, the investigator asked herself if it would happen in other elements. After a search of many other minerals, Madame Curie found that materials which contained thorium also behaved in a like manner; that is, they gave off radiation just as the uranium compounds did.

At this point, Marie Curie decided she had found all the known elements which emitted these mysterious radiations and so she asked herself the next very obvious question. What are these unknown rays that have been located really like?[32] She gathered together many materials which radiated these mysterious rays and found that they always contained uranium or thorium, but she also found an unexplained bit of information. One of the minerals, pitchblende, was several times more radioactive than an equal quantity of pure uranium was. Here, indeed, was a problem which had not been anticipated. After careful consideration of all the information at her command, Madame Curie hypothesized what was the only logical explanation. She stated that she believed that in many of the minerals she had investigated there was a completely unknown substance which was causing the minerals to have "an activity three or four times greater than that of uranium."[33]

If the pattern of action which Marie and Pierre Curie followed during their investigation to find the "hypothesized substance"—as Madame Curie called it—is examined, an important aspect of how a scientist works and how science should be taught emerges. When they began their search they did not know any of the chemical or physical properties of the hypothesized substance. All they knew was that it emitted rays, which they had to work from. They also knew that the unknown substance was found in the radioactive part of pitchblende. So they began with what they knew and extracted the radioactive part of the pitchblende.

This example should be heeded by all who propose to teach science to elementary school children. Children are not able to intellectualize about a problem or a situation. They must be provided with the opportunity to begin their learning of science in reference to concepts about the world. When a new year is begun, the experiences to be

---

[31] Ibid., p. 146.
[32] Marie Curie gave these mysterious rays a special name. She thought of the rays as being "radiated" out from the material and as being very "active." She called them "radioactive."
[33] Beiser, op. cit., p. 146.

provided for the child must begin as a reflection of what has been accomplished the previous year. Do not misinterpret this last remark. We are not saying that you need to know what specific facts the children have been exposed to—they probably would not remember them anyway. Rather, ask yourself what experiences they have had; for learning occurs in young children only through experience. We shall devote an extensive amount of space to desirable science experiences for children later in this book. A curriculum based upon this reflective procedure is, of course, best for those children who do not transfer schools; it is difficult for those pupils who do. But in designing a system for the teaching of science in the elementary school, one must be designed that has the best possible educational foundation; teachers then can be concerned about providing help for the transfer student and others who do not fall within the prescribed pattern. The procedure being recommended—that is, always building one science experience on a previous one—finds its greatest applicability in moving from one activity to another and in interpreting a finding in a late part of an investigation in terms of a finding in the early part of the investigation. Here is often the clue that a skillful teacher uses to assist a child over a difficult spot in interpreting what an observation, a measurement, or a particular piece of information means; that is, the pupil must be urged to think of what he already knows about the problem.

Marie and Pierre Curie thought about what they already knew and, as a result, they extracted that part of the pitchblende which was radioactive. As they studied this isolated material, they observed the element bismuth, but accompanying the bismuth was another element with well-defined chemical properties and which was about 400 times as radioactive as uranium. This new element Madame Curie named polonium in honor of her native country, Poland.

The Curies had started with the facts that Becquerel had described in his discovery—certain crystals containing uranium-radiated activity. From this they moved to the finding that the element thorium also acted in a similar manner. From the fact that the radioactive materials could expose a photographic plate, the Curies began the study of these rays which culminated in the discovery of a new element.

Notice that in their investigation the scientists used facts at every step, but the facts were not treated as though they should be revered. The facts were used to state hypotheses, to gather information, and to generalize, but the facts used or discovered were not an end in themselves—only a means to an end.

One of the most important aspects of learning how to learn is to

All the data gathered in an investigation must be examined.

internalize that every possible approach to a problem and all the data gathered must be examined. If the Curies had not done this they would have missed the discovery for which they are best known. In separating the radioactive material from the pitchblende, the element barium, in addition to bismuth and polonium, was also separated. The barium had not been especially considered during the investigation of the bismuth, and the investigators turned their attention to that pitchblende residue. What they found astonished (and probably delighted) them—the barium was much more radioactive than the polonium. The Curies knew, however, that barium is not radioactive. They concluded that the residue from the pitchblende, "although for the most part consisting of barium, contains in addition a new element which produces radioactivity and which furthermore is very near barium in its chemical properties."[34]

Because this new element they had found was so intensely radioactive, they called it *radium*. Pierre and Marie Curie knew that the radium must be contained in the residue left when uranium was

[34] Gerald Holton and Duane H. D. Roller, *Foundations of Modern Physical Science* (Reading, Mass: Addison-Wesley, 1958), p. 660.

extracted from pitchblende. They asked the Austrian government if they could have one ton of this residue from the uranium plant at St. Joachimsted in Bohemia. They worked for nearly four years distilling, crystalizing, and redistilling the pitchblende residue, and finally they isolated about 1/300th of an ounce of radium, although it was not entirely pure. (The pure metal was not isolated until 1910.) But their hypothesis had been correct. There was indeed a radioactive element mixed with the barium which was much more intense than the radiation from polonium or uranium. The highest award that a scientist can receive is the Nobel Prize, and in 1903 Becquerel and the Curies were jointly awarded the prize for physics in recognition of their work in the discovery of radioactivity. Marie Curie was awarded the 1911 Nobel Prize for chemistry, for the discovery of polonium and radium and for the preparation of pure uranium. These awards are testimony to the fact that their recipients had found the proper perspective of facts in science.

These investigators had taken the facts they knew, defined the problem in terms of these facts, stated an hypothesis in terms of the facts, and finally stated their findings in terms of the facts. But notice that at no time during this entire process did any of the three scientists (or Pasteur) treat the facts they were using as end points. When accepted ideas did not explain the problem (e.g., the accepted idea in Pasteur's time that yeast was a chemical substance), the scientists whom we have investigated did not hesitate to cast them aside and hypothesize new ideas that explained the results of an experiment or an observation that had been made. Facts are meant to be used in this way—that is, to ask questions with and about, to use in designing the solution to a problem, in stating an hypothesis, and in generalizing about the data which the experiment or observation provided. Facts are *not* meant to be memorized, revered, and savoured; *they are meant to be used!* Too often in teaching science we forget this and treat the facts of science as though memorizing them will gain for children an understanding of what science is and what power it has.

There was a time in the development of science when the idea that the fact was the all-important item was widely accepted. In 1836 the French chemist Jean Baptiste André Dumas stated that hypotheses were just "pretty guesses" and the road of science should lead men "on to fact!"[35] This reverence for facts says that a collection of factual knowledge is power and that "to know" is what is important. The examples of the scientists which we have studied do not support

[35] Feinberg, op. cit., p. 38.

this position. The scientific work that has been examined can be characterized as, Can we use what we know to prove what we do not know and, if what we know cannot be used to prove the unknown, is there indeed something wrong with what we know? Facts, then, are keys, keys to unlock the door of the unknown. But keys are meant to be used and, if they are not, those doors behind which lies the explanation of the unknown will remain locked forever.

Unfortunately, in too many science courses taught in our schools and colleges, the attitude just expressed is not shared. These courses present the learner with the significant, established facts of a given area and assume that when these facts have been mastered, the discipline of science has been "learned." The facts of science represent conclusions and so any course or textbook which presents only the significant facts of that particular discipline is presenting to the learner a rhetoric of conclusions. Such an experience is an important one in reading but, as we have seen science practiced, is hardly a significant learning experience in science. As you proceed with your study of science for the elementary school child, remember that the facts of science are important as long as they are used, but they are unimportant as ends in themselves. Studying only the facts (or products of science because facts are what science produces) of science gives the child a very distorted view of science because facts are only the working materials of the scientist.

Furthermore, what represents the facts of science today may not be regarded as facts tomorrow. In other words, facts change and, if only the facts of science are taught, the educational residue which the learner has left when those facts change will not be very valuable. Since he did not learn how or why the facts he learned were accepted as facts, he does not have the ability to replace the now obsolete facts with new ones. He has then only learned some interesting vocabulary.

If science is not facts, what is it? Our study of four scientists allows an answer to that question to be advanced. At the end of our study of Pasteur the tentative conclusion was drawn that science was a special method by which a problem was analyzed; an experiment imagined; an hypothesis synthesized; experimental results classified, compared, analyzed, and evaluated; generalizations formed; and future results inferred. The works of Pasteur, Becquerel, and the Curies seem to confirm that science is principally a mental process by which problems are solved, in which facts are used in producing the solution, and which produces facts as a result. The facts that are produced as a result of the processes of science often are the explanation of the motivation of the scientist. Most scientists agree that "they are motivated by a compelling desire to search for truth simply as an end in itself. . . . The primary purpose of science has little to do with weapons or washing machines; it is just to know and to understand."[36]

In teaching science, the desire to know and understand, must be aroused in children and this can only be done if they are provided with opportunities to investigate. For this is where scientists fulfill this desire to find out; this is where they have the opportunity "to explain a complexity of facts by a simplicity of causes."[37] This is the motivation which a scientist has, that is, the *opportunity to explain* what he does not know. That motivation sustained the Curies for four years while they labored to separate radium from the residue left when uranium was extracted from pitchblende; such deep motivation sustained Pasteur while he sought to prove that living organisms, not inert chemical forms, were spoiling Monsier Bigo's fermenting beet juice. The search for the fact is often back-breaking labor (in the case of the Curies), but the ultimate joy of explaining the unknown which can be at the end of the road is motivation enough to sustain scientists.

If finding the factual answer to a problem is so motivating, why, then, is not the teaching of the discovered facts also motivational? It can be, but presenting facts that are already known to the student as the only side of science does not make use of one of his innate characteristics—the desire to investigate. In every person there is a natural inclination to investigate; if scientists did not have this natural bent, they would not recognize a problem when they encountered one. A child (or an adult) cannot develop the ability to recognize problems and follow through to a solution unless he has the opportunity to participate in investigative activities. Without the ability to use the processes of science (problem-solving skills) neither learner nor scientist will ever be able to profit from the true experience which Doctor Vannevar Bush calls "the sheer joy of knowing."[38] Science, then, provides as its principal contribution to man's understanding of the universe certain mental processes that assist in solving the problems of that universe. (If you put an interpretation on the word "universe" which is broader than the natural universe, the applicability of science in other areas becomes evident.) These processes represent the true dimensions of science and can be described as methods of working

[36] Russell Fox, Max Garbundy, and Robert Hooke, *The Science of Science* (New York: Walker and Co., 1963), p. 3.

[37] Ibid., p. 3.

[38] Vannevar Bush in C. L. Strong's *The Amateur Scientist* (New York: Walker and Co., 1963), p. 3.

which " 'lead to certain distinct habits of mind' and is of prime value in education."[39] Such "habits of mind" can be developed by the study of science if developing understanding of its processes rather than its products is concentrated upon.

Major Processes of Science

From studying the samples of scientific investigation included here, you can immediately see that not all individual scientists work in *exactly* the same manner. The exact procedures (or methods) of science cannot be discussed. But there are certain major mental *processes* which every practicing scientist goes through sometime during any investigation. Every scientist, however, has his own specific time in the investigation for using each major process. We contend that experience with and the acquisition and understanding of these processes by children represent the major educational values to be derived from the study of science. These major processes are:

1. *Problem identification and hypothesis formation.* In an elementary school classroom the teacher will normally select those educational experiences which will lead a child to realize that he is faced with an unfamiliar situation; in other words, the teacher in developing the pupil's understanding of science as a process will confront him with a problem. This procedure will probably not (and perhaps should not) happen all the time and at all grade levels; pupils must be given significant experiences in observing and translating their observations into communications before problems can be stated. There are times, however, when kindergarten or elementary children can recognize a problem. A group of first graders was confronted with a collection of seedlike materials and asked what they were. Some of them said, "Seeds," and others said they did not believe the irregularly shaped objects were seeds. Which ones were seeds? Here was a group of children with a problem which they could understand and for which they could design a series of experiments. There are times, however, when problems in the early elementary grades are not formulated so easily. Here, also, was a time when an hypothesis could be immediately stated because of the past experiences of the children. But hypothesis formation must not be pushed at children; they must feel they are ready to make an estimate of what the solution to a problem might be. The age at which a child can be expected to hypothesize will be discussed later in this book. This procedure demands that the child have a reasonable acquaintance with the problem before he states an hypothesis; guessing without reason has little (if any) educative value

[39] Platt, op. cit., p. 350.

and should be discouraged. Science, then, has as one of its principal processes problem identification and hypothesis formation.

2. *Experience has proved that the data which experiments and observations provide in one instance would be repeated if the experiment or observation were repeated.*[40]   Children must be taught to classify and compare data which come from their observations and experiments. This assumes that if a learner repeats his observations and/or experiments that he will again get the same results. The child must discover that when a pattern does not evolve from the comparison of data from two or more experiments, perhaps his hypothesis is incorrect, his problem is not well defined, or his investigation is not extensive enough. The learner must develop the understanding that the laws governing the universe function with precision and regularity; that is, nature is not capricious. Those of us who attempt to use data to establish and interpret those laws are often inadequate to the task. Samplings may be inadequate or we may be sampling from different "funds" of information which Nature holds, but we must have faith that if we provide the same set of conditions in any given situation the same data will be collected from that situation. The most important task of the teacher is to lead children to discover order and pattern among a seemingly chaotic collection of information. The teacher must believe that children will neither develop the belief that their data can be replicated nor learn to interpret data if they are not allowed to have actual experience in replicating data and interpreting those data

3. *Beliefs that arise from the interpretation of data must be verified.*   To collect, classify, compare, and interpret information is not enough. After a pattern develops among data which suggests a solution to a problem, that hypothetical solution must be verified.[41] A set of conditions similar to those under which the data were gathered must be provided and the solution to the problem (which the data originally gathered suggested) must be once again found in the data delivered by the second experimental (or observational) situation. Verification must always precede generalization.

4. *The hypothesis when verified is a general solution to the problem.*   There is an inherent danger in this portion of the scientific process; children can gain the impression that science is composed of

[10] Several of the items which appear in this section of this chapter have been heavily influenced by Ernest Nagel, "Major Items in the Process of Science," *Theory into Action in Science Curriculum Development* (Washington, D.C.: National Science Teachers Association, 1964).

[41] Just as no two scientists work alike, no two teachers work alike. Experience in working with children has shown the authors that the children best learn the nature of an hypothesis and its formation if they are encouraged to formulate it at this point. Waiting until this point in a learning exercise to formulate an hypothesis also serves to discourage wild guessing.

a series of general solutions to problems; that is, science is an enterprise which can be completed. The impression must be left with the learner that the general solution to one problem is only the introduction to the next. In other words, the pupils must be made to understand that "Science is an ongoing and cumulative enterprise, in which the answers to one set of specific problems may acquire great importance because of the light those answers throw on a large class of other problems."[42] This cumulative nature of science allows scientists to develop comprehensive conceptual schemes (models of nature) to explain natural phenomena and into which individual solutions to problems concerning a limited aspect of nature can be incorporated and interpreted. Experience in formulating conceptual models to explain patterns or regularities and a familiarity with the major conceptual schemes already developed through the cumulative work of scientists constitute valid objectives of science education. The achievement of those objectives needs to begin in kindergarten with problems and materials which the child can operate with. Those problems and materials must become more complex as the thinking of the learner develops. As the child progresses through the school system and becomes familiar with the conceptual schemes of science, he will begin to feel that he understands his environment. Evidence abounds to support our hypothesis that the majority of today's citizens do not understand our environment.

There are, no doubt, many ways in which the primary educative values of science can be stated with equal validity. The foregoing four points represent one such statement. In 1966 the Educational Policies Commission made an equally valid statement of the educational gains which are to be derived from the study of science. That organization described its beliefs in the following manner:

> The schools should help to realize the great opportunities which the development of science has made apparent in the world. They can do this by promoting understanding of the values on which science is everywhere based. Although no particular scientist may fully exemplify all these values, they characterize the enterprise of science as a whole. We believe that the following values underlie science:
> 1. Longing to know and to understand
> 2. Questioning of all things
> 3. Search for data and their meaning
> 4. Demand for verification
> 5. Respect for logic
> 6. Consideration of premises
> 7. Consideration of consequences.[43]

[42] Nagel, op. cit., p. 31.
[43] Educational Policies Commission, op. cit., p. 16.

The spirit of science can be caught only through investigation.

If you compare the foregoing statement with the four major processes of science developed in this book, you will immediately see that these two sets of criteria almost completely overlap each other. Each set of criteria has, however, "the defect that neither individually nor jointly do they provide a fully adequate guide to action."[44] The two foregoing statements—that of the authors and that of the Educational Policies Commission—represent the broad, general dimensions of science. How each of them could contribute to the educative process has been described.

Several questions must, however, be answered before we can conclude that the area of science can and/or should be included in the educational pattern of a child. If science is to be taught it must be taught within the framework of our schools. If, then, a learner has experience with the processes of the scientific enterprise, this experience must enhance his achievement of the purposes for which schools exist. Are, then, the purposes of the present educational structure and the outcomes which can be attained by the study of science compatible? In order to answer that question we must look carefully at why we have schools.

[44] Ibid., p. 16.

Teachers must never forget they are teachers of *children*, and the content that teachers select to assist a child in achieving the purposes of education must be suitable for the child to study. A child needs to have learning experiences that match his physiological, emotional, and intellectual maturity. When can a learner be expected to state reasonable and logical hypotheses? During what period in the intellectual development of a child should the teacher expect him only to make observations and report what he has seen? What types of data-handling techniques can be expected of the various age groups? Do the contributions which science can make to the education of children match their characteristics and provide operational answers to the foregoing questions? The answer to that question will be found only by a careful examination of the physical, emotional, and psychological characteristics of the child.

If any academic area is to be included in the elementary curriculum, it must have certain specific objectives. What would such objectives be for elementary school science? Before that question can be answered, the previous questions posed must be explored. These topics will all be examined in subsequent chapters.

2 | Science and the Ability to Think

Most American citizens spend the majority of their first 18 years in school. Within the last thirty years, the number of persons seeking education beyond the twelfth grade has sharply increased. But not only is the amount of time which our citizens devote to education increasing, the amount of material resources which are poured into the nation's schools is also rapidly rising. The fields of publishing, film production and equipment, and apparatus manufacture are but a few that depend heavily on "the school business" either partially or completely for their existence. The teaching population represents one of the largest common interest groups in our country and the common professional organization for teachers, the National Education Association, is the largest professional organization in the world. In addition to the NEA, most discipline and special interest groups within the profession operate their own unique educational organizations.

When all of these facts are examined, there can be no doubt that the American educational enterprise constitutes a major concern of the citizenry of the United States. So important is that enterprise that those within the profession must consistently address themselves to the question "Why do we have schools?" because only if the responsibilities of schools are examined from within the profession can a course of action for continuance of a program, or a change in purpose and/or direction be implemented. What, then, is the purpose (or purposes) for having schools?

A determined group of English settlers arrived on the eastern shores of this country in 1620. There is no doubt that informal and neighborhood education went on during those years immediately after the Pilgrims landed, and the first elementary school was opened in New York (Nieuw Amsterdam) in 1638. In 1642 what is now the state of Massachusetts passed the first law in the Western Hemisphere which required that children be taught to read and write. In 1647 Massachusetts required every town of over fifty families to establish a school to accomplish the task of teaching children to read and write. The first residents of this country were a very religious group, and the law of 1647 is often called the "Old Deluder, Satan" law. It was so named because these early American citizens felt that if children could read the Bible, they would be better equipped to cope with that "Old Deluder, Satan."

If you were to trace the historical development of the American public school, you would find that many of the laws and customs which have shaped it have been no more a part of a general educational scheme than was the Old Deluder law. The history of American education also reveals that many important educational decisions were based on expediency rather than on a sound, farsighted educational philosophy. But as William McElroy, director of the National Science Foundation, has stated: "Today's education must now be geared to the needs of the individual throughout his life, as he lives it in a changing, science-based society."[1] Perhaps the pressures on society in the early centuries of this country were not as great as they are today. But regardless of the reason, the schools of this country have not been built to serve the future; they have evolved to suit the present. John W. Gardner stated this entire concept neatly when he said, "The somewhat blind evolutionary process of the educational past is no longer suited to the needs of our fast-changing society."[2] What Gardner is saying is that we can no longer afford the luxury of not knowing where our schools are headed. We must know in what direction we are going and, what is more important, why we are headed there. In short, we must know what the purposes of American education are.

We can not simply evaluate the effectiveness of our schools by judging how the capabilities of our children compared to those of children of the same age a century ago or in another country. We must educate our children not only to live in a science-based, rapidly-changing society, but a society in which each person bears the responsibility of government by the people. Does this not make the purposes of American education somewhat unique?

[1] William D. McElroy, "Science, Society and Education," *The Bulletin of the National Association of Secondary School Principals*, 54 (May 1970), 25.
[2] John W. Gardner, "National Goals in Education," *Goals for Americans* (Englewood Cliffs, N.J.: Prentice-Hall, 1960), p. 100.

Commonality in Education

Whatever educational direction we choose, that direction leads us toward the mental, physical, and social development of the learner. If these three types of development are examined, it will be seen that they are not mutually exclusive.

Suppose, for example, that we make the assumption that the child's physical development can proceed independently. Under the authority of the school and teacher, the child can be made to perform the type of exercise and eat the kind of food that will provide him with a reasonably healthy body (assuming, of course, that his body does not have organic defects). If, however, he does not develop an understanding of and proper mental attitude toward physical health, what he does outside the school environment can detract from, if not completely frustrate, the attempt of the school to develop him into a sound physical specimen. An even more serious consideration is what will become of this learner when he has completed his education or reaches a point in that experience where physical activity and education are no longer demanded by the school. If during his education the learner has not developed a reasoned approach toward physical fitness, when he is left to make his own decisions his body is likely to suffer.

A type of logic identical with the foregoing can be applied to the social development of children. Teachers and schools can impose a definite code of behavior upon pupils and enforce that code. Or, in other words, children can be *made* to conform to behavior standards that are not their own. Frequently the quiet classroom is thought of as being the classroom where children are learning and have learned to get along with their peers. In many cases the only reason that the classroom is quiet and children are not having severe differences of opinion is that the teacher will not permit it. Learners in a situation such as this have not been allowed to develop an understanding of or a mental attitude toward the importance of living with other people. The school has provided a code of behavior for the children—they did not need to develop their own. When these young citizens leave the schools, they lose the behavior standards they have been living by, and the insecurity that accompanies such an event often causes severe problems. And why shouldn't problems develop? These learners must now provide themselves with a basic mental attitude which should have been developed in school; they must now develop an understanding of what they must do for their fellow human beings in order to be treated as they wish to be treated. From a series of nonsupervised learning experiences (often painful and sometimes fatal) these young members of society collect information (data) that will ultimately enable most of them to develop behavior patterns, based upon reason, that are not offensive to society. The crime rate among young adults is evidence that not all of them develop such reasoned behavior.

So even if the educational enterprise were to put its primary emphasis on the physical and social development of pupils, its results would be less satisfactory if those pupils did not simultaneously develop their mental facilities—the intellect. The concept of mental capacity, the mind, in education is "not unlike that of a keystone in an arch: the whole structure depends upon it; remove it and all collapses."[3]

We can, therefore, conclude that regardless of the educational direction we select, we will be abruptly confronted with the inescapable truism that any educational process must be directly concerned with the mental development of the learner and how this mental development must take place. And on this latter point, the conduct of an individual's mental development, there is a wide divergence of opinion because "not everyone agrees on the basic nature and function of the mind."[4]

What is the mind and how does it function? The first part of that question, what is the mind, is a very broad, philosophical, and in many respects, theological question that is clearly beyond the scope of this work. Our purpose here is to develop an understanding of the function schools are to perform, and we have seen that that function is clearly tied to the notions of mental development. Clearly, then, our attention must be confined to the latter part of the introductory question—how does the mind function? On that question there are today, and have been for many years, two clearly defined schools of thought. For want of better "labels" we shall call these positions the "classical" and the "modern."

The Classical Position on Mental Development

If you were to explore fully the position of the classicist on mental development, you would encounter such scholastic giants as Plato, Socrates, Thomas Aquinas, René Descartes, John Cardinal Newman, and, to a degree, Robert Hutchins. The thoughts and writings of the

[3] C. J. Brauner and H. W. Burns, *Problems in Education and Philosophy* (Englewood Cliffs, N.J.: Prentice-Hall, 1965), p. 28.
[4] Ibid.

classicists seem to center around two cardinal notions—the mind as substantive matter, and truth.

The classical tradition holds that the human mind at birth is an intellectual void with a certain degree of potential, and whether or not that mind reaches its potential depends upon how it is educated. The purpose of education, then, according to the classicist, is the training of the mind. Serious contemporary scholars of education would, no doubt, accept this basic classical purpose of education; the fundamental differences between the two positions rests in *how* that purpose is accomplished.

Adherents to the classical position view the mind as "something" to be developed, and, consequently, they accept that such development requires exercise. In other words, the mind, says the classicist, is like a muscle and, as with most muscles, the best method of developing it is with exercise. The traditional school, therefore, made wide use of subject matter that required the learner to perform intellectual gymnastics. Many times these mental gymnastics were extremely intricate and, from a traditional point of view, these intricacies were desirable exercise for those whose minds were being developed. Euclidean geometry, Greek, and other such bodies of subject matter are extremely necessary in this form of education because they require the learner to use his best intellectual-gymnastic ability. In short, the classical position on mental development is that the mind is a muscle that is developed, strengthened, and toned by mental exercise, and such mental exercises develop the potential powers of reason which are inherent in every human organism.

The development of the implicit powers of reasoning in the human being represents the first step on the road to achieving true mental discipline. The second step is stocking the mind with definite, unquestionable knowledge that represents absolute and final truth. It is in this second step, and the relationship of this step to the first one, that the classical and modern schools of thought find their primary divergence. But in order to allow ourselves to understand this divergence fully, we must first investigate the point of view of the classicist with respect to what knowledge is to be used for the "mind-stocking" process.

That knowledge which is of the greatest importance, according to the classical position, is metaphysical (intangible, or abstract) rather than empirical. Information gained empirically is useful, says the classicist, but is of considerably less importance than that knowledge which results when the powers of pure reason are applied to abstract problems. The type of knowledge which is best to stock the human

Empirical information is of vital importance to the mental development of children.

mind with is that which is known to be "ultimate truth." The position of the classicist has been summed up succinctly as, "Denigration of sensory experience, empiricism, and empirical knowledge in favor of pure reason, rationalism, and metaphysical knowledge is the bench mark of classicism."[5] Simply stated, the classicist does not feel that man can come to a complete understanding of the world around him by using only his own senses and information gained empirically. There are self-evident truths known to man which are independent of his own ability to reason, and these ultimate truths represent the type of knowledge with which the mind should be stocked. When the well-trained mind (one that has had the proper "exercise") is placed in contact with proper knowledge, the person who can function in all types of situations will emerge. This is the position taken by college teachers who spend their contact hours with students lecturing them about the generalities of a subject or supervising students who are following cookbook-type directions in a room called the "laboratory." That teacher firmly believes that once the learner has the facts he will be able to remember and use them when he needs them. The classi-

[5] Ibid., p. 35.

cist's educational philosophy can be summarized as teaching is telling, memorization is learning, and being able to repeat something on an examination is evidence of understanding. The primary goal of the traditionalist is the transmission of information.

The traditional position on education does not seem to take into account that the development of the mind and the mind-stocking process can go on simultaneously. If the classicist recognized that position, he would be admitting that sensory experience could provide empirical knowledge which represents proper material with which to stock the mind. This admission would place empirical knowledge on a par with metaphysical knowledge, and this equality the traditionalist is not willing to accept. Some classicists do advance the argument that only a well-developed mind (one that can reason) will know *how* to use the knowledge with which it is equipped. This deviation from the strict, classical position places a higher priority on the development of the ability to reason than on the possession of knowledge. Furthermore, says the left-wing traditionalist, a mind that can reason is capable of attaining knowledge when its utilization becomes desirable or imperative. The majority of adherents to the classical point of view, however, reject this latter position because it emphasizes the *means* rather than the end of having the human mind contain acceptable products.

The dispute regarding how the human being knows what he knows is not new. John Locke, in *An Essay Concerning Human Understanding* (Chapter 1, Section 2), asked the question this way: "Let us suppose the mind to be, as we say, white paper void of all characters, without any ideas, how come it to be furnished? Whence has it all the materials of reason and knowledge?" The traditionalist, even in Locke's era, would say that the materials of reason had to be put there. Today's traditionalist would say that those materials could be put into the mind only after it had been developed. John Locke took quite a different view. He answered his own question with, "To this I answer in one word, from experience; in that all our knowledge is found, and from that it ultimately derives itself." Locke was presenting to traditional education that experience, which produces empirical knowledge, was the essential ingredient in learning. He was not seriously listened to in the seventeenth century, and the present-day traditionalist still believes that education is the process of mind-stocking.

In summary, the classical position on mental development is that the human mind must be well disciplined (have acquired the ability to reason) and well stocked with true knowledge. But of the two components of mental development, the traditionalist believes that the possession of the products of pure reason (not empirical knowledge) should take precedence over the development of reasoning ability. Perhaps this priority of "product" over "process" partially explains the popularity of the lecture as a pedagogical tool and encyclopedia-like textbooks as effective aids to learning. The classicist believes that placing a well-developed mind in proximity with true knowledge is the proper environment for developing a truly educated individual. If the traditionalist does direct his attention to the development of *how* to reason, he has definite factual material "built into" the learning experience which makes using empirical knowledge either unnecessary or partially unnecessary. The classical position on mental development does not accept that stocking the mind can occur as a concomitant outcome with developing the ability to think and reason. To do this the classicist would need to admit that empirical knowledge is of a first-order value; he is unwilling to do this, but the modern position on learning eagerly embraces that knowledge can be gained from sensory experience and empiricism.

Another View of Mental Development

Before the actual position of many contemporary educators on mental development can be fully understood, their most basic disagreement with the classicists must be examined. Because the traditionalist believes that the human mind is an object that can be sharpened, he accepts that it is, as Whitehead expressed it, a "dead instrument."[6] This position is not acceptable to most contemporary thinkers in education; in fact, some denounce it vigorously. For example, "I have no hesitation in denouncing it [the position that the mind is a dead instrument] as one of the most fatal, erroneous, and dangerous conceptions ever introduced into the theory of education."[7] Whitehead, however, did not only denounce the classical view; he firmly stated what he believed the mind to be when he said, "The mind is never passive; it is a perpetual activity, delicate, receptive, responsive to stimulus. You cannot postpone its life until you sharpen it."[8]

The position of most contemporary educators, then, has its roots in the thesis that the human intellect is active and receptive and, if it is

[6] Alfred N. Whitehead, *The Aims of Education and Other Essays* (New York: Macmillan, 1929), p. 8.
[7] Ibid., p. 9.
[8] Ibid.

to be developed, such development must be accomplished through direct, active involvement in those experiences which result in intellectual growth. The types of activities which can be used to produce mental development depend upon the age of the learner and the level of development he occupies. Regardless of his age or level, if development is to take place, the learner must have experiences that engage his active, receptive mind. (How the level of development a learner is occupying can be determined and what that means for the classroom will be the subject of Chapter 3.) The fact that experience is a prominent factor in developing the intellect was expressed by Locke in the seventeenth century and Jean Piaget[9] and John Dewey in the twentieth century. Dewey said that the business of education was to form mental habits and he called that formation the training of the mind. He described those habits as

> effective habits of discriminating tested beliefs from mere assertions, guesses, and opinions, to develop a lively, sincere and open-minded preference for conclusions that are properly grounded, and to ingrain into individuals' working habits methods of inquiry and reasoning appropriate to the various problems that present themselves.[10]

The foregoing quotation demonstrates that most present-day educators are at least as deeply concerned with training the mind as is the traditionalist. There is, however, also contained in the quotation those ideas which clearly show the basic differences between these two positions on mental development. The traditionalist does not accept sensory experience and empirical information on an equal basis with self-evident and/or metaphysical "truth." The modern viewpoint not only accepts empirical knowledge as being valuable, but states that the business of education is to concentrate upon developing *in the learner* habits of inquiry which enable *him* to be able to discriminate between guesses, assertions, opinions, and tested beliefs. That statement tells us that the learner must learn to make such decisions himself. He must, therefore, be given those learning experiences that will demand that he make decisions on the basis of the information he has at hand and not only on the basis of self-evident axioms with which his mind has been stocked. When the learner begins to exhibit such intellectual habits, the contemporary educator regards such behavior as evidence of mental development.

[9] Piaget has also identified social transmission, maturation, and equilibrium as contributing to intellectual development. Those factors will be examined in Chapter 3.

[10] John Dewey, *How We Think* (Boston: Heath, 1910), pp. 27–28.

Simply stated, the primary difference between contemporary and traditional views on mental development is the frame of reference from which the learner reasons. The traditionalist believes that complete mental development occurs only when the sharpened mind is filled with self-evident axioms and facts and those are used as a basis for reasoning. The contemporary position rests on the belief that developing within the learner the ability to discriminate between tested beliefs and assertions, guesses and opinions represents true mental development. Inherent in the contemporary view is the position that individuals must be taught to rely more upon their own sensory experience and empirical knowledge and less upon metaphysical information.

Acquiring Information

Does the view of education held by most present-day educators make provisions for the learner to acquire information? That is the question the traditionalist usually asks when he is questioning the worth of modern educational beliefs. Where is the learner to get the basic information he needs to answer questions he will ask if he is not given such information? Basically, these are questions that involve the curriculum, and they will be explored in depth in Chapters 5 and 6. These questions are, however, inseparable from modern views on education and, consequently, deserve a brief treatment here.

The information that the learner acquires when he is educated in a school adhering to contemporary beliefs is gained simultaneously with the training of his mind. Providing the pupil with educational experiences which allow him to learn how to discriminate tested beliefs from assertions and/or opinions implies giving him those experiences which demand that he consider evidence which has a direct bearing upon some unknown situation. Now this unknown situation must be drawn from some recognizable discipline or, in other words, some established body of content. The task of the curriculum maker is to identify what can be taught from established bodies of content to which age group, and he must be aware that the view of education of most present-day educators strongly supports the thesis that all disciplines have value at all grade levels. Or, as Jerome Bruner has stated it, "We begin with the hypothesis that any subject can be taught effectively in some intellectually honest form to any child at any stage of development."[11] Bruner is saying, for example, that

[11] Jerome S. Bruner, *The Process of Education* (Cambridge, Mass.: Harvard University Press, 1962), p. 33.

science taught in the first grade must be recognizable as science to a scientist. If it is not so recognizable, it is not being taught in an "intellectually honest form." We shall return to the types of science which can be utilized in the elementary school and which represent intellectually honest form, in Chapters 5 and 6.

If, then, the pupil is placed in a curriculum that allows him to collect information about an unknown situation, and to formulate tentative notions, he will most certainly be developing the discriminating mind the modern school is interested in. But also the experiences he is having with content will, simultaneously, be providing him with those pieces of information that he needs to stock his mind. When the learner emerges from such an educational experience, he will have developed his ability to reason (think) and will also have his mind stocked. But the material the learner's mind has acquired will be meaningful and functional because it is the same material that was used in developing in him his ability to think. He has not been asked to postpone the life of his mind until, as Whitehead said, it has been sharpened. The material that has been used to let a delicate, receptive, active mind live is the same material used in the sharpening process. The content which the learner has acquired has been gained (and understood) by his reflecting on what has been done, and from those reflections real understandings of the unknown situation being considered are developed. Reflection on what has been done is an extremely important part of the educative process. John Dewey emphasized this when he wrote, "To reflect is to look back over what has been done so as to extract the net meanings which are the capital stock for intelligent dealings with future experiences."[12] The foregoing quotation from Dewey also delineates an extremely important point—that is, information acquired from a learning situation which emphasizes thinking is usable in "further experiences." Not only is the information itself usable, but understanding the procedures used in gaining such information represents a major educational gain.

When we discuss the possibility of profitably using a given piece of information gained from one experience in another, we are talking about the way in which things are related. To be able to develop in learners the ability to see how seemingly unrelated factors in any given discipline (or between disciplines) are related is leading them to develop a true understanding of the structure of knowledge. Bruner has said, "Grasping the structure of a subject is understanding it in

[12] John Dewey, *Experience and Education* (New York: Macmillan, 1938), p. 100.

a way that permits many other things to be related."[13] But learning material in a manner that will allow it to be used in the future or learning the structure of a discipline will occur only when the mental development and information-gathering processes occur simultaneously. Each of these desirable portions of the general topic called "mental development" is complementary to the other. Where, then, do pupils attending schools that are adherents to the modern theories of education get their information? From those experiences that also provide them mental development.

Freedom of Mind

So far, in our discussion of the responsibilities of schools, we have indicated that education must foster mental development and concurrently equip the learner with an understanding of the structure of the disciplines. The fact that goals must be reached simultaneously has also been established. That these goals represent general direction for the educational enterprise cannot be denied. Yet they do not provide the specific directions that are necessary if daily classroom teaching is going to accomplish them. Furthermore, we have not taken into account the sociological environment in which the schools must function in achieving these general goals. Let us begin, then, delineating specific objectives from our general-direction statements by freely admitting that the schools of this country must serve all of American life—the schools are for all the children of all the people.

To provide educational experiences for *all* the children in this country means that those responsible for the curriculum must consider (in addition to the intellectual side of the educational picture) the physical, emotional, vocational, leisure time, and citizenship needs of the school population. Providing curricula[14] that will enable the learner to achieve goals that satisfy his needs (immediate and long term) while in school represents a tremendous undertaking. The schools do not have the facilities and financial resources to provide such a sweeping educational establishment and, if they did, the learner would not have the time to utilize it. Furthermore, if the school attempted to supply preparation for life which provided for each finite need of our future citizens, it would be setting itself up as a foreteller of the future. Today's educators cannot know the specific needs of tomorrow's citizens and, furthermore, attempting to provide each learner

[13] Bruner, op. cit., p. 7.
[14] We define curricula as "all activities provided and supervised by the school."

with the abilities necessary to make him able to cope with every future problem he will face assumes that learning ceases when the learner leaves school. Neither of the foregoing propositions is true. The schools must *not* attempt to foretell the future, and learning *does* continue after formal education has been completed. If, however, the citizen of tomorrow is going to be able to cope with the future, he must be able to learn from the experiences he has every day. Only when he does this will he achieve his fullest potential and greatest happiness. But if John Q. Citizen is going to learn effectively from his day-by-day experiences, *he must have learned how to learn!* This, then, represents several objectives for the learner toward which the school can lead him, and learning how to learn is certainly compatible with the school providing experiences which lead to mental development. (Possibly learning how to learn *is* mental development.)

But general objectives do not provide the exacting kind of guidance that teachers need in planning pupil learning experiences and when actually engaged in the process of interacting with children, which is teaching. What do you lead the learners to do? *Specifically, in what types of activities should they be engaged?* Answering that question is extremely important because it tells *you* something about *your* educational philosophy.

Please take time to write an answer to the foregoing question because only by involving yourself in this discussion can you have your educational beliefs supported or changed.

The answer to the last question asked, from our frame of reference, is: It depends on what you think is important. If you believe that the most important responsibility of an elementary school teacher teaching science is to transmit the facts and generalizations from the subject matter to the children, the activities that your pupils should engage in are quite clear. You must provide them the opportunity to hear about and see demonstrated every important fact and generalization from the discipline; a textbook is an excellent guide for this type of activity. You are engaged in the mind-stocking process. The person who works with children in the manner just described believes his primary responsibility is the transmission of information about the discipline.

If, however, you believe that the function of the school is, as was stated earlier, to lead pupils to learn how to learn rather than transmit information, you are faced with a different set of responsibilities. Those responsibilities tell you that *by using the content of science* the children in your classes must learn to live in a *free* society. Freedom implies individual liberty to do and think many "things," but perhaps all of these things will be included if we simply say that true freedom provides the individual with *freedom of choice*. But in order for an individual to be able to exercise freedom of choice responsibly and judiciously, he must have developed freedom of mind. Each individual in our society must develop freedom of mind for himself, and the degree to which our society will prosper depends upon how well each citizen develops that attribute. Although the schools cannot develop freedom of mind for an individual, they can provide the conditions under which that development can take place. But what is a "free mind?" What are the criteria which describe a free mind and to which the school experience can make a direct contribution?

If a mind is free it is able to apply certain definite rational powers to the solution of problems and the making of decisions. Those rational powers have been defined as "recalling and imagining, classifying and generalizing, comparing and evaluating, analyzing and synthesizing, and deducing and inferring."[15] The rational powers, then, describe a person who has developed freedom of mind, and they also describe another type of individual because the Educational Policies Commission has defined these rational powers as "the essence of the ability to think."[16] Seeing how studying science can assist in rational power development is not difficult if science is taught as the scientists described in Chapter 1 practiced it and as contemporary scientists practice it, that is, as a form of investigation.

Outline how investigations such as those of Pasteur, Becquerel, and Curie actually demanded that rational powers be used.

There can be no doubt that the individual who is developing his ability to think is moving toward optimum mental development. He will be developing that ability to discriminate between tested beliefs and assertions, guesses and opinions which John Dewey insisted must be developed. He will also be developing that freedom of mind which the citizens of our democracy must have if our culture is to be preserved and propagated. The development of the rational powers of the mind (the development of the ability to think) then represents "the common thread"[17] of education.

Have teachers in the past not striven to develop the ability to think? If one judges by the instructions which are given elementary school children, he would perhaps conclude that "thinking" is a de-

[15] Educational Policies Commission, *The Central Purpose of American Education* (Washington, D.C.: NEA, 1961), p. 5.
[16] Ibid.
[17] Ibid., p. 12.

sirable activity in the classroom. One frequently hears such instructions as: "Now, think before you answer," or "Don't just give me the first answer that comes to your mind, think about the question for a time." The fact is, however, that teachers simply request logical thinking as if it is an innate ability rather than something to be developed. The development of the ability to think will not be accomplished unless, and until, "the school focuses on it."[18] (To date the success of *any* educational system in developing the individual's rational powers has been something less than spectacular.) Here, then, are the specific guidelines which must guide our daily classroom teaching. The development of the individual rational powers within our pupils represents the specific objective toward which our teaching must be pointed. But how does a teacher use this specific objective?

Stating that anything our educational system accomplishes must be accomplished through the curriculum is almost prosaic. But, also, there can be little doubt as to the reality of the statement—curricula represent the tools with which the teacher has to work. These tools must be employed in a manner (methodology) which leads the learner to achieve the purpose for which the school has been established. Let us recognize, then, that *the central role of the school is to develop in children the ability to think, and that curricula must be selected which will allow that responsibility to be discharged.* In addition, methods of employing the proper curriculum must be used which will permit it to make its optimum contribution to the development of thinking ability. If we also accept that the ability to think is defined by the rational powers, we then have specific criteria to guide us in selecting curricula, instructional techniques, and teaching materials.

When units of study are chosen, learning aids are secured, and classroom procedures are decided on, the rational powers represent an important and valuable standard against which to measure their potential effectiveness. Teaching materials and techniques that stuff the mind of the learner without giving him the opportunity to develop some of his rational powers are nearly valueless. Sometimes using purely information-centered materials can be justified because they provide the learner with information which is "nice to know" or make an enjoyable experience possible. Many of the currently available motion pictures provide the learner with nice-to-know information and are fun to watch. School time spent on using such teaching materials can be justified because they provide a change of pace in a school day and they frequently can be used as a culminating experience for a unit of study which has concentrated upon developing rationality.

18 Ibid.

A teaching device, such as film, can pull together in a few minutes all information about a discipline which the learner will have acquired in a few weeks or months of investigation. The actual investigation provided the learner with the opportunity to develop his rational powers and gather a great deal of factual information; the film could easily review and summarize the findings of the investigation for him.

We must not, however, delude ourselves into thinking that providing factual-centered learning experiences *about* investigation substitutes for the investigation itself. Our central responsibility is to lead the learner to develop his rational powers, and only actual investigatory experiences can do that. There is little doubt that frequently 90 percent of the time of the school has been spent upon the development of 10 percent of the rational powers (recall), and 10 percent of the time is devoted (if any time is spent at all) to the development of the other 90 percent of the rational powers. This type of activity in our schools cannot and will not produce citizens who have developed freedom of the mind. Possessing the ability to recall is important— extremely important—but recall cannot substitute for the other rational powers when a free mind is needed.

Saying that the central purpose of the school (the development of the ability to think) represents the *sole* purpose, or that purpose to which the greatest priority is given, is to misunderstand the use of the term "central." *The development of the learner's rational powers is basic, or central, to his achieving any other purposes which the school and/or society may wish him to achieve.* Regardless of what we wish the learner to achieve—selection of a vocation, deciding upon leisure-time activities, or understanding his civic responsibilities—that achievement will take place only to the degree to which the learner has developed his rational powers. This, then—the development of the ability to think—represents the unifying purpose (the common thread) which ties together all learning experiences provided by our educational establishment. If every teacher in every class in this country made the development of the ability to think central to his teaching, the goals of the modern educator would be achieved and, because of the information that the learner would gather (in a meaningful way), the classicist would find less fault with our schools.

Science and the Rational Powers

If we accept that the central role of the schools is developing the learner's rational powers, then these powers must be used as criteria

Since classifying is one of the rational powers, it must be developed. In order for children to learn classification, they must be given the opportunity and the material.

to evaluate the disciplines to be studied. We must then ask whether or not science is a discipline that can contribute to the development of the ability to think.

In Chapter 1 we saw that science progresses by a special method of investigation and that special method is one in which a problem is *analyzed;* an experiment is *imagined;* experimental results are *classified, compared,* and *analyzed;* an hypothesis is *synthesized* and tested and the results of these tests *evaluated; generalizations* are formed; future results are *inferred,* and mental models to explain what has been found are *imagined.* If you will study the mental processes that an investigator must carry on while searching for an answer to a problem, it becomes immediately evident that those mental processes are the rational powers of the free mind. The structure of science, then, *if taught as a form of inquiry,* or investigation, *is a natural vehicle to use when leading the learner to develop his ability to think.* But if the discipline of science is to be used to teach habits of inquiry and develop the child's rational powers, it must be taught as a form of investigation. Acquainting children with the facts of science which have been found by investigation, and asking for those facts to be returned on examinations, does not teach them how to inquire. What will be learned if fact giving and receiving are emphasized in science teaching is the generalizations that science has developed, and not *how* those generalizations were established.

Teaching science as a form of investigation demands that each child in the classroom must make individual inquiries for himself. He must be placed in a situation where he will have to observe some type of experimental situation and interpret his observations as he sees them. In short, the learner must be allowed to inquire in his own unique way. When an individual conducts an inquiry he usually does it to find out something *he* does not know. This is exactly the manner in which the word "inquiry" must be interpreted when it is applied to learning. The inquiries of elementary school children are not expected to find something new to the world—only something new to the child. The entire inquiry process and its relationship to teaching will be closely examined in Chapter 4. As you might suspect, the teacher has an important and unique role in an inquiry-centered learning situation. That role will be considered in Chapter 7. For the present it is sufficient to say that if the discipline of science is to be used to develop the rational powers of children, it must be taught by a method that fosters inquiry (the structure of the discipline of science). That teaching method is often called the *inquiry method*.

The Objectives of Elementary School Science

From what has been said in Chapter 1 and in this chapter, three objectives of elementary school science can be synthesized.[19] Since science is a natural vehicle to use to develop the learner's powers, the first objective of elementary school science can be stated as: *To develop in the learner a command of the rational powers.* From what has been said about the relationship between inquiry and rational power development, you have probably concluded that using inquiry fosters rational power development and that the systematic use of the rational powers is inquiry. The second purpose of elementary school science, therefore, is *to develop in the student the ability and confidence to inquire.* But the vehicle of science must use subject matter to accomplish these objectives. Thinking and learning do not happen in a vacuum; we think with facts, notions, and ideas. In selecting the curriculum that will allow the learner to develop his ability to think, the notion that learning takes place in terms of those

[19] Donald G. Stafford, Don Kellogg, John W. Renner, et al., "Wings for a Dinosaur," *BIOS*, October 1970.

things with which we are already familiar must be kept in mind. This immediately tells us that the content of science selected for study should be related in some way to the learner's environment and those factors which affect his environment. There are, of course, times during the education of a child when he must, in order to develop an understanding of his environment, become acquainted with ideas not directly obtainable from his immediate, direct experiences. These ideas or concepts help the child develop a structure into which new information can be stored and interpreted and from which information can be retrieved. Karplus summarizes these content notions from the teaching frame of reference.

> Two aspects of the teaching program should be distinguished from one another: The experiential (student experience with a wide variety of phenomena . . .) and the conceptual (introduction of the student to the approach which modern scientists find useful in thinking about phenomena they study).[20]

If the learner has a thorough acquaintance with his own environment, he will have a much better experience background for stretching his imagination, later in his educational program, up to the far reaches of the universe and down to the realm of the atom. The third principal objective, then, which can be listed for elementary school science is: *To develop an understanding of the changing nature of the environment in terms of matter, life, energy, and their interaction.*

Many other objectives for elementary science teaching could be listed. Examples of these are: To develop scientific literacy, to develop scientific attitude and open-mindedness, and to develop skill in the use of the methods and processes of science. These are perfectly good, sound objectives; but if you study the three general objectives listed here, you will discover that the objectives just expressed will be accomplished if our general objectives are achieved.

So far in our discussion of elementary school science, we have considered the discipline of science and the institution in which it will be taught—the school. We have seen that science in its most refined form is an intellectual process and that the schools must concentrate upon developing the rational powers of the free mind (intellectual ability). Science, we have demonstrated, is a natural and logical curriculum vehicle to use in leading the learner to develop his ability to think, and, in addition, the inquiry experiences provided can lead the learner to understand a great deal about his environment.

[20] Robert Karplus, "Three Guidelines for Elementary School Science," *SCIS Newsletter*, no. 20 (Spring 1971), University of California at Berkeley.

There is, however, still one element of the content-teaching-learning enterprise which has not been considered. *That element is the child!* Are the learning experiences that the study of science can provide, even though they will lead a learner to develop his rational powers, proper experiences for young children to have? (Remember, we are concerned here with children from kindergarten through the sixth grade.) In other words, are science and children "right" for each other? To be able to answer that question, we must briefly refresh ourselves on the fundamental characteristics of children. Those characteristics we shall explore in the next chapter.

3 | The Child

When teachers isolate the way in which their profession can contribute to society, they ultimately settle upon the changes they can bring about in children as being the most important contribution that teachers can make. The next question is what kinds of changes are desirable and possible. In Chapter 2 we discussed the central role of the school, which is to develop in each learner the ability to think, to make the maximum use possible of his rational powers. We described science as curriculum that can be used to achieve that purpose —to promote intellectual development.

One school of thought believes that the best evidence that can be found that learning has occurred is to state in behavioral terms everything that is desirable for the child to learn. That is, all objectives should be behavioral objectives. Suppose, for example, that an upper grade elementary science class observed and experimented with daphnia. What types of behavioral changes should be expected?

The child should be able to

1. state hypotheses concerning the response of a single animal to changes of an environmental variable.
2. construct and demonstrate tests of stated hypotheses.
3. state the results of experiments he conducts.[1]

The rationale for behavioral objectives is that by achieving them the broad, general purpose of education discussed in Chapter 2 would be achieved. And so it may. There is, however, a danger "inherent in the behaviorist approach to education itself, with its insistence that the goals of education not only can, but should be defined in precise

[1] Commission on Science Education, *Science—A Process Approach*, Part Six, Second Experimental Edition (Washington, D.C.: American Association for the Advancement of Science, 1964), p. 861.

behavioral terms."[2] If those leading the children toward those be-havioral objectives rigidly insist upon their achievement and measur-ing all achievement in terms of them, that insistence "is a prescription for training and not for education."[3] If, however, the teacher looks at the lesson as a vehicle to develop in children "values, self-confidence, abilities to reason, analyze, and learn,"[4] then statements of behavioral objectives can be useful. They can be guidelines that the teacher uses to evaluate the general direction in which the learning is going and to use as a basis for adjusting learning activities to the needs of the children. Again, although behavioral objectives can be useful, they can also promote classrooms that are just as rigid, dogmatic, and sterile as the traditional show-and-tell type of classroom they seek to replace.

Interaction and Structure

Behavioral objectives, as was suggested above, do give a general direction in which the learning should proceed. When that notion is combined with a more inclusive view of how children learn, a teach-ing strategy evolves which makes achieving the central purpose of the school possible. But how do children learn? Jean Piaget believes that to explain learning, intellectual development must first be understood. Piaget's position is that

> development is the essential process and each element of learning occurs as a function of total development, rather than being an element which explains development.[5]

In other words (although improving on Piaget's statment is difficult), the intellectual development that a learner undergoes explains *what* he can learn rather than the learning explaining and accounting for his development. Assuming, then, that the material to be learned is clearly within the intellectual development pattern of the learners (and how that determination is made will be discussed later), how do they learn and gain knowledge about the material?

Piaget's basic hypothesis about learning is that to know something is to act upon it and/or interact with it. Knowing an object, event, or

---

[2] Charles Silberman, *Crisis in the Classroom* (New York: Random House, 1970), p. 201.
[3] Ibid.
[4] Ibid., p. 202.
[5] Jean Piaget, "Development and Learning," *Journal of Research in Science Teaching*, 2, Issue 3 (New York: Wiley, 1964), 176–186.

situation is not simply looking at it and making a mental copy of it. Suppose, for example, that you wished to teach the properties of hard, soft, smooth, and rough to first-grade children. You can drill the children on *rough* means "bumpy," *smooth* means "even," *soft* means "squeezable," and *hard* means "difficult to break." Children can make mental copies of those properties and probably do well in any recitation or examination. (In fact, much of what masquerades for "learning" words is just that—making mental copies of words through vocabulary drill.) Property words learned in this fashion will probably soon be forgotten. But what is more detrimental—assuming that he remembers the words—is that when the child meets the concept of *rough* in a context other than the one he was told about, he does not know how to interpret it; that is, he does not know what to do with the information he has just received. He does not have a *mental structure* for *rough*, and so *rough* is not a concept but a memorized word. In other words, when the "thing" whose properties are copied is changed, no mental structure exists which the learner can use to process the information received from the new "thing."

Instead of having the learner mentally copy the properties of "things," suppose they began at the first grade to act upon liquids by mixing them, to interact with crystals by grinding them, to act upon sandpaper by feeling it, and in general involving themselves with the property concept. All the while this interaction is going on, the learner is finding out not so much the specific properties (that would be copying reality) of the objects studied but something about the concept of property itself. Property is hard, soft, sticky, rough, scrunchy, sweet, sour, and so on. Now he is developing broad mental structures for the property concept and when he meets something in the future relating to property, he has a structure to use in processing those data. This view of knowing is precisely what Bruner meant when he said "knowing is a process, not a product."[6] Learning, therefore, proceeds by the interaction of the learner with something and his construction of mental structures from and to accommodate the results of those interactions. The material and/or ideas that are selected for the learner to interact with must obviously be at his level of intellectual development, or structures *cannot* be developed. You cannot, for example, expect a first grader to interact with the calculus and build structure from the interaction.

But how does an individual build mental structures? Piaget's funda-

6 Jerome Bruner, *Toward a Theory of Instruction* (Cambridge, Mass.: Harvard University Press, 1966), p. 72.

mental thesis about knowledge is: "To know an object is to act on it."[7] Learning, in other words, comes from interaction with the world and the objects in it. Now, that interaction and the perceptions the child gets from it form what Piaget refers to as a *schema* (plural, *schemata*). Schemata "form a kind of framework into which incoming sensory data can fit—indeed must fit."[8] Now, these schemata can be used to *assimilate* new data the child acquires. But in that process the existing schemata must *accommodate* to them. Thus the framework of schemata are continually changing their shape making them better able to assimilate new data. In assimilating new data and accommodating to them, a schema not only changes itself but may assimilate other schema and thereby change an entire structure rather than just itself. This change in structure demonstrates that "schema, then, is the generic unit of structure."[9] Inhelder and Piaget describe the utilization of the foregoing, and its relation to experience, when we identify an orange like this:

> What we are doing is to assimilate the orange we see to a perceptual schema . . . the orange is perceived as presenting the familiar configuration of an ovoid with a corrugated skin and an orange color. This configuration has acquired its stability as a result of previous perceptual experience. But it is closely linked to a number of . . . schemata: peeling the fruit, cutting and chewing it, squeezing out the juice, etc.[10]

Children are producing and changing structures from birth. Piaget has stated that "learning is possible only when there is active assimilation."[11] Since assimilation and its accompanying accommodation lead to changes in structures, an operational definition of education could easily be the changing of structures. This change of structures occurs by analyzing, synthesizing, comparing, classifying, evaluating, and utilizing all the rest of the rational powers. So utilizing the learning model of Piaget enables teachers to lead children to achieve the central role of the school.

Cognition

Quite apparently, Piaget's learning model is *cognitive*. Now the learning model that has governed the formulation of curricula and

[7] Piaget, "Development and Learning," op. cit., pp. 176–186.

[8] John L. Phillips, Jr., *The Origins of Intellect: Piaget's Theory* (San Francisco: W. H. Freeman, 1969), p. 9.

[9] Ibid.

[10] Barbel Inhelder and Jean Piaget, *The Early Growth of Logic in the Child* (New York: Norton, 1969), p. 10.

[11] Piaget, "Development and Learning," op. cit., p. 185.

the classroom behavior of teachers for most of the history of education in this country is the stimulus-response model. This learning
model perhaps finds its optimum utilization in programmed instruction. Adopting achievement of the rational powers as the general
purpose of education requires that schools shift from the stimulus-
response model to one that has as its primary function the development of cognitive structures. You have just seen that Piaget's learning
model has as its focus the change of structures. In expressing his
disagreement with the stimulus-response model, and contrasting it
with his cognitive model, Piaget says:

> Classically, learning is based on the stimulus-response schema. I think
> the stimulus-response schema, while I won't say it is false, is in any
> case entirely incapable of explaining cognitive learning. Why? Because
> when you think of a stimulus-response schema, you think usually that
> first of all there is a stimulus and then a response is set off by this
> stimulus. . . . I am convinced that the response was there first. . . .
> A stimulus is a stimulus only to the extent that it is significant and it
> becomes significant only to the extent that there is a structure which
> permits its assimilation, a structure which can integrate this stimulus but
> which at the same time sets off the response. . . . The stimulus is really
> a stimulus only when it is assimilated into a structure and it is this
> structure which sets off the response. Consequently, it is not an
> exaggeration to say that the response is there first. . . . Once there is a
> structure the stimulus will set off a response, but only by the intermediary
> of this structure.[12]

Stimulus-response, then, is a viable learning model only because of
the existence of cognitive structures, and those cognitive structures
are built and changed by the learner only through the action on and
interaction with materials, ideas, objects, and all types of "stuff"
found in a learning environment; that is, by building and changing
schemata. When a learner is learning by interacting with his environment, he is inquiring. *Inquiry*, then, can be thought of as the classroom methodology to promote the building and changing of cognitive
structures. If, however, you look more closely at what inquiry actually
is, you find that it is asking about something, receiving information,
and processing that information. The seeking, receiving, and processing of information require that the child compare, classify, evaluate,
analyze, synthesize, and utilize all the rational powers. Inquiry, then,
is the methodology necessary for the development not only of cognitive structures but also of the rational powers. That probably does not

[12] *Ibid.,* p. 182.

come as a big surprise to you because you have probably begun to build schemata about the relationship between cognitive structure development and rational powers development.

Explain how the development of cognitive structures and the development of rational powers are or are not related and compatible.

We shall return to the utilization of inquiry in the classroom in later chapters.

Equilibrium

Earlier in this chapter, we discussed how Piaget's learning model explains how structures are built from their generic units—schemata —and how structures change through assimilation and accommodation. But the question needs to be asked why does the human organism accommodate his thinking to his assimilations? Basically because of the individual's desire to be in a state of mental and physical harmony, or *equilibrium*, with his environment. If an individual is mentally or physically uncomfortable with his situation, he tends to act to establish equilibrium again.

Suppose that a teacher is leading children to develop the concept of property, and the need for the concept of "pentagon" arises. If the children do not have the concept of pentagon in their cognitive structures, this event, or perturbation, produces in many of them a state of disequilibrium. Now, in order to establish a state of equilibrium again, they and/or the teacher must *invent* the concept of "pentagon," which of course means using the proper language.

After the *conceptual invention*, the learners are back in equilibrium and they can now employ the concept and make all types of *discoveries* with and about it. But in making these discoveries, they sharpen their own structures having to do, perhaps, with geometrical shape. The learners also begin to find other concepts with which they were in equilibrium before but which are now out of equilibrium with how they view and interact with their environment. Here is a new perturbation, and the individual must act to reestablish equilibrium. Phillips explains the equilibrium states thus:

> Structures continually move toward a state of equilibrium, and when
> a state of relative equilibrium has been attained, the structure is sharper,
> more clearly delineated, than it had been previously. But that very
> sharpness points up inconsistencies and gaps in the structure that had
> never been salient before. Each equilibrium state therefore carries with it
> the seeds of its own destruction.[13]

[13] Phillips, op. cit., p. 10.

The teacher, therefore, has the responsibility to provide activities that lead the learners to reach disequilibrium and that will produce information that can be interpreted so that equilibrium can be reestablished. But this new state of equilibrium has developed for the child a changed cognitive structure (reoriented schemata) that is sharper and richer than the one he was disequilibrated from. The learner now views objects, events, and situations from this new structure and sees gaps, inconsistencies, and contradictions, which again puts him out of equilibrium. Thus, as Phillips has said, each new equilibrium carries with it the procedure for self-destruction.

Earlier, inquiry was presented as the methodology for cognitive development. Now, inquiry in its most basic form must consistently present the inquirer with objects, events, and/or situations to *explore* and for which he does not have schemata to accommodate. If he seems to make such an accommodation to an assimilation easily, he is probably not inquiring at all but is perhaps only recalling. In the process of inquiring, therefore, structures are disequilibrated, and for inquiry to reach its fullest potential, equilibrium must be reestablished. In fact, equilibration is the thread that weaves the inquiry teaching design together because the purpose of inquiry is to involve the learner so completely in the learning that his understandings grow deeper and deeper. But in order for a person to deepen an understanding, he must move himself from the position of being in equilibrium with his environment because only when disequilibrium occurs does the learner's structure grow sharp enough to see inconsistencies in the way he understands something.

Notice that in the foregoing paragraph the statement is made that the *learner must move himself* from a state of equilibrium; you cannot move him. This, of course, means that just telling the learner that his views of something are skewed does no good; he himself must make that discovery. He must be confronted with contradictory or new evidence that will disturb his equilibrium. That new and/or contradictory evidence must be *his own*, and the only way he gains that evidence is through inquiry; that is, through exploration, invention, and discovery. Through successive disequilibrations the child's cognitive structures are changed. This constant change of structure leads to intellectual development and explains why a stimulus *seems* to be delivered to a response. As Piaget said in the quotation earlier in this chapter, the response is already present; the stimulus does not generate the response. But that response would not have been there if structures had not been built up through experiences that caused equilibration and disequilibration time and time again. Thus the stimulus-response view of learning is incomplete and inadequate without the concept of cognitive structures.

Equilibration, according to Phillips, is an "overarching principle." It is the one concept that ties all the pieces of the cognitive view of learning together and furnishes data that allow us to see why inquiry-centered teaching is the methodology of cognitive development. One of your moment-to-moment tasks in the classroom is to seek opportunities with *individual* learners to establish, destroy, and reestablish equilibrium. It is a task that must be accomplished individually, and represents the only way to intellectual development.

Factors Affecting the Changing of Cognitive Structure

In the discussion so far we have assumed that intellectual development is dependent on the changing of the learner's cognitive structures. These structures, we have also seen change through equilibration and disequilibration; hence the equilibrium concept is one of the important factors in cognitive development. But equilibration is not independent of other factors even though it is the fundamental idea in changing cognitive structures. The *maturation* process also influences the intellectual development of a child. Later in this chapter the relationship between chronological age and the intellectual level of the child will be considered.

To help you isolate the next factor that influences cognitive development, you are asked to do an experiment. What do you hear when you read this sentence? The government should outlaw automobiles because they are the major contributors to air pollution which is probably injurious to our health.

Make a written record of what you hear. Read the statement to three other persons and record what they told you they heard.

We have done such an experiment, and our results were that the persons we asked heard different things. Some of them focused their attention on government, others argued that electric-powered automobiles are not contributors, some said that many factors in our environment are injurious to our health, and others insisted that many objects and functions in our society are doing more damage to our air than automobiles. In other words, the same words called to mind different focuses of attention for different people. Word meaning is not in the word itself; it is in the person hearing it. (How did your results correlate with ours?) We, all of us, attach meaning to anything from our own language frame of reference; we are truly trapped in our language. That is a tremendously important notion when you begin to think about changing a person's cognitive structure. Earlier you saw that structures are changed by disturbing the learner's equilibrium. Now, that equilibrium can be disturbed by communicating with him; but if his language development is severely retarded, he is difficult to communicate with and difficult to disequilibrate. Consequently, changing the cognitive structures of learners with language deficiencies is more difficult than with learners who have no such deficiency. How is language developed? Through social interaction with other human beings. Piaget has called this factor "social transmission."[14] A learner cannot be disequilibrated if he is not in a position to receive information, and if his language development is not sufficient to perceive what is being said he cannot receive the information.

You have probably heard the statement that every teacher should be a teacher of language. Most teachers interpreted the phrase "a teacher of language" as meaning that they should teach grammar, and a few of them did. If teachers would interpret the universal direction to teach language to mean they are responsible for leading a child to describe and receive information about his environment, they would be doing much more than teaching language; they would be moving the learner into a position where he could have his cognitive structures changed through the disequilibration-equilibration process. By teaching a learner language he can use in describing his environment, we mean, of course, that this language development will occur as a result of conceptual invention (and not as pure vocabulary drill) that is a result of *experiences* the learner has had.

That factor—experience—is the fourth factor which Piaget states has an influence upon cognitive-structure development. There are, according to Piaget, two types of experience—*physical* and *logico-mathematical*.[15] Physical experience is what is had when a learner interacts with objects in his environment and the environment itself. This type of experience is essential to the very young learner. Through such interaction he begins to develop structures about objects, environments, and their interactions. Physical experience is also the type that many adolescents need because their intellectual development has not reached the point where experience involving logic has any meaning for them. In fact, any adult, when encountering a new and unusual notion, will have or attempt to secure physical or inter-

14 Piaget, "Development and Learning," op. cit., p. 180.
15 Jean Piaget, "Foreword," Millie Almy, *Young Children's Thinking* (New York: Teachers College Press, Columbia University, 1966), pp. v and vi.

active experience because when he is learning about something new, basic cognitive structures (schemata) must be built.

At some point in a child's education he begins to learn such things as when he counts four groups of three objects he gets the same total as he does when he counts three groups of four objects. He has learned that performing some action (rearranging) on the objects does not change their total number. While he is still manipulating objects, he is learning from the actions and not from the objects themselves. Such experiences Piaget has called *logico-mathematical*—experiences where knowledge comes from the assimilations and accommodations resulting from the actions, and not from the objects themselves. In the foregoing example, Piaget says that when the child learns

> that the sum is independent of counting he is discovering the properties of the actions of ordering and uniting. He is learning something from the actions themselves, rather than from the objects independent of these actions.[16]

You probably noticed that in the last paragraph the term *actions* was introduced and the example given was a physical action; that is, rearranging the objects. We also have stated that the learner acquires knowledge from the action. Or, as Piaget has said, "a child learns very little . . . when experiments [investigations] are performed for him, . . . he must do them himself rather than sit and watch them done."[17] Learning from logico-mathematical experiences takes place only when the actions are internalized; that is, the learner takes the actions into his cognitive structure and he is now able to make decisions on the basis of his internalized actions and not on the basis of the physical manipulations. Such internalized actions are called *operations* and are the foundations of logico-mathematical experience. These experiences require that the learner coordinate his actions very carefully in order to avoid contradicting himself. He must, in other words, utilize a good deal of self-regulation, or else contradictions will continually dominate his reasoning patterns. (Self-regulation is the learner's own mechanism for utilizing the equilibrium concept.) As he exercises his self-regulation, he checks his logic and seeks out contradictions that might be present. Finding those contradictions enables him to sharpen his structures and thus throw himself out of equilibrium and put himself back in. This, however, will occur only when the learner can internalize his actions and reverse his reasoning to get from any point in his line of reasoning back to the beginning.

[17] Ibid., p. v.
[16] Ibid., p. vi.

Children in the early years of school cannot reverse their thinking, which explains why they cannot have logico-mathematical experiences.

Perhaps by this time you are asking yourself, "What the dickens do these four factors (equilibration, maturation, social transmission, and experience) have to do with teaching elementary school science?"

Record your answer to the foregoing question. Play the game straight, and don't read on until you have formulated and recorded your answer. Remember, you are your own evaluator.

Throughout most of this chapter, the learner has been referred to as having equilibrium destroyed and reestablished by interacting with objects and the environment. The emphasis has been on the *learner* interacting. This means that the teacher must ascertain the students' level of language development and then provide the experiences commensurate with his language and maturity levels that will permit him eventually to reach the point where he can sharpen his own structures by learning from operations instead of having to continually rely on the information he gets directly from objects. That is, the learner must be allowed a *maximum of activity* to investigate and interact with the materials of the discipline being studied. As you saw in Chapter 1, the basic structure of science is investigation. Therefore, when it is taught as investigation it is an activity that promotes intellectual development. This general teaching direction applies not only to the way children get information from objects—that is, through physical experience—but also to logico-mathematical experience. Piaget sums up his feelings on this latter experience thus:

> In the area of logico-mathematical structures, children have real understanding only of that which they invent themselves, and each time that we try to teach them something too quickly, we keep them from reinventing it themselves.[18]

In other words, the notions that Piaget has about how experience aids the intellectual development of the learner demand that science in the elementary school be taught from its basic structure—investigation. But how is the concept of investigation turned into classroom methodology? You have probably assimilated enough information from what has been said so far to have developed an answer to that question, because all the necessary elements have been introduced.

When one investigates he does so to find out something he does not know. The first activity he engages in is to *explore* thoroughly what he is investigating and collect all the information about it he can.

[18] Ibid., p. vi.

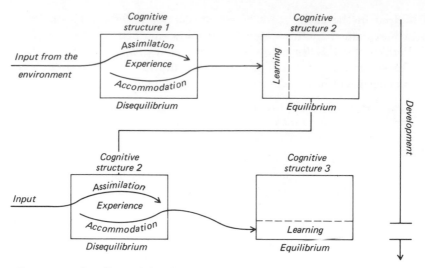

Figure 3–1. Intellectual development.

He then arranges that information in some way in order to find some pattern that will enable him to *invent* some kind of explanation. After the invention of an explanation he tests its accuracy and usefulness by seeing what kinds of *discoveries* he can make with it.

The foregoing discussion is a description of an investigation. But, more important, it is an explanation of the inquiry process and inquiry-centered teaching. Exploration, invention, and discovery, then, are phases in the inquiry process and represent the teaching methodology that must be used to achieve intellectual development. (We shall return to a more detailed description of the inquiry process in later chapters.) The discipline of science, then, properly utilized can make a great contribution to intellectual development. Figure 3–1 diagrammatically summarizes what has been said so far about Piaget's learning model. This diagram shows that the process of cognitive development and/or modification begins by an input from the learner's environment. The input is assimilated into the existing cognitive structure (cognitive structure 1) and modified by it. In turn the structure is also modified by the disequilibrium produced by the input and as accommodation to reestablish equilibrium occurs. As a result of this experience, a new cognitive structure (cognitive structure 2) is produced which is now capable of interacting with input in a new way. Learning is the change produced in cognitive structure (cognitive structure 2). But cognitive structure 2 now permits the learner to interact with the world in a different way and assimilate different types of inputs from it. Through the accommodation necessary to reestablish equilibrium, a refined cognitive structure (cognitive structure 3) emerges. Thus intellectual development (the ability to think) proceeds by continued modification of the cognitive structure.

Levels of Intellectual Development

Earlier in this chapter maturation was referred to as one of the factors that control intellectual development. Figure 3–2 demonstrates how the picture of shifting cognitive structures model just presented relates to an age continuum.

As structure modification proceeds along an age continuum, new types of cognitive-structure modifications become possible which greatly enhance the learner's ability to process information. Even though development itself is a continuum, the emergence of these new structures at certain age levels is the basis for Piaget's stages of intellectual development model. One must keep in mind, however, that the model is superimposed on the continuous spectrum of age and that the transition from one stage to another is gradual rather than abrupt—new structures do not come into existence spontaneously at a particular age. Even though physiological maturation—increased differentiation and complexity of the nervous system—has opened the possibility for development of new, more powerful structures, the actuation of the new structures by experience through the existing structure is essential. Each new "stage" must be built on fully developed existing structures. Children of the same age and in the same class in school, therefore, could be functioning intellectually at completely different stages of development.

The stages-of-development model is most frequently associated with Piaget, but the notion of stages of development is not unique to him. He has, no doubt, been most responsible for popularizing the idea. The picture of intellectual development that Piaget has constructed comes from over forty years of research during which he and his co-workers "accumulated the largest store of factual and theoretical observations extant today."[19] His methods of data collection are unique and are largely clinical; Phillips has described that method of operation thus:

> He observes the child's surroundings and his behavior, formulates a hypothesis concerning the structure that underlies and includes them both, and then tests that hypothesis by altering the surroundings slightly

[19] Phillips, op. cit., p. 4.

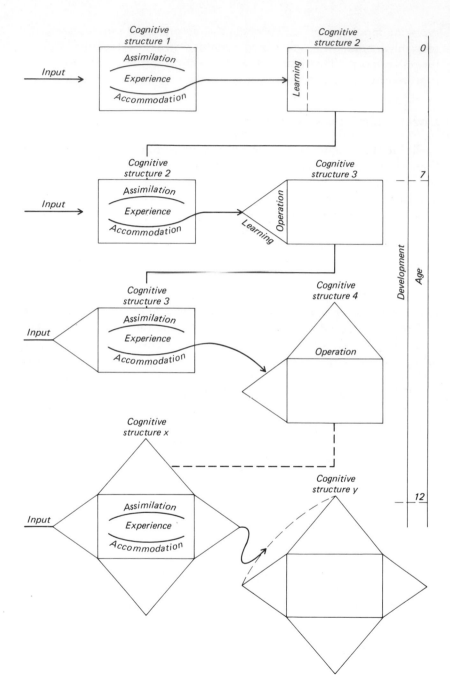

Figure 3–2.

—by rearranging the materials, by posing the problem in a different way, or even by overtly suggesting to the subject a response different from the one predicted by the theory.[20]

Perhaps, for our purposes, Piaget's procedure for gathering data could be described as giving the child a task to perform which involves materials and reasoning, letting him perform the task, and then asking him what he did and why he did it that way. What is important for you as a teacher is that Piaget's model of intellectual development comes from *direct* association with learners of all ages. You are going to be directly associated with learners, and it is important that any model you use to guide you in selecting and employing content and materials be relevant to children.

The first level

The first stage of intellectual development in Piaget's model begins at birth and continues until the child is approximately 2-and-a-half years old. Piaget has called this period the *sensory-motor* phase. During this phase the child learns that objects are permanent—that just because an object disappears from sight does not mean that it no longer exists. Acquiring the characteristics of object permanence explains, for example, why a child approximately a year old will cry when his mother leaves. This separation anxiety, however, does not occur earlier because until that point out of sight, out of mind adequately describes the child. During the sensory-motor period, language begins to develop[21] (a development that is far too complex to explore fully in this book). Basically, however, the child learns how to attach sounds to the objects, symbols, and experiences he has had. But this inventing of appropriate sounds for something depends, as does later learning, on the child's having an experience with that something. During the sensory-motor period the first signs that intellect is developed and does not just occur begin to emerge. Now, certainly, the way a sensory-motor child goes about learning is quite different from the way learning occurs in an adult. But throughout all the stages of Piaget's model the fact becomes obvious that later learning cannot occur "unless 'early learning' has been accomplished."[22] This means that for culturally deprived children who have not had the benefit of a rich environment which will assist them in

---

[20] Ibid., p. 10.
[21] Ibid., pp. 13–49. Phillips presents a thorough picture of the sensory-motor child.
[22] Ibid., p. 17.

developing the beginnings of a language system, the school may need to provide many experiences that go far beyond the conventional reading readiness programs *before* traditional "school" activities can begin. There is little likelihood that you will be working with sensory-motor children. You need, however, to be aware that this is the stage in which intellectual development begins to emerge; and unless certain goals are accomplished in this stage *by the child*, later learnings must wait. Perhaps we, as teachers, need to spend more time determining when the learner is ready to begin and less time being concerned with the specific content being covered.

The second level

Before the second stage of intellectual development in Piaget's model, which is called *preoperational*, is investigated, two factors must be thoroughly understood—the age at which the child enters each stage and passes from stage to stage. There is only one stage in Piaget's model whose starting point can be precisely stated—the sensory-motor stage. It begins at birth and ends *around* 2-and-a-half years of age. A 2-and-half-year-old child will *begin to enter* the preoperational stage, and his exit from that type of thinking *begins around* 7 years of age. In other words, in the model exact, precise ages at which a learner will progress from stage to stage cannot be stated. The child himself determines his progress through the stages. In his model Piaget describes the relationship of the stages and age thus: "although the order of succession is constant, the chronological ages of these stages varies a great deal."[23] As you read the remainder of this discussion about Piaget's model of intellectual development, keep in mind that a child does not move *completely* from one stage to another. The evidence available suggests that a learner can easily be in the sensory-motor phase on some traits and preoperational on others. Rather than thinking about a child as moving *from* one stage *into* another, think of him as moving into a particular stage on certain traits. As his development progresses, he moves deeper and deeper into a particular stage on some traits as he moves into the stage on other traits. There is not, in other words, a chronological line and as he passes it he has moved from one stage to another, much as he is permitted to vote when he reaches 18 years of age.

In this paragraph the notion of "trait" is referred to. What is a trait? Based only on what you know so far, describe what you feel the "traits" referred to are.

[23] Piaget, "Development and Learning," op. cit., p. 178.

To lead to an understanding of Piaget's use of the concept of "trait," we will utilize the preoperational stage of intellectual development.

Earlier in this chapter the concepts of *action* and *operations* were invented. An action is something a child does which is mainly physical. When a child takes an action into his cognitive structure and is able to reverse his thinking at any point in the action and get back to the starting point, he has performed an operation. An operation is an intellectual procedure—an action may not be. Consider this example. Maybe at some time in your education experience you were exposed to a mathematical formula you did not completely understand, say, one like $S = \frac{1}{2} at^2$, $x = (-b \pm \sqrt{b^2 - 4\ ac})/2a$, or $a = dv/dt$. Now suppose that in order to take part in the great trivia contests called examinations, you had to use such a formula. We are willing to wager that you memorized the formula and several examples and then when necessary searched the problem presented to you for clues to enable you to apply a formula. In others words, you acted upon the problem with a number of formulas until you found a match. While there is a slight hint of operation in matching formula and problem, what was just described is primarily an action.

This example clearly points out the difference between an action and an operation.

> When he [the child in the example] was . . . . a small child—he was seated on the ground in his garden and he was counting pebbles. Now to count these pebbles he put them in a row and he counted them one, two, three, up to ten. Then he finished counting them and started to count them in the other direction. He began by the end and once again he found ten. He found this marvelous that there were ten in one direction and ten in the other direction. So he put them in a circle and counted them that way and found ten once again. Then he counted them in the other direction and found ten once more. So he put them in some other arrangement and kept counting them and kept finding ten. There was the discovery that he made.
>
> Now what indeed did he discover? He did not discover a property of pebbles; he discovered a property of the action which he introduced among the pebbles. . . . the subsequent deduction will consist of interiorizing these actions and then combining them without needing any pebbles.[24]

When actions become "interiorized" and pebbles are no longer necessary, mental operations have begun to be formulated. Operations must be completely reversible and internalized by the learner. The name of the second stage of intellectual development in the Pia-

[24] Ibid., pp. 179–180.

getian model—preoperational—is wonderfully descriptive of what children at this age are like. They cannot mentally operate with ideas that require them to take information into their cognitive structures and do simple mental experiments with them. Perhaps the best description of a preoperational child is that he is *perception-bound*;[25] that is, he sees, he decides, and he reports. In short, *he thinks, but he cannot think about his own thinking.*

A complete description of all the intellectual characteristics of the preoperational child is far beyond the scope of this book. If, after studying what is here, you wish to investigate further the characteristics of preoperational children, it is suggested that you consult the book written by John L. Phillips, Jr., which has been referred to throughout this chapter, or *The Psychology of Intelligence*, the book in which Piaget explains his intellectual model and the characteristics of the stages within the model. For the purposes of using the Piagetian model in selecting and utilizing content and instructional methodology, five basic characteristics of the preoperational child warrant examination:

1. Egocentricism
2. Irreversibility
3. Centering
4. States in a transformation
5. Transductive reasoning[26]

Egocentrism in the young child is one of his most prominent preoperational traits; the child sees the world from only one point of view—his own. The world as far as he is concerned revolves around him and he is unaware that he is a prisoner of a single frame of reference for viewing the world. In other words, the child cannot see another's point of view, take that point of view and coordinate it with his own and that of others. He has his own opinion which his perception has given him and he feels no responsibility to justify his reasoning nor look for contradictions in it. A preoperational learner has developed a certain language pattern with which he communicates and he does not have the ability (or see the need) to adapt his language to the needs of his listener. Considering his single frame of reference for viewing the world, the language patterns of a preopera-

---

[25] The authors wish they could take credit for inventing this phrase, but cannot. They first heard it used by Dr. Celia Stendler Lavatelli in the film *Piaget's Theory: Conservation*, produced by John Davidson Films, San Francisco.

[26] Do not forget the equilibration concept while studying the stages in the Piagetian model. Remember, we early called it the overarching concept of intellectual development.

tional learner are entirely predictable. The learner in this stage of development gains his perception-bound view of the world and his environment by interacting with it—and that type of experience must always be provided. He cannot gain any understanding of anything by being told about it or given its abstractions; he thinks only about what he perceives from his observation of and interaction with his surroundings.

The egocentric trait of a child continues throughout the preoperational stage, which ends between 6-and-a-half and 7-and-a-half years of age. Teachers of this age group must be continually aware that they must provide experiences that permit the child to have a maximum of physical experience and a minimum of (if any) logico-mathematical experience. That fact raises serious questions about the viability of some of the firmly entrenched activities that are found in the early years of schooling. Reading, for example, begins as basically a set of abstract sounds that are represented by a series of abstract symbols. After all, why is a series of lines hooked in a certain way called "A," "B," or "C"? That series is defined, and we believe that the definition is an abstraction and that the child must take another's point of view in order to internalize it. That requirement contradicts the preoperational learner's egocentric trait. Is there a possibility that reading difficulties that can plague a person his entire life are begun when an egocentric, preoperational learner is placed in a situation where those in charge demand that he begin to internalize abstractions he cannot comprehend? Comprehension of an abstraction demands that the learner take it into his cognitive structure and operate with it. According to the empirical data on which the Piagetian model is based, a preoperational learner is not able to perform intellectual operations. Perhaps much of the time spent in the first grade teaching reading could be better spent giving the children physical experiences with objects (some of which might be with letters) and social interactions that will lead them to develop a language structure that is much expanded from that they bring to school.

Reading, however, is not the only subject area that needs to be critically examined from the preoperational child's egocentric point of view. Remember that the egocentric child is perception-bound, hence his understandings of the social world must be developed from experience. A social studies program for early elementary grades which concentrates on such topics as "Children of Other Lands" is of questionable value. Perception by young children of children of other lands is not possible.

The second trait of the preoperational child which has great importance from the curriculum-methodology frame of reference is that of *irreversibility*. In order for a human organism to begin to do intellectual operations, he must be able to reverse his thinking. The irreversibility of thought is beautifully illustrated by this dialogue with an 8-year-old boy:

> Have you got a brother?
> Yes.
> And your brother, has he got a brother?
> No.
> Are you sure?
> Yes.
> And has your sister got a brother?
> No.
> You have a sister?
> Yes.
> And she has a brother?
> Yes.
> How many?
> No, she hasn't got any.
> Is your brother also your sister's brother?
> No.
> And has your brother got a sister?
> No.[27]

The dialogue with the child continues until he finally recognizes that he is his brother's brother. This dialogue with a 4-year-old girl also nicely illustrates the irreversibility concept.

> Have you got a sister?
> Yes.
> And has she got a sister?
> No, she hasn't got a sister. I am my sister.[28]

Reversibility means that a thought is capable of being returned to its starting point. For example: $8 + 6 = 14$, and $14 - 6 = 8$. The thought started with 8 and returned to 8. Preoperational children cannot reverse their thinking. Consider what that says to those planning a mathematics program for early primary grades. Much of our society has a real hang-up on mathematics. Is there a possibility that mathematics activities are introduced into the early elementary grades which require mental reversibility in order to achieve understanding, and since the learners cannot mentally reverse they memorize for the

[27] Jean Piaget, *Judgment and Reasoning in the Child* (Paterson, N.J.: Littlefield, Adams, 1964), p. 86.
[28] Ibid., p. 85.

trivia contests? Could it be that such an experience creates hang-ups about mathematics which individuals never conquer?

Isolating the irreversible trait in a young child's thinking is not difficult and is informative. The following procedure will enable you to do it. The materials you will need are simple—two equal quantities of modeling clay or plasticene (we have found that using different-colored pieces facilitates communication with the child).

> Form the pieces of clay into two balls and explain to the child that you want to start the experiment with one ball just the same size as the other. Allow your subject to work with the two balls until he believes they are just the same size. Now, deform one of the balls; a good way to do this is to roll one of the balls into a long, cylindrical shape.
>
> Next, ask the child (a 5-year-old child will probably be best to work with) if there is more clay in the ball, more in the roll, or if there is the same amount in each (be sure to give him all three choices), and ask why he believes as he does.
>
> Record the child's answer.

A child who has not developed the thinking trait of reversibility will tell you that there are different amounts in the two clay shapes. Our experience has been that most preoperational children will select the cylinder shape as the one containing more clay.

The subject you tested (if he is preoperational) is not able to make the reversal in his thinking from the cylinder-shaped object that now exists back to the clay sphere that did exist. He cannot do the analyzing and synthesizing that would permit him to reconstruct the sphere mentally, although he knows that it existed. This can be proved by asking the child to restore the roll of clay to its original shape; he will produce a sphere and now tell you there is the same amount of clay in each. This age child thinks, but he is so irreversible he cannot think about his thinking.

Why does the learner *usually* focus his attention on the cylinder-shaped object rather than on the ball? The event is explained by utilizing another trait in the preoperational model—*centering*. When the one clay ball was deformed the child probably fixed his attention on the detail of length, and his rigid, perception-bound thinking structure prevented him from seeing anything else about the transformed object. Educational experiences provided for young children must avoid using materials and/or activities that encourage the centering trait. If, for example, colors are used, they should all be attractive and appealing. Teachers must not be surprised when a child focuses his attention on one aspect of an object, event, or situation; he is only acting as a preoperational learner can be expected to act.

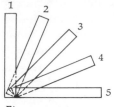

Figure 3–3.

Insisting that a child decenter and consider other aspects of an object will not prove fruitful if the teacher is so insistent that the child says he sees some other property just to get the teacher to leave him alone. Centering is a characteristic of preoperational children, and those working with them should expect to find it. Does a child's inability to reverse his thinking cause him to center or does his centering trait cause irreversibility? Who knows? Besides, is it important? Both traits exist—and which comes first is really not relevant because obviously they are not mutually exclusive.

The extreme perception-boundness of a preoperational child is well illustrated by the trait known as *states in a transformation.* Figure 3–3 represents a wooden rod that is standing vertically (position 1) and then released (positions 2, 3, and 4). The rod eventually comes to rest at position 5. Obviously, the rod was in a *state* of rest when it was held in position 1 and is again in a rest position in position 5. If a series of pictures is taken of the following object, it would be seen to pass through many other states as represented by positions 2, 3, and 4. In other words, the series of states in the event resulted in a *transformation* from the stick standing erect to its horizontal position.

If a preoperational child is shown the experiment, after having been informed that he will be asked to draw a diagram of it, he will not draw what is shown in Figure 3–3, nor will he indicate in any way what successive states the stick went through in being transformed from position 1 to position 5. Our experience in asking children to do this task has been that they draw only positions 1 and 5. They see only the beginning and final states and do not see the transformation. This particular preoperational trait (which also shows irreversibility and centering) is particularly important when young children are studying science and doing experiments, for example, a plant-growing experiment. There is little need in trying to get them to see the importance of the several states in the transformation; they cannot do it. They will perceive the first and final states and nothing else. The process that allowed the final state to be a function of the intermediate states cannot be seen by preoperational children. That trait seems to call into doubt insisting that young children do detailed experiments; they will see the beginning and the end, but as long as they are preoperational, they will not learn anything about the process of experimentation.

In his book entitled *Play, Dreams and Imitation in Childhood* (translated by C. Guttegno and F. M. Hodgson), Piaget relates the following incident that occurred when his daughter Jacqueline was just past 2 years old:

> J. wanted for her doll a dress that was upstairs: she said *"Dress,"* and when her mother refused to get it, *"Daddy get dress."* As I also refused, she wanted to go herself *"to mummy's room."* After several repetitions of this she was told that it was too cold there. There was a long silence, and then: *"Not too cold." "Where?" "In the room." "Why isn't it too cold?" "Get dress."*[29]

As far as Jacqueline was concerned there was no difference in the logic between a warm room makes securing the dress possible and getting the dress makes the room warm. Jacqueline was reasoning from particular to particular and not from general to particular (deduction) or particular to general (induction). Piaget has called the particular to particular reasoning *transduction.* This type of reasoning begins to appear in the child with the beginning of language and lasts until about 4 years of age. In our study of children, we have often used Piaget's classification tasks. One of these is showing a child a great number of wooden beads (we usually use red) and a few of another color (say, blue). Ask the child if there are more wooden beads or red beads. A truly preoperational child will tell you there are more red beads and when asked why, we often get the response "Because they are prettier"—a perfect transductive response. As a teacher, do not be surprised if you encounter such transduction in kindergarten and first-grade children. If you do, be patient; usually it disappears with the increased experiences a school environment can provide over what the preschool environment supplied.

Identifying preoperational thinkers

Identifying whether or not the preoperational thinker can see the relationship between states and transformations is a simple task; you do the falling stick experiment with the child and then ask him to

[29] Jean Piaget, *Play, Dreams and Imitation in Childhood* (New York: Norton, 1951), pp. 230–231. (Original French edition was published in 1945.)

Administering conservative reasoning tasks to a child can tell you much about him.

tell you what happened. Identifying egocentricism, irreversibility, centering, and transduction, however, is not as easy as using the falling stick experiment.

There is, however, a procedure that can be used to identify preoperational children. You have already met one of the techniques used—that is, the clay balls activity which was used to illustrate irreversibility in thinking. That activity can be described as illustrating the *inability* of a preoperational child to hold mentally the image of an object and see that distorting the object does not change the amount of material it contains. "Mentally holding" the original image of an object is called *conservation,* and preoperational children do not conserve—that is, they make decisions about the distortion of the object on the basis of what they perceive. This rigid, perception-boundness, however, is due to their irreversible thinking, tendency to center, extreme egocentrism, not seeing a transformation among several states, and transductive reasoning. In other words, isolating a child who does not use conservation reasoning will allow you to describe his stage of intellectual development in terms of the five preoperational traits already described and his ability to conserve. Conservation, then, is an overt manifestation of whether or not a child is a preoperational thinker. As was said earlier, this stage of development begins at about 2-and-a-half years of age. In describing the beginning of a child's ability to conserve, Piaget has also provided information about the end of the preoperational period.

> There always comes a time (between 6 and one-half years and 7 years 8 months) when the child's attitude changes: he no longer needs to reflect, he decides, he even looks surprised when the question is asked, he is *certain* of the conservation.[30]

The beginning of the ability to conserve and the beginnings of the child's entry into the third stage in the Piagetian model (concrete operations) occur, then, in the late first or second grade. For purposes of designing a first-grade curriculum for most of the year, the teacher can consider that the children are preoperational.

You have seen one activity (the clay balls experiment) that will reveal the child's ability to conserve. That activity tells you whether or not the learner conserves *solid amount*. We have found that task and five other Piagetian tasks to be very useful in identifying pre-operational thought. These tasks are the conservation of number, liquid amount, area, length, and weight. The descriptions for all of those tasks follow. As you read them, keep in mind the definition of "conservation" which may be stated thus: A child who conserves can hold a concept regarding an object in his cognitive structure, while a second object, like the first, is distorted and he can see that the distorted object is still like the nondistorted object in many specific ways.

Conservation of Number Task[31]

Have the children line up 6 black checkers in one row and 6 red checkers in another row, as shown in Figure 3-4. Ask the child if he agrees that there are the same number of red checkers as there are black checkers. After he agrees, stack the red checkers, one on top of

[30] Jean Piaget, *The Psychology of Intelligence* (Paterson, N.J.: Littlefield, Adams, 1963), p. 140.

[31] The utilization of these tasks is illustrated in the film *Piaget's Theories: Conservation*, produced and distributed by John Davidson Films, Inc., San Francisco. The directions for these tasks have been tried by several hundred elementary school teachers and we appreciate their suggestions and contributions. We are especially indebted to Dorsee Bennet Cohenour and Sandra Thompson Quigley who, after extensive tryouts with children, assisted in rewriting the directions for each test.

Figure 3–4.   Figure 3–5.

the other, and leave the black checkers as they were; the checkers will now appear as in Figure 3–5. After the checkers have been rearranged, ask the child if there are more red checkers, more black checkers, or if the numbers of black and red checkers are equal. If he reports that the numbers are equal, he conserves number. Be sure to ask him why he believes as he does not only on this task but also on all the others. Getting the child to explain why he thinks as he does will tell you a great deal about his state of intellectual development.

Conservation of Liquid Task

Pour the same amount of water in 2 containers of equal size. For convenience, you may wish to color the water in one container red (see Figure 3–6). Ask the child if he agrees that the containers are the same size and that they contain the same amount of liquid; let him adjust the levels if he wishes. After he agrees that the amounts are equal, have him pour the clear liquid into a taller, thinner container (see Figure 3–7) and ask him if there is more colored water,

Figure 3–6.   Figure 3–7.

more clear water, or if the amounts are equal. A report that the amounts are equal shows that the child conserves liquid; a report that there is more water in one of the containers demonstrates a lack of liquid-conservation ability.

Conservation of Solid Amounts Task

This task has already been referred to. Prepare two pieces of clay containing the same amount of clay and roll them into balls of equal size. For convenience, you may wish to use two colors of clay, i.e., blue and red (see Figure 3–8). Ask the child if he agrees that there is the same amount of blue clay as red clay; let him make any adjustments in the balls he wishes to in order to convince himself the balls are of equal size. Next, deform the piece of red clay by rolling it into what you may want to call a "snake" (see Figure 3–9). Ask the learner if there is more clay in the ball, in the snake, or if there is the same amount in each. Recognizing that the amount of the solid remains constant indicates solid-amount conservation ability.

Figure 3–8.   *Figure 3–9.*

Conservation of Area Task

Show the child two fields of grass (green construction paper) of *equal size*; be sure he satisfies himself that the fields of grass are the same size before going on. Explain that each field of grass is owned by a farmer; Mr. Green owns one, and Mr. Jones owns the other. Both Mr. Green and Mr. Jones build a barn on their fields. Place a barn made of red construction paper or toy barn on each field and explain that the barns are exactly the same size (see Figure 3–10). Ask the child if there is still the same amount of grass that is not covered on each field, or if one or the other has more. Record his answer. Next, tell the child that Mr. Green and Mr. Jones each build another barn; Mr. Green built his second barn right next to his first barn. Mr. Jones left a space of grass between his two barns (see Figure 3–11). Again ask the child if there is still the same amount of uncovered grass on each field. Explain to the child that Mr. Green and Mr. Jones each build a third barn and place them in the same manner as they had before (see Figure 3–12). Ask the child if there is still the same amount of

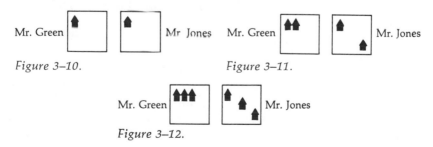

Figure 3–10.   *Figure 3–11.*

Figure 3–12.

uncovered grass on each field or if one or the other has more. A statement that there is still the same amount of uncovered grass demonstrates the learner's ability to conserve area.

Conservation of Length Task

This task requires a wooden dowel 12″ long and four dowels of the same diameter each 3″ long. The exact lengths are not important, but the combined lengths of the four smaller dowels must equal the length of the long dowel. Two identical toy cars are also helpful. Place the long dowel and the pieces parallel so that the combined length of the pieces just exactly equals the length of the long piece (see Figure 3–13). Be sure the child agrees that the line of pieces is exactly the length of the long piece; let him make adjustments if necessary. Inform the child that the dowels represent roads and there is going to be a race. Place identical toy cars (say, a red one and a blue one) at the same ends of the roads and then pose this question. "If the cars travel the same speed, which car, the red one or the blue one, will reach the end of the road first? Or will they reach the ends of the roads at the same time?" The child will generally agree that the cars will reach the ends of the roads at the same time; if he does not, discuss it with him until he sees that they do. If he does not ultimately agree that the cars reach the ends of the roads at the same time, abandon the task.

Next, move two pieces of the four-piece road as shown in Figure 3–14 and ask the question about the race. If a child states that the cars will reach the ends of the roads at the same time, he conserves length.

Figure 3–13.   Figure 3–14.

Conservation of Weight Task

Give the child two balls containing equal amounts of clay; two colors of clay, say red and green, facilitate communication in this task. (See Figure 3–15.) Add and subtract from each of the balls until the child agrees that the balls weigh exactly the same. Next, take the two balls

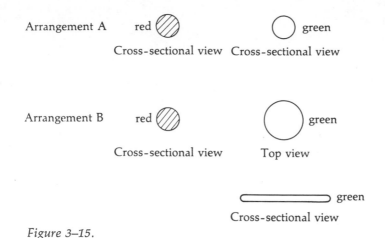

Figure 3–15.

of clay from the child and flatten one of them into a pancake or distort it in some other way. Don't let the child lift the two clay objects after distortion. Next, ask the learner if there is more green clay, more red clay, or if the amounts are still the same. Failing to recognize that the amounts of red and green clay are still equal shows that the child does not conserve weight.

The conservation tasks you have just read are neither meaningful nor functional until you employ them with children. You are probably thinking that the tasks are so simple that anyone can do them. All that thought proves is that *you* are not preoperational!

Administer the tasks to three children and record your results. A 5-year-old, a 7-year-old, and a 9-year-old will probably give you an age range that will allow you to see preoperational thought and thought moving into the concrete operational stage. After the child has given you his reasons for believing as he does on each task, be sure to give him the opportunity to explain his reasoning to you.

Your results will increase in meaning if you combine them with those of your colleagues. The combination of data will also show you that age alone does not determine when a preoperational learner leaves that stage. The data combination will also show you that just because a child conserves on one task does not necessarily determine what other tasks he will satisfactorily complete. Our experience with the tasks suggests that the first conservation usually made is number, and the second and third conservations are liquid and solid amount. But our results on the order in which conservation on the other three is achieved show no definite pattern.

Table 3–1

Age— months	Sample size	Conservation of					
		Number	Solid amount	Liquid amount	Length	Area	Weight
60–64	12	3	2	2		1	1
65–68	12	7	2		2	2	3
69–72	12	6	3	4	1	2	1
73–76	12	8	7	7	3	6	3
77–80	12	8	5	5	3	2	6
81–84	12	9	5	5		3	5
85–88	12	11	11	9	6	9	10
89–92	12	11	9	11	9	8	11
93–96	12	9	9	8	7	6	8
97–100	12	12	12	11	9	8	11
101–104	12	12	11	8	5	7	8
105–108	12	11	9	9	7	8	10
109–112	12	11	10	10	7	7	6
113–116	12	11	11	10	7	7	7
117–120	12	12	12	10	7	6	9
121–124	12	9	12	11	7	8	9
125–128	12	11	11	10	9	7	11
129–132	12	12	11	11	12	10	10
133–136	12	12	12	12	8	7	12
137–140	12	12	10	10	10	10	12
141–144	12	12	12	12	12	12	12

SOURCE: John W. Renner, Judith Brock, Sue Heath, Mildred Laughlin, and Jo Stevens, "Piaget *Is* Practical," *Science and Children* (October 1971), p. 23.

These data were gathered by a group of experienced test administrators, all of whom cannot be acknowledged. The authors are especially grateful, however, to Jo Stevens, Judith Brock, Mildred Laughlin, and Sue Heath, Kennedy Elementary School, Norman, Oklahoma.

The data shown in Table 3–1 are informative when a frame of reference for studying them is considered. The 252 children represented in that table are a random sample of children from the Norman, Oklahoma, school system. Those doing the evaluations used identical objects and standardized their questioning techniques. They worked from the set of directions for the conservation tasks you have just read.

If you adopt the interpretation policy that all twelve children in any given row must complete a task satisfactorily before the group can be regarded as exercising conservation reasoning, it appears rather late for some tasks. In evaluating data from the responses of children to a type task just slightly different from conservation reasoning, Piaget used the following procedure. "We have followed the accepted custom of considering a test successfully passed when 75% of the children of the same age have answered correctly."[32] This means that in Table 3–1 conservation reasoning is achieved when nine children (in the 12-child sample) in any row respond satisfactorily. (The number in the cells of Table 3–1 are those responding correctly.) In each row, however, the number should not fall seriously below nine once it has been achieved. We have taken the position that eight is not seriously below nine but that seven is. We fully recognize that our interpretation is arbitrary. If you disagree, please make your own and operate with it on what follows.

If Piaget's "75%" rule of thumb is adopted, the data in Table 3–1 take on a meaning that tells those concerned with curriculum a great deal. Conservation of number, for example, is not achieved until 84 months of age (7 years). What does that tell you about using numerical experiences with children in science experiments? Length conservation is not achieved until 136 months (11 years 4 months). Where do you usually find the teaching of systems of measurement? But throughout the conservation tasks, the children are being evaluated upon their ability to reverse their thinking, decenter their attention, cease using transductive reasoning, and overcome all the other characteristics of a preoperational thinker. A child who does not reverse his thinking does poorly in science experiments; he can observe and report what he saw. All the conservation tasks indicate a child's ability to do thinking reversals; those reversals get more difficult as the complexity of the tasks increases.

Explain the mental reversals in each conservation task and how difficult an experiment each successful conservation allows a child to perform.

In short, conservation tasks can be used to determine whether or not a learner is preoperational. That statement seems to deny the existence of conservation as a trait in itself; that is partially true. *Conservation is a trait of preoperational children,* but its greatest usefulness is to identify preoperationalness. Phillips explains this relationship.

[32] Piaget, *Judgment and Reasoning in the Child,* op. cit., p. 100.

. . . the Pre-operational child tends to be dominated by his perceptions, to center on a single attribute of a display and to "reason" transductively. In order to conserve, he must shake off that domination. He must decenter, and he must realize that an object can change in one respect without changing in other respects.[33]

The curriculum, therefore, must provide opportunities for the children to work within their limitations and must also provide experiences that will ultimately lead the children to lose their perception-boundness. The following lesson plan for first-grade science represents such an experience.

LESSON PLAN FOR FIRST-GRADE SCIENCE[34]

Advance Preparation

Select groups of objects to provide as wide a variety as seems reasonable. Buttons, beans, rocks, shells, wires, wood blocks, metal pieces, bottle caps, birthday candles, and pipe cleaners are available in the kit. You can also add rubber bands, crayons, paper clips, chalk, and 3" x 5" cards to the array. Use all or just some of these objects during the first session. Place each kind of object on a separate tray, and display these in front of the room. Put a tray, plastic dish, and magnifier on each child's desk.

Teaching Suggestions

Beginning the activity. Ask the children what objects are on their desks. Discuss the properties of the dishes and magnifiers as well as their similarities and differences. Allow the children some time to explore with the magnifier before you give them any instruction. . . .

Describing properties. Ask each child to select one object from his collection. Volunteers may show their objects to the group, describing the properties they observe. Pick up one object from your collection, and ask each pupil to choose a similar one from his collection. Call on a child to tell you about the properties of his object. . . . Repeat this procedure with several pupils. Choose other objects from your collection in order to discuss as extensively as possible a list of properties.

[33] Phillips, op. cit., p. 115.
[34] Reprinted with permission from *Material Objects Teacher's Guide*, pp. 29–30, by the Science Curriculum Improvement Study, published by Rand McNally & Company, Chicago. Copyright 1970 by the Regents of the University of California.

Defining sorting. If necessary, introduce a definition of sorting by citing a simple example, such as "The class is made up of children. We can sort the children into boys and girls." Or you can sort crayons by colors, as a classroom demonstration. Now invite each child to sort the objects on his tray. Many children will sort according to the properties already mentioned; others will use different criteria. When the children have sorted all the objects, suggest that each child display his tray to a neighbor. Each child then tries to guess how his neighbor sorted. Encourage the children to discuss their guesses and the reasons for them. After a few minutes, suggest that they tell each other how they sorted. Informal conversation and description among children is most important to their continuing development of language skills. You also have an excellent opportunity at this time to provide individual help to those children who need it. After this informal discussion, some children can describe their sorting methods for the class, or you can proceed to the sorting-by-specific-properties activity.

Sorting by property. Name a property (color or shape, for example), and ask each pupil to group some or all of his objects into piles on his desk while thinking of this property. Let individual children describe how the objects in their piles differ from one another. If they cannot sort or describe the objects at this time, do not become concerned since they will have many more opportunities for similar experiences.

The day-to-day science work in the classroom can consist of any activity that helps children become aware of objects and their properties. The number of sessions spent on this activity depends upon the needs, interest, and abilities of your particular pupils.

Earlier in this chapter experience was presented as one of four factors that influence intellectual development, and two kinds of experience were listed—physical and logico-mathematical. In the curriculum example just given, the experience at first inspection seems to be largely physical, and perhaps it is. There is, however, a real element of basic logic that the child encounters in such a learning experience.

Inspect the curriculum example for opportunities to break away from the five preoperational traits listed earlier. Also compare this lesson to the data in Table 3–1. Does this first-grade lesson demand thinking traits the first-grade child does not have?

Do experiences like the example given produce results that are significant enough to warrant including them in the curriculum of the school? We asked ourselves that question and selected the entire *Material Objects* unit quoted earlier as our curriculum vehicle.[35]

[35] Don G. Stafford and John W. Renner, "SCIS Helps the First Grader to Use Logic in Problem Solving," *School Science and Mathematics* (February 1971), 159–164.

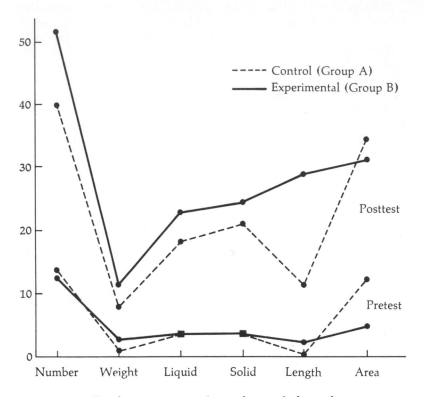

Figure 3–16. Total conservations for each sample by task.

Two groups of 60 first-grade children were selected from schools having the same socioeconomic background, general type of educational program, and caliber of teachers. The children's ability to conserve was measured in early September 1968. Group A excelled group B in the number of children who conserved number and area; on the latter task, group A exceeded group B by a very wide margin. Group B excelled group A in the number of conservations demonstrated in weight and length, and the two groups had the same number of children conserving solid and liquid amounts (see Figure 3–16). Group A was given a typical, conventional first year program, and Group B was given the same program *except* that the unit on *Material Objects* constituted the science program instead of science taught from a book. Another way of viewing the principal difference in the educational program provided these groups is that group B studied a program that was concerned with providing an abundance of physical

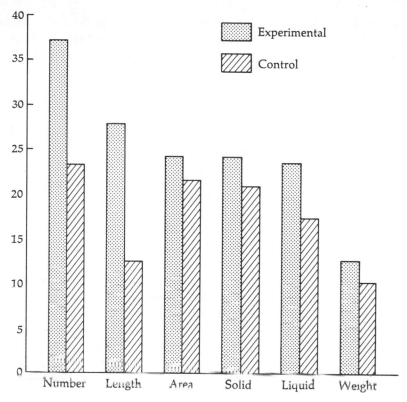

Figure 3–17. Numerical increase in conservation.

experiences as well as an introduction to logico-mathematical experience. Group A had a science program that required children to look at pictures in a book and talk about what was in the book, but did not have any direct experiences with the objects discussed in the book; this latter statement succinctly describes programs based on a book only. The conservation ability of both groups was measured again in January 1969. At that time group B, the group having studied *Material Objects,* markedly excelled group A in all conservations except area, and the margin between groups B and A now was very small in contrast to being very wide at the beginning of the experiment. But perhaps the most significant result of the experiment is that group B *outgained* group A in developing the ability to conserve on *every* task (see Figure 3–17) in spite of the fact that the Otis-Lennon scale measured group B as having a mean IQ of 103.2 and group A as having a mean IQ of 106.2. Since the only difference that could be found in the educational program the two groups experienced was the *Material Objects* unit, the conclusion was drawn that a program emphasizing physical and the introduction to logico-mathematical experiences leads children to develop the ability to conserve on the six Piagetian tasks used.

The conservation concept is a potent tool in the hands of a teacher who knows how to use it. He can identify preoperational and concrete operational learners and he immediately knows something about their thinking processes. The type of curricula which can be used with this type of thinker can then be identified. There is no use in asking a pre-operational thinker to become involved in an educational activity that requires him to reverse his thinking—he just cannot do it. He can observe, perceive, and report his perceptions. He needs educational experiences that will utilize his perceptions, and those experiences might put him out of equilibrium if he were not preoperational. Putting a preoperational child out of equilibrium is impossible because he does not internalize his perceptions and do mental experiments with them to test their equilibration properties in his present structure; he does not do mental operations. Activities like those cited in the lesson from *Material Objects* tend to give the learner physical and simple logico-mathematical experiences that lead to a change of structures and also to disequilibrium. Being able to provide all the foregoing for a child is possible if the teacher knows and uses the characteristics of preoperational thought.

The third level

You have probably learned more about the preoperational child than you wanted to know! There is a reason for treating the pre-operational period of intellectual development as thoroughly as has been done—those understandings about preoperations make understanding concrete operations much easier. The *gross* way to think about a concrete operational child is he is what a preoperational thinker is not; that is, he can decenter, equilibrate, do mental reversals, begin to reason inductively and deductively and not trans-ductively, see the relationship between states in a transformation, and his egocentric structures begin to thaw out—he can begin to see objects as other people do. He also conserves. You have seen, however (Table 3–1), that conservation ability does not develop in all areas at one time. A child, then, does not move from the preoperational to the concrete operational stage all at once. Rather, he begins to leave the preoperational stage and enter into the concrete operational stage. He continues this movement for some time and moves deeper and deeper into concrete operations.

The concrete operational thinker can truly do the mental operations that Piaget insists represent the beginning of logical thinking (viewed from an adult frame of reference). He can take ideas about things or data from an investigation into his head, move them around, do mental experiments with them, and make statements about what he believes. The concrete operational thinker can think about his thinking. Piaget describes concrete operations like this:

> In a third stage the first operations appear, but I call these concrete operations because *they operate on objects and not yet on verbally expressed hypotheses.*[36]

All of the concrete learners' ability to make mental reversals and do all the other types of thinking preoperational thinkers cannot do will be frustrated unless they have the actual objects to work with. As Piaget said in the foregoing quotation, concrete thinkers operate on objects and not on verbally expressed hypotheses. Verbal learning for this group is of no value.

This stage of intellectual development begins somewhere between 6½ years and 7 years 8 months and continues, according to Piaget, until 11 to 12 years of age. Friot and Renner corroborated this age range and suggested that it might even be extended when they found that in a sample of 258 eighth and ninth graders, 253 of them exhibited concrete operational thinking, and their average age was approximately 14 years 6 months.[37] McKinnon and Renner provided data that suggest that the upper age limit on concrete operations is much higher for some people than for others. They found that 50 percent of 131 entering college freshmen were concrete operational and that only 25 percent were definitely at the formal level.[38] The generalization can be safely made that concrete operations represent the stage of thinking which nearly all elementary school students occupy. The probability is pretty great that a good percentage of senior high school students are also thinking on a concrete operational level. In fact, a study we conducted during the 1970–1971 school year to

[36] Piaget, "Development and Learning," op. cit., p. 177. (Italics added.)

[37] Faith Elizabeth Friot, *The Relationship Between an Inquiry Teaching Approach and Intellectual Development*, doctoral dissertation, University of Oklahoma, 1970.

[38] Joe W. McKinnon and John W. Renner, "Are Colleges Concerned with Intellectual Development?" *American Journal of Physics* (September 1971), 1047–1052.

Table 3–2

Grade	Sample size	Formal operational or marginal	Concrete operational	
			(number)	(percent)
7	96	16	80	83
8	108	25	83	77
9	94	14	77	82
10	94	26	68	73
11	99	29	70	71
12	97	33	64	66

SOURCE: Adapted from *Teaching Science in the Secondary School* by John W. Renner and Don G. Stafford. Copyright © 1972 by John W. Renner and Don G. Stafford. By permission of Harper & Row, Publishers, Inc.

determine what type of thinking students in grades 7–12 do, showed results as given in Table 3–2. The formal operational column in Table 3–2 can be misleading. Note carefully that the numbers listed there represent those students who were *formal operational* (the fourth stage in Piaget's developmental model) or who were just entering into it. If only those students in the sample who were completely formal operational were listed the results would be

Grade 7— 3 students
8— 6
9— 9
10—10
11—12
12—18[39]

If you consider what has been said in the last paragraph, the curriculum implications for the elementary grades are quite clear. The first generalization that can be made is that the curriculum experience must consist of direct experimental kinds of learning, and learning that allows the child to interact with the objects of the several disciplines is inquiry.

Earlier in this chapter the statement was made that you would understand why so much time was spent on the preoperational stage of thinking. Stop reading at this point, pick up your pencil and organize your thoughts about why understanding the preoperational stage is so important and record those thoughts.

[39] For a complete description of these data and how they were gathered, see Appendix A.

The fourth level

The preoperational thinker often indulges in the wildest kind of fantasy which often has no basis in fact. If the world does not suit him, he just imagines it to be different until he has the type of fanciful world he wants. The concrete operational thinker is concerned with the actual data he extracts from objects, organizing those data, and doing mental experiments with them. This learner does not formulate hypotheses from his experiences; he accommodates his thinking to events in the real world. He can categorize, compare, seriate, and perform all various thinking acts that will lead to the extraction of information from objects and to rational power development if he is given experience with concrete objects. In short, the concrete operational child does not take departures from reality as the preoperational thinker does even though those departures have no lawful or logical basis.

The last level of intellectual development in Piaget's model is called formal operations and "begins at about 11 or 12 years."[40] Note that Piaget's age level for entry into formal operations is somewhat lower than ages quoted earlier. This need not disturb you; Piaget himself has given great thought to the lack of consistency at which learners enter the various stages and sums up his feeling thus: "although the order of succession is constant, the chronological ages of these stages varies a great deal."[41] Formal operational thinkers have the ability to take imaginative trips, but the basis for their trips is firmly rooted in the reality of information they receive from the world around them. John Phillips explains the formal operational thinker as being "capable of departures from reality, but those departures are lawful; he is concerned with reality but reality is only a subset within a much larger set of possibilities."[42]

A preoperational thinker cannot think about what it is he thinks. A concrete operational thinker can think about his thinking as long as objects are present for him to manipulate. *A formal operational thinker can think about the consequences and/or implications of his thinking.* He can think in the abstract—he does not need to have the objects to manipulate; he can take data and treat the pattern those data have as only one possible pattern they might form. As was said earlier, reality is only one possibility as far as the formal, abstract

[40] Piaget, *Psychology of Intelligence*, op. cit., p. 148. The data shown in Table 3–2 lead us to wonder about this age.

[41] Piaget, "Development and Learning," op. cit., p. 178.

[42] Phillips, op. cit., p. 101.

thinker is concerned. *The possible is as real to him as the here and now.* Perhaps another way that may be useful in helping you think about the formal level is to remember that the preoperational thinker cannot do mental operations, whereas the concrete thinker can perform mental operations with the information he has received from concrete objects. The formal operational thinker not only performs mental operations with reality but can perform operations on the operations used in mental experimentation. Only when learners achieve the formal operational level of thought can they deal with abstract ideas, and our information suggests that that does not occur, at the earliest, until sometime during senior high school.

The concrete operational thinker can obtain information, classify it, seriate it, and so on, but, according to Piaget, formal operations

> consist essentially of "implications" (in the narrow sense of the word) and "contradictions" established between propositions which themselves express classification, seriations, etc.[43]

Jerome Bruner describes formal thinking as the same type of logical operations that "are the stock in trade of the logician, the scientist, or the abstract thinker."[44] In short, the learner who has passed into the formal operational stage can reason from ideas and does not need objects.

When careful consideration is given to what has just been outlined as describing formal operations and then the science curriculum found in today's schools is considered, some interesting, disappointing, frightening, and enlightening factors become apparent. The intellectual levels model of Piaget tells us that any experience that children below the formal operational level have needs to be an experience with objects of the discipline which he can seriate, classify, analyze, compare with other objects, evaluate and, in general, *act upon*. Those experiences are necessary if the learner is going to progress through the stages of the Piagetian model. If schools truly embraced the intellectual levels model and selected science curricula that would lead children to achieve the stage of formal thinking, the school day would be structured much differently than it is today. First of all, there would be much less emphasis placed on science textbooks and "learning" from them than is presently true. Do not interpret the foregoing remark to mean that we are saying books are not important—they are. But we are saying that school activities which focus their atten-

[43] Piaget, *Psychology of Intelligence*, op. cit., p. 149.
[44] Jerome Bruner, *The Process of Education* (New York: Random House Vintage Books, 1960), p. 37.

tion on the acquisition of the material in textbooks with little experience except reading about the disciplines' objects are not providing experiences that will enable children to move through the various intellectual developmental stages.

Earlier in this chapter we quoted Piaget as saying that every time we try to teach a child something too soon, we keep him from reinventing it himself. A learner invents an explanation only when he is in disequilibrium, and putting himself back in equilibrium with inventions and discoveries sharpens his ability to look at what is being considered. But in addition, the continual process of equilibrating and disequilibrating (through exploration, invention and discovery, that is, inquiry) moves the child upward through the several stages of intellectual development. Inquiry, then, is the methodology of intellectual development because it provides the opportunity for the learner to disequilibrate and equilibrate himself. Put in another way, inquiry is the methodology of equilibration.

None of the foregoing will happen, however, if the curricula selected in the schools do not provide experiences for the learners *at their level of intellectual development.* In Chapter 2 *the rational powers* were introduced as *one criterion* for selecting curricula to use with your students. Here, then, is a *second criterion—the curriculum used* (content and materials) *must be compatible with the developmental level of the learner.* Only then will the child progress through the several stages of development and reach the formal operational stage. The child must work with content *at his level;* only then will he progress to the next level. He does not need to work with concrete operational content while he is preoperational in order to become concrete operational—in reality he cannot do so. Providing the learner with experiences, or his providing them for himself, at his operational level, is the only way he will progress to the next level. If a child were left to his own devices—that is, without school—he would probably provide himself the proper experiences to become concrete operational. We *hypothesize* that unless a learner has ample and proper concrete operational experience at that level, he *will not* become formal operational; he will not be able to make decisions that require the degree of abstract thinking that citizenship in this country requires. The number of concrete operational college students found in the study of McKinnon and Renner suggests that many of today's schools are not providing the experiences needed at the concrete operational level and that will enable the learners to become formal operational. We also believe that many schools and teachers are providing formal operational experiences for concrete operational learners, and the result is that little learning is taking place. Could "pushing content down" result in providing formal operational experiences for concrete operational learners? Carefully consider that possibility when you select science content to teach in your classroom.

Formal thinking has two constructs that are useful in its identification. The first of these constructs results from the understanding that a formal thinker has of the importance in his experimentation of keeping all factors constant except one—the one being varied. He has, therefore, a frame of reference which says that, all other things being equal, we can then say that such and such a variable has (or does not have) an effect on the outcome of the experiment. The ability of a child to handle the "all-other-things-being-equal" contrast, can lead you to suspect you are working with a formal operational learner. The second construct that is useful in identifying formal thinking and those who use it is that of the proposition. In fact, formal operational thinking is often called propositional thinking. Propositional thinking can be most easily thought of as being of this form: "If (such and such is true), then it follows that (such and such is true); therefore, this (action is dictated, or suggested)." The "if, then, therefore" construct demands that the person using it depart from reality and push himself into the formation of hypotheses. Such is the ability and prerogative of the formal operational thinker.

What kinds of experiences are needed to actuate the level of formal operations? The answer is simple—the doing is not. Carefully selected activities which will allow the child at his present level of development to participate successfully but which will also tempt him to extend his thinking by carefully measured increments are needed. For example, those students who have progressed far into the concrete operational stage should be given practice in framing general statements from data they collect, and in making and testing logical deductions from those statements.

Identifying the formal operational thinker

Identifying the formal operational thinker is a more complex matter than identifying those in the concrete operational stage. The work done to date in finding tasks that will select formal operations has been less comprehensive than that done at the preoperational–concrete-operational boundary. At the present time Robert Karplus of California and Jan Smedslund of Norway are among those addressing themselves to the task of inventing ways of identifying formal think-

The conservation of volume task helps identify the beginning formal operational thinker.

ers. There are, however, several simple things you can do to give you information about a learner's ability to think formally.

As a learner just enters the formal operational stage, he will begin to conserve volume. The equipment required to allow the learner to attempt that task is two cylindrical containers, each about one-half full but containing *equal amounts of liquid,* and two small weights of *equal volume but different weights* which can be lowered by a string or wire into the cylinders. (See Figure 3-18). Have the pupil adjust the

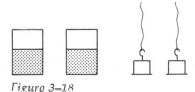

Figure 3-18

levels of water in the two containers until he feels they are identical; be sure he understands that the weights are identical in volume but different in weight. Next, ask him what will happen to the water in the cylinder if one of the weights is submerged into one of the containers and after that answer (which will, of course, be that the level will rise), ask him if the heavy weight or the lighter weight will raise the level more or if each will raise the level the same amount. A thoroughly concrete operational thinker will report that the heavier weight will raise the level more, and one who has just begun his entry into formal operations will report that each will raise the level the same amount. Next, have the student lower the lighter weight into one cylinder. Now, give him a rubber band and have him mark the spot that he believes the water will rise to in the second cylinder. Lastly, have him lower the heavier weight into the container and if he had predicted incorrectly, ask him what he thinks caused the levels to come out equal.

Two additional tasks are included here which we feel you can use to identify a learner who has moved into the formal operational stage. The first of these is called the *reciprocal implication* task. This task is based upon the principle that when a solid, moving object (like a marble) strikes a straight, solid barrier (like a wall) at an angle (*i*) and is reflected, the object will be reflected from the wall at the same angle (*r*) it struck the wall. The experimental setup is shown in Figure 3–19.

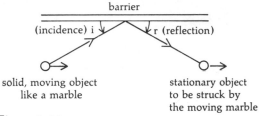

Figure 3–19.

The task the student is assigned is to strike a stationary object with the moving object, *but* the solid, moving object must be made to strike the wall *first*. After the student has performed the task, he then must be asked to analyze the problem and formulate a rule that will assure his success with each trial. The work that Inhelder and Piaget[45] have done with this task has led them to conclude that the statement of the equality of the angle (*i*) which the incoming object makes with the wall and the angle it makes (*r*) when leaving the wall will not be formulated until the student's thinking has entered well into formal operations. Inhelder and Piaget also tried this task (they used an especially constructed apparatus that they described as "kind of a billiard game!"[46] with preoperational and concrete operational children. They report that preoperational thinkers do not see the path of the moving object as straight line segments but describe the object's entire path as a curve. At this stage of development, the child takes into consideration the "starting point and the goal, but not the rebound points."[47] Concrete operational thinkers report that the path of the moving object is two straight lines; these thinkers

[45] Barbel Inhelder and Jean Piaget, *The Growth of Logical Thinking* (New York: Basic Books, 1958), pp. 3–19.

[46] Ibid., p. 3.

[47] Ibid., p. 4.

succeed in isolating all the elements needed to discover the law of the equality of the angles of incidence and reflection, yet they can neither construct the law *a fortiori* nor formulate it verbally. They proceed with simple concrete operations of serial ordering and correspondences between the inclinations of two trajectory segments (before and after rebound), but they do not look for the reasons for the relationships they have discovered.[48]

Not until the thinking of students becomes formal will they look for the way the two angles are reciprocally implicated. This task requires the learner to organize his data, do mental experiments with them, and finally develop an hypothesis and put it in shape for testing—a truly formal operational task.

The last formal operational task we have found useful is one that requires the learner to do something, watch the results, isolate the factors (or variables) which can be changed, and *exclude* those which do not influence the results. This task is called the *operation of exclusion*. The apparatus used is a series of different-sized weights that can be suspended from a solid support by different lengths of string and allowed to swing back and forth; that is, the apparatus is a pendulum. (See Figure 3–20.) The student is shown all the materials

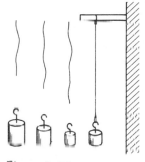

Figure 3–20.

and asked to make a pendulum. After he has it operating he is asked what controls how fast the pendulum swings. He is told he can use any of the weights and string lengths he wishes to assist him in solving the problem. As the student inspects the problem he will see that he has a range of variables to play with. The length of the string, the size of the weight, the height from which the weight is released (amplitude), and the force of the push he may give the weight, all probably represent variables that he may isolate. The one that controls the

[48] Ibid., p. 8.

rate at which the pendulum completes its swing is the length of the string; none of the others has any effect. The formal task that the student has is to formulate hypotheses that will lead him to exclude all factors from his thinking except length of the pendulum's cord.

A preoperational thinker, according to Inhelder and Piaget,[49] will attribute all variations in the motion of the pendulum to the push it is given when starting out. The concrete operational thinker will find the inverse relationship between the length of the string and oscillation of the pendulum—the longer the string the slower its motion and the shorter the string the more rapid its motion.[50] But a learner in this stage of development will not attribute the motion of the pendulum to length only; he gives rather casual roles to the weight and starting point and cannot exclude them from the length as the significant factor.

What has been said above about identifying the formal operational learner is only a beginning. There are other tasks that can be used; the ones presented here were those for which the materials would be readily available. If you have read the procedure we have used for our own formal operational research in Appendix A, you noticed that we used the sinking-floating problem (the elimination of contradictions) rather than the reciprocal implications task. We did this because our preliminary research told us that evaluating for the elimination of contradictions was more efficient than the reciprocal implications task. (Most certainly the materials are easier to secure and manipulate.) Our judgment was in error; that is why we recommend the reciprocal implications task here. There are also many points in the interpretation of data from formal operational tasks which should be considered before making an intricate determination of what position on the formal operational spectrum a student occupies. Such a detailed account of the formal operational stage we feel is beyond the scope of this book. We urge you to study carefully Part I (Chapters 1–6) of the Inhelder and Piaget text cited in footnote 45. What has been presented here are tasks you can administer quickly and for which you can interpret the data easily. That interpretation can guide you in selecting content and materials for your classes.

Recent research in identifying operational thinkers

Recent research findings indicate that the educational experiences provided by the upper elementary and secondary schools have not nurtured formal thinking in students. You have already seen the

---

[49] Ibid., p. 69.

[50] Because of the relationships between the length of the string and the length of the weight, strings shorter than 18″ should probably not be used.

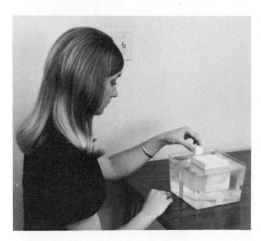

The elimination of contradiction task has been useful to us in our study of formal operations.

results of the work of Friot, McKinnon, and Renner, and Appendix A reviews our most recent project.

Karplus and Karplus,[51] using procedures very similar to Piaget's, isolated transitional substages from concrete to formal operational thinking by use of a simple puzzle concerning four islands. The subjects were asked questions concerning the possibility of traveling from one island to another, and their answers were to be based on information provided in statements by the investigator.

The written responses to the questions posed concerning the puzzle were categorized according to the type of thinking used. The subjects ($n = 499$) tested ranged from fifth grade through college physics teachers. The categories of the responses are roughly as follows:

N	No reasons given
I	Reasons not logical
IIa	Transition to concrete models
IIb	Concrete models
IIIa	Transition to abstract logic
IIIb	Abstract logic

The students who participated in the test were from suburban schools. The groups (10–12) were in college preparatory classes. The group 12P were twelfth-grade physics students. The two adult groups were as follows:

NSTA	Convention Participants at 1969 NSTA Symposium on Piaget
AAPT	American Association of Physics Teachers

[51] Elizabeth F. Karplus and Robert Karplus, "Intellectual Development Beyond Elementary School I: Deductive Logic," *School Science and Mathematics*, LXX, 5 (May 1970), 398–406.

Table 3–3

Category	Grades 5–6	Grades 7–9	Grades 10–12	12P	NSTA	AAPT
N	24	3	1	9	10	0
I	40	39	9	15	4	3
IIa	11	26	13	6	18	6
IIb	18	19	62	47	54	51
IIIa	7	15	11	15	8	27
IIIb	0	0	3	8	6	13

SOURCE: Elizabeth F. Karplus and Robert Karplus. "Intellectual Development Beyond Elementary School I: Deductive Logic." *School Science and Mathematics*, LXX, no. 5 (May 1970), 402.

There is a gradual transition in the group median from category I for the 5–6 group to IIa for the 7–9 group and IIb for the 10–12 group. Karplus says: "It is clear from this study that intellectual development in abstract reasoning, as defined by the 'Islands Puzzle,' reached a plateau in the high school age group and did not progress much further. In addition, the plateau is at a disappointingly low level."[52] Only 14 percent of the 10–12 group utilized formal logic or abstract reasoning to solve the problem which is essentially the same as the 7–9 group at 15 percent.

Karplus and Peterson[53] assessed the ability of students at grade levels from fifth to twelfth to solve a simple ratio problem. The procedure was to administer the problem to groups of subjects and to collect written responses. These responses were categorized using essentially the same categories as were used by Karplus and Karplus in the Islands Puzzle.

The ability to solve this ratio problem using abstract logic was not demonstrated by a majority of the students until grades 11 and 12. As Karplus and Peterson state:

> Few readers experienced in teaching mathematics and science will be surprised by the findings of this study. Nevertheless, it may be disappointing that successful proportional reasoning is not achieved until the last years in high school even though the subjects of ratio and proportion make their appearance in most mathematics programs in the sixth grade and in junior high school. It seems, therefore, that there

---

[52] Ibid., p. 403.

[53] Robert Karplus and Rita Peterson, "Intellectual Development Beyond Elementary School II: Ratio, A Survey," *School Science and Mathematics*, LXX, 9 (December 1970), 813–820.

Table 3–4

Category	Age 10–12 Grades 5–6	Age 14–16 Grades 9–10	Age 16–18 Grades 11–12
N	2	0	1
I	38	13	5
IIa	22	25	9
IIb	30	25	5
IIIa	2	14	5
IIIb	6	23	75
	$n = 129$	$n = 80$	$n = 154$

SOURCE: Robert Karplus and Rita W. Peterson. Personal Correspondence.

Table 3–5

	Grades (number)						
Percent	4–5 (116)	6 Suburban (82)	6 Urban (95)	8–10 Suburban (75)	8–10 Urban (128)	10–12 Suburban (153)	10–12 Urban (67)
N	2	1	5	0	0	3	1
I	31	36	41	4	16	3	15
IC	9	5	12	11	21	1	12
A	16	26	20	25	30	10	31
S	33	26	16	24	25	3	20
SA	4	0	3	4	3	0	12
P	5	6	3	32	5	80	9

SOURCE: Robert Karplus and Rita W. Peterson. "Intellectual Development Beyond Elementary School II: Ratio, A Survey." *School Science and Mathematics*, LXX, no. 9 (December 1970), 817.
NOTE. Category symbols are defined as follows: N = no explanation; I = intuition; IC = intuitive computational; A = addition; S = scaling; SA = addition and scaling; P = proportional reasoning.

is a serious gap between secondary school mathematics curricula and the children's reasoning ability.[54]

This might also explain why students below senior high school have difficulty with density, acceleration, and other such concepts that require proportional thinking.

Table 3–5 shows a comparison of suburban and urban groups taking the ratio test. The categories are roughly I, preoperational, to P, formal thought. There does not appear to be a substantial difference in the urban, suburban groups through grade 6, but the differ-

[54] Ibid., p. 818.

ence in the high school groups is substantial. It appears to us that the educational program in the urban schools provides little opportunity to develop formal thinking at all.

On the basis of these research findings, the generalization can be safely made that concrete operations represent the stage of thinking which most junior high school students occupy. From their research the inference can be made that a considerable percentage of senior high school students are thinking on a concrete level. Our most recent research (Appendix A) supports that hypothesis.

As a professional teacher you have the responsibility to promote learning, that is, to teach. To do so you must take the child where he is and guide him toward maximum intellectual development. We have already indicated that the inherent teaching method in discharging this responsibility is inquiry. In order to use inquiry successfully, you must use it functionally. To promote the development of such functionality is the purpose of Chapter 4.

4 | The Elements of Inquiry

If two parallel lines are cut by a transversal line, the opposite angles formed are equal. Perhaps you have encountered such a definite statement in your study of mathematics. If you have not, you probably learned your basic geometrical ideas through one of the "new" mathematics programs. The foregoing theorem from plane geometry has traditionally been taught (and learned) in a manner that can be classified as "deductive." The proposition to be learned is stated, a proof of its authenticity is presented to the learner, and several "problems" (actually exercises wherein the procedure used in the proof was applied in recipe fashion) are "done" to impress the importance of the proposition upon the pupil. This type of learning imposes on children what John Dewey called "adult methods." Children learn such material because it is imposed on them and not necessarily because they understand and/or like it. When the learner forgets the proposition about the two parallel lines and their transversal (and the "forgetting rate" of such abstract learning is high), he has nothing left from his school experience—his educational residue is zero. The principal reason for his zero residue is that he had no direct sensory experience in finding out that certain angles in the figure are equal; the learning he had was imposed learning.

Contrast the foregoing procedure for learning this important geometrical idea with the following:

> Examine the lines on a piece of ruled paper. These lines have exactly the same direction; they are parallel. . . . Darken a pair of lines on the ruled paper. Draw a straight line diagonally across these two lines. Label the angles formed. With your protractor measure the angles. What statement can you make about these angles?[1]

[1] Elementary School Science Project, *Charting the Universe* (Urbana: University of Illinois, 1963), p. 18.

Inquiry versus Authoritarianism

The foregoing quotation from *Charting the Universe* represents an approach to learning the "opposite angles" generalization which recognizes that if the learner finds out the generalization for himself, he will be developing his rational powers (his ability to think). That development will take place because he must actually collect and classify data, compare the classifications, synthesize an answer to the question on the basis of the data, and ultimately take a stand on the question which is based upon what *he* truly believes and not on what someone has told him. In this type of learning situation, the child is not only developing his rational powers, but, simultaniously, he is also developing an understanding of the content involved because he is evolving the content as he works. In addition to developing an understanding of the content and his rational powers, the child is learning how to find out information he does not have and increasing his confidence in his ability to inquire; in short, he is learning how to learn.

The first procedure for learning the geometrical proposition described in the introduction to this chapter represents the imposition upon the learner of those generalizations that adults feel he "should know." The child is expected to accept such generalizations, and to make accepting them more valuable to him, a proof of their preciseness is presented. This type of learning represents the traditional procedure for "learning" subject matter. Following through the logic of the proof of a given proposition is intended to sharpen the intellect of the learner; the proposition itself, when memorized, represents the type of subject matter with which the mind should be stocked. Notice that the "stocking" and "sharpening" processes are quite separate. The logic of the proof does not necessarily make the proposition any easier to remember, nor is it intended to; the proof is presented only as an example of the type of activity the mind should be able to perform. The classicist believes that repeated experiences like this will ultimately improve a mind if it can be improved. Meanwhile, the proposition represents the type of material with which to stock the mind.

This latter type of learning procedure represents "authoritarianism." The authority representative of the adult society present in the classroom (the teacher) not only prescribes the material to be learned, but also dictates the manner in which it is to be learned. Compare that type of educational environment with the classroom atmosphere that will result when the teacher leads the children to the geometrical proposition by using the previously quoted statement from *Charting the Universe.* In this situation the children draw the lines, make the measurements, and arrive at the proposition by themselves with the teacher assisting only when necessary. That type of teaching represents "inquiry." Often the inquiry method is criticized because the teacher relinquishes control of the content to the learners. As the example of inquiry teaching illustrates, this criticism is not justified. The teacher selects the generalization to be arrived at in the inquiry situation just as does the teacher in the traditional case. There is no dilution of the principle being taught in the inquiry situation. There is, however, a vast difference in the manner in which the teacher goes about teaching the principle and achieving the objectives. That difference is exactly what inquiry teaching represents—a teaching methodology. Content is learned, but the *method* the teacher uses enables the learner to achieve more than content understanding; he also develops his ability to think.

Inquiry and Science Teaching

Inquiry as a methodology was discussed briefly in Chapter 3. Here we shall return to a discussion of inquiry for a closer, more detailed examination with emphasis on its role in teaching science in the elementary school. First, it should be stated that, contrary to popular usage, "discovery" and "inquiry" should not be used as synonyms. The term "discover"—obtaining insight or knowledge for the first time—brings to mind a generally self-directed activity (mental or physical) of the logico-mathematical type culminating in a new insight. "Discovery" activities, then, from the Piagetean frame of reference are very valuable learning experiences. But discovery learning experiences, valuable as they are, are only a part of the cyclic spectrum of experiences which make up "inquiry" as a teaching method.

Suppose, for example, a teacher has as a major goal to help his pupils grasp the structure of science. According to Bruner, "grasping the structure of a subject is understanding it in a way that permits many other things to be related to it meaningfully. To learn structure, in short, is to learn how things are related."[2] The "things" to which Bruner refers are the conceptual building blocks of the subject developed through firsthand explorations and logico-mathematical experiences. Such concepts can also evolve through intuitive understandings, and are often difficult to express verbally because they are not clearly

---

[2] Jerome Bruner, *The Process of Education* (Cambridge, Mass.: Harvard University Press, 1962), p. 7.

The exploration phase of inquiry is valuable and fun for children.

in focus and there is no language available in the mind to express them. If the understanding of the concept does not progress beyond exploration and/or intuitive stage, it is, of course, not readily related to other concepts. Also, if no language is available to the learner to summarize and express his ideas, he can not clarify his understanding through communication with others. A simple act at this point can help the pupil over this learning barrier. He can be provided a label or word that can be used to summarize his intuitive ideas or notions. This label, or "conceptual invention," is usually provided by the teacher. Labeling a concept (giving a name to an idea or a collection of ideas) not only helps bring the ideas into focus for use in thinking, but it also provides the basis for communication with others concerning the concept. The label used can be one agreed on by the pupils in a particular class, or it can be a label in common usage by the scientific community.

Once the concept has been labeled, it becomes for the pupil one of the more clearly defined parts of the structure of science. Through subsequent discovery activities, the concept can be extended and refined and the relationship between the concept and others can be grasped; that is, the learner can grasp the structure of science. The labeling of concepts (invention) in inquiry teaching greatly increases learning efficiency and provides the basis for communicating ideas to others. But invention without the necessary prior exploration to allow the child to become familiar with the objects being investigated is of little value.

What follows are two very brief examples of inquiry teaching which show the place of invention in the inquiry method.

The invention phase of inquiry is as useful in small groups as it is in large ones. Hara Geneva Evans invents the concept of property.

Example One[3]

A group of children was experimenting with two magnets. Imagine that these magnets were mounted on small wheels (roller skates work nicely). The pupils in their exploratory experimentation with magnets found that magnets attract each other. This attraction showed an interaction between the two magnets: "something" caused them to move toward each other. What is the something that made the two magnets move together? The children noticed that they could not feel or measure the length of the something, but they also found that a nail responded to either magnet, that is, the nail was attracted to the magnets. One of the children suggested that the something was a "magnetic." At this point the teacher agreed that the "something" which was attracting the nail was indeed magnetic and proposed that the something be called the "magnetic field." Eventually the children would probably have named the something the "magnetic field" of

[3] Example One has been paraphrased from J. M. Atkin and Robert Karplus, "Discovery or Invention?" *The Science Teacher* (September 1962), 45–51.

Inventions will lead children to discoveries. The histogram being used here to solve a problem in area was just a conceptual invention a few days earlier.

the magnet, or the teacher could have fished for it by asking questions. There was, however, no point in letting the children struggle. They had discovered that there was something unique about the two horseshoe-shaped pieces of metal which made them interact. As you can see, letting the children work and/or search for the proper name of the something would have been pedagogically inefficient. The teacher *invented* the name "magnetic field." Experiments can go forward during which the children can discover much more about the magnetic field. Will the magnetic field attract pennies? How far from the magnet can a steel nail be placed and still have the magnetic field attract it? It is in the exploratory experiments that lead up to the *necessity* for the invention, and in those experiments following the invention, that discoveries are made and the rational powers are developed.

Example Two

A group of prospective elementary teachers was given a convex lens and told to find out all they could about it. In addition to describing the appearance of the lens, taking its dimensions, and finding out that when it was held at a reasonable distance from the eye everything viewed through it looked diminished in size and inverted, they also

One of the teacher's responsibilities is to provide material from the environment for investigation.

made a very important observation. The lens, they found, would project the image of an object upon a card. This image was in full color, diminished in size when compared to the size of the objects, and inverted. These investigators also found that as long as the object was about 4 feet (or more) from their lens, the distance between the lens and the image was always the same. Distances of the object from the lens ranging from 4 feet to several miles were tried and the result was always the same—the distance from the lens to the image projected upon the card was constant. The teacher asked the students how they would define the quality of the images they had been viewing and they replied, "Sharp and in focus." At this point the teacher recalled to the investigators what they had told him—that the distance, or length, between the lens and the clearly focused image was always a constant when the object was more than 4 feet from the lens. Here was clearly a point where the teacher either could let the students investigate further until they uncovered the principle of focal length for themselves or invent the principle for them. The latter course was followed. The teacher told the group that what they had just discovered was the focal length of a lens. Then he led the students to compare the magnitude of the focal length with the magnitude of the distance the object was away from the lens. When, for example, the students observed that when an object was 30 feet (914 centimeters) away from a lens of 5 centimeters focal length, the object distance was infinitely greater than the focal length, they developed a concise definition of focal length—the distance the image is from a lens when the object is at infinity. That concept allowed the investigators to study the relationships that exist between the focal lengths of two lenses and three lenses. The discoveries and rational power development occurred before the invention and after the invention. The invention of the concept of focal length increased the efficiency of the learning situation and enhanced the discovery activities utilizing the concept. The invention probably assisted the learning most by reducing the frustration of not knowing what to call or how to use certain findings.

The inquiry method illustrated by the examples above can be mentally divided into three interrelated phases:

1. *Exploration*—during which a learner probes into an area new to him and in so doing develops a reservoir of ideas about changes he observes or interactions he infers.
2. *Invention*—during which a label or concept is agreed upon or provided to bring the ideas into focus for developing conceptual structure and for efficient communication.
3. *Discovery*—during which the concept invented is expanded and related to other concepts. These discovery activities can, of course, lead to new ideas which in turn might require a conceptual invention.

Inquiry teaching is therefore cyclic in nature.

Figure 4–1.

You have probably been asking yourself, "What *specifically* does the teacher do? What does the learner do in an "inquiry" science class?" Our model (Figure 4–2) breaks down these functions into a sequence that works well for us. This model, however, is not meant to be a recipe you can follow to teach by inquiry. In order for it to be of assistance to you, *you* must adapt it to *your* own classroom style; it can, however, provide you with guidelines for beginning to teach by

Teacher and Learner Functions in an Inquiry-Centered Classroom

	Teacher	Learner	
Exploration	1. Provides materials from environment and establishes minimal guidelines for exploration	Explores materials	**Learner Feedback**
	2. Questions learners individually to give directions; listens and observes	Investigates observed phenomena	
	3. Asks for report from class, and acts as moderator for report	Reports results of investigations and/or observations	
	4. Asks questions concerning meaning of data	Searches for patterns or generalizations in data. Proposes hypotheses	
	5. Questions class concerning how hypotheses concerning patterns can be tested	Proposes experiments and tests hypotheses *Observes and records related data*	
Invention	6. Asks for report of tests. Provides labels for concepts developed in exploration. Encourages use of *eye of mind* (i.e., what do you see in your mind) to construct a model for explanation of patterns Discusses model(s) presently in widespread acceptance	Discusses concept or model invented as it applies to explorations completed	
Discovery	7. Provides materials for concept or model expansion	Enlarges concept or model through explorations guided by model or concept	
	8. Questions concerning interconcept relationships and their relationships to original materials provided	Grasps interconcept relationships and fits into developing structure of major conceptual scheme and doing so uncovers another missing piece in the conceptual puzzle and the exploration begins again	

Figure 4–2.

inquiry. After you have used the method for a time, you won't need our model because you will have begun to look at inquiry through your own eyes and construct your own model.

More will be said about teacher responsibilities in Chapter 7 and about the inquiry classroom in Chapter 8.

The inquiry-teaching model in Figure 4–2 allows you to equate specific, overt teacher and learner acts with the exploration-invention-discovery teaching strategy. It also indicates where evaluation fits into the entire scheme. In inquiry teaching the most important function of evaluation is to provide feedback to the learner in order to permit him to make adjustments in the procedures he uses to find out. Figure 4–2 indicates where we have been able to utilize feedback from the teacher to the student and where the student begins to get feedback from the inquiry to himself. In Chapter 8 these evaluation notions will be picked up again and enlarged to demonstrate how the teacher who teaches by inquiry can also evaluate that way.

As you have no doubt already concluded, "exploration," "invention," and "discovery" are themselves labels or conceptual inventions. So too is the term "inquiry teaching." In practice it is often difficult if not impossible to isolate exploration and discovery as distinct activities.

Inquiry in Elementary School Science

When a child enters school he is somewhat acquainted with many of the wonders of science and technology. He has, most likely, come from an environment that includes automobiles, television sets, dentists, physicians, lawnmowers, electrical appliances, birth, growth, and many other examples of pure and applied science. As we have already said, one of the characteristics of children which makes science a natural area for them to study is their natural curiosity. Children are curious about all of the items just listed, and many more. Are we, then, to expect children to learn through inquiry the answer to everything about which they are curious—that which has been found out only by the best minds the world has known? Certainly not!

Jerome Bruner took a definitive stand on the expected outcomes of inquiry when he said, "I do not restrict discovery to the act of finding out something that before was unknown to mankind, but rather include all forms of obtaining knowledge for oneself by the use of one's own mind."[4] We cannot, therefore, expect the children in elementary school classes to make original contributions to the accumulated scientific knowledge of the world. What will be found, no doubt, is already known and probably is in some textbook whose intention is to present its readers with a rhetoric of the conclusions of science. In short, do not expect your pupils to discover something new in their investigation.

You can expect the children in your classes, however, to discover things that are new to them or to obtain insight about a given topic for the first time. If, for example, a child learns that too much water is just as harmful for certain types of plants as not enough water, that, for him, is a significant discovery. He has not found anything that botanists have not known for centuries, but, to the child, his finding represents something entirely new and, most probably, exciting. A class of sixth graders conducted extensive investigations on whether or not a mealworm could see. Their final interpretation of the data they collected would not have surprised a zoologist, but to those children their inquiry was a significant and stimulating one. Their inquiry motivated them to investigate many other aspects of mealworm development and behavior. They found, for example, that at a particular time the mealworm shed his skin and ultimately changed his shape. They watched several of those strangely shaped organisms for an extended period of time and were delighted to find that the "other form" (as they called the strangely shaped organism) of mealworm became a beetle. At that point, proper names for the various stages of the development of the organism were invented. Throughout the weeks of investigation into the life cycle and behavior of the mealworm, nothing new to the realm of science was discovered by these sixth grade boys and girls, but what they did discover was new to them.

If we cannot expect new knowledge to be found, what will the inquiry method of teaching allow the learner to discover about science? Whenever a group of children investigates a problem and finds that a fact leads to a question and the answer to that question presents another problem that must be investigated, the children are learning that their findings are related. In addition, the members of the group are becoming aware that science is not to be learned from a book; it can only be understood by employing the procedures of careful investigation and interpretation of the data their investigations

[4] Jerome S. Bruner, "The Act of Discovery," in D. F. Ausubel and R. C. Anderson, eds., *Readings in the Psychology of Cognition* (New York: Holt, Rinehart and Winston, 1965), p. 607.

provide, that is, inquiry. These children are learning that science is basically a process. These two factors—findings in a scientific investigation are related and science is a process—constitute the true structure of the discipline of science. Children who are taught science by the inquiry method will discover for themselves the true structure of the discipline. In addition, educational experiences provided by the process of inquiry are tremendously motivating and, therefore, encourage children to pursue their investigations. The previously mentioned sixth-grade class, as a result of asking themselves whether or not a mealworm can smell, conducted an extensive investigation into the exact materials in which mealworms can live. The materials used ranged from soil to red pepper! The investigation was made at the insistence of the children; their teacher had earlier concluded that such an investigation would not interest them.

What can children discover if taught science by the inquiry method? Two very important factors of which no amount of telling could have convinced them. These factors are (1) the structure of the discipline of science, and (2) the fact that scientific investigations are tremendously interesting.

In addition to the foregoing accomplishments, children taught by the inquiry method will discover for the first time *for themselves* a great deal of factual information. Does information discovered for ourselves hold any special place in our educational experience? Bruner's answer to this question is that "if man's intellectual excellence is the most his own among his perfections, it is also the case that the most uniquely personal of all that he knows is that which he has discovered for himself."[5] In other words, learning by inquiry not only will develop the rational powers of the child's mind, teach him the structure of the discipline of science, and let him experience the tremendous thrill that can accompany scientific investigation, but he will consider the knowledge he accumulates the most significant of any of the knowledge he has. All of the foregoing represent what the proper employment of the inquiry method can lead the learner *to discover for himself*. But what will the utilization of inquiry-centered learning experiences allow the child to develop which extends beyond these goals that are basically concerned with the content of science itself? What will inquiry-centered learning *do for the child* which other teaching methods would have difficulty providing?

Stop at this point and ponder these questions. Discuss them with your classmates and teacher and write answers to them before going on. Keep those answers in mind as you continue in this chapter.

[5] Ibid.

The remainder of this chapter is devoted to investigations that will lead you to discover the true nature of inquiry. No attempt has been made to arrange these experiments in order of difficulty or importance. Neither will these laboratory experiences lead you to discover all there is to know about inquiry teaching; rather, they will give you enough insight into the notion of inquiry to enable you to begin thinking about it. You are not expected to gain a thorough understanding of the scientific principle being investigated in each experiment. The problem you will be investigating in each case is the vehicle being used to allow you to familiarize yourself with the inquiry method of learning. You will find, however, that you cannot fully appreciate how useful the inquiry method is until you gain a reasonable grasp of the content. But this understanding of the content will be acquired by using the inquiry method and will, in turn, enable you to better determine the usefulness of the method. As we said earlier about the structure of the discipline of science, we find the elements of the discipline by using the process of the discipline, but the processes in turn provide us a framework within which we can relate the elements found and so construct the structure of the discipline. Hence we cannot say which is more important—an understanding of the content of the experiment or the processes of inquiry by which the content is found. Each enriches and deepens the other.

Physical Science Investigations

INVESTIGATION 1

Part I
You will be given a tape measure which has the length units of the metric system on one side and length units of the English system on the opposite side. Study these two systems carefully. Measure the height of a door in metric units and English units. Measure five other objects (all longer than a meter) in both systems of measurement. Study the data you have collected and determine how centimeters (cm) are related to inches. You must use ONLY the data *you* collected to make that determination.

Part II
In this portion of the experiment you will make measurements, but use only the metric system. Measure the circumference and diameter of a cup, a water glass, a plate, a saucer, and three other objects, none having a diameter less than 50 cm. Next measure the circumference and diameter of three large circular objects such as a bicycle wheel,

automobile wheel, or some other object having a diameter greater than 50 cm. Using *only* the data collected in this experiment, investigate whether or not there is a relationship between the circumference and diameter of a circle. If you find a relationship, is there a difference in it between objects of small diameter and those of large diameter? How would you describe any relationship you find? *Be sure you take all measurements carefully.*

INVESTIGATION 2

For this experiment you will need a ring stand, a ring, several pieces of string (various lengths but none shorter than 18 inches), and 3 weights of various sizes. Construct a pendulum by tying a string of known length to a weight and attach it to one of the rings on the stand. Pull the weight to the side and release it. Determine how long it takes the weight to swing *from* the point it was released *back* to that point. That amount of time is called the "period" of the pendulum. Keep the weight on the pendulum the same and increase its length. (It is suggested that you double the length of the string holding the weight.) Be sure you record all lengths of string you use. Determine the period of this pendulum. Increase the length again by a significant amount (keeping the weight constant) and again determine the period.

Repeat the foregoing procedure twice, but use a different weight in each case. The 3 weights used should be significantly different to allow any possible differences they cause in period to be evident.

On the basis of the data you have gathered, formulate an hypothesis about the period of a pendulum. Verify or disprove your hypothesis by selecting a completely different length of string and weight.

If you had a pendulum clock which was always slow, what kind of adjustment would it need?

INVESTIGATION 3

Part I

At the beginning of the period you will be given a convex lens and a white card. Study the lens carefully and find out all you can about it. Take it outside if necessary. Make any measurements which you feel will add to your understanding about what the convex lens is and how it functions.

Discuss your findings with your laboratory partners and clearly understand why you agree or disagree with them. After you have gathered all the information you need, return to the discussion area for a class summary of the findings about the convex lens. Do you see a pattern in the data gathered?

Part II

Fasten two convex lenses together with scotch tape. (Use an optical bench in this portion of the experiment. Secure one from the instructor.) Focus an image from a distant object on the card with the two lenses taped together. Now separate the lenses and focus an image with each of them. What relationships can you see between the images formed individually by the lenses and the image formed by the combination of two lenses? Be sure you can prove your relationships.

INVESTIGATION 4

Using an optical bench, place an object on one side of the lens and a white card on the other side. Focus an image on the card. Describe that image. Take all the measurements you can while the image is visible on the card (distances, size of object, size of image, etc.). Now see if you can find any other point where there is an image. If you find a second image, describe it and repeat the measurements you previously took. *Carefully* record all your data. Leave the apparatus set up and study your data. What kinds of interpretations can you make of your data? What kinds of generalizations about convex lenses can you make? Be sure your data agree with your laboratory partner's data or clearly understand why you disagree with him. Check any data you feel should be checked.

INVESTIGATION 5

At the beginning of the experiment you will be given a meter stick and something with which to support it.[6] Balance the meter stick. How far from each end is the balance point of the stick? While the meter stick is still balanced, hang different weights on each side of the balance point. *Be sure to always keep the stick balanced!*

Do this five times. Each time use different size weights and different distances on opposite sides of the meter stick support. Be sure to write down each time the amount of weight you used and how far it was from the balance point. What hypothesis can you form about how this lever works? Is there a definite relationship between the weights and the distances? Test your hypothesis by using different weights and distances, but keeping the support at the stick's natural balance point. Further test your hypothesis by moving the support to a point other than the natural balance point. Be sure to keep accurate records of all the data you collect. Now study all the data you have collected and interpret it.

[6] A commercially designed meter stick can be conveniently used here because it has an English measuring system scale on one side and a metric scale on the other.

INVESTIGATION 6

In interpreting the data from Investigation 5, we saw that the relation found which explains the action of levers did not hold when the fulcrum was not at the natural balance point of the lever. We also saw that the weight of the lever had not been considered and agreed to study its affect upon our investigation. The question also came up as to what part of the weight of the stick really had to be taken into consideration when making our computation. Here you are going to study the problem of what the weight of a meter stick means. When we say a meter stick weighs 120 grams, what have we said? If only 10 centimeters of a meter stick are on one side of the fulcrum of a first-class lever, can we neglect that piece, or must it be taken into consideration?

Complete the following steps:

1. Obtain a meter stick, balance edges, weight holders, weights, etc.
2. Carefully balance the stick on the fulcrum without weights on either side of the fulcrum.
3. Record the exact location of this natural balance point of the meter stick.
4. Now move the fulcrum to the 40 centimeter point and balance the stick using a weight holder and 1 weight.
5. Place the fulcrum at the 20 centimeter point and balance the stick using 1 weight and the holder.
6. Place the fulcrum at 2 other points. Balance the stick each time with 1 weight and the holder.
7. Study your data carefully and state a tentative hypothesis about what you have found.
8. Design a way to check your hypothesis.

INVESTIGATION 7

Did you notice that when one side of a first-class lever is pushed down, the other side moves up? This is called "changing the direction of an applied force." Therefore, in addition to being able to multiply the applied force, a first-class lever can also change its direction.

This is a first-class lever:

If a first-class lever were rounded out on the top and the bottom it would become a wheel.

In this experiment you are going to work with first-class levers that have been turned into wheels. When a wheel is used to change the direction of force, it is called a "pulley."

You will be given a set of pulleys, a scale, and some weights. Set up each diagram that is shown and, using the scale, measure the amount of force necessary to lift a definite amount of weight. Use the same amount of weight with each arrangement of pulleys (use a rather large amount

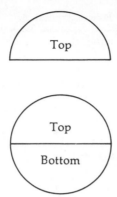

of weight). Why is it important to use the same amount of weight
each time and a rather large amount of weight?

How do the forces in Diagrams 1 and 2 compare? What are the
fundamental differences in Diagrams 1 and 2? What is the mechanical
advantage of the pulley in Diagram 1? What is the mechanical advantage
in Diagram 2?

Now set up the pulleys as shown in each of the following diagrams.
Use the same weight you just used in answering the same questions for
Diagrams 3 through 7 that you answered for Diagrams 1 and 2. Be
sure to record all the data the experiment gives you.

INVESTIGATION 8[7]

One of the really important characteristics which we hope science will
develop in children is the ability to interpret data. In this experiment
you are going to generalize on the basis of the interpretations you make
of certain data.

Place a level teaspoonful of cornstarch in a baby food jar. Also place
a teaspoonful of talcum powder, baking powder, and baking soda each
in its own individual baby food jar. Using a medicine dropper, dampen
each powder with a few drops of water and observe what happens.
Next add four or five dropperfuls to each powder and observe the
results. Repeat this experiment using white vinegar, and an iodine
solution. Prepare a table of your results. Be sure to classify your data
in the most usable form.

After you are completely familiar with your data secure a sample of
unknown material from each of the containers labeled A, B, C, and D.

[7] This laboratory exercise was developed from the concept in Lesson 10, "Interpreting Data 3—Identifying Materials," *Science—A Process Approach*, Part
Five (Washington, D.C.: American Association for the Advancement of Science, 1966), pp. 97–104.

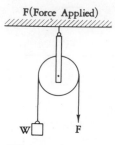

F(Force Applied)

W□   F

Diagram 1.

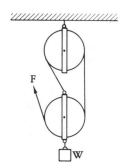

W(Weight Lifted)

W□

Diagram 2.

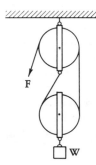

F

W

Diagram 3.

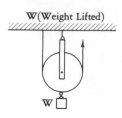

F

W

Diagram 4.

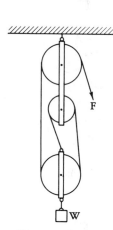

F

W

Diagram 5.

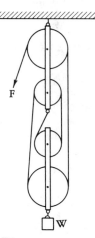

F

W

Diagram 6.

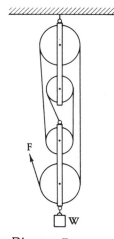

F

W

Diagram 7.

These samples either are or contain the four powders used in the first part of the experiment. Identify which of the unknown samples are or contain the powder used earlier.

Using the water, iodine solution, and vinegar, identify which of the following foods contain starch: apple, flour, bread, sugar, and salt.

Take a sample of liquid from each of the bottles labeled P, Q, and R. Using the four powders used in the early part of the experiment, identify the unknown liquids.

INVESTIGATION 9

Complete the following steps:

1. Place a 1-kilogram weight on a small car. If necessary, place a piece of cardboard on the top of the car to provide a smooth surface for the weight to rest on. The surface should not have vertical ends. With a piece of string attached to the front of the car, start it with a jerk.
2. Repeat the procedure, but this time start the car very gradually until it has a pretty good speed. Now, by means of a string attached to the rear of the car, stop it very quickly. What happens to the weight?
3. Repeat the two previous procedures using 2- and 3-kilogram weights.
4. Interpret your data and make a tentative hypothesis as to what they mean.
   Devise an experiment of your own to test the validity of the hypothesis you have drawn. After you have tested the validity of your hypothesis, what generalization can you draw?

INVESTIGATION 10

You will be given two eggs each having a different color. These eggs may both be hard boiled, one or the other of them may be, or they may both be uncooked. You are to find out the condition of the eggs you receive. You may use any three methods you wish to make your decision *except breaking the eggs*. You must return the eggs, unbroken, to the instructor. When you finish the experiment be prepared to explain what your three methods were for determining the condition of the eggs, the data you received from those three methods, and why you made the inferences you did.

INVESTIGATION 11

The solubility, the amount of a substance that will dissolve in a given amount of solvent at a given temperature, can be determined in the following manner.

Place 10 ml of water into a test tube. Then fill a plastic pill bottle with one of the substances for which the solubility is to be determined. Weigh the bottle and substance together and record this weight. Add the substance slowly, closing the test tube with a rubber stopper after each addition and shaking with a rocking motion. Continue adding small amounts of the substance until no more will dissolve and a very small amount settles to the bottom after shaking. Weigh the pill bottle and its contents again and record the amount (grams) required to saturate. Using those data, calculate the number of grams of the substance that will dissolve in 100 cc of water. Determine the solubility of the substance at 5 additional temperatures, several degrees apart. Place the data on a graph.

Determine the solubility of the following:

a. Table salt

b. Sugar

c. Baking Soda

Can a generalization be made concerning solubility of the substances at a given temperature?

Is there an observable pattern between the solubility and temperature of the substances investigated?

Make a prediction based on the graph of the solubility of one or more of the substances at a temperature other than the ones used. Then measure the solubility at this temperature and determine the validity of the estimate.

INVESTIGATION 12

Water that contains hardness minerals will not form lasting suds with soap until soap has combined with all of the hardness minerals. The reaction product usually forms a milky suspension in water.

The hardness of water may be tested by comparing the number of drops of a standard soap solution required to produce a suds lasting 30 seconds.

Prepare a standard soap solution by dissolving one level quarter teaspoonful of granulated soap in 10 cc of distilled water. Place 5 cc (ml) of the water to be tested for hardness into a test tube covered with a rubber stopper. Then add the standard soap solution dropwise, closing the container and shaking after each drop until a lasting suds is produced. Determine the number of drops of standard soap solution required to produce lasting suds for samples of water taken from a variety of sources such as:

tap water	ditch water
distilled water	river water
farm pond water	well water
lake water	melted refrigerator frost
rainwater	

Organize your individual data in some way (or ways) and
a relationship of pattern. These relationships or patterns wi
explored in class where the data will be pooled.

Life Science Investigations

Investigating animals

INVESTIGATION 13

The word animal refers to any living object that is not a plant.
Compile a list of objects, any objects, and then sit down with several
friends and put them into categories of living and nonliving. Be sure you
give reasons for putting an object into the living or nonliving category.
Remember, if you put, for example, any object into the living category
for a particular reason, you cannot put any object into the nonliving
category for that reason. Make a list of all the reasons for putting an
object into one of the categories. At the end of the investigation, your
explorations should have led you to have invented a classification for
living and nonliving objects. Next, pick any object in the room and,
using your classification system, explain why it is one of the categories,
living or nonliving.

INVESTIGATION 14

In this investigation you are going to work with fruit flies
(*Drosophila*). You first need to prepare the food mixture for the flies.
A recipe for food follows.[8] This recipe prepares enough food for
approximately twenty vials 8 cm tall and 3 cm in diameter when
approximately 2 to 3 cm of food are placed in the bottom of the vial.

Solution 1
    1 quart of hot water
    10 grams of agar
    2 teaspoons of Methyl Parasept

Solution 2
    28 grams of yeast
    10 ounces of cold water
    mix these two ingredients until there are no lumps and then add
    4 ounces of molasses

[8] Department of Zoology, University of Oklahoma, Norman, Oklahoma.

Solution 3
> 8 ounces (*by volume*) of cornmeal
> 16 ounces of cold water
> mix until there are no lumps

Be sure that the agar in Solution 1 has *completely* dissolved; then add Solutions 2 and 3 and cook until the entire mixture is fairly thick.

Place the food mixture in the vials loosely. Put on the lids and allow cooling to room temperature to take place. Next, place about one dozen fruit flies to each bottle used. During a period of several weeks, observe the changes in the fruit fly vial system and determine what happens. Do the flies remain unchanged? What new organisms appear? How are all the organisms related to each other and to the fruit fly? Your data should enable you to make some definite statements regarding the life of a fruit fly.

INVESTIGATION 15

The animal you will meet in this investigation is called a *Daphnia*; you may have heard this animal referred to as a water flea. Study your *Daphnia* with a magnifying glass and draw a diagram of him. Identify his mouth and how he eats. Over a period of days, observe the *Daphnia* and determine how he reproduces. Next, place a few *Daphnia* in a container of clear, aged water for a day. What changes do you observe in the *Daphnia*? Place some algae in the container and observe the changes in the *Daphnia*. What do the data from this observation allow you to infer about the structure of the *Daphnia's* anatomy?

At the first of the investigation, place about three guppies in some clear, aged water and leave them for about two or three days. DO NOT FEED THEM. Next, place the guppies with the *Daphnia*. What happens? Draw a diagram showing the relationship among algae, *Daphnia*, and guppies. Invent a name for that relationship.

INVESTIGATION 16[9]

For this investigation you will need a good supply of *Daphnia* and three containers that can be clearly and obviously labeled small (like a pill vial), medium (babyfood jar), and large (jelly jar). Fill each container

[9] This experiment was developed from the concept in *Populations Teacher's Guide*, pp. 29–33, by the Science Curriculum Improvement Study, published by Rand McNally & Company, Chicago. Copyright 1969 by the Regents of the University of California.

with water which contains a lot of algae and arrange a cover so air can pass into the water. Place about twelve *Daphnia* (be sure you know exactly how many) in each container and observe the *Daphnia* for a period of weeks; be sure to add algae-filled water as the *Daphnia* eat the algae in the containers. What do your data allow you to infer about the relationships among jar size, algae, and *Daphnia*? Be sure to compare the results of your investigation with several other people. Be prepared to discuss why this comparison is important.

INVESTIGATION 17

The realm of insects is a fascinating world to study. Insects have many interesting and exacting patterns of living which, when understood, can furnish information that can be used in helping to understand animal behavior. Bees, for example, have a pattern of life which is nearly a culture. Each bee has his role, and when that role is fulfilled, he dies. There are many similar examples in the insect world.

Before anything can be determined about the specific behavior of an organism itself, information must be available about the organism. What does he look like? How does he move? What type of food does he eat? After such questions as these are discovered, specific hypotheses can be advanced and tested about the specialized behavior of the organism.

In this experiment you are going to work with an organism called a "mealworm." The mealworm is the larva stage of a beetle (*Tenebrio molitor*). He is reasonably good-sized, active, cooperative, and quite a good subject to experiment with. You are asked to find answers to these questions.

1. Does the mealworm have eyes?
2. What processes does the mealworm go through in moving?

You will be given a paper plate, a small pile of bran, and a mealworm. Please ask for any additional materials you feel you need. The following general procedures may be helpful in guiding your work.

1. Place the bran on one side of the plate and the mealworm on the other. Watch him and describe his actions.
2. Form a hypothesis as to whether or not the worm has eyes and design some short experiments to test that hypothesis.
3. Observe the motion of the mealworm and inspect him carefully. On the basis of those data, describe how he moves.

When you have collected enough information to satisfy yourself that you have discovered answers to the two questions asked, form the interpretation of those data into logical statements. Be sure to give adequate reasons for your beliefs.

If you could spend additional time with these mealworms, what additional activities and/or experiments would you suggest?

INVESTIGATION 18

In Investigation 3 you saw that *Daphnia* eat algae and guppies eat *Daphnia*. That relationship among algae, Daphnia, and guppies is called a *food chain*. Select thirty living things—plants and animals—and draw a diagram. Among them showing who eats whom. For example (⟶ means "eats"):

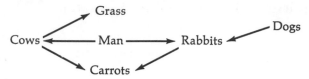

Such an arrangement is called a food web. Make a food web from your thirty living things. If you wish to practice first, enlarge the web we started. When is the food web completed?

INVESTIGATION 19[10]

You have probably found the animal used in this investigation when digging in flower beds, around shrubs and trees, and in other places in your yard and garden and called him a roly-poly. Another name for him is an *isopod*. In this investigation you are going to study his response to temperature.

Use about three sheets of heavy aluminum foil and prepare a tray about 6 cm wide, 65 cm long, and 4 cm deep. Mark the tray off into 6 cm numbered segments in order to give yourself a frame of reference to discuss the results of the investigations. Place one end of the tray on crushed ice or an ice chunk and the other end very close to (but not touching) a 75-watt white light bulb. Be sure to keep the inside of the tray dry. Why is that important?

Use about twelve isopods and place them first in the warm end of the tray, then in the cold end, then in first one segment, and then another. Be sure to give the isopods plenty of time to find where in the tray they are comfortable. What do your data allow you to say about isopod's responses to temperature?

INVESTIGATION 20[11]

You also use isopods in this investigation; you are going to study their response to moisture. Prepare an aluminum foil tray just as you

---

[10] This experiment was developed from the concept in *Environments Teacher's Guide*, pp. 49–54, by the Science Curriculum Improvement Study, published by Rand McNally & Company, Chicago. Copyright 1970 by the Regents of the University of California.

[11] Ibid.

did in Investigation 19 and fill it with good soil. (Plant-potting soil works best.) Starting on the left end of the tray, thoroughly soap about one quarter of the dirt, make the next quarter just wet, the next quarter just damp, and leave the remaining quarter dry. Use about twelve isopods and place them at different times in each of the four segments of the tray. Observe them carefully. Be sure to give the isopods enough time to find where in the tray they are comfortable. What do your data allow you to say about isopod's response to moisture? In Investigation 19, you were advised to keep the tray dry. Think back through this investigation; why were you so advised? What variable was constant in Investigation 7 that was allowed to change here? What variable was allowed to change in Investigation 19 but was held constant here? How could Investigations 19 and 20 be combined to make a perfectly valid investigation which would require either of the two variables just mentioned to be held constant? What would you be testing?

INVESTIGATION 21

Repeat Investigation 19 using some other insect such as the *Tenebrio molitor* beetle from Investigation 17. What general statements about insects' responses to temperature can you now make?

INVESTIGATION 22

Repeat Investigation 20 using some other insect such as the *Tenebrio molitor* beetle from Investigation 17. What general statements about insects' responses to moisture can you now make?

INVESTIGATION 23

Design and carry out an investigation that will permit you to make meaningful statements about the response of isopods to light.

Investigating plants

Throughout these investigations you will need to make judgments about whether or not the techniques and procedures being used in each investigation are proper. Those judgments will be made on the basis of quantitative and/or qualitative information you get from the plants themselves. You must before beginning each investigation decide what factors you will use to judge the data you will receive. You might wish to consider plant height, and/or color; condition of the leaves; stem diameter; amount of growth per day, week or some other period of time;

or some other set of criteria which would uniquely apply to your particular plant. No one can select those criteria but you, and once you have decided on criteria remain with them as long as they are adequate. Do not be afraid to discard one (or more) criterion if it does not permit you to gather the kind of data which allow you to make meaningful statements about the investigation being made. Remember that from each investigation you ultimately should be able to make a type of generalizing statement about the investigation. Be aware of when exploration, invention, and discovery occur and why they are necessary.

INVESTIGATION 24

Wash four quart jars very thoroughly and rinse them with great care. Be sure no soap remains in the jar. If possible rinse each jar with just a little alcohol to make sure the soap is all gone. Rinse the jar with water again. Fill each jar about one-half full of water and let stand for about two days. Fill a fifth jar with water and let it stand also. Mark the level of the water on each of the first four jars and keep it at that level by adding aged water from the fifth jar. Be sure to always refill the fifth jar after use.

Now obtain a liquid called chlamydomonas (clam-i-DA-mi-nas). Put about twelve drops into each of the four jars. Place two of the jars in direct sunlight and the other two in darkness or semidarkness. Watch them for a period of a few days and observe what happens. If the water in the two pairs of jars begins to change, what could you do to find out what is causing the change? All the data you will have will come from your observations. Be sure to state carefully any hypotheses you might have about the differences in the jars. Design any procedures you need to collect data to test your hypotheses. Include in your report why you believe you were directed to place *two* pair in each environment.

INVESTIGATION 25

You had better start the investigation with fifteen paper cups in which you can plant bean seeds. DO NOT SOAK THE BEAN SEEDS BEFORE PLANTING THEM. Most any type of bean will do, but we have had best results with bush beans. Be sure you use the same kind of soil in each cup. Why is that important? We have had best results with potting soil, which any garden supply center will have. Plant *two* bean seeds in each cup about ½-inch deep. Why plant two seeds? Arrange your cups in direct light and in a warm place.

The problem is to find out how much water will produce the best results. Give each of three cups the following amounts of water. Be sure each cup has holes in it for drainage. (1) What you believe to be absolutely much too much. (2) What you feel is too much but not as much as in (1). (3) What you believe is just the right amount. (4) What you believe is not enough. (5) What you feel is definitely too little. Be sure you isolate all the other variables you believe are involved and be sure they are controlled except the moisture. Continue your experiment until you have definite, irrefutable results. Why were you asked to use three plants in each moisture category?

INVESTIGATION 26

Repeat Investigation 25 but use plants which are healthy and well established in their environment. You will need a single place to keep the plants in order to control the environmental variables. After you have selected such a place, move the plants to it and give them about a week with normal care to acclimate themselves before the experiment is begun. Why is this important? Decide upon the five amounts of water just as you did before and proceed.

INVESTIGATION 27[12]

In this investigation you are going to use clover seeds. You will also need 21 plastic vials 3" by 1" (drug stores are good sources of supply), a shoe box and enough aluminum foil to line it, a small aluminum foil tray about 3" deep which is small enough to fit into a hole cut into the cover of the shoe box, a styrofoam carton with a cover, three small thermometers, and a daily supply of ice (approximately two tray fulls).

Half fill each vial with previously moistened potting soil and plant about 15–20 clover seeds, pushing them just under the surface. Make very sure to keep the soil moist throughout the experiment.

Place six of the vials in a bright place where the room temperature is reasonably constant. Lay a small thermometer in an empty plastic vial and place it with the six other vials.

Cut seven holes in the top of the styrofoam container just the shape and size of the plastic vials. Place six of the vials which have clover seeds planted in six of the holes and a vial containing a thermometer in the seventh. Place enough ice in the container so the bottoms of the vials do not touch it. The level of the soil in the vials should be just even with the surface of the container's cover. Keep ice in the container at all times. Be sure to add a little on weekends. Place this container with the other vials which are at room temperature.

Line the shoe box with aluminum foil and cut several holes in the sides. Cut a hole in the top to exactly accommodate the small aluminum foil tray. Fit the tray into the shoe box cover. Place a 60-watt light source in the box and leave lighted *throughout* the experiment. Be sure the light bulb does not make direct contact with the aluminum foil tray. Place six vials with soil and clover seed and a seventh one containing a thermometer in the tray. Be sure to start all three parts of the experiment at the same time.

What kinds of data can you gather? What are the variables? Which variables are not controlled? Why are the thermometers necessary? At the start of the investigation, state your hypotheses about what you think its results will be. What would be a good statement of what is being investigated here?

INVESTIGATION 28

Repeat Investigation 27 using vials containing healthy clover plants instead of clover seeds. Follow Investigation 27 exactly including isolating the variables and answering the questions asked there.

INVESTIGATION 29[13]

Soak about 30 bush bean seeds in water for from 24 to 36 hours. Soaking beans is best done by placing several paper towels in the bottom of a container, covering them with more paper toweling and then, soaking the towels. Do not let the beans stand in water because they need air.

Split the bean seeds in half. Each half of the bean is called a cotyledon. Another structure is also found in the open seed. Separate the last structure from the cotyledons; do this for about ten seeds. Next, plant the cotyledons in several containers and the unnamed structures in several others. Next, plant several cotyledons with the unidentified structure still attached. Also plant several containers of whole, soaked bean seeds. Paper or plastic cups which have drainage holes work nicely for this experiment. We recommend using potting soil. Watch the progress of the planted objects. Which seed parts grew? Which did not grow? What name could be invented for the unidentified structure found in the bean seeds? Why are both cotyledons and the unidentified structure found in the bean seeds? Why are both the cotyledons and the unidentified structure necessary in the seed?

[13] This experiment was developed from the concept in *Communities Teacher's Guide*, "What Is a Seed?" and "What Seed Parts Grow?" pp. 10–16, by the Science Curriculum Improvement Study, published by Rand McNally & Company, Chicago. Copyright 1971 by the Regents of the University of California.

INVESTIGATION 30

For this investigation you need a good, healthy crop of rye grass, some good, well-established clover plants, and some other type of plant—we have found geranium plants to be satisfactory. Be sure to have two containers of each type of plant. Find an ideal place for the plants to grow in the same way. By ideal we mean proper temperature, proper lighting, and the answer to the amount of water to be used which you arrived at from Investigation 25. Find a second place in the room where the temperature is satisfactory but that is in the dark. Place one of each kind of plant in the dark and one in the light. Observe and compare the pairs of plants daily. Be sure to keep records which provide you with adequate information. What do your data tell you over a period of weeks?

INVESTIGATION 31

Begin this investigation with three different types of plants (eight plants of each kind) already growing. The types we suggest are beans, peas, and clover. Be sure the plants are all growing in the same kind of soil, are in the same types of containers, and have been growing in the same environment. Why are the cautions listed in the last sentence important? Now divide the plants into four pairs of each kind. Select some chemical fertilizer, which can be purchased at any garden supply house. Give one pair just exactly what you feel is the correct amount of the chemical, a second pair just a little more, a third pair quite a bit less, and a fourth pair much too much. Why is having one pair of each kind of plant receiving just what you think is the proper amount important? If no differences are noted at the end of a ten-day period, give all the plants a second application of the chemical. Collect all data carefully and draw some generalizations regarding plants and chemical fertilizers.

INVESTIGATION 32

In this investigation you are to determine the affect that the type of soil has on seed and plant growth. We suggest you use at least two types of plant; e.g., peas and beans. Secure three different types of soil from areas around you; e.g., sandy soil, loam, black soil, clay, and pure sand. In addition, use potting soil. Why is using potting soil important or even necessary? Plan three containers of each seed in each soil type. Why use three containers? Be sure the containers have proper drainage holes. Select a place in the room that has a fairly uniform temperature and adequate light. Keep the soil moist and make regular investigations over a period of several weeks. Be sure to include references to seed and plant growth in your report.

INVESTIGATION 33

In this investigation you will need two small fruit-juice-size cartons for water, a drinking straw and some bromothymol blue (BTB). Fill the container about one-half full of water and add about ten drops of BTB. Blow your breath slowly and gently through the straw and observe what happens. Do not get impatient. A change will occur. Next use a balloon pump, a filled balloon or some other means to pass air (not your breath!) through a second container of water and BTB. What can you conclude? Let the containers set for from 24 to 48 hours. What changes do you see? What does your evidence tell you? Of what use is the water-BTB solution?

INVESTIGATION 34[14]

You must have completed Investigation 33 before undertaking this investigation. You need three containers with lids (pill vials from the drug store serve well), aged tap water, BTB, and two sprigs of Anacharis (or some other healthy water plant). Place a sprig of Anacharis into two of the three containers which have been completely filled with water and BTB (about 5–6 drops per vial). Containers should be so full that there is no air space between the fluid and the cover when the cover is secured. Fill the remaining container carefully every day for a few days days and record your results. What invention do your data enable you to make? Why was the third container important?

INVESTIGATION 35

You need to have completed Investigations 33 and 34 before doing this one. You need a large, well established potted plant (like a geranium), a small vial of water and about 5–6 drops of BTB (the vial should be as wide and shallow as possible), a good strong stick 12"–18" long (depending on the plant), and a good strong, large, clear-plastic bag. Push the stick into the dirt around the plant far enough to enable it to hold the vial containing the water and BTB about halfway between the dirt and the top of the plant. Fill a second vial completely with water and BTB, cover it tightly and place it on the stick. Place the plastic bag completely over the plant, stick, and vial and fasten its opening very tightly. The plant must now be placed in constant light. Inspect the plant

[14] This experiment was developed from the concept in *Ecosystems Teacher's Guide*, "Inventing the Oxygen-Carbon Dioxide Cycle," pp. 47–51, by the Science Curriculum Improvement Study, published by Rand McNally & Company. Copyright 1971 by the Regents of the University of California.

and BTB solution every day and record anything you observe. What invention about the life process of plants do your data allow you to make? Of what use was the covered vial of BTB solution?

INVESTIGATION 36

This is a paper and pencil and library investigation. You need to accept that a plant grows from a seed. Next select the fruit of a plant like an apple or a tomato. The fruit must contain seeds. Dissect the fruit and count the total number of seeds. Now go to a reference source and find out how many such pieces of fruit a plant will bear (in a lifetime in the case of the tomato or in one season in the case of the apple tree). Compute the total number of seeds the plant will bear in one season. That is called the *biotic potential* of that plant for a given season. Be sure you understand that term before going on.

Assume that each seed will produce the same number of fruits the next season. What is the biotic potential of a plant in two years? In three years? In five years? What has nature done to make sure the biotic potential of any plant does not reach 100 percent? How is this problem related to population growth and control?

Imagine this situation. In a large forest there are many rabbits. But in the same forest there are foxes, wolves, mountain lions, deer, and all other types of creatures. Some well-meaning persons decide that the foxes and wolves should be eliminated because they are eating the rabbits. A large fox-and-wolf drive is begun and those animals are eliminated. What will happen to the forest? Be sure to treat all the variables in your explanation. Mountain lions are natural predators on deer. Next, assume that the mountain lions are eradicated. Ultimately, what will happen to the deer? Invent a general concept that explains what these examples have been leading you to explore.

5 | Essential Science Experiences: Observation, Measurement, and Experimentation

Three primary purposes of the science curriculum in the elementary school were listed in Chapter 2, as follows:

1. To develop in the learner a command of the rational powers.
2. To develop in the student the ability and confidence to inquire.
3. To lead the child to develop an understanding of the changing nature of the environment in terms of matter, life, energy and their interactions.

Any content used in the elementary school classroom must allow and encourage the achievement of one or more of these purposes. The converse is also true—if what is being done in the science classroom is not leading children to the foregoing purposes, it has no educational value. Sometimes things are done in the classroom just for fun, and we heartily applaud that reason. But do not delude yourself that you are doing anything but having fun. Many science textbooks written for elementary school science introduce such concepts as the atom and the molecule. Such concepts are among the greatest abstractions of all science, and, as such, are of no value to preoperational and concrete operational children. Furthermore, if you again consider the purposes for which elementary school science is taught, such content does not fit with the children who are there.

The above-mentioned purposes of elementary school science serve as more than goals to lead children to achieve. They also serve as criteria that can be used to evaluate the content being taught and how it is being used. Exploration, invention, and discovery represent inquiry, and only when a child experiences them will he develop the ability and confidence to inquire. So when content and teaching procedures are selected for use in the elementary science classroom, the previously stated purposes serve as evaluative criteria. One ought not be afraid to apply them rigorously to the materials and techniques you select for your pupils to interact with.

There is, however, one question that as yet has not been explored. What specifically does a child *do* when he explores, invents, and discovers? From the frame of reference of the teacher, what kinds of *experiences* do you provide for children to encourage them to undertake exploration, be ready for conceptual invention, and able to make discoveries? We believe there are six specific experiences which are essential when teaching by exploration, invention, and discovery, and which would make the classroom activities recognizable by a scientist as science. Those essential experiences are observation, measurement, experimentation, interpretation, model building, and prediction. This chapter and the next are devoted to those experiences.

Before reading on, stop and write an explanation of what each of these six terms means from the frame of reference of classroom implementation.

Observation

If you are interested in acquiring information about an object you are not familiar with, the most obvious thing to do is to look at it. Your observations can give you a great deal of specific information and can lead you to discover other types of investigations which will give you much more information. Observations, however, can be made in many ways other than visually. Feeling, squeezing, poking, and rubbing are but a few of the methods (other than visual) which can be used to make observations. Observation is the first action taken by the learner in acquiring a new understanding. The curriculum must provide opportunities for the child to have extensive experience making observations. How are such learning experiences provided?

It is axiomatic that if a child is going to learn how to observe, he must have experience observing. He must be given the opportunity to watch, feel, squeeze, poke, and do anything else he needs to do which will enable him to describe the object he is observing. Furthermore, the object the child is observing must be one he feels comfortable with. The object must not be so foreign to the observer that he is afraid of it or uncertain of what he can or should do with it. When a young child comes to school he is probably more familiar with the objects found in his environment than he is with anything else; he is a collector of string, buttons, stones, small bottles, often small living things, and so on. The beginning observations that children can be

Observation is an essential learning experience in science and it also interests children. (Photo courtesy Science Curriculum Improvement Study, University of California, Berkeley.)

led to make, then, can be made on the common material objects found in their immediate environment. What follows is a description of a lesson which would be taught in the first grade and which is devoted solely to improving the learner's ability to observe and then describe what he has observed.

GRANDMA'S BUTTON BOX[1]

Teaching Materials

For each child:
  Approximately 20 assorted buttons
  1 cardboard tray

Teaching Suggestions

Sorting by color. Distribute a tray and a handful of buttons to each child. Discuss with the class the properties of the buttons as well as their similarities and differences. Then suggest that the individual button collections be sorted by color. Children should choose their own methods and numbers of groups. For example, some may group all red

[1] Reprinted with permission from *Material Objects Teacher's Guide*, p. 28, by the Science Curriculum Improvement Study, published by Rand McNally & Company, Chicago. Copyright 1970 by the Regents of the University of California.

buttons into one stack and all other colors into another. Some may sort each color into a different pile; others may even separate colors into shades. Accept all these choices as correct, and encourage individual pupils to describe their sorting procedures.

Sorting by other properties.   After the previous discussion has been completed, ask the children to sort their buttons according to another property. The number of groups and the properties they use should again be left completely to the pupils. Offer suggestions only if a child seems very confused. Afterwards ask a few children to describe the methods they used and let others participate in the discussion. As your pupils exchange ideas they will probably ask for more opportunities to sort buttons.

Individualizing the use of buttons.   Children may also group the buttons according to specified numbers of properties. Color might be one property, color and shape designate two properties, and so on. Ask children to tell you what properties they used for their groupings. If a child has trouble sorting his button collection, try giving him only eight or ten selected buttons during another session. Allow the children access to the buttons during free class periods. This additional work will help them analyze and further diversify their sorting methods.

Children who participate in learning experiences such as these are having their abilities to describe phenomena developed. This, of course, demands that a vocabulary that will allow the observer to express himself adequately must also be developed. In such a learning situation the vocabulary that is acquired really belongs to the learner because it answers a felt need. If, for example, a child is describing a button and uses the word "bumpy" when the word "rough" is more appropriate, the invention of the word "rough" by the teacher will be accepted by the child and that word placed meaningfully in his vocabulary.

In addition to providing experience in observation, the foregoing lesson demonstrates the contribution that experiences such as these can make to the development of the rational powers of the learner. The categorization of the buttons demand that properties be analyzed, buttons be compared with each other, each comparison be evaluated and, finally, that a generalization be reached about exact classifications.

One criterion established for the evaluation of the elementary school science curriculum is that the curriculum must provide experiences that will allow the learner to better understand his environment. How can concentrating upon developing the learner's ability to observe provide such environmental experience? One of the activities that *Material Objects* provides children is called the "Object Hunt." This activity is best described by quoting directly from the teacher's manual.

AN OBJECT HUNT[2]

Teaching Materials

For each child:
1 opaque plastic bag
1 magnifier
1 cardboard tray

Teaching Suggestions

When the class has reached the area you have chosen for the hunt, give each child a plastic bag for his collection. Tell the children that each one may choose as many as ten objects, and emphasize that each individual should work alone.

Restrict your remarks to interesting objects that cannot be collected. Point out that birds, trees, buildings, and clouds are objects. Some children may be inspired to collect feathers, leaves, and bits of brick.

Introducing the magnifier. After the class returns from the hunt, give each child a cardboard tray, and encourage the children to spread out and examine their objects. Give each child a magnifier, taking a few minutes to demonstrate how one uses it for careful observation. Encourage the children to use the magnifiers when they observe objects.

Introducing sorting. Tell the children to think of one property and then sort their objects accordingly. One child should tell and show how he sorted his objects; as he reports, write on the board the property used for sorting. This method of sorting can be used later by everyone. Follow the same procedure as you call on other children. Some objects may be placed in an "undecided" group. This category may result in a class discussion, which you should encourage.

Combining the collections. After the objects from the hunt have been sorted, put the trays with labels chosen from those suggested by the children. For example, these labels may be "smooth," "brown," "sticky," "undecided," "crunch," and "bumpity." Each child should have an opportunity to place one or several objects on an appropriate tray. Encourage the children to discuss their reasons for sorting.

Property hunt. Another way of using the outdoors is to go on a property hunt. Divide the class into groups, and let each group select

[2] Ibid., pp. 26–27.

a property. When your pupils have collected only objects having that property, they should display the objects on a tray in the classroom. You can put a label identifying the property on the tray.

. . .

Optional Activities

Object walks. You may take your class on an object walk preceding or following the object hunt. This activity is intended to acquaint the children with the vast array of objects in their environment. Some objects are observed and described but not collected. Such walks can be particularly useful if your school is in an urban or built-up area where collecting objects is not feasible, as around the center-city school. For example, parts of buildings, such as doors, or iron ornaments, can be identified and described.

If the suggestions given above are followed, the children will certainly have experiences that will help develop their powers of observation, improve their rational powers, and give them information about their environment. A learning activity such as this does not know regional bounds; the flowers, animals, seeds, and fruit that are discovered and then discussed will be those indigenous to the area in which the school is located. In other words, such learning activities really increase the child's knowledge of his immediate environment because he is actively involved in them.

The study of the properties of material objects need not be confined to investigating only those materials and objects in the environment which are not immediately obvious to the child, that is, those which he must learn to identify and describe before he has an adequate grasp of his immediate surrounding and the world in which he lives. The learner can, however, be introduced to the more subtle aspects of his environment in such a manner that his ability to observe is enhanced. The study of material objects proposed as a first-grade course in science by the Science Curriculum Improvement Study (SCIS) provides children with experiences wherein observations are made on living things (which can come from the immediate environment), colors, metals, wood, powdered substances, liquids, gases, plastics, seeds, plants, and many other materials. If the curriculum is constructed using such learning activities, it certainly develops the learner's powers of observation. In addition, these learning experiences develop the child's rational powers and uncover for him many aspects of his environment. We can conclude, then, that learning experiences aimed at making a child a critical observer are an essential part of the elementary school science curriculum. Since science progresses by hypotheses based on and tested by data provided from observations and measurements, there can be no doubt that a scientist would regard the development of observational abilities in children as "good science."

Measurement

Just by looking at, feeling, squeezing, listening to, and poking (i.e., qualitative observing) an object can yield most important information. There are situations, however, where data from qualitative observations do not tell us enough about the object under consideration. We may need to acquire such information as the length, the weight, and the width of the object. With these data we can compare the object with other objects, classify objects observed on the basis of specific criteria, and synthesize the various general characteristics for the classifications established.

After taking measurements of any object an investigator (adult or child) is able to make statements that are much more definitive than those he was able to make based only on qualitative observations. We cannot, for example, look at a plant today and specifically say it has grown a definite amount since yesterday. Our senses might tell us the plant has grown, but they certainly would not tell us how much. In order to be able to state how much a plant has grown in three days or a week, we must be able to refine the measurements that our senses allow us to take. Not only are our senses inadequate to make a measurement as small as daily plant growth, but they are also woefully inadequate in estimating accurately large measurements, such as the distance to the sun, the velocity of sound, or the weight of an elephant. Measurements are necessary to extend our senses down to the infinitesimal and up to something approaching the infinite, because our senses are not reliable as measuring devices except in a very approximate way.

Measurements can be considered observations, but they are *quantitative* observations that can be repeatedly taken in the same manner at different times, and the results received will be approximately the same. There will be variations that occur in measurements due to growth (i.e., occurring in a living organism, if that is what is being measured) or due to inaccuracies or inconsistencies that occur in the application of the measuring standard. The concept of variation by itself and in measurement is an extremely important one, and we shall return to a discussion of it later in this chapter. To enable children to learn how to use observations from measurements in the same manner as the qualitative observations previously discussed are used, the elementary school science curriculum must provide appropriate learning experiences for pupils at all levels.

Young children have an extremely wide range of interests, and within that range is an interest in growing organisms. Very interesting and valuable learning experiences can occur if each child is given an envelope containing about a dozen seeds and seedlike objects.[3] The children are then asked to sort objects into categories and identify which of the objects they feel are seeds and which are not. After sorting has been completed (in this portion of the activity the children are using their rational powers of comparing and classifying), each child is then invited to state which of his objects he feels are seeds. Responses such as "This can't be a seed because its edges are rough," "Seeds aren't black," "This is a seed because it has funny little marks on it," are representative of the responses the children will give during this activity. At this point the teacher should ask (if one of the children hasn't), "How could we find out which of your objects are seeds?" and eventually the class will suggest planting all the objects and seeing which ones grow.

What follows is an interesting activity for first graders; they thoroughly enjoy setting up their experiment and observing which seeds mature and which do not. They will, early in the experiment, want to dig up some of the objects planted to see which of them have started to grow. Much good inquiry-centered teaching can be done while this is going on, and it keeps the children's interest in the activity very high. In a few days, the children will have decided which of the objects were seeds. At this point the teacher gives each child (or two children) additional objects like those found in the envelope which *were* seeds. This will allow the pupils to see whether or not there are any general characteristics about seeds which they could establish. This seed-identification activity, although extremely valuable, is but preparatory to the introduction of the measurement aspects of the unit.

Introducing the measurement portion of the unit to the children is extremely important. The general procedure for the teacher to fol-

[3] The ideas explained in this section are based on an elementary school science unit entitled *Growing Seeds* prepared by the Educational Services Inc., Watertown, Mass., and published by McGraw-Hill Book Co., Inc., Webster Division, Manchester, Mo., 1966.

The essential experience of measurement can be an interesting experience for children.

low is to ask the children questions that cannot be answered without measurement. There are, however, some difficulties in following this procedure in this unit and in introducing the entire concept of measurement to young children; they do not at first see the need for measuring or think measuring is very important. These difficulties can be overcome, however, if the teacher directs their attention to their *own* plants with such questions as "Whose plant is biggest today?" "Has your plant grown since last week?" and "How do you know?" Eventually one of the children might suggest measuring the plants, or the teacher may have to introduce the procedure himself.

After the children have accepted the fact that by measuring the plants they can answer questions about how their plants are growing, the problem of how the measuring is to be done has to be solved. With first-grade children it is probably unwise for the teacher to introduce a formal measuring unit, such as inches (they usually do not conserve length). All that is needed is a system by which the growth between measurements can be compared. Each child is given an envelope containing many strips of colored construction paper and asked how he can use these to measure the growth of his plant. He will eventually come to the conclusion that he can place one end of a paper strip at the base of the plant and draw a mark on the paper which represents the height of the tallest leaf. While this idea will usually come collectively from the children, the teacher will probably have to suggest that each strip be dated to enable them to know when the various measurements were taken.

In studying the growth of his plant, the learner must compare the various measurements he has taken, synthesize these measurements

Temperature is a quantitative measure children can make and understand.

into a complete picture of his plant's growth, and evaluate whether or not his plant is growing as well as the other plants in the room. Rational power development is an inherent attribute of this science activity.

In addition to the foregoing, this learning activity has another dimension that can be used to introduce the mathematical concept of graphing to children. After several measurements have been taken, the teacher should ask the children what they can do to compare their measurements. The pupils will usually line up the measured strips of paper on their desks in some arrangement. At times these arrangements will not be too meaningful. The teacher can then ask how the strips can be arranged to make a picture of how their plants grew from measurement to measurement. Not too much time is needed before the entire class has the strips arranged in chronological order. At this point the teacher can suggest (if the children have not already done so) that these strips be pasted upon sheets of paper so that a permanent picture of the growth of each plant might be made, and this picture can then be easily added to as more measurements are taken. In this activity, measurements—how they are recorded and how these recordings can be interpreted—have been integrated in an understandable, meaningful way for the children. Measurement is a valuable curriculum area—one in which children can become interested and with which they are comfortable.

A group of fifth graders were convinced that they could accurately and consistently measure any object they chose. Their teacher realized that here was a serious defect in the understandings these children had about measurement. He knew that telling them that they probably could not achieve *exactly* the same results by measuring the same object, using the procedure two or more times, would not contribute to their understanding of the information that measurements can give us. The teacher suggested that they measure each other's heights to test their decision that measurements can always be accurately made. The first measurements were taken and given to the teacher; two days later the heights of the class members were again measured and these data given to the teacher.

The day following the second measuring, the teacher wrote the two sets of measurement data on the chalkboard. The height measurements for the first child showed that he was 2 inches taller the second time he was measured than he was at the first measurement. The other measurements showed comparable variation. Seeing that the first set of height measurements could be used to develop an understanding the pupils needed, the teacher focused the attention of the class upon those data. He asked the children how they would explain the difference in the measurements of the boy's height. That question did not even need consideration as far as the pupils were concerned; the answer was quite simple—the boy grew! Completely accepting that response from the children, the teacher asked them how tall that boy would be in two months if he had grown 2 inches in two days. The pupils computed that the boy would grow 60 inches— 5 feet—in two months! Since he had grown less than 5 feet in over 10 years, the children did not think that expecting him to grow 5 feet in two months was reasonable. The teacher had achieved the most difficult part of his objective for their lesson; that is, he had led the children to suspect that the data they had gathered were faulty. He next led the children through a third height-measuring activity, and this produced, in many cases, a third set of measurements. The teacher then asked the children if they had in any way altered their beliefs about how accurately measurements can be taken. The class agreed that generally the same measurement will not produce exactly the same results each time.

From a scientific point of view the foregoing represents an extremely important concept: measurements made of objects can have extreme variation. There was, in the exercise, great opportunity for the children to compare, evaluate, classify, analyze, synthesize, and generalize. In other words, the idea of measurement provides ample opportunity for children to develop their rational powers, that is, to develop their ability to think. There is also a second facet of variation which is not related to how accurately a measuring standard can be applied. That facet is that objects that are apparently alike may vary tremendously. Do you know, for example, what the relationship is between the size of a pea pod and the number of peas it contains, or how many leaflets will be formed per leaf on an ash or mimosa tree? These represent to us extremely good topics to get children interested in the entire idea of measurement and variation.

There are several excellent reasons why the topic of variation should be the vehicle for teaching the more formal concept of measurement. First, upper grade pupils are fascinated with the idea that objects that appear to be alike differ greatly. One teacher introduced the idea of variation to his pupils by counting the leaflets on mimosa leaves, and the class became so interested that the teacher did not need to search for a way to introduce them to how they could represent the variations they had found. The children were very eager to learn about a technique that would let them record their data in a manner that would tell them a story of their investigation; the technique they used was the histogram. The foregoing example represents the second reason why the study of variation is an excellent vehicle to use in studying measurements: studying variation demands that methods be devised to record findings in a manner that will present the data in a meaningful way.

Methods must also be devised for making measurements if the information collected is to be meaningfully discussed with and used by persons other than those doing the measuring. It is impossible, for example, for two children to communicate to each other how the rocks that each of them has differ if they do not agree ahead of time on the standard of measurement they wish to use. The study of variation will lead children to discover that before the variations can be discussed, a standard for discussion must be established. In the latter years of the elementary school, the standards used can be the more formal standards of measurement—the metric and English systems—which are common to science.

Children need curricula that will provide them with the understanding that measurements and their inherent variations are part of our environment. The early years of the elementary school science curriculum are properly devoted to the children making generalizations based upon qualitative observations. The primary grades as well as the upper grades can provide children with experiences that will lead them to develop the understanding that generalizations can be just as properly based upon quantitative observations. They will discover that quantitative observations (measurements) are in many ways superior to qualitative because measurements can be taken in the same way again and again. Observing an object or action the same way more than once is, at best, extremely difficult. The assignment, sometimes made in the upper elementary school, "Memorize the basic units of measurement in the English and metric systems and how they are related," will not produce the types of understandings about measurement and variation which we wish children to develop. the fundamental nature of measurement and variation and also give

What types of learning activities will lead children to understand the learner the opportunity to develop his rational powers? What follows are several sample lessons that illustrate the types of learning activities that can be conducted to make learning the nature of measurement and variation meaningful to children. Each lesson shows the relationships that exist between these concepts. These lessons introduce the study of the measurement of surface area.

WHICH LAKE IS BIGGER?[4]

Show your pupils the picture of the two lakes [Figures A and B] and ask which is bigger, and how they could find out for sure. Try to stimulate interest in the problem of surface measurement. From this point, start a discussion about the various ways the pupils might use to find out which lake is bigger. Direct the discussion so that all the children come to understand that by "bigger" you mean having more surface, or room for more boats or swimmers. You should encourage students to propose methods for finding out which lake is larger. All methods they suggest, whether or not the methods are usable, should be accepted and written by you (in the child's words) on a chart. This should encourage a goodly number of proposals. Once a set of proposals is developed, the class can discuss each method in turn. Interested pupils should be encouraged to try their suggested methods. It is important to explore the good and bad points (either by discussion or trial) of the various methods. The approaches should not be considered as either right or wrong. Instead, emphasize aspects of each method which make it more or less useful for the particular situation.

The discussion should bring out the possibility of using objects, as is later done, to cover the two surfaces, and then counting and comparing the number of objects used for each lake. Beans were first used in teaching this lesson. Other objects which are available in quantity could

[4] Reprinted with permission from *Variation and Measurement Teacher's Guide,* Trial Edition, p. 43, written and published by the Science Curriculum Improvement Study. Copyright 1964 by the Regents of the University of California.

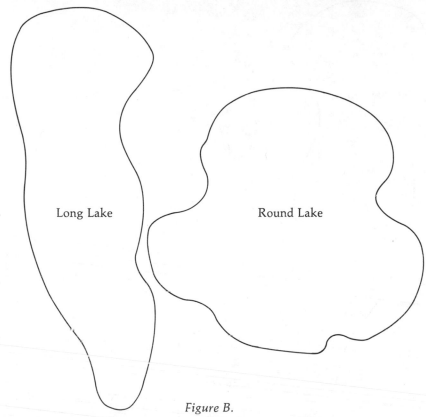

Long Lake

Round Lake

Figure B.

Figure A. Which lake is bigger? How can we find out which lake is bigger?

also be chosen, but it is helpful if the first standard chosen varies in size. The use of such a standard will help illustrate the value of a clearly-defined and reproducible standard such as labels, which are used later.

You will notice that the primary objective of this lesson is to lead children to think about the idea of area and how it can be measured. In other words, the teacher's guide material which has been reviewed is that needed for an exploration lesson in the exploration-invention-discovery (i.e., inquiry) teaching strategy. You also noticed that the problem under consideration here deals with the measurement of area. Keep in mind that these lessons are only used as examples; a complete inquiry study of measurement (which *Variation and Measurement* represents) deals, of course, with all facets and not just those notions involving area. The next lesson is one in which the children actually start taking measurements.

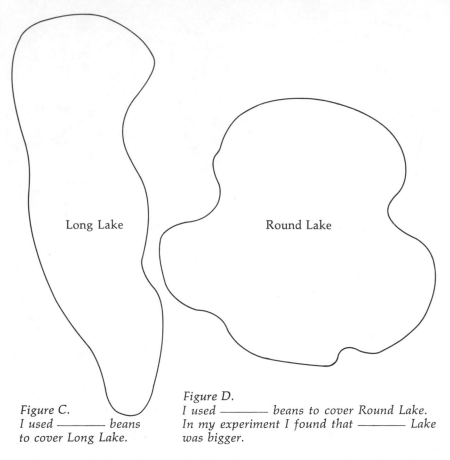

Figure C.
I used ———— beans
to cover Long Lake.

Figure D.
I used ———— beans to cover Round Lake.
In my experiment I found that ———— Lake
was bigger.

*Refer to Chapter 3 and consult the data given there to determine when
area is conserved. Then decide at what age level the lesson just quoted
can be used most productively.*

MEASURING THE LAKE IN BEANS[5]

Tell the children that pages 5–50 and 5–51 [Figures C and D] are
copies of one picture of Long Lake and one picture of Round Lake. Give
each pupil a paper plate filled with dried lima beans. Ask the children to
use the lima beans in order to find out which lake is bigger. Observe the
method they use in taking the beans from the plate and using them to
cover the pictures of the lakes. After they have covered the entire lake
with beans, they should count and record the number used. During the
activity you should encourage children who try to allow them to work

[5] Ibid., p. 44.

out the method for themselves. Questions about what to do with a space too small to fit a bean may arise. Let the children discuss these questions, and help them realize some of the limitations of beans as a standard. Postpone any discussion of results until all the pupils have finished counting and recording the number of beans used for each lake. Ask the children which lake they think is bigger, and have them put their answer on page 5–51 [Figures C and D] in the student manual.

The foregoing and following lessons outline the need for and value of a standard unit of measure. It is extremely important that the children discover for themselves how necessary and convenient a standard unit of measurement can be. They must be led to realize that when they were measuring the area of the lakes with lima beans they could not communicate in a meaningful way. Measurements, like any data in science, are of limited value unless they can be communicated to others in a meaningful fashion.

The next lesson leads the young investigators to discover the advantages of using a standard unit of measurement.

VARIATION IN NUMBER OF BEANS USED TO COVER LAKE[6]

Ask individual pupils to tell you which lake they found to be bigger. [Figure D.] If there is a difference of opinion, encourage all answers. Remind the children that all their pages are reproductions of the same picture of Long and Round Lakes. Discuss whether or not they think it should take the same number of beans to cover each picture of one lake. Ask a few children to tell you how many beans they used to cover Round Lake. From the answers it will be apparent that there is a rather wide variation in number of beans different pupils used. Using pages 36 and 38 [Figures E, F, and G] in the student manual, determine the lowest and the highest number of beans used by an individual to cover each of the lakes. This information determines the extremes of a number line for each lake, which is placed on the board. The pupils can copy these two scales by filling in the numerals under the lines on page 37 and 39 [Figures F and H] in the student manual. Have the pupils construct a separate histogram for the number of beans used to cover each lake. . . . Once the histograms have been constructed, ask the children to discuss the range of results found for each lake. The wide variation in number of beans used by different individuals now becomes apparent to the class. Use this information to develop a discussion about the use of beans as a standard of measurement. You can demonstrate the difference in bean sizes at this time. Discuss at length, using demonstrations or experiments, the effect this size variation has on the number of beans

[6] Ibid., pp. 44–46.

The smallest number of beans used to cover Long Lake was _____
The largest number of beans used to cover Long Lake was _____
I used _____ *beans to cover Long Lake.*

Figure E.

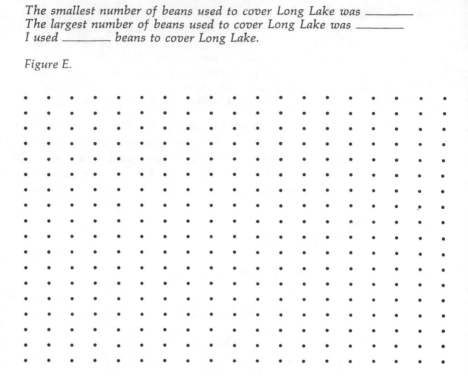

Figure F. Histogram of the number of beans each pupil used to cover Long Lake.

used by different experimenters. The demonstration should help them to see the relationship between bean size and the number needed to cover a surface. You might use two different sizes of beans to cover the same surface. The effects of the shape of the beans and of their sliding around should also be mentioned. The shape prevents complete covering of the surface (unless the beans go outside the boundaries), while the sliding around tends to increase the number used.

Ask the class to suggest standards which would not involve the problems found with beans. All suggestions should be considered and the good and bad points of each pointed out by the pupils. Two of the criteria which may evolve from the discussion are the need for a uniform shape and some way of keeping each unit in place. Self-gummed labels can now be suggested by you as an example of a standard which will work better than beans. The group can develop the plan for testing the new standard of surface measurement. The plan should include the actual measurement of the lakes' surface area with the new standard.

The largest number of beans used to cover Round Lake was _____
The smallest number of beans used to cover Round Lake was _____
I used _____ *beans to cover Round Lake.*

Figure G.

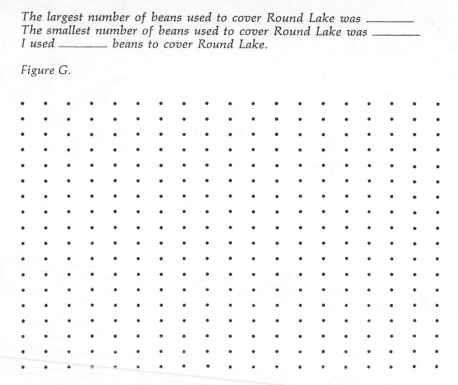

Figure H. Histogram of the number of beans each pupil used to cover Round Lake.

The histograms developed in this lesson provide a way of predicting the number of beans another experimenter would use to cover Round Lake or Long Lake. Of course, the way the pupils use the histogram for prediction provides an evaluation of the lessons on variation.

The need for a uniform standard unit of measurement has now been established by the children themselves and a standard (gummed labels) has been suggested. The children now need experience working with the standard in order to discover for themselves its advantages. The following lesson provides that experience.

ANOTHER MEASUREMENT OF THE SURFACE OF THE LAKES[7]

With pages 40 and 41 [Figures I and J] in the student manual the pupils again measure the surface of Long and Round Lakes, using the

[7] *Ibid.,* pp. 46–48.

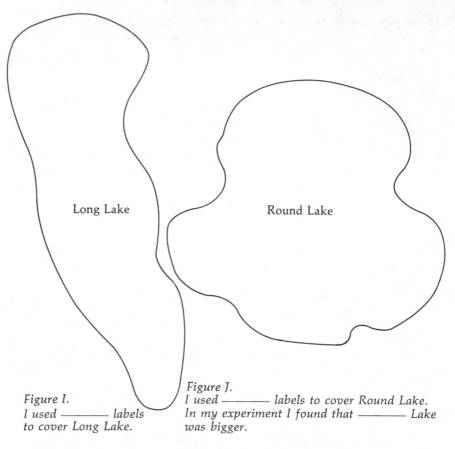

Long Lake

Round Lake

Figure I.
I used ———— *labels*
to cover Long Lake.

Figure J.
I used ———— *labels to cover Round Lake.*
In my experiment I found that ———— *Lake*
was bigger.

labels in the same way as the beans. Tell them to try to cover the surface of the lakes without overlapping the labels. Some overlap will still occur, but not so much as if you had not mentioned this. You should discuss the problem of spaces too small to fit a whole label; hopefully, this problem will have already become apparent to some of the children and the discussion will thus be more meaningful. Suggest that smaller labels are needed for the small spaces. The group may or may not reject this idea. If they do not reject it, remind them of the problem of the different sizes of beans. You can encourage other suggestions for solving the problem. Someone can suggest using parts of labels to fill the spaces. The pupils should be cautioned to use as many whole labels as possible without overlapping, before using parts of labels. Each time they divide a label into parts they should make a mark to indicate they used another label, and use all the parts before dividing another. Directly counting parts to determine how many labels were used is almost impossible. After covering the surface of each lake, the pupil counts the number of whole labels used and he adds the marks which represent the labels he tore up to fill the small spaces. The total number of labels used to cover each lake is recorded by each individual on pages 52 and 53 [Figures I and J].

After each pupil has recorded his results and answered the last question on page 53 [Figure J] a discussion of the results ensues. As different pupils report the number of labels they used to cover each lake, the small difference in number of labels used by various individuals will become apparent. Histograms of the results can be developed if you feel this necessary. Usually the contrast between the use of beans and the use of labels is so apparent that the histograms are not really needed. The advantages of using labels instead of beans should be discussed. If some children have trouble understanding the difference, further experiments using both standards will help them.

A discussion of the disadvantages found in the use of labels is also important. Pupils who have made obvious errors in counting or using the labels should be encouraged to try the experiment again.

. . .

Asking what to do if you don't want to stick anything to the surface can be used to introduce the use of a grid ruled on clear plastic. The boxes on the grid should be the same size as the labels. The pupil places his grid over the surface to be measured and counts the number of squares used to cover the surface. Of course, the parts of the squares used are important, too. The child must estimate the number of whole squares to which the parts are equal. This is difficult, but a reasonably good approximation can be made if he counts all the part squares involved and cuts the results in half. This involves a level of sophistication for which many children will not be ready, and therefore the use of the grid is optional at this level.

There can be little doubt that learning activities such as the foregoing provide the elementary school child with opportunities to develop his rational powers. If you carefully inspect the four sample lessons, you will see many opportunities for children to compare, classify, infer, generalize, imagine, synthesize, and evaluate. The topic of measurement, then, does represent an area of knowledge which can be used as a vehicle to lead children to develop their rational powers. In addition, these lessons are rich with opportunities to use the exploration-invention-discovery instructional concept. The lessons that utilize the lima beans are clearly exploration lessons. Their principal value is in leading the children to gain familiarity with the ideas of measuring and in allowing the teacher to invent the concept of varia-

Many objects can be used to teach measurement. Here two children cover Long Lake and Round Lake with labels and will discover the value of a standard unit of measure.

tion. The children immediately see that to reduce the variation you must use objects that are regular. So labels are introduced. In other words, the invented concept of variation immediately leads to the discovery that the results would have less variability if the measuring objects (the beans) had less variability. What a meaningful way to discover the need for systems of measurement.

Take particular notice that if these lessons are not taught in an exploration-invention-discovery way, they are nearly valueless. What is the value of knowing that there is less variation when pictures of two lakes are covered with labels than when covered with lima beans? The answer is "none." In that question and response is found the answer to what should go on in school. Those things should go on which teach a child *while* they are going on and not by the end product they produce. The end product of a learning experience will then be meaningful and will have contributed to the learner's intellectual development; only he understands it in terms of how he reached it. That is what Jerome Bruner meant when he said, "Knowing is a process, not a product."[8] But the lakes problem not only represents good education; it also represents good science because measurement

[8] Jerome S. Bruner, *Toward a Theory of Instruction* (Cambridge, Mass.: Harvard University Press), p. 72.

is certainly an essential tool in science. Furthermore, as has been emphasized throughout this book, the structure of science is investigation that leads to inductive inferences. These activities certainly do that.

Experimentation

Much can be learned about any object by observing it qualitatively and measuring it. Both of these methods of discovering information, however, are concerned with describing an object or condition *at the present moment*; they do not encourage the learner to put two or more objects together to see what will happen. Asking the question "What would happen if . . . ?" in the most meaningful way (which is the abstract hypothesis) is probably done at the earliest, only by late concrete or early formal operational thinkers. But very young children ask questions regarding what happens when two things interact, and often, as in the case of a baby, do not verbalize the question. They do not have any abstract hypothesis they are testing—they simply want to know what happens. When young children have those types of experiences, they are building a structure that will let them ask "What would happen if . . . ?" in the abstract manner a truly formal operational thinker asks it.

The two experiences, observing and measuring, do not necessarily encourage an investigator to want to experiment, but deciding "what has happened" to an object demands that observations and measurements be made. The relationship, then, between experimenting and observing can be summarized thus: Experimenting demands that observations and/or measurements be made; observing and measuring do not demand that experiments be performed.

We have already seen that measuring and observing are essential activities in a modern elementary school science program, but since these activities do not demand experimentation, is it necessarily an essential part of such a program? To answer that question, we must ask ourselves what is meant by an experiment. Webster defines experiment as "an operation carried out under controlled conditions in order to discover an unknown effect or law, to test or establish an hypothesis, or to illustrate a known law."[9] Notice that experimentation is active; it is "an operation carried out." We also know that learning is an active process, and since experimentation is an active process we

[9] *Webster's Seventh New Collegiate Dictionary* (Springfield, Mass.: Merriam-Webster, 1963), p. 239.

are led to hypothesize that experimentation can be used as an approach to learning. Before, however, any operation or activity can be carried on meaningfully, there must be an understanding of *why* carrying out the activity is necessary. (After all, running is also an active process and learning does not necessarily result from it.) There must be, in other words, a carefully defined situation which those participating in the operation understand and which they agree will not be further understood unless "something" is done. That something to be done is, of course, experiment.

Now, the next question that must be asked is what experiment is to be done? Where are the procedures to come from which will be followed? Perhaps the best answer to that question is from the imagination of the investigators. Those solving a problem or investigating a situation must analyze it, evaluate other approaches to the problem which have been used (if any have been made), and synthesize from the foregoing and their imaginations a method and/or procedure to be followed in the investigation. Experimentation, then, is really an attitude on the part of the experimenter; it is an attitude that leads the investigator to ask himself what he has to do in order to change the types of observations and/or measurements he can make. An experimentalist is one who is constantly altering in his mind those conditions surrounding an object or activity and asking himself what would happen if certain of those conditions were changed. We have discussed only that part of experimentation which deals with formulating the experiment. There is, of course, at least one additional phase to experimenting which must be considered, and that is determining what the results of the experiment mean. The ideas germane to the *interpretation* of data are so important to the elementary school science curriculum that an entire section of Chapter 6 will be devoted to that topic.

There is no need to ask whether or not what has been discussed here is an activity which would be recognizable by a scientist as science. The control of conditions (variables) is one of the basic building blocks in the enterprise of science. Activities wherein the learner must manipulate variables give him a much better idea of what science is (and how he likes such activities) than does verifying something he already knows or has been told. In addition, designing and carrying out experiments in the manner described above provide the pupil an excellent opportunity to develop his rational powers. We have then satisfied two of the criteria used to evaluate an activity for elementary school science. Whether or not experimentation contributes to the learner's understanding of his environment has not yet been explored.

Experimentation is an attitude and children will obviously develop it through investigation, particularly if their teacher investigates with them.

Our lives are spent making decisions—decisions about our relationships with people, about our individual actions, and about our relationships with our environment. Decisions also must be made as to whether or not the data produced by an experiment really help answer the question that was asked. Such decisions are, to elementary school children, very real and important ones. Experimentation, then, can provide pupils with actual experience in decision making. While experimentation does not contribute to the understanding of our environment *as such*, each experiment done deals with a portion of that environment and can contribute to our understanding of that portion if what is done under the name of experimentation is really experimental. In addition, learning why experiments are necessary contributes to an attitude of open-mindedness, which is an essential attribute of citizens of a democratic society. Experimentation, then, is a desirable activity that must be carried out in the elementary school science curriculum. What are the types of experimentation which can be done in elementary school?

A group of fourth, fifth, and sixth graders was asked what plants needed in order to live. Among the many responses given was "water." The teacher asked the pupils if they really felt that water was necessary to the growth of a plant. When the children replied in the affirmative, he simply asked, "Can you *prove* that water is really necessary for plant growth?" The next few days saw the children engaged in planning experiments that would give them data to be used to prove their hypothesis that plants need water in order to live. Experimental procedures were drawn up, records were designed, and the experiment was under way. The children were convinced that they were right when they started the investigation, but this did not dampen their enthusiasm in the least. In fact, because they felt so strongly about their convictions, the experiment quickly gained momentum; the children were working on a problem with which they felt comfortable. As a result, they directed their attention closely to the experimental procedures to be used and the data to be collected. At the end of the experiment, all the experimental plants were placed in the front of the room; all the plants that had not received water during the experiment were placed on one table and all the plants that had been watered were placed on a second table. The visual evidence was overwhelming. There was, however, one plant that had been given more water than the rest—it was dead! That experimental finding led the children to ask whether or not a plant could be given too much water. Here, now, was a problem to which the young investigators did not feel they knew the answer.

They had established their faith in the experimental technique in the previous experiment and were now ready and willing to engage in an experimental activity to find the answer to this problem. Once again experiments were designed (from their imaginations), experimental procedures established, record forms designed, and the investigation was underway. There was, however, no definite hypothesis advanced for this problem as there had been in the first one. Here, then, is an example of true scientific activity in the classroom. The activity goes from problem to experiment to problem to experiment, and so on. The children are investigators, the problem is theirs, the data are interpreted by them, and the solution to the problem is truly *their* property. But what is more important than the solution to the problem is the fact that the children *identified, designed,* performed, and *evaluated the results from* the experiment. Learnings such as how to perform an experiment (and the rational powers development which comes from it) are far more lasting than the factual answer.

Experimentation in elementary school science can take many forms and what follows are several examples of experimental situations that have been used effectively with children. These sample lessons demonstrate how the scope of the child's experience can be enlarged by using experimentation as a teaching device. They also demonstrate effectively the importance of observation and record keeping in experimentation. But the most important factor made clear by these experiments is how the child must be involved in the learning activity if he is to develop his rational powers and an understanding of the material being studied.

ROCK CANDY AND SUGAR CUBES[10]

As children experiment with rock candy and sugar cubes, they recognize that the material in an object remains the same as the object's appearance changes. They realize that although two objects appear to be different they may still be composed of the same material.

Teaching Materials

For each team of two children:
1 mortar and pestle
2 cubes of sugar
2 pieces of rock candy
2 plastic spoons
2 cardboard trays
2 paper towels
2 magnifiers

Teaching Suggestions

The children will work in teams of two. Give each team two trays, two cubes of sugar, and two pieces of rock candy, and suggest that the children examine both kinds of objects with their magnifiers. Ask the children to report the similarities and differences they observe.

Grinding the sugar cube. Give each team two plastic spoons and a mortar and pestle. Tell the children to put one cube of sugar into the mortar and to break the cube into six or eight pieces with the pestle. (If necessary, show them how to do this). When the cube has been broken into smaller pieces, the children should examine these objects and describe to each other the similarities and differences between the smaller pieces and the remaining sugar cube.

The sugar cubes and rock candy are solids, as are the granulated and powdered sugar into which they are ground. Also note that even the smallest pieces of sugar or rock candy are objects. You may point out to your class that this is another instance where parts of objects are individual objects.

[10] Reprinted with permission from *Material Objects*, op. cit., pp. 66–67.

Some small pieces of sugar should be placed on a cardboard tray. Then the team members can take turns grinding the rest into a fine powder. Using the plastic spoon, they can scrape the powder onto the same cardboard tray holding the small pieces. The mortar and pestle should be wiped with a dry paper towel to remove any powder that still remains. The team's second sugar cube should be placed on the tray with the sugar powder and pieces of sugar.

Grinding the rock candy. Each team now goes through the same steps with the rock candy. It is important that the children examine the rock candy with magnifiers as it is broken down. Each child participates in the grinding process. It is also important that, using the second spoon, the children put the powder and small pieces onto the other cardboard tray along with the second piece of rock candy.

Discussing the results. To conclude the session, let each child examine the powder and small pieces on both trays by using a magnifier, by touching, and by rubbing the powder between his fingers. As the children describe the properties of the powdery materials, listen carefully to their language and compare it to the words they used to describe objects at the beginning of the unit. Such informal comparisons will give you information about the growth of the children's language abilities during the course of the program.

The young investigators participating in this experiment have learned that often appearances can be deceiving. Materials that appear to be different can often be the same and materials that appear to be the same can be quite different. Equally important, however, the children, through an active process of doing something, discovered the experimental findings for themselves. They have, in other words, demonstrated to themselves that experimental procedures can be used to acquire specific information. The manipulations in this experiment were comparatively simple and crystals were easy materials to work with. The following experiment, taken from a fourth year unit, illustrates the types of experimentation with living things which elementary school children can do. This experiment demonstrates the importance of record keeping and the design of apparatus for an experiment as well as the necessity for controlling variables.

THE ENVIRONMENT OF ISOPODS[11]

In this discovery activity, the children apply their understanding of range as they suggest possible ways to test the response of isopods to

[11] Reprinted with permission from *Environments Teacher's Guide*, pp. 49–53, by the Science Curriculum Improvement Study, published by Rand McNally & Company, Chicago. Copyright 1970 by the Regents of the University of California.

different intensities of light and water. They compare their findings and determine the optimum range of each of these factors for isopods. Differences in the ways the experiments are conducted lead to a review of the concept of variables and to the idea of controlled experiments. After reviewing their data, the children infer what the environment of an isopod consists of.

Teaching Materials

Light Test	*Water Test*
For each team of six children:	For each team of six children:
10 isopods	10 isopods
1 sheet of black paper	1 runway
10 red dots	4–6 labels
4–6 labels	1 vial
1 runway	soil
scissors	marking pen or crayon
marking pen or crayon	paper towels
For the class:	For the class:
. . .	. . .
1 roll of aluminum foil	1 roll of aluminum foil
5 planter cups	5 planter cups
5 planter lids	5 planter lids
tape	tape

Advance Preparation

Prior to each experiment, put ten isopods into each of five planter cups.

Teaching Suggestions

There are several ways to conduct the activities in this chapter. The class can run the experiments as described, or your pupils may wish to determine which environmental factors they will test and develop their own techniques. If the children work individually or in small groups, each experiment should be repeated several times so enough data are accumulated to make comparisons possible.

Isopods and light. Explain to the children that they can investigate the response of isopods to another environmental factor—light. Let them discuss possible ways to do this. The children's comments should give you some insight into how well they have grasped the range concept. For example, do the children suggest that the isopods be tested in a range of light intensity?

Experimental setup. Divide the class into teams, and distribute the materials (except isopods) for the light test. Have each team refold a runway[12] so the lines do not show. (If the runways were lost or damaged, or if you wish to provide for more teams, give each team a 6 by 18 piece of aluminum foil to build a new one.) To provide a range of light intensity, show the children how to set up the runways as follows:

1. Fold the black paper into a trough slightly larger than the runway. (The ends of the black paper trough will have to be cut, folded, and taped in order to fit over the ends of the runway.)
2. Toward the end, make a hole in the bottom of the paper trough about 2 inches in diameter.
3. Place the paper trough upside down over the runway.

The runway now has only one source of light—the hole at one end. The part of the runway directly under the hole is lightest, and it becomes progressively darker toward the opposite end.

When the teams have set up their runways, the children will have to translate the range of light intensity into terms that everyone understands. Let the children decide into how many sections they will divide the runways and what to call each section. They may use a felt pen or crayon to mark lines on the runway bottom, labeling the spaces (bright, medium, dim, and dark, for example). The children might prefer to measure distances from the hole and name the light intensity accordingly. For example, the area directly below the hole would be brightest, 6 inches away would be darker, and so on. If the children decide to name more than four sections, add the necessary vertical lines to the chart.

Testing isopods. . . . give each team ten isopods. Tell each team to lift the paper trough and drop the isopods into the runway. Suggest that individual children be responsible for recording isopod positions in each section of their team's runway. After about five minutes a child should carefully lift the paper trough so all the children can quickly record the isopods' positions in the runway. . . .

Return the isopods to the classroom container, and save the runways for use in the water test. . . .

When the children have completed recording their findings, gather them for a discussion. Ask the children if the data on the chart suggest the optimum range of light for isopods. This question should stimulate a discussion. There are various ways you can direct the discussion depending on the children's answers:

1. If all the isopods appeared in the darkest (or lightest) part of the runway, the children will probably conclude that this is the optimum range of light for isopods.

[12] How to construct the runway was described in the previous lesson in *Environments Teacher's Guide*, op. cit., p. 43.

2. If the isopods were randomly distributed in the runways, the children may conclude either that isopods do not respond to light or that all teams did not run the experiment in the same way.

If the latter is the case, let the children suggest possible differences in their experiments, and remind them that such differences are called variables. They might suggest variables such as the position of the hole in the paper trough, the size of the hole, the available light in the area where the experiment was conducted, or where the isopods were placed at the beginning of the experiment.

The children's responses in this discussion should give you feedback about their understanding of controlled experiments. The idea of controlled experiments is considered in several SCIS units. If your pupils have had experience with *Subsystems and Variables* or *Populations*, they should be familiar with this idea. Remind them that in a controlled experiment only the variable being tested should change; all other conditions should remain constant. For example, if beetle response to light is being tested, then the temperature and other variables should be the same in all tests; only the light factor should vary.

Your pupils may want to run additional experiments to control some of the variables they pointed out.

Isopods and water. If your pupils are interested in investigating isopod response to another factor, suggest that they try to determine the optimum range of water for this animal. Let the children discuss possible ways to conduct the water test. If they do not suggest providing a wide range in the amount of water, this would be a good time to review the range concept.

Experimental setup. Divide the class into teams, and distribute the equipment (except isopods). Teams whose runways have been damaged may construct new ones. If children do not have ideas of their own, you might show them how to set up the water experiment as follows:

1. Cover the bottom of the runway with about one-quarter inch of soil.
2. Divide the runway into four approximately equal sections and label these soaked, wet, damp, and dry.
3. Pour water into the "soaked" section and mix it in (fingers work fine) until the soil is saturated (water begins to stand on the surface). The amount of water needed to saturate the section will vary somewhat depending on the depth and dryness of the soil. Begin with about one vial of water.
4. Mix only half as much water into the soil of the "wet" section.
5. Sprinkle a very small amount on the "damp" section.

Testing the isopods. . . . distribute ten isopods to each team (use fewer if necessary, but each team should test at least five). After the children have placed the isopods in the runways, they should wait about ten minutes before recording the positions of the isopods. . . . If some teams wish to run several tests, placing the isopods in a different section each time, have them record their data on separate sheets. . . .

Return the isopods to the classroom container. These organisms will be used again in Part Five.

Discussion. . . . After recording has been completed, let the children describe how the isopods responded. Do the class data show the optimum range of water for isopods? Ask the children what they think the response of isopods would be if their environment became very dry or was flooded.

Living things are fascinating to children and working with them fascinates them even more. The foregoing experiment involves the child in one of the most important experiences he can have in science (one to which we will devote a section in the next chapter), that of data interpretation. He has to decide what the data he receives from the experiment really mean. But before attempting an interpretation, he must realize that what went on while watching the isopods represents the only data he will have to work with. He can develop this realization only if *he* does the experiment; that is, he sets it up and watches what happens. Experimentation means pupil experimentation and teacher demonstration. In experimentation the children have the opportunity to compare, analyze, synthesize, evaluate and use the other rational powers, but that will happen only if they do the experiment.

The isopod experiment is one that will involve the children and let science truly reach its maximum potential as a curriculum vehicle to lead children toward achieving formal operational ability.

Some content concepts in science are so important that a child must become familiar with them if he is to be truly scientifically literate. Energy is such a concept. But energy is also one of the greatest of all abstractions in science. You have probably heard energy defined in many different ways, and most definitions are inadequate. Reflect on the discussion in Chapter 3 about the intellectual level of children in elementary school. You immediately see that they are mainly concrete operational, and that type of learner must have concrete objects to interact with. Energy is an abstraction, so it would seem to be beyond the grasp of the elementary school child. But energy is basic to understanding many of the concepts of science which need to be understood before the learner can truly understand his environment.

The seemingly impossible situation just described beautifully demonstrates why experimentation is one of the experiences that are essential in elementary school science. The learner is given an experience during which he can experiment manipulating variables to *do* a certain "thing." After he has such a rich experimental background, he can be confronted with the question of what makes accomplishing the particular "thing" possible. The concept of energy can be invented for him at that point. The concrete operational child has, therefore, moved toward the acquisition of an abstract concept using concrete materials and experiences. We do not mean to suggest that this concrete operational learner has acquired a formal operational understanding of a formal operational task (which energy is). Rather, we are suggesting that the experience of experimentation has enabled the concrete operational learner to acquire an understanding of those portions of a formal task which match his ability. This is probably the manner in which a child acquires formal operational ability. The lesson that follows is an example of the first type of experience which children must have in order to enable them to accomplish what has just been described. Notice that the word "energy" is not used in this experiment.

MAKING PAPER AIRPLANES[13]

Each child designs, constructs, and tests a paper airplane. The class then holds several contests to see which plane flies the greatest distance. Following the contests, your pupils discuss variables that affect the planes' flight distance. Spend at least one class period on the activity.

Teaching Materials

For the class:
   64 sheets of paper, 8½ x 11"
   scissors

Advance Preparation

Select a suitable area for testing the airplanes. The playground, a gymnasium, or a multipurpose room are preferable to the classroom, where the flight distance is limited by room size and furniture. Plan to use an indoor area on a windy day, however. It is important that all sheets of paper be of the same size and weight.[14] Sheets of duplicator or mimeograph paper are suitable.

[13] Reprinted with permission from *Energy Sources Teacher's Guide*, pp. 32, 33, by the Science Curriculum Improvement Study, published by Rand McNally & Company, Chicago. Copyright 1971 by the Regents of the University of California.

[14] Although not suggested in *Energy Sources Teacher's Guide*, the authors have extended the experiment by letting paper type and shape be a variable.

Teaching Suggestions

Making the airplanes. Show your pupils the paper they will use to construct airplanes and explain that they will have a contest to see whose plane flies the greatest distance. Tell them to write their names on the planes and to follow two rules: (1) each plane must be made from one sheet of paper; (2) no other objects may be added to the paper (no tape, glue, or paper clips).

Encourage a child who has no design ideas of his own to team up with another pupil for assistance. The pair will have two sheets and can therefore try out two designs in the contest.

Flying the planes. (Take the extra sheets of paper to the launch area for use after the first contest.) Your students should launch all planes in the contest in the same direction from one starting point. The activity will proceed quickly if the children line up behind the starting point and take turns. Allow the planes to remain where they land so everyone can see how far they went.

Give recognition to the designer of the winning plane after everyone has participated. Have your pupils point out which planes traveled the greatest distance and which the least, so they can infer which were the most successful designs.

Invite them to modify their designs or to build another airplane if they have new ideas they would like to try. Allow a few minutes for the necessary construction work, and then hold a second contest so your pupils may determine the value of the changes they made. Let them recognize the winner of this contest, but postpone discussing the results until after your return to the classroom. Winning planes might be saved for further examination.

Discussion of variables. To open the discussion, write the heading *Variables That Affect the Flight Distance* on the chalkboard. Ask your pupils to identify the variables that affected the flight distance of their airplanes in the contest. If necessary, explain that a variable is something that can be changed from one experiment to the next or that is different for one airplane compared to another. Invite children to furnish examples and write these under the title on the board, but be prepared to provide one or two yourself in case they need these to get started. You might, for instance, mention the height from which a plane was thrown, the launching speed, and/or the wing spread of the plane. . . .

Evaluation. Ask children who changed one or more variables between the two contests to tell which were changed and to describe the effect the change or changes had on the flight distance. Take note for your records which children already associate a particular consequence with a change in a variable—for instance, a wider wing means short flights, or a longer tail results in steady flight.

There is no set length that an experiment must have. The experiments from *Material Objects* which have been described can be comfortably done in less than one hour. On the other hand, an experiment such as the energy experiment can take several days or weeks. In the plant-water experiment mentioned earlier, the children observed the experiment in progress for several weeks. During that time data were collected by keeping carefully designed records that were used in formulating an answer to the problem. A group of sixth-grade children wanted to determine what relationship existed between the mealworm, its pupa, and the beetles that were found in the same container. They placed mealworms in each of several jars and pupa in each of several different jars. These jars were carefully studied and eventually the life cycle of mealworm (larva) to pupa to adult beetle was worked out. The question where the mealworm came from then arose. The meal in which the insects *(Tenebrio molitor)* lived was carefully inspected and the children isolated what they thought were the eggs. These eggs were isolated in a suitable environment and, in due course, mealworms emerged. Here, then, is an example of a long-term experiment that can be effectively used in the classroom. Experiments can be simple and quick, such as rolling two balls toward each other to determine whether or not an interaction takes place; or time consuming, such as determining whether or not one-half cup of water per day will kill a small, potted cactus. The important thing for the children to understand is that an experiment is a time when information is gathered to enable them to find out something or to solve a problem, and the teacher must realize that to conduct a successful experiment the children must assume the attitude that the solution to a problem depends upon the data the experiment gives them.

Hidden deeply in learning by experimentation is the basic notion of hypothesis formation. Do not confuse hypothesis formation, which can come from the types of experiments just described, and what Piaget has called "reasoning in a hypothetico-ductive manner."[15] This latter type of reasoning results from thinking beyond the present and being able to consider what is only one avenue open to him for thinking. He is, of course, a formal operational thinker. There can be no doubt that the hypothesis he developed can be the ultimate in abstract thinking; that is, he can reason with proposition and does not need concrete data.

[15] Jean Piaget, *The Psychology of Intelligence* (Totowa, N.J.: Littlefield, Adams, 1968), p. 148.

We contend that there is another level of hypothesis formation which is just as valid as the abstract type and which young children can do. They can take concrete data from experiments and form concrete hypotheses about what they believe those data mean. Furthermore, they can then test their concrete hypotheses in a concrete way. These are, we believe, the types of experiences which will lead a child to become the "individual who thinks beyond the present and forms theories about everything, delighting especially in consideration of that which is not."[16]

Hypotheses can be formed in many ways and at various times during an experiment; the plant-growing experiments discussed earlier in this chapter illustrate two of the points at which hypothesis formation can take place. In the first experiment the children felt they knew that plants needed water to live and grow. They had, in fact, stated an hypothesis before the experiment began because they had seen lawns being watered and then needing to be cut, house plants being watered, and so on. This question was not outside the range of their experience, and because of that they had a justifiable reason to state an hypothesis at the beginning of the experiment. There are other experimental situations where the investigator has not had enough experience with the problem to be able to state a reasonable hypothesis. Any hypothesis stated at the beginning of such an experiment would be a pure guess. Hypotheses that are the most productive in helping to guide experimental work (which will produce data to be used in solving a problem) are those that are stated from a belief based on a reason. Often much experimental data must be collected before the investigator has any beliefs about a problem and an hypotheses can be formed.

As the previously mentioned upper grade children moved on to discussing whether or not plants could be given too much water; no hypotheses were advanced at the beginning of the experiment. Data were gathered and the problem explored in some detail; in other words, experience was gained before any hypotheses were formed. Proper hypothesis formation (i.e., hypotheses that are formed for a reason) is not an intuitive trait of the human organism. It is a learned behavior and, as with all learned behaviors, to truly learn how to do it the learner must have experience doing it. Children must be encouraged to state hypotheses on the basis of past experience and/or the information that the experiment they are presently conducting produces for them.

[16] Ibid.

Is there a place in teaching the art of hypothesis formation for the truly "intuitive flash" that some persons have? Absolutely! True intuition is not a frequently found trait, and when it is encountered it should be nurtured. How is a truly intuitive hypothesis recognized? The hypothesis itself cannot be identified, but the attitude and sincerity of the person stating it can be. If a child really is convinced that his idea is a sound one, he will not be easily discouraged from holding it. He will probably tell his peers and teacher that he is not really sure why he believes as he does—he just "feels" that his belief is true. Perhaps the most easily recognizable mark of an intuitive conviction is that the person holding it will be perfectly willing to subject that conviction to test. In fact, the pupil stating the intuitive hypothesis will probably be the leader of the group in designing an experiment to test it. There is some evidence to support the notion that intuition cannot be given to a child; it is essentially innate. Teachers, however, have a responsibility to nurture and cultivate this precious gift when it is found. To repeat—the intuitive hypothesis itself cannot be easily identified, but the attitude and sincerity of the child stating it can be.

Children should be encouraged often to state more than one hypothesis at a time. In fact, scientists often use this technique as the following quotation demonstrates.

> The investigator at the outset puts himself in cordial sympathy and in parental relation (of adoption if not by authorship) with every hypothesis that is at all applicable to the case under investigation.[17]

What Chamberlin is suggesting is that whenever an investigator, regardless of his age, is solving a problem, he must not be satisfied to confine his activities to just one set of ideas. He must test all hypotheses that he feels have a bearing on the problem. This notion fits very snugly into the scheme of encouraging children to think for themselves. If only one hypothesis is adopted by a class as a possible solution to a problem, there is a great possibility that out of N children, N minus 1 will be disappointed. The one child who will be pleased and motivated is the child whose hypothesis is adopted. Repeated experiences such as this could easily dampen the enthusiasm of many of the children in the room and, as a result, their attitude toward learning could become "tell us" rather than "let's find out."

When children, like scientists, are investigating a problem, many benefits can be derived from the utilization of multiple hypotheses.

---

[17] T. C. Chamberlin, "The Method of Multiple Working Hypotheses," *Science*, *148* (May 7, 1965), 756. (Originally published in *Science*, February 7, 1890.)

Perhaps the greatest benefits that can accrue to an elementary school child are that his motivation is retained, and if one of the least popular hypotheses should prove fruitful, he sees the value of investigating more than one idea. Forming and testing hypotheses, then, is an important phase of experimentation and, as such, must have a place provided for it in the elementary school science curriculum.

Compare the descriptions you wrote of observation, measurement, and experimentation with what has been said here.

6 | Essential Experiences: Data Interpretation, Model Building, and Prediction

The last chapter explained the contributions that experimentation can make to the development of pupils' ability to make sound decisions. There can be no doubt about the importance of every person being able to make his own decisions, but just making decisions is not enough. The success of our type of society depends on citizens who make decisions on the basis of the information available—not with a predetermined mind or prejudices. The Educational Policies Commission expresses the foregoing thought this way.

> No society is today composed predominately of individuals who are guided in most of their behavior by scientific modes of thought or action. Other bases, conscious or unconscious, seem to guide most persons in most of their activity. Even where it is deepest, the penetration of the rational spirit may be shallow in comparison with its potential.[1]

There is, of course, no way a person can be *completely* freed from his prejudices in making decisions; regardless of how objective we try to be, we are usually less than 100 percent successful. If, however, we take seriously our responsibility to teach the child to think, science education can increase the extent to which his decisions are based on information. In other words, we can provide learning activities in which children can actually experience how a given problem can be solved (or a question answered) using just the data the activity provides them. This educational procedure will not eliminate the effect of prejudice upon decision making, but the influence of prejudice can be reduced when this educational procedure is followed throughout the individual's educational experience.

[1] Educational Policies Commission, *Education and the Spirit of Science* (Washington, D.C.: NEA, 1966), p. 11.

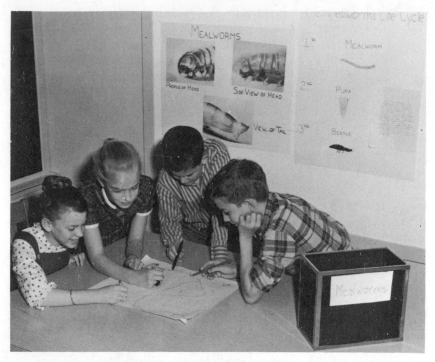

In order to be useful, data must be interpreted.

Interpretation of Data

So far in this discussion you have been led to view the activities of decision making and interpretation of data synonymously, and in many respects they are. If a decision is reached on the basis of the information at hand, then these two activities are synonymous and it is the development of this method of decision making to which the study of science by children can make a major contribution. To enable science to make its greatest contribution, however, teachers must understand that the *children* must interpret the data an experiment delivers. If the teacher makes the interpretation, all the learner derives is the end product (or fact) of the interpretation. We, as teachers, must remember we learn by experience and if children are to develop their abilities to interpret data (and make decisions), they must be given the opportunity to *interpret data*. Teachers often raise the question of the danger of children incorrectly interpreting the data and arriving at a wrong answer. Is such a procedure dangerous and/or undesirable?

No one, of course, likes to arrive at an incorrect answer—especially teachers. There is a good reason why teachers feel as they do—they (as children and students), were probably never allowed to accept an incorrect answer as having any value. Anything they needed to know was presented to them as a correct fact, and when a person has grown up in a tradition such as this, learning to appreciate the value of an incorrect answer (i.e., incorrect from the adult's point of view) is difficult. Such an attitude is unfortunate for two reasons: (1) it puts a premium on information, and (2) it represents a misunderstanding of what an answer is. Point (1) will not be discussed here because the questionable value of teaching factual information was treated in Chapter 5. In addition to what has already been said, however, consider another aspect of overemphasizing information. When a premium is placed on factual information the importance of recall to the learner is greatly overemphasized. Recall is one of the rational powers, but it is only 1 of 10 (10 percent). In many classrooms across the country developing the 10 percent of the ability to think occupies more than 90 percent of the school day. The inequity of such a procedure is immediately evident.

The second reason listed above, however, is an extremely important one to consider, at this point in our discussion, because the final result of data interpretation is an *answer*. But in order to fully appreciate and understand what data can do for us, we must have a relatively solid notion of what an answer actually is. To have an answer you must first have a problem or question, and *an answer to that question or solution to the problem is what the data (information) which have been gathered tell you it is—nothing more*. If an experiment has been used to acquire those data being considered, then perhaps variables can be manipulated in some way to enable more and/or different data to be accumulated. But when all the data that can be obtained from all the various experimental processes that can be designed are gathered, the answer to the question depends strictly upon what those data tell you. This belief does not exclude the use of common sense and/or intuition in interpreting the data. If, for example, an investigator receives an intuitive flash while performing an experiment, that experience may completely change his experimental procedures. But the final answer arrived at will still be directly dependent on the manner in which the data received from the experiment (which has been redesigned to accommodate the "moment of intuition") are interpreted.

Science is a fruitful area to explore in order to demonstrate the use of intuition in investigation; the work of such men as Newton, Faraday, and Einstein are excellent examples of how intuition is used to solve a problem or advance a theory. In every case, however, the final result (answer) accepted depended on how the data received, whether following a procedure designed by intuition or cold logic, were interpreted. We, as teachers, must teach science as it is practiced; that is, the answers that our students give us should be based upon the information (data) their observations, measurements, and experiments have given them. If we reject the answer formulated from the data and substitute (without test) what we feel is the answer, we are using the discipline of science incorrectly. In addition—and more important from an educational point of view—we are prohibiting our pupils from gaining confidence in their ability to solve their own problems through the interpretation of data. Such pedagogical procedures are harmful to the development of the children's rational powers—their ability to think—which is the principal purpose of all education. So if a wrong answer develops from the data that are collected and the pupils give that answer with extreme sincerity, we, as teachers, must accept it. When a wrong concept or fact has been developed, what should be done?

The child must not be allowed to harbor an incorrect concept, but experience has shown that telling the learner he is wrong will not allow him to correct that concept. Probably he will overtly accept your decision as adult authority, but he certainly will not *really* begin to disbelieve what his collected information has told him and accept what you say. If a pupil is going to learn to classify, compare, evaluate, and use all the rational powers, he must be given experience classifying, comparing, and evaluating without the feeling that what he does is really not important because the teacher will tell him whether or not his data are correct and interpret them for him. This notion about teaching tells us that if applying the rational powers to data delivered by an experiment has the adverse effect of leading children to an erroneous concept, there is only one way for the learners to correct that concept for themselves. *They must be provided the opportunity (or observation) to apply their rational powers to data from a second experiment[2] that will result in developing a contradiction to the first experiment.* The pupils must then decide which evidence is correct, and they have absolutely no basis for making such a decision. The only way they can approach the solution to that

---

[2] We use the word *experiment* to mean any action that a learner undertakes to get information short of looking up an exact answer in a book. Do not visualize lots of apparatus, special rooms, and furniture when experiment is mentioned; they may be there. But experiment, like the word *laboratory*, is probably more a state of mind than anything else.

problem is to repeat both experiments (observations or measurements).

If the data an experiment delivered are leading the learner to an incorrect concept, then something that was done in the experiment was done improperly. Leading the children to see the necessity of repeating the experiments will also give the class an opportunity to review their procedures. If the class-determined procedures are carefully reviewed, the probability of reoccurrence of procedural errors (which will again result in the learners' arriving at an unacceptable concept) has been reduced. Therefore, if a teacher is going to lead the learners away from a self-developed concept that is unacceptable to science, he must have available a second experiment which, although using a different route, will provide data to enable the children to arrive at the acceptable concept.

One of the pervasive concerns expressed in this book is that elementary school science experiences contribute to the development of the child's rational powers. We have referred several times to how the data interpretation can make such a contribution. When the activity of data interpretation is viewed in its entirety, however, it can best be described as "making sense out of what you found." The Educational Policies Commission has neatly described how such mental activities contribute to the development of the rational powers when it stated, ". . . the abilities involved in perceiving and recognizing pattern in a mass of abstract data are of considerable importance in learning to analyze, deduce, or infer."[3]

So far we have been concerned with the educational dividends that accrue to the learner through experiences in interpreting data. Teachers, however, have another and equally valid concern. How do we teach data interpretation? We shall start formulating an answer to that question by asking what constitutes data. *Data are the information that is derived from an experiment or observation.* The observations that are made and/or the experiments that are done may be very carefully directed—that is, there may be a previously defined problem to solve or question to answer. Observations and experiments, however, may be done just to see what is happening or what will happen; that is exploration. Data from such instances are valuable. Each child in a sixth grade was given two mealworms and a pile of bran and told to observe them carefully. Out of these observations grew such questions as "Can a mealworm see?" "Does a mealworm hear?" "Is

[3] Educational Policies Commission, *The Central Purpose of American Education* (Washington, D.C.: NEA, 1961), pp. 17–18. [See Appendix C.]

he sensitive to heat?" Here, then, is an example of the value that can be derived from letting children make observations. The data they collect can be used to formulate specific questions. After the specific questions had been identified by the sixth-grade group, data were next collected and interpreted to answer those questions. The most basic premise, then, to be remembered in teaching data interpretation is that at the beginning of the interpretation exercise, all data, regardless of their origin, are valuable.

In order for data to be interpreted they must be available for inspection. They must be arranged in such a way that there exists the possibility of their telling the interpreter a story. Children should be required to keep data about like experiments (or like parts of the same experiment) together, and measurements or observations of the same variable in the same place. Suppose, for example, the children have decided that they want to know at the end of an experiment how tall a plant has been at several stages throughout the experiment. The pupils should have a special place to keep these data. Then at the end of the experiment, the data can be carefully inspected, and because only data involving height are being studied, if a pattern is present its chances of being found are enhanced. The first prerequisite in teaching data interpretation is keeping adequate and complete records.[4] These records then can be studied individually by the children for any notion of a pattern that might exist.

As adults, we know that we learn from each other; so do children. An excellent classroom technique that takes advantage of this trait is group interpretation of data. In this approach the teacher uses the chalkboard and serves as the class secretary. Each group of children states what was found, and the teacher records it. At the end of such a session there are many data available for inspection and study. The entire class has the same data, and the attention of the entire group (including the teacher) can be focused on any part of the information. The class is then able to decide whether or not any of the variables being considered require the collection of additional information. The following example demonstrates the value of group interpretation of data.

A group of children were trying to decide whether a mealworm found a pile of meal by chance or sight. They decided that the mealworm would have to be placed in three different conditions of brightness—in the light found in their classrooms, in a nearly dark en-

---

[4] Mary Clare Petty, *How to Record and Use Data in Elementary School Science* (Washington, D.C.: National Science Teachers Association, 1965).

vironment, and in total darkness. Each child participated in the experiment. A mealworm was placed on a piece of white paper in the classroom and followed with a pencil until he either found the meal or ran off the paper. Each child then took the mealworm home and repeated the experiment in semidarkness (the only light used was a candle placed behind the investigator, and the mapping was done in his shadow). For complete darkness, the children decided to place a mealworm and a pile of bran in a shoebox and close the lid. From the previous two experiments there had been a notion developed of about how much time the mealworm required to find the bran. At the end of that time, the box was opened. Many of the young investigators, however, gave the animal much more time, "Just," as they put it, "to be sure." All the data were returned to school and the chalkboard became a data-collected chart and the teacher a recorder. After all the data were on the board, the pattern was so random that the pupils immediately concluded that the mealworm found the bran by chance. Many of the children had believed that conclusion (which for them was an hypothesis) before collecting the data, but when they received the support of their classmates' data, their hypothesis was confirmed. Each child had contributed to the understanding of all the others and himself through group interpretation of data. This latter method certainly does answer the criteria previously established for data interpretation—it encourages children to keep the values for observations about variables together, and it makes the data available for inspection.

There are, then, two procedures for teaching data interpretation—the individual and the group. In the individual method each child keeps his own records and, with the assistance of the teacher or classmates, interprets, hypothesizes, and concludes from them. What the child receives from this procedure is directly dependent on him. In the group procedure, each child contributes his findings to the entire group, and what he gains is as much dependent on the data of others as it is on his own. This latter method, in addition to being useful in demonstrating the values of working together, leads a pupil to discover the scientifically sound concept of the value of more than one set of measurements or viewpoint. While there are values to be gained from each child's interpreting his own data, those values as well as several others will be achieved by group interpretation of data. Also remember that social interaction is necessary in learning.

The following lesson illustrates the type of learning experience children need to develop an understanding of data interpretation.

THE ENVIRONMENT OF BEETLES[5]

You gather feedback about your pupils' ability to solve problems as they design their own experiments to test responses of beetles to light, temperature, and water. With your help the children suggest ways to construct class charts so that data from these activities can be displayed. The children determine the optimum ranges of the factors for beetles and make inferences about the kind of environment beetles require.

Teaching Materials

The necessary equipment will vary depending on the experiments the class designs but will probably include the following:

Temperature and Light Tests
50 mealworm beetles
 1 roll of aluminum foil
   black paper
   heat/light sources
   reflector boxes
   rocks
 2 pieces of chart paper
   labels
   thermometers
   dots
   marking pens or crayons
   scissors
   tape

Water Test
50 mealworm beetles
   one-pint plastic containers
 1 piece of chart paper
   dots
   paper towels
   tape

Teaching Suggestions

By the time your students reach this point in *Environments,* they should begin designing their own experiments based on their previous experiences. In this chapter they have a chance to propose, design, and carry out experiments. Your role is to help the children choose one or two experimental designs that will help them answer questions.

[5] Reprinted with permission from *Environments Teacher's Guide,* pp. 61–63, by the Science Curriculum Improvement Study, published by Rand McNally & Company, Chicago. Copyright 1970 by the Regents of the University of California. A second model lesson for data interpretation will be found in American Association for the Advancement of Science, *Science—A Process Approach,* Part F, Lesson C, Interpreting Data 5, "Magnetic Fields—The Nature of the Earth." Published by the Xerox Corporation, 1970.

Beetles and light. Write the question "What is the optimum range of light for beetles?" on the chalkboard. As your pupils discuss their experimental designs, they should also discuss some of the following problems:

What equipment can we use?

How many heat/light sources are available?

How many children should work together?

How large and how high must a container for these beetles be?

How can we make it dark for the beetles?

How can we provide a range of light intensity?

Should all the environmental factors be the same except light?

How shall we record the data?

The experiment. One of the most interesting aspects of this activity will be the children's excitement. Their interest may diminish if they are very much delayed in getting started. If the children have not decided on several experimental designs in about ten minutes of discussion, release them to think individually, using their hands and selected equipment. Activities such as handling the beetles, cutting black paper, making beetle houses with light and dark rooms, and noticing where the beetles crawl trigger the imagination. Experimental designs and some data will emerge from such preliminary investigation. During the experiments, or while in conversation with you, the children may notice and correct some of their design flaws.

After the experiments are completed, return the beetles to the classroom container. . . .

Discussion. Let each team describe its experiment and report the data collected. The data may show that beetles go to both dark and light areas. If that is the evidence and the children trust their experimental designs, then that is the answer to the original question. During the discussion, however, children may mention variables that were not controlled in a team's experiment. Encourage this kind of analysis, and if the children decide they can't trust their designs, allow them to improve in their ability to solve problems by carrying out this kind of activity.

Beetles and temperatures. Your students will design techniques for investigating the response of beetles to temperature. They may wish to use runways, rocks, or something else of their own design.

To help the children design testing techniques, follow the same approach you used in the light experiment. As the children offer suggestions . . . for experiments, be alert to comments that will give you feedback about their ability to design an experiment and their understanding of the range optimum-range concepts. Teams should discuss ways of providing a temperature range and the number of tests they feel are necessary for reliable data. They should also be concerned about controlling variables. Such as how and when to take temperature readings and where to start the beetles in the experiment.

Discussion. The children can use their student manuals to help them report their experiments and the data they collected. Ask the children if they can determine the optimum temperature range for beetles from the class data. While you observed the groups conducting their experiments, you may have noticed that some of the children did not provide a range of temperatures or control certain other variables. You may have to ask a few questions to initiate a discussion about these problems if the children do not do so.

Beetles and water. As the teams attempt to design experiments to test the response of beetles to water, you may find them speaking of "wet" and "dry" rather than in terms of a range of water. Refer them to previous experiments, leading them to include the idea of range in their design.

The following simple test provides a means for investigating a range of water. It is presented here as a guideline for children wishing to design their own experiments.

1. Place a crumpled paper towel at each corner of a 1-pint container. One towel should be dry, one damp, another wet, and the fourth soaked (be careful not to drip water from the soaked towel onto other towels or the bottom of the container).
2. Place at least five beetles in the center of the container. Wait about ten minutes before recording the positions of the beetles. . . .

When the experiments are completed, return the beetles to the classroom container. . . .

A beetle's environment. . . . Display all the data collected during the beetle experiments. Ask the children to suggest what a beetle's environment might be like, basing their comments on their data. . . .

The foregoing exercise is uniquely concerned with children acquiring the ability to interpret the data that a particular experiment gives them. Such learning experiences constitute a very excellent beginning to understanding the fundamental principles of data interpretation. Interpreted data can lead to either or both of two additional experiences that are essential if a child is to develop a functional understanding of the nature of the discipline of science. Those experiences are *model building* and *predicting*.

Model Building

You have probably inserted a coin in a vending machine and received a candy bar, a coke, or some other article.

Write a description of what you believe happens inside the machine to deliver you a candy bar when you insert a coin.

The evidence you have is that you put a coin in a slot and candy comes out a different opening in the machine. The explanation you have just written is your *model* of what the inside of the machine looks like and what goes on in it to enable it to deliver candy to you. The probability is great that your model and the working parts of the machine do not closely resemble each other. That is really not important as long as the model you have built supports the evidence you have and as long as that support continues. Model building is an important scientific process which those practicing science use frequently and to great advantage.

Probably the best known model of science is that of the atom. That model has changed many times throughout science whenever change was necessary to accommodate new data. There was a model of the atom constructed by Sir J. J. Thompson which has a mass of material with negative charges scattered through it. Rutherford proposed the planetary model of the atom. In his model the nucleus was positively charged and the negative charges were whirling about the nucleus in several different orbits, much like the planets whirl about the sun. Bohr, Sommerfield, and others have proposed models of the atom which allowed them to accommodate to the particular data they had.

A second model that science has found useful is the magnetic field.

Take two very strong horseshoe magnets—one in each hand—and bring them toward each other. Now reverse one of the magnets and repeat the experiment. Now construct a model of what you believe is between the magnets.

The model of what surrounds a magnet is, of course, a magnetic field. If you wish to test your model, place a magnet under a glass plate and sprinkle iron filings over it. How would you now change your magnetic field model? Next place a bar magnet under the glass plate and sprinkle iron filings over it. How does your magnetic field model explain what you see? How can you change your model to accommodate the new evidence you now have?

Electric current, light, how light passes through lenses, radio and television waves, how atoms of elements hold together to form compounds, and sound waves are all examples of models that science has constructed to explain physical phenomena and interactions among those phenomena.

Construct a model of electric current. Then use it on this model (which was suggested to us by a child) of current from a dry cell. "Half of current needed to light a flashlight bulb comes from each post of the dry cell."

As you can see, the process of model building is an extremely important part of science and represents an experience that is essential to its study.

Model building is, however, also important for another reason. Children in grades above the first generally require concrete objects to work with and concrete ideas to discuss. They must, in other words, have experiences that provide them concrete evidence. Attempting to teach, for example, the topics of atoms and molecules in the elementary school, at anything above the verbal learning level, is futile because the children cannot obtain any direct evidence of the existence of atoms and molecules. Electric current, while an abstraction, can be taught in the fifth and sixth grades because it can be invented as the interaction among a wire, bulb, and dry cell which causes the bulb to light. The evidence that an interaction exists is the bulb lighting. Now the thoroughly concrete operational child can invent (or understand an invention made for him) a thoroughly concrete model that explains the interaction he sees.

When a child builds a model he will, of course, build it in terms of some system he has had experience with. The following quotation nicely summarizes the importance of model building to children. "Scientific models permit children to relate their present observation to their previous experiences with similar systems. Models satisfy the children's need for thinking in concrete terms. Models also lead to predictions and new discoveries about the system being investigated."[6] Model building is perhaps the highest-order invention possible. An exemplary lesson to use in teaching model building follows.

"INVENTING" SCIENTIFIC MODELS[7]

Your pupils briefly review their experiences in solving circuit puzzles and then observe while you test a special puzzle. They try to figure out what might be inside in order to explain their observations. After you point out that their ideas are scientific models, you invite them to make predictions, suggest additional tests, and think up new models that better explain the test results. . . . Finally, your pupils evaluate models

[6] Science Curriculum Improvement Study, *Models: Electric and Magnetic Interaction Teacher's Guide*, published by Rand McNally & Company, Chicago. Copyright 1971 by the Regents of the University of California.

[7] Reprinted with permission from *Models: Electric and Magnetic Interaction Teacher's Guide*, pp. 51–55, by the Science Curriculum Improvement Study, published by Rand McNally & Company, Chicago. Copyright 1971 by the Regents of the University of California.

depicting the connections inside the base of a flashlight bulb. They identify deficiencies in unsatisfactory models presented in the student manual and propose improved models. Depending on your pupils' interest, spend one or two class periods on the activities of this chapter. . . .

Teaching Materials

. . .
1 electric-circuit puzzle
  aluminum foil
1 push-pull system
1 circuit-tester set
1 battery holder

Advance Preparation

Assemble a circuit puzzle[8] as a means of introducing the model concept. We suggest you use a simple puzzle. . . .

The simple puzzle has connections from A to B and D to F. . . . Test the connections to make sure they function and then tape the folder closed. . . .

Assemble a circuit tester,[9] but for convenience place the battery in a holder rather than on a circuit base. Practice your demonstrations with the puzzle folder and the circuit tester; it is not easy to hold them at the same time as you manipulate the bulb before a group of onlookers. You might tape the battery (in its holder) to the back of the puzzle folder to simplify the operation.

Draw four or five puzzle outlines on the chalkboard in places your students will find accessible.

Teaching Suggestions

Reviewing puzzles. Invite several students to describe their experiences when they made and tested circuit puzzles. Ask them to

8 A circuit puzzle is a sealed cardboard box or folder with six holes on one side. A brass paper fastener is inserted in each hole and its leaves are bent out on the inside of the box. The fasteners are labeled A, B, C, D, E, and F. Wires on the inside of the box can then connect any of the fasteners, making a complete circuit.
9 A circuit tester is a dry cell and a bulb connected by a minimum of three wires which enables the conductivity of any object to be tested.

tell what means they invented to solve the puzzles, how well they succeeded, and what aspects gave them most difficulty.

Electric-circuit puzzle. Show your pupils the new puzzle and tell them you will test it with the circuit tester. The children must try to explain why the bulb does or does not light during your tests. It will be up to them to figure out the connections inside. They need not tell everything that is inside the puzzle, but just enough to explain their observations. . . . carefully try combinations AB, AD, BD, and BF, making sure that all children clearly see that the bulb lights in the first test and remains dark in the last three. Repeat any of the tests that the children question, but do not try the other combinations just yet. Your pupils should imagine how the puzzle might have been built, basing their opinions on the results they observed. Invite them to describe their ideas by a diagram. . . .

Invention. Ask several children to put their ideas on the board. . . . Then let them describe how their diagrams explain the test results, or let someone else who had the same idea explain it. The rest of the class, and especially those students who come up with very different diagrams, should evaluate the ideas presented.

After this brief discussion, tell the class that their ideas for explaining results are called *scientific models* and write this phrase on the board. If the children's diagrams differ from one another, point out that scientists may also think up two or more models to explain the same observations. Then tell your pupils that a scientific model can be used for predicting experimental results.

. . . invite your pupils to use their models to predict the results of further tests on the puzzle. Accept their predictions, especially for new combinations of holes (AF and DF), and record them on the chalkboard. After you have written several predictions, you might ask for a show of hands from children who agree and from those who disagree, and tally the number of each beside the prediction. Finally, carry out the actual tests. . . .

Models for the light bulb. *Student-manual, page 13.* Invite your pupils to evaluate models for the concealed parts of their light bulbs. Ask them to turn to page 13, where several diagrams of such models are pictured and to cross out the diagrams that contradict their past observations. Any pictures not crossed out are considered "acceptable" models, at least for the present. A diagram for another "acceptable" model might be drawn. . . . At the bottom of the page students should list some of their reasons for eliminating models.

The foregoing lesson demonstrates effective procedures for teaching children to invent models in physical science. The lesson which follows demonstrates how model building using biological science is taught.

"INVENTING" THE WATER CYCLE[10]

The children try to evaporate water at one end of a container and condense it at the opposite end. On the basis of this and previous activities, the water cycle is introduced. The water cycle the children observe is then compared to the water cycle in the ecosystem in which they live. Two class periods will be required for this activity.

Teaching Materials

For each team of two children:
  2 fluted containers
  1 plastic cup
  1 rectangular label
For the class:
  2 lamps
    pitcher to be filled with water
    thermometers (optional)
    ice (optional)
    masking tape

Teaching Suggestions

Introducing the activity. Remind the students of the experiment they did with Freon. Then show them the available equipment and ask if they can think of a way to get water in a cup to evaporate and to condense at one end of a container.

Designing the experiments. Student-manual, page 12. Allow time for the children to discuss how they might do the experiment. Let teams pick up the equipment and begin their experiments as soon as they have a few ideas. Some might wish to take the temperature on various surfaces of the container with a thermometer. Some children may want to use ice to produce a greater temperature range within the container. Suggest that the containers be taped shut with masking tape. Tell the children to label their systems with their names.

[10] Reprinted with permission from *Ecosystems Teacher's Guide*, pp. 54–57, by the Science Curriculum Improvement Study, published by Rand McNally & Company, Chicago. Copyright 1971 by the Regents of the University of California.

Each child should make a record of his team's experimental setup. . . . Even if you think that the way the children have planned their experiments will not produce "desired" results, let them realize their errors on their own. Some children can verbalize how water evaporates and condenses, but are unable to do it operationally. The errors they make will provide you with feedback. For example, if a child places a heat source at the opposite end of the container from where the water is, you will know that he does not understand the conditions necessary for evaporation.

Observing and discussing results. Have the children examine the apparatus on the next day. Give them a few minutes to study their experiments and to determine if the results they obtained were what they expected. They should record their results. . . . Ask a few children to describe how they set up their systems—they may diagram these on the chalkboard—and then describe their results.

Invite the children to comment on the various procedures that were tried and to consider the differences in the results. Some students may not yet realize that heat is required to evaporate water and that the surface on which the droplets form must be cool. If some teams wish to repeat their experiments with modifications, you may wish to allow them to do so before proceeding to the invention. Possibly the whole class would like to try again.

"Inventing" the water cycle. Draw the experimental setup shown in the *illustration*[11] and review with the children what happened to the water in their experiments. Ask them to compare this system with the Freon system.[12] How are the two systems alike? How are they different? Tell them that when water evaporates and then condenses, we call this a *water cycle.* The water cycle is a way of thinking about water evaporating and condensing, over and over again.

Ask children for examples of the water cycle in an ecosystem. You might ask what becomes of the local rainfall once it reaches the ground. The children may say that rainwater (1) flows through streams and gutters into the ocean and finally evaporates into the air, (2) soaks into the soil and then evaporates into the air, or (3) is absorbed by plants and animals and then is returned to the air. Follow through with each example until the rainwater again falls to the ground.

To emphasize the importance of the water cycle, you might ask some of the following questions:

How do organisms living far from a body of water obtain the moisture they need? How does the water travel there? Could the water cycle

[11] The Teacher's Guide for this unit shows a diagram of a closed, rectangular, clear-plastic container containing a beaker of water at one end. A bright light is shining on the water.

[12] The Freon system the children worked with was a plastic bag in which liquid Freon was placed. After the Freon evaporated and expanded the bag, an ice cube was placed on the outside of the bag to show condensation.

exist if there were no organisms on earth? Could land organisms exist if there were no water cycle?

The relationships that exist among the several variables that cause water to evaporate, condense, and evaporate again represent a scientific model. You have probably encountered other such models. But have you thought of them as models that were invented to explain observed interactions, or were they given to you as absolute truths? The former is scientific, the latter is not.

Invent a model that will enable you to explain how an adding machine functions.

Prediction

The interpretation of data, as we have seen, can lead to model building. There is also another use that can be made of interpretations coming from data, and that use is exactly the same as the use that can be made of any past learning in increasing our ability to function more effectively in the future; that is, we use past learnings to predict what our future behavior should be. The interpretations that we make of our past experiences form the basis for our everyday behavior. A common example illustrates this very well. When you are standing at a corner waiting to cross the street and the light regulating the traffic turns red, you feel free (after a visual inspection) to cross. Ask yourself why. In the past you have had direct experience that tells you that moving automobiles stop when confronted with a red light. From that data-interpretation experience, you predict that the moving automobiles you are watching will also stop when the traffic light becomes red. You are so convinced your prediction is true that you are willing to risk your own personal safety by stepping into the street in front of the automobiles that are approaching the red light. This behavior on your part did not come without a great deal of experience which occurred over a long period of time.

So it is with predictions that can be made from data received from experiments. If children are going to learn to predict future events and base those predictions on scientifically collected and interpreted data, they must be given the freedom to make predictions; we, as teachers, must provide experiences that will give them that experience. The following exercise has been taken from *Variation and Measurement*. This particular exercise has been selected because it gives a concrete illustration of how group interpretation of data leads to prediction.

Prediction is an important part of science. How many times will the little pulley go around for every single turn of the large one? (Photo courtesy Science Curriculum Improvement Study, University of California, Berkeley.)

LESSON 6. VARIATION IN RAISIN BREAD[13]

In this lesson the children study variation in the number of raisins in raisin bread. Give each child a slice of bread and ask him to count the number of raisins on the surface of each side of the bread. The pupils should record the number of raisins counted for each side of the slice. . . . All visible raisins and parts of raisins should be counted. If it is not possible to differentiate the sides of a slice by its shape, you should cut off a corner of the slice to provide a reference point. . . .

While each child is putting his data on the board for the histogram, ask the others to indicate the approximate location of the raisins in their bread by drawing them on the outlines of bread provided in the student manual. . . . In addition to demonstrating and recording the variation in the number of raisins and in the distribution of the raisins over the surface of the slice, this activity is an introduction to the use of a reference point (the outline or the cut corner) and later will lead to the

[13] Reprinted with permission from *Variation and Measurement Teacher's Guide,* Trial Edition, pp. 24–26, written and published by the Science Curriculum Improvement Study. Copyright 1964 by the Regents of the University of California.

use of a coordinate system and the kinds of mapping and graphing of distributions and variables which are then possible.

This lesson should help to develop the idea that the kinds of predictions one can make and the probable accuracy of these predictions is to some extent determined by the kind of distribution and the number of observations. For example, in the experiment illustrated in [Figure K] there is no clear central tendency in the range of distribution. All that one can say for this sample is that most results fell between 15 and 25. This allows the prediction that another slice taken from the same loaf would probably contain somewhere between 15 and 25 raisins on either surface.

Of course, when a distribution is spread out over a wide range like this one for raisin bread, one cannot be as specific in his predictions as in the case of a distribution with a narrow central tendency such as the one obtained in Lesson 4, Variation in Green Beans.

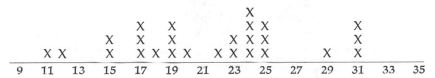

					X			
X	X		X X		X		X
X	X	X	X X X		X
X X	X	X X X X	X X X X		X	X

| 9 | 11 | 13 | 15 | 17 | 19 | 21 | 23 | 25 | 27 | 29 | 31 | 33 | 35 |

Figure K. Histogram showing the frequency of the numbers of raisins in slices of raisin bread as counted, recorded, and graphed by first graders. The raisins counted by each pupil (13) on each side of one slice, are recorded, as separate observations (X); n — 26 (two counts per pupil) as graphed.

You will notice that the foregoing sample lesson does not differentiate between the experience of data interpretation and prediction. Had such a differentiation been made, it would have been artificial. In actual practice, one cannot tell where one of these activities ends and the other begins, and this is extremely advantageous. A learner should be no more conscious of when he is interpreting and when he is predicting than he is of which of the rational powers he is using at any given time. A mind that is capable of problem solving does not view a problem solution as the utilization of many individual mental capacities; rather, it views the problem and continuously brings into service those capacities that are needed as they are needed. A continuous type of experience in science drawn from the experience areas outlined in this chapter—observation, measurement, experimentation, data interpretation, model building, and prediction—should be provided for children. The learner should not necessarily be aware of which of these facets of science he is dealing with. Rather, he should use and develop the skills from any of the areas whenever the problem being considered demands that they be used. (Certain of these experiences are more beneficial at one level of maturity than at another. We shall return to that point later in this chapter.)

Predictions are made in order to make an estimate of the events to take place and/or results to be achieved. You will immediately recognize that the description of a prediction does not differ greatly from that of an hypothesis, and your observation is quite correct. There is, however, a fundamental difference between them. An hypothesis is generally based on very limited experience with a particular problem or situation (as has been previously stated), and sometimes it is based on intuition. In other words, an hypothesis is a belief of an investigator of what the answer to a question actually is; he doesn't need too much evidence to support his belief, but enough to make him want to investigate further and guide him in that investigation. Sometimes the information that an experiment delivers in its early stages is not definitive enough to allow one hypothesis to be stated; rather, the data suggest several hypotheses that can be tested. An hypothesis, then, could be described as a *tentative assumption stated to enable the investigator to test its validity.* Stating hypotheses that are believed to be false is often useful in an investigation because proof of such falsity narrows the number of possible explanations for a problem. Hypotheses are sometimes called "working hypotheses."[14] Such a literal interpretation of the term is quite useful in understanding it; that is, an hypothesis is a statement that guides future work.

Predictions, however, do not have the tentative, "work-guiding" nature of hypotheses; they are not stated for the primary purpose of being tested—hypotheses are. A prediction is made on the basis of ideas that have been tested over and over again. When, for example, the weather is predicted, those predictions are based on data from such variables as temperature, humidity, time of year, wind velocity, and direction. The effect of each of these factors on weather has been thoroughly investigated, and while that investigation was progressing many hypotheses about them were tested. Now, however, meterologists understand the effect of the various factors upon the weather and need not further hypothesize about them. Rather, the effect of such thoroughly tested factors can now be treated as facts and *used* to predict the weather. An hypothesis, then, is an assumption to allow the validity of a fact to be tested, and a prediction is the *utilization of tested facts in order to forecast the future behavior of an individual, the results of an experiment, or the outcome of an event.*

What is the value to a child of learning how to predict? Why is

[14] See T. C. Chamberlain, "The Method of Working Multiple Hypotheses," *Science,* 148 (May 7, 1965), 756.

experience in this area an essential part of his experience in science? Perhaps the most basic reason for including experience in predicting in a child's science education is that prediction is a definite, integral part of the structure of the discipline. In many ways, prediction is at the apex of the scientific process; all that is done in a scientific investigation leads the experimenter toward the goal of stating results of a similar situation in the future. Since we feel that the elementary school science curriculum must be recognizable as science by a scientist (i.e., the integrity of the discipline must be maintained), prediction must be a part of that curriculum.

What is necessary in order to make a prediction? Tested facts must be gathered, classified, compared, analyzed, and evaluated. Those facts selected must then be synthesized into a generalized statement about the situation being considered. This generalization then allows the investigator to reason from the general to the particular about what will happen in a future situation. This is, of course, deduction. In other words, making a prediction demands that many of the child's rational powers be used. The experience of predicting, therefore, assists children in the development of their rational powers and leads learners to construct a more complete picture of the structure of the discipline of science than they would if prediction were not included.

As with the other essential experiences in science, if a child is going to learn how to predict, he must be given experience predicting. The raisin bread lesson included in this chapter is an excellent example of the experience a child needs. A second example of an excellent prediction experience follows.

THE ANGLE OF THE STOPPER POPPER[15]

Your pupils experiment to determine the effect that a changed angle of the stopper popper has on the flight distance of the stopper.[16] They try to control the other important variables. Then they compare their

[15] Reprinted with permission from *Energy Sources Teacher's Guide*, pp. 81–83, by the Science Curriculum Improvement Study, published by Rand McNally & Company, Chicago. Copyright 1971 by the Regents of the University of California.

[16] The "Stopper Popper" consists of the barrel and plunger from a medium-sized syringe that has the end opposite the plunger completely opened in order to allow a solid rubber stopper to be inserted. The syringe is mounted on a board that can be moved from the horizontal position to any angle up to and including 90°. The movable board has one of its ends hinged to a second board that remains in the horizontal position. The movable board can be secured at any angle by a support and by tightening the wing nuts which hold it to the horizontal board.

measurements by marking them on a grid chart and identify the angle that brings about the longest flight distance. Spend about one class period on this chapter.

Teaching Materials

Student manual, page 19
For each team of two children:

1 stopper-popper set
1 measuring tape

For the class:

grid chart[17]

How does the angle of the stopper popper effect the flight distance of the stopper? Do a series of experiments to find out. Try to transfer the same amount of energy to the stopper in all the experiments.

A. Which variable will you change?_____
   Which variables should be kept the same?_____

   _____

   _____

B. Record the flight distance you measure for each angle.
   Test each angle at least twice.
   Then find the average flight distance for that angle.

stopper popper angle	flight distance to the nearest foot		degree
0 degrees			
20 degrees			
40 degrees			
70 degrees			
80 degrees			

C. List the stopper popper angle in order from the longest to the shortest flight distance.

   Long_____medium_____short_____

Figure L.

[17] A large piece of paper ruled like graph paper which is used to plot the results of the children's experiments.

Advance Preparation

If you believe your pupils would benefit from advance practice with the measuring tapes, consult the "Operational Activities" section for suggested additional activities. Check the wing nuts on the ramps and tighten them if necessary. Label one axis of the grid chart with angles and the other with distances as shown in the diagram.

Teaching Suggestions

Control of variables. Student-manual page 19. [Figure L] Invite your pupils to read page 19, where experiments for investigating the effect of the stopper-popper angle are introduced. . . . Then explain that they can find the effect of the angle only if the same amount of energy is transferred to the stopper each time; otherwise the varying results might arise from differences of energy transferred rather than from changes in the angle. Invite your pupils to answer the questions about the variables (part A), or perhaps discuss the answers with them before they write down their ideas.

When the children are ready, ask one or two to tell their answers to the class, and invite evaluative comments from others. Encourage them also to describe how they would make sure that the variables that are to be kept the same remain unchanged.

Next, refer your pupils to the data table on page 19 where they will record their measurement to the nearest foot. We suggest that the children average the data of two trials for each stopper-popper angle, but the procedure may be modified if they have other ideas. (Explain briefly how the average is found if this topic has not been discussed in the mathematics program.) Finally, ask a few children to *predict*[18] which angle will give the longest flight distance and to explain their predictions. Write some of the predictions on the chalkboard, for later comparison with the actual results.

Children's experiments. Ask your pupils to bring their manuals as they go to the launch area, and distribute the equipment there. Remind the children to use the stopper poppers carefully and not to launch stoppers at one another. Help children with the measuring tapes. It may be necessary to remind them to keep the other variables the same while the ramp angle is changed.

After all teams have completed their measurements, the class should return to the room so each child can complete his record on page 19.

Comparison of results. To initiate a comparison of the data, post the labeled grid chart and call on children to report their results. You might then ask one or two teams to dictate their flight distance for all five

[18] Italics added.

angles; as they do so, mark an X for each result on the line referring to that angle. These first few marks give the children a preliminary view of the trend of the data.

You could use the same method to tally the results from the other teams. If that appears to be too time consuming, you might ask the teams to tally their own results informally before the next science class.

After the data have been recorded, and perhaps during the next science class, invite children to evaluate the success with which they controlled variables, and to explain why the longest flight distances were found at intermediate angles between 0° and 90°. They might also compare the findings with their predictions.

Optional Activities

Target games. A target, either an area drawn on the floor or a cardboard box, must be hit twice in succession by a stopper shot from a given spot. Once they succeed, the children might move the target and adjust their stopper poppers to hit the new target position without further trial.

Using the measuring tape. The measuring tapes may be useful teaching aids in your mathematics program, or you may wish your pupils to practice with them before continuing the stopper-popper activities. Invite the children to measure the dimensions of the classroom, various items of furniture, and other objects that are longer than the tape. Students may report their measurements in inches or in feet. Groups investigating the same distance may compare their results on a histogram, converting their data from inches to feet, and vice versa, if different units were used for the same measurement. You can introduce the procedure of averaging and give the children practice in calculating averages through these activities.

In the foregoing exercise, you will immediately see the fundamental premise of prediction being utilized; the child is asked to predict only after he has the factual information available. He is not asked to make any predictions about the relationship between angle and flight distance until he has had experience exploring with the stopper popper and has recorded data from his exploration. Then he is ready to invent a relationship and predict with it. This is, of course, another way of saying that before we can make a prediction about a situation, we must understand and have tested the several facts involved in that situation.

There is a relationship among the three experiences discussed in this chapter that is important when implementing programs in classrooms to teach them is considered. Of the three experiences, interpretation is the most basic. Before models can be constructed or predictions can be made, data that are understood are essential. This, of course, means that the data must be interpreted. Progression from data interpretation to the other two experiences is strictly an individual matter. Some learners build models and predict with them; others find predictions useful in model building. The relationship can be expressed diagrammatically as shown in Figure 6–1 (→ should be read as "leads to"). The relationship among these three essential

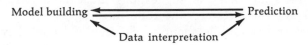

Figure 6–1.

experiences starts with interpretation but is an individual matter from there.

Think of some behavior you have that is based upon a prediction. Then determine where you got the data to allow you to make that prediction.

Placing the "Essential Experiences" in the Elementary School

In Chapters 5 and 6, we have proposed that the elementary school science curriculum be developed around the learning experiences of observation, measurement, experimentation, data interpretation, model building, and prediction. The elementary school science curriculum must be chosen to allow its previously stated objectives to be achieved, but, in order to maintain the integrity of the discipline of science, children must have experience in all six of these areas.

There remains a very pragmatic question that must be answered to enable these "essential experiences" to make their maximum contribution to the intellectual growth and development of a child. At what grade and/or age level are children given experience in these six areas? Should the science program at every grade level contain a degree of experience with all of these areas? Or should areas as obviously complex as model building and prediction be left for the older elementary school children? Are materials available to enable teachers to concentrate upon developing child competencies in these areas? We have indicated through the sample lessons included here, that there are some materials available, and this question will be reconsidered in Chapter 9. For the present we shall turn our attention to the first question. Where in the elementary school should children have the essential experiences in science described in this chapter?

A definitive answer to the foregoing question cannot be formulated because all children are different. A first-grade group of children in one section of the country may be completely unlike any other first-grade group of children anywhere else. Furthermore, large differences exist among the children in any given grade in an elementary school. Therefore, what will be said here about the specific grade placement of the various experiences in science must be tempered with the good judgment of the classroom teacher and his consultant. Do not be misled into believing that the suggestions made here refer to the mythical average child. Rather, the following suggestions are based on what research has told us about all children and how they learn. Our concern is to outline a general view of the sequence of science education experiences for children which will make a maximum contribution to the development of their rational powers. We are particularly concerned with outlining an educational program that can be used to accelerate all boys and girls in the area of science. For, as Celia Stendler has said, "sixteen-year-old thinkers can never be made of six-year-olds, no matter how carefully the educational program is planned."[19] But there are definite intellectual gains that children can make by being engaged in an explicit, carefully planned educational program. Regarding such a program, Professor Stendler has said that "if at the present time, as a result of chance experience, some adolescents build into their nervous systems a structure of logic capable of handling abstractions, more youngsters could do so, if these experiences were not left to chance."[20]

Although no one can outline in detail the specific, day-to-day experiences the children in any given classroom should have, certain general guidelines can be laid down which will prevent chance from being the primary factor that determines whether or not children will have science experiences that will help to develop their rational powers.

What is said here is largely based upon the work of Jean Piaget. The next few paragraphs will also serve as a review of what was said in Chapter 3. The first level of development with which we must concern ourselves is the preoperational stage. Understanding this phase of child development is important for primary-level teachers and particularly first-grade teachers. In the preoperational stage a child is basically concerned with "establishing relationships between

[19] Celia B. Stendler, "Elementary Teaching and Piagetian Theory," *The Science Teacher* (Washington, D.C.: National Science Teachers Association, September 1962), 37.

[20] Ibid., p. 37.

experience and action; his concern is manipulating the world through action."[21] This stage of development begins about the time the child starts to develop his language ability and continues until he can begin to manipulate symbols. In other words, when a child enters the first grade he is an object-manipulator. Science is greatly concerned with the study of objects because the world around us (the investigative field for science) is made up of objects, from subatomic particles to the earth itself. A child's first experiences in science, then, should be concerned with objects and since upon entering the first grade he is a manipulator of objects, it is only natural that he be given the opportunity to study and manipulate them. How does a first grader study an object? When given an object the first act he will perform is to look at, or observe, it. So the first of the essential experiences in science which the child should have is *observation*. Of course, all the necessary observational abilities cannot be provided for during a child's first few years of school. While this experience is the first one for a child to have, opportunities to have it must be provided throughout the learner's educational experience. Remember, as was previously discussed, that observation involves all the senses, and not just seeing. Preoperational children have mastered the basic principles of a language (an extremely difficult act) by the time they enter school. They can talk about what they have observed. Letting them talk about their observations using words that have been newly developed for them or that they have invented is beneficial to their language development. You will remember from Chapter 3 that one of the factors involved in learning is social transmission. Talking is certainly a part of social transmission. Here, then, is a second expectation a teacher can have for a preoperational child—he can report.

Since the child is a manipulator of objects, the ideas of measurement can be started in the first grade. These measurements will be quite crude and approximate and must definitely involve objects. The comparison of the height of a plant with a stick, a piece of paper, or a soda straw involves comparing the plant with another object and the manipulation of one or more objects. Do not expect preoperational children to make repeated application of some standard unit of length in measuring an object. That involves the conservation of length, which preoperational thinkers do not do. The techniques for and systems of measurement, which the child will need in later academic life and as a citizen, will be more thoroughly understood when met if the

---

[21] Jerome S. Bruner, *The Process of Education* (Cambridge, Mass.: Harvard University Press, 1962), p. 34.

basis for measurement is developed in the early primary grades. This experience, like observation and reporting, should continue to be provided for preoperational learners.

In the concrete operational stage, the child is capable of performing some type of operation as opposed to his preschool behavior, which was merely active. The child's attention can be focused on a problem and/or situation which will cause him to do something definite "to see what will happen." Such operations furnish the child with data about the real world which he can internalize and use in the solution of problems. Bruner defines internalize as "the child does not have to go about his problem-solving any longer by overt trial and error, but can actually carry out trial and error in his head."[22] This stage of development extends from about ages 6 to 12 or 15 years[23] and, obviously, the activities the child can undertake during this period can develop in sophistication as he passes through it. But what do these characteristics of child mean with respect to the essential experiences in science outlined here?

In most cases children have *entered* the concrete operational stage by late in their first year of school. Since that means they have begun to see the various states in transformation (which is what an experiment is), they can begin to do single experiments during the latter months of the first grade. One of Piaget's basic premises about concrete operational children is that they can use operations as a means of finding data to assist them in solving problems. An example of that premise is, as was discussed earlier, that if first-grade children are presented a group of seedlike objects (some of which are seeds) and asked how they could determine which were seeds, they will suggest planting them. Here is a concrete operation that 6-year-olds are very willing to undertake. This age child will not normally hypothesize because he sees the problem as an entity. He does not see the several variables and/or divisions of the problem—he sees it as a whole. He cannot, then, hypothesize about any given portion of the experiment; he can only say the seedlike objects will or will not grow. The child has no reason for making such a statement—he has no information which would lead him to make it—and any statement he would make is a wild guess and not an hypothesis. Children should not be encouraged to make such wild guesses at an early age because bad intellectual habits could be formed that will have to be broken when they begin to form simple hypotheses.

[22] Ibid., p. 36.

[23] The data shown in Appendix A suggest that the upper limit of the concrete operational stage may be higher than 15 years of age.

The experiment described produces data and, according to Piaget, concrete operational children have the ability to use these data to assist them in answering their questions. When they do this, they are interpreting data. Experimentation and data interpretation, therefore, can be introduced into the elementary school science program at the late first-grade level—when the children have entered the concrete operational stage. There is some evidence to support the notion that these two experiences will be most efficient if they follow a period of experience in observation and perhaps some acquaintance with measurement. Perhaps the basic idea of size is all the work with measurement which a child needs before beginning experimentation. This basic idea can be thoroughly taught by a comparative exercise during which the teacher will ask such questions as "Who is the tallest?" "Which book is heavier?" and "Which stick is longer?" After such introductory experiences the results the child's experiments provide can be used as a vehicle to lead him to begin to understand measurement as a tool to be used to interpret those results.

The sequence, then, of the essential experiences in science is observation, the basic idea of size in measurement, simple experimentation, and data interpretation. The experiences provided in each of these areas can be started in the first grade and need to continue and become increasingly sophisticated as the child progresses upward through the educational system.

As the child moves upward through the elementary school and continues to have inquiry experiences, he moves deeper and deeper into the concrete operational stage. In the latter years he can begin to take data interpretation and construct models and/or make predictions. He also begins to synthesize simple hypotheses. But the models he builds, the predictions he makes, or the hypotheses he states will be concerned with the objects and operations he is presently concerned with. He is deep into the stage of concrete operations, but he has not yet entered into the early phases of formal operations. In a study we conducted of 588 secondary school students we found that only approximately 25 percent of them had entered the formal operational stage. Do not expect, therefore, fifth and sixth graders to construct mental models, make predictions, or synthesize hypotheses about anything *except* reality. They will not usually take that step into the unknown and begin to relate what is possible but not real to them. Do not put your level of expectation beyond those of prediction or the construction of models which can be made by children using the information and objects they have *directly* in front of them.

As primary children increase in verbal ability and develop their rational powers, *some* will begin to hypothesize, build models, and predict (particularly hypothesize) using abstract information and ideas; but such learnings at this level will be a result of what Stendler calls "chance experiences." When a teacher finds such learning in a child he should encourage and not discourage it, but do not let this happening be your expectation level. You are going to be working with concrete operational children; do not expect too much model building and prediction. Of extreme importance, however, is that late concrete operational children have model building and prediction experiences; those experiences are essential in moving them toward achieving formal operational ability.

A literal interpretation of the sequence for introducing the essential experience in elementary science discussed in this chapter is discouraged because, as was said at the beginning of this section, no two children, classes, schools, and/or sections of the country are alike. If a class of first graders is encountered who has the capacity to predict, that characteristic should not be discouraged. Conversely, if a group of 11-year-olds cannot make adequate observations or take and use measurements with accuracy and finesse, this deficiency in their educational background should not be ignored because "they should have had that." To be sure, the teacher in a classroom is a teacher of content. But he is a teacher of that content to CHILDREN and to ignore what a child *can* do because he is not old enough or to neglect what a child *cannot* do because he should have already developed that ability is an evasion of responsibility. The sequence of experiences in science recommended here is intended for general guidance and not as a blueprint for the science education of all children.

A Reflection

In Chapters 5 and 6, the experiences that constitute a good elementary school science program and where in the school those experiences should be provided have been examined. What has been said here constitutes the skeleton for that larger body known as the science curriculum, and that body will have to be completed by each individual teacher in his own classroom. No one but the teacher knows what the exact day-to-day needs of his pupils actually are. The concern that each teacher in a system must have, however, is that the learners encounter in their years of elementary school all six of the essential experiences discussed in Chapters 5 and 6. This means that the teachers in a given school system must work closely together in developing and maintaining a coordinated program in kindergarten through the sixth grade. Where will teaching materials be found to implement such a program? Within the last few years several national projects have been organized to devote their attention to the development of materials for an elementary science program which will provide the experiences discussed in these chapters. As was indicated earlier, the work of these projects will be the subject of Chapter 9.

7 | Teacher Responsibilities in an Inquiry-Centered Science Program

Within the last thirty years the importance of the role of the teacher has attracted the attention of research scientists, governmental officials, scholars, parents, and the various communications media. Although much of what has been said and written has been overtly directed at how to "improve our schools," the real question being asked (which is hidden beneath that altruistic façade) deals with what an effective teacher does. The description of what an influential teacher does has little meaning in itself unless we know *why* he has adopted his particular pattern of behavior. In other words, until we know what a teacher's educational objectives are, studying his behavior during the teaching act would not be especially fruitful. If, for example, you watch a teacher conduct a science lesson during which the children are naming the planets in our solar system and their various distances from the sun, you are led to suspect that this particular pedagogue places a high value on children accumulating information. This teacher has interpreted his role in teaching as transmitting information to his pupils; his educational objectives are met when the children under his guidance can supply him on an examination with what he has supplied them during his classes. This teacher's responsibilities are confined to designing procedures to assist his pupils in memorizing material as effectively as possible. If his teaching procedures are evaluated with the foregoing responsibility in mind, we can make judgments with respect to how effectively he is accomplishing his purpose, and we can isolate the specific elements that are present and necessary in this type of teaching. While the foregoing philosophy of science teaching is not endorsed in this book, the example does point out how the responsibilities of a teacher are governed by his educational purposes.

Contrast the educational purposes (and the resulting responsibilities) of the teacher in the foregoing example with those of a teacher conducting the following series of three lessons in a second-grade classroom.

Exploration

EXPERIMENTING WITH COMMON OBJECTS[1]

In this exploratory activity, children experiment with simple objects and observe changes that are produced. At the same time, they spontaneously describe their observations to classmates or to you in small-group situations. This chapter will require one class period.

Teaching Materials

For each team of two children:
1 cardboard tray
1 tumbler (to be partly filled with water)
   colored candy balls
2 "mystery pictures"
1 piece of aluminum wire
1 small magnet
1 flashlight bulb
1 battery (size D)
1 scissors
3 or 4 paper clips
1 rubber band
1 card (3" x 5")
   plastic clay (1–2 ounces)
1 sharpened pencil

Advance Preparation

Each set of objects should include the items from the kit; in addition, the batteries, which are very important, must be purchased. It is not necessary that each team has all the other items. The items are provided in sufficient quantity to complete sixteen sets. The "mystery pictures," which are printed six to a sheet, must be cut apart. (When water is spread on them, colors appear.) Cut the aluminum wire into five-inch

[1] Reprinted with permission from *Interaction and Systems Teacher's Guide*, pp. 31–32, by the Science Curriculum Improvement Study. Published by Rand McNally & Company, Chicago. Copyright 1970 by the Regents of the University of California.

pieces and twist one end of each piece once around the base of a flashlight bulb. (When connected with a battery, as shown, the bulb will light.)

Prepare one set of objects for each team of two children. Partly fill the tumblers with water or plan to pour the water while the children work. You will be able to save time by asking two or three children to assemble the sets on the trays.

Teaching Suggestions

Distribute the trays and invite the children to experiment with some of the objects. They may add items from their pockets and desks but should not take more than three or four objects from a tray at one time. Encourage the children to use as many combinations of objects as they wish.

Individual children may wish to show you their experiments. Encourage these children to discuss the objects they are using. You might also suggest that a child try another experiment with the same objects. If he can't think of one, you might suggest, "See if you can make the paper clip become a magnet by rubbing your magnet back and forth across it."

Invention

"INVENTING" THE INTERACTION CONCEPT[2]

A brief review of the children's earlier experiments sets the stage for the invention. You then introduce and illustrate the concept that objects interact when they do something to each other. Children observe and describe changes that occur during the demonstration experiments. They also interpret pictures of interacting objects in the student manual and later draw their own pictures. Plan to use one or two class periods. Optional activities by individuals or small groups may take extra time.

Teaching Materials

For demonstration purposes:
  1 spring
  1 support stand
  2 carts
     vinegar in squeeze bottle
     concentrated bromothymol blue solution (BTB) in squeeze bottle

[2] *Interaction and Systems Teacher's Guide,* op. cit., pp. 34–37.

1 large magnet
3 tumblers
1 pitcher (to be filled with water)
1 pail
1 tray of objects
 paper towel

Advance Preparation

Prepare some materials from Chapter 4 [the previously quoted lesson] for review demonstrations. You might use the light bulb, wire, and a tested battery; water and an unused "mystery picture;" and a 3" x 5" card and scissors. For the first new demonstration, you will need one cart, the spring, and the support stand. Set up the support stand and hang the spring from the screw eye.

Another demonstration employs the large magnet and the second cart. Remove the keeper bar from the maget by twisting it. Put the cart on a level surface. Practice attracting the cart with the magnet by holding the magnet above and in front of either end of the cart. Keep withdrawing the magnet so the cart does not catch up with it as it rolls forward. You may also use the magnet to pick up the cart up by its axles.

The last experiment is demonstrated after the interaction concept has been introduced. It employs separate, dilute solutions of bromothymol blue dye (BTB) and vinegar. The dilute solutions are prepared by squeezing three or four drops of each liquid into separate tumblers, each about one-third full of water. When these solutions are poured into a third container, the dye turns yellow. Try it. The BTB solution should be blue, but if your tap water is slightly acid, the BTB solution will appear green. In that case use distilled water for the experiment.

Teaching Suggestions

Review and demonstrations. To establish a familiar context for the invention that follows, use a group of objects from Chapter 4 [previously quoted lesson] to demonstrate an experiment. Or, a child might demonstrate his experiment. . . . Hold up the objects and ask the children what changes are occurring during the experiment. If they seem not to understand the question, describe the change yourself—for example, "The bulb is now lit." Then proceed to one or two or two other experiments and ask again about the changes that occur.

New demonstrations. Next, you may perform one or two of the new demonstrations you have prepared. First, identify one cart and the spring as the objects to which the children should pay special attention. Ask the children to watch closely as you hang the cart from the spring. Remove and reattach the cart two or three times, so everyone has a chance to notice that the spring stretches. Briefly discuss the changes that occur and then set the objects aside, after taking the cart off the spring.

Second, pick out the magnet and the other cart and use the magnet to attract the cart several times as you did before. Again, ask the children what changes they notice.

Invention. By now, you and the class have observed and discussed the changes that took place during several experiments. Tell the children, while indicating one set of objects with your hand, that you will use the word interact whenever objects do something to each other, as in the case of the chart and the spring. Write *interact* on the chalkboard and let the children pronounce it.

Illustrate the meaning of the word interact by repeating some of the earlier demonstrations. Ask the children to identify moments when the objects are interacting and also moments when they are not interacting. Finally invite them to describe their evidence. As an example of objects that interact, firmly hold the cart and the magnet so close to one another that you can feel the attraction even though you do not let them come together. Let the children see you "straining" to keep them apart as you ask them about interaction. . . .

After this explanation, tell the children that you will show them another system of objects that can interact. Display three tumblers on a paper towel and prepare separate dilute solutions of BTB and of vinegar in two of them. Ask the children to watch carefully as you mix the liquids by pouring them into the third tumbler. Let them describe the changes they observe. Do they interpret these to mean that the liquids interacted while you poured them together?

Follow-up experiments. Encourage all the children to experiment with the support stand, the spring, a plastic tumbler with a string handle taped on (to serve as a container for weighing crayons and other objects at the end of the spring), the magnet, and the cart. You may leave these on the class science table for a few days. . . .

Discovery

ALUMINUM AND COPPER CHLORIDE SOLUTION[3]

Children investigate the interaction between aluminum and copper chloride solution. They observe evidence of interaction, afterwards reporting it in their manuals. By comparing and evaluating these reports

[3] *Interaction and Systems Teacher's Guide, op. cit.,* pp. 77–79.

your pupils are led to try further experiments in which they attempt to identify the interacting objects.

Teaching Materials

For each team of two children:
1 tumbler with copper chloride solution
2 aluminum cups
2 stirring sticks
1 cardboard tray

Teaching Suggestions

The children's experiment. To begin this activity, distribute the equipment and remind each team to keep the tumbler on the tray. Tell your pupils to put the aluminum cups into the copper chloride solution and to look for evidence of interaction in their experiments. They may use the sticks to stir the mixture. Because there is a possibility of splattering, they should not put their faces close to the liquid. After a few minutes the accumulation of copper on the aluminum cup will become evident; the children will not have to look closely to see it.

Experiment Report   Date_____

System of interacting objects_____
_____

Evidence of interaction_____
_____
_____
_____

Picture story

Figure M

. . . This time each child will write his own report on page 19 [Figure M]. Save the experiment systems for discussion and for later optional activities.

Discussion. During the discussion of the interactions that occurred, the children should refer to their reports. Some pupils may ask questions about which objects were interacting. These questions reflect their thoughts that possibly not all objects listed in the report were interacting to produce the temperature rise, the brown material, or other evidence. Encourage the children to answer their own questions and to test their ideas experimentally (see suggestions under "Optional Activities").

Optional Activities

Identifying the interacting objects. The systems reported by the children on page 19 may include copper chloride, water, aluminum cups, tumblers, stirring sticks, and possibly other objects. To determine the role played by each of these objects in the interaction, your pupils have to discover what would have happened if some of the objects had not been present. By observing evidence, or the lack of evidence of interaction in these other experiments, your pupils could infer which objects are essential to the interaction. This is a difficult task, however, that should arise from the children's questions and end when their interest lags.

If your pupils think that only the aluminum and copper chloride interacted, they might sprinkle some dry crystals into a dry aluminum cup. (Because even very slight amounts of water promote the interaction, it is important that the cup be completely dry.) After a while, they should pour out the crystals and examine the separate materials for evidence of interaction. In other trials, they might put copper chloride into one of the paper-cup liners or put the aluminum cup into tap water.

Although a considerable amount of information might have been accumulated by the learners during their participation in the preceding lessons, the teacher has not accepted the transmission of information as his primary function. Instead, the teacher using these lessons has as his principal educational purposes the development of the children's rational powers and their scientific literacy. Children actively participating in the foregoing activities must be using at least the rational powers of comparing, analyzing, synthesizing, imagining, recalling, and inferring. In addition to using the rational powers, the children are becoming acquainted with process-oriented concepts that are a fundamental part of the structure of science. Only when the educational purposes of the teacher using the foregoing lessons are understood can we assess what his classroom responsibilities are.

Since the philosophy of science teaching advocated by this textbook is richly exemplified in the preceding sample lessons, we shall devote the remainder of this chapter to isolating and examining the teacher responsibilities which must be accepted if learning experiences such as those of the sample lessons are going to be educationally valuable.

The role or responsibility of the teacher broadly and very simply stated is to promote learning. But how can a teacher effectively promote learning without becoming a "purveyor of information" or a "supplier of answers"? To isolate the data needed to understand how this can be done, we must examine such factors as the influence of the learning environment, the relationship of the teacher to the child and the child to the teacher, specific duties of the teacher before teaching begins, and duties during the teacher-learning process.

The Learning Environment

The human being is an interesting animal in many respects, and one of his most remarkable characteristics is that his behavior tends to be a mirror of his environment. When young children step into a place of worship most of them whisper, walk as quietly as possible, and do not exhibit many of the behaviors they would happily show just beyond the church door. On the other extreme, when children are "turned loose" on the playground, happy yelling, wrestling, running, jumping, and many other types of overt behavior which would have been offensive *to the child* in church or in the schoolroom are freely and openly expressed. There are many other examples of this phenomenon and there would be exceptions to any generalization drawn about it, but to a large degree, children exhibit the type of behavior which they feel their environment demands. If, then, we wish children to develop their rational powers and learn the structure of the discipline of science by investigation, their classroom environment must be one that encourages and respects investigation as well as makes it possible. The Educational Policies Commission has described such a classroom environment:

> The school which develops the ability to think is itself a place where thought is respected and where humane values implicit in rationality are honored. It has an atmosphere conducive to thinking and it rewards its pupils for progress toward the goals it values.[4]

[4] Educational Policies Commission, *The Central Purpose of American Education* Washington, D.C.: NEA, 1961), p. 16. [See Appendix C.]

The teacher begins establishing "an atmosphere conducive to thinking" the first day of school chiefly by his attitude toward the pupils. If he begins his class by giving the children an opportunity to identify themselves and explain anything they would like to about themselves and/or their families, they begin to feel that the teacher is interested in *them*. Furthermore, the teacher who accepts what the children have to say in the first few class hours will have begun to establish in their minds the extremely important concept that the teacher is really interested in what *they* think. The teacher, in other words, can demonstrate at the very beginning of the school term that he is eager to listen to what the children have to say.

The teacher's willingness to listen to the children and his ability to utilize what they have said in carrying the classroom activities forward is the first principle in establishing a classroom environment conducive to investigation. Listening to the children's contribution to the classroom discussion aids in establishing rapport with the children, but it also does much more. It tells the children that they, as well as the teacher, have a responsibility in carrying out the activities of the class. Developing the ability to listen to what children have to say is not easy for an adult—adults usually feel that the learning can proceed much more rapidly if they interpret what has been said and, in short, tell the children what they should know. We, as teachers, must constantly remind ourselves that the principal goal we are reaching for is to assist children in learning why they know what they know (learning how to learn), and that goal can best be achieved if we use the contributions of the children in advancing their understandings of the topic under consideration. We cannot, however, utilize the children's contributions if we do not listen and find out what they are. The information that can be received by listening to the children will also tell the teacher how well the pupils are understanding the concept being developed or the object being inspected. This is the principal type of information which a teacher can use to assist him in guiding the classroom work at a precise moment or planning future learning activities for his class, and the children are the only ones who can supply that information. The first principle, then, in establishing a learning environment conducive to investigation is: *Listen to the children.*

Experience with children will very soon lead any adult to conclude that the child can easily identify a phony person. The old fairy tale "The Emperor's New Clothes" is an excellent example of this ability of children. What could there be about a teacher that a child might identify as "phony?" If the teacher is going to establish an environ-

If the teacher establishes an environment in which children can learn to investigate, he too must be a willing investigator.

ment that is to teach children to investigate, he too must be a *willing* investigator. If the children do the investigating, collect and interpret the data, and form hypotheses and/or generalizations about the problem under consideration, and the teacher then rejects the results of what the children have done, the pupils are going to conclude very quickly that the investigation process is a fake. They will begin to think that the teacher knew the answers all the time and unless data are produced which allow them to conclude what the teacher wants them to conclude, their investigation has failed. If the teacher is sincere about teaching children to investigate (and he must be if developing the rational powers of children represents his primary educational purpose), *all the results that are produced must be accepted.* When the teaching process is based on an investigation, the teacher will function best if he becomes an investigator with the children. How does a teacher do this?

After the problem has been identified (and the necessary materials secured), the children are the ones to carry on the investigation. But the teacher can be a contributive part of the investigation if he works with the children asking them direct questions about their work; for example, the teacher might ask whether or not there might be a more convenient and/or better way of carrying out a measurement or con-

An inquiry-centered science class will involve the teacher in many class activities, including that of class recorder.

structing an apparatus than the one they are using. In other words, the teacher who exhibits interest and concern in the investigative process is the one whom children will identify as being genuinely a part of that process.

The teacher can best show his willingness to be an investigator during the time when data are being interpreted. When data are available for inspection and evaluation, they must be arranged in an order that will allow all the children to view them at the same time. A technique that is quite useful to allow data to be efficiently displayed and to enable the teacher to become a part of the investigation is for him to use the chalkboard and become the class secretary. The pupils should first be led to identify the several factors (variables) about which data have been gathered and then be asked to suggest procedures for arranging these data in a convenient order. If no suggestions for the arrangement come from the class, here is an excellent opportunity for the teacher to become an actual part of the investigation; he can suggest a method for arranging the data and urge the children also to contribute to the discussion. If the teacher freely changes the data-arranging procedure to conform to the wishes of the class, he will have concretely demonstrated that he too is an investigator.

An additional (and perhaps the most important) teacher behavior that will contribute to the pupils' acceptance of him as an investigator develops when the data placed on the chalkboard (or chart) are interpreted. This is a crucial time in maintaining a classroom environment that encourages or discourages active investigation by the children, and the teacher will demonstrate to the pupils which of these he wishes to do by his attitude toward the data collected. If he shows that he does not have faith in the information the children have gathered (by actually stating that he doesn't really believe the information or by acting skeptically about it), he has lost the investigative spirit within his classroom. But if he accepts the data as any member of the group does and continually asks what those data tell them, he has shown that he accepts not only the information found but also the group's investigative procedures.

This attitude on the part of the class leaves two definite avenues open for the teacher. He can lead the pupils to summarize their data and, if the problem or situation under study warrants it, form a generalization, or he can ask another question which must then be investigated. (We shall return to the point of asking questions that require additional investigation.) If, however, the teacher realizes the children are reaching an unacceptable generalization or conclusion, he has a second approach open to him which he can use and still be accepted by the children as an investigator; that is, he can suggest an additional investigation to confirm their findings just as he would do when the investigation led them to a generalization acceptable to the discipline of science and, of course, to the teacher. (The children must not be aware that the teacher views their results as unacceptable.)

If a second investigation is performed and data are produced which are contrary to the data from the first experiment, the class then has a *real* problem that can be solved only by making both investigations again. The second time the first investigation is performed, the chances are good that it, too, will produce acceptable data (i.e., supportive of the data from the second investigation) because often incorrect data are the result of a procedure improperly employed. The experience gained in conducting an investigation four times (twice for each procedure used) increases the probability that procedures will be properly followed and results will be acceptable. The teacher, in order to show that he is an investigator, must be an accepter of data. In summary, then, if a teacher is going to maintain an investigative environment (and atmosphere) in his classroom, *he must be an investigator himself.*

Perhaps the reader has begun to ask himself what we mean by an investigation. We define an investigation as any act an individual performs to secure information that will enable him to describe or understand something better than he did before his inquiry. First-grade children determining the properties of a squash or sorting several kinds of nuts, bolts, and washers are conducting as authentic an investigation as are sixth graders when they search for those stimuli that will make a mealworm back up, high school students determining the molecular formula of water, or a research scientist searching for a substitute for natural fuels. The value in the learning process of a scientific investigation is not determined by its complexity, but rather by its appropriateness to the intellectual level of the investigator.

The learning environment that is conducive to encouraging children to investigate is one in which the child realizes that what he has to say is important and will be listened to. Proper investigative learning conditions demonstrate to a pupil that his teacher is also an investigator and, as such, is interested in the results of the investigation; he is not one who passes judgment on those results. In short, the best learning environment for investigation is established and maintained by a teacher who is a model of investigation with whom the children can identify. This kind of teacher has as a dominant part of his vocabulary such questions as "How do we know?" "How can we find out?" "What do these data mean?" and "Can we find further evidence to support our interpretation of our data?" One of the better summary statements regarding the responsibilities of a teacher for maintaining a classroom environment conducive to learning science as an investigative process was made to us by an undergraduate student. Nancy Baldwin Butler summed up her feelings this way: "A teacher cannot ask children to hypothesize if she never guesses and allows critical analyses of her guesses."[5]

Responsibility for Selecting Topics for Investigation

Teachers who are serious about providing educational experiences in science for children which will develop their rational powers will have discharged one of their most important responsibilities before meeting the pupils for the first time. That responsibility is the selection of the

[5] Nancy Baldwin Butler, paper submitted while a student in Education 244 ("Science in the Elementary School"), University of Oklahoma. Mrs. Butler went on in her paper to distinguish between the "guesses" she was referring to in this quotation and "wild guesses."

topics in science (the curriculum) which the children will investigate. There are three general criteria to be used in the selection of subject matter:

1. The content must be useful to lead the learner to develop his rational powers—it must lend itself to investigation.
2. The learner should gain an increased understanding of and appreciation for his environment as a result of having the learning experiences provided.
3. The science studied in the classroom must be recognizable as science by a scientist; that is, the integrity of the discipline of science must be maintained.

Although the foregoing three points represent important criteria that must be observed in order to lead children to the achievement of the principal goal of education—the development of the ability to think—there is another, more specific factor the teacher must constantly keep in mind. That factor, which was discussed extensively in Chapter 3, is that the educational experience (content) must match the intellectual maturity-level of the child.

What are the responsibilities of a teacher in providing experiences in investigation? Principally, to introduce into the classroom those topics to investigate which can be effectively utilized by the age group being taught. Preschool and kindergarten children are chiefly concerned (according to Piaget) with manipulating the world through action. The investigations these children perform should give them experience in manipulating familiar objects and discovering all manner of information about them. This kind of experience can provide a child with the opportunity to develop the vocabulary necessary to communicate the findings of his investigations to his peers. Although the data are not sufficient to warrant a general statement about the increase in vocabulary which investigative experiences in science at the kindergarten and early primary grades provide, evidence is mounting that such learning experiences make an important contribution. Kindergarten children react best to objects that come from their environment and that they have selected. The responsibility of the kindergarten teacher, then, seems fairly clear: the investigative experience provided for children at this level should be confined to familiar objects, and many of those objects should be provided by the children.

But what about children in grades 1 through 6? Are there notions about them similar to those about the kindergarten child? If you will think back to Chapter 3, you will remember that after the preoperational stage of child development, the concrete operations stage begins and continues through probably the sixth grade and quite probably longer. During the concrete operations stage the pupil can carry out operations (acts which provide him data) rather directly. He can manipulate objects, observe growth and condition of living organisms, take measurements and, in general, perform any operation that will give him data. The pupil can then organize and use these data to assist him in the solution of problems. Quite obviously a first grader cannot collect data and use them to solve as complex a problem as can a sixth grader, but he can solve problems. As we have seen (Chapter 5) first graders can determine which of many seedlike objects are seeds by planting all the objects and watching them grow. This problem was quite direct and the data gathered were also straightforward. But the character of the concrete operational stage is there. These children manipulated objects (seeds, water, pots, and soil) to provide them data to solve a problem, just as did a group of fifth graders who wished to see whether or not a geranium plant would grow under an artificial light. The levels of sophistication of the problems were different, but the method of operation of the learner was the same and characteristic of the concrete operations stage: *objects were manipulated to produce data to solve a problem.*

At no time in these experiments did either group attempt to operate on a hypothetical or abstract level—they did not hypothesize what would happen. They manipulated objects, gathered data, and used the data to explain the situations being investigated. Throughout grades 1 through at least 4 and possibly 5, the investigative experiences of children can be broadened to include many problems from his environment. Teachers need not wait until the child suggests investigating a particular problem or area; these areas can be selected by the teacher and presented to the children. In many cases selection of the areas by the teacher is desirable because the children have not had the necessary experience to know what they should be studying. Experience has shown that what determines the child's interest in a problem is not affected nearly as much by what the problem is as it is by the manner in which the teacher presents the problem to the child. At the level of concrete operations, then, the teacher has the responsibility of providing investigative experiences that will allow the children to manipulate objects in order to produce data that can be used in the solution of a problem.

Children in the sixth, and sometimes the fifth, grade present teachers with a unique curriculum responsibility. This age group is approaching the upper limits of the concrete operational stage, and possibly a few are just entering the formal operations state. These pupils can begin to develop simple hypotheses. Younger children will in some cases state rather unsophisticated hypotheses. They should not be discouraged from doing so, but when they state hypotheses they must be led to understand why such a statement can be made. The first age level where true (but simple) hypotheses can be stated is at the beginning of the formal operations stage. At this stage of development children have the opportunity, in fact, should be urged, to hypothesize, and experience has shown that they will. The following example demonstrates their willingness to hypothesize.

A colony of mealworms was kept in a large black container that was covered with a piece of black paper. The children were studying the behavior of these organisms and observed each day that as they removed the cover from the container many mealworms would be found on the top of the meal. The worms, however, did not stay on the top of the meal; a few minutes after the cover had been removed, the children observed that the worms all burrowed into the meal. After about two days of observing this event the young investigators hypothesized that mealworms' eyes were sensitive to light just as our eyes are when we come from the dark into a bright room. The teacher then asked the children if they were sure the mealworm had eyes. The pupils agreed that they assumed he did have eyes but could not prove it. Here the ability of sixth-grade children to begin to utilize basic hypothetical reasoning became evident. The mealworm must have eyes, they hypothesized, because if he did not it would mean that his entire body was light-sensitive which did not seem logical to them. One child emphatically stated that our eyes are the only part of our bodies that is light-sensitive. Here is a clear case of children operating upon, as Bruner calls them, "logical operations," which require that the learner must be able to deal with simple abstractions.

The children agreed to investigate whether or not the mealworm had eyes, and after many child-designed experiments, they concluded that perhaps the worms did have eyes but, if so, they were nonfunctional; that is, the worms were blind. The investigators were again faced with the question of why the mealworms seemed sensitive to light. Here again the ability of sixth graders to handle beginning formal operations became evident. They hypothesized that perhaps the worm's underdeveloped eyes and/or his body were sensitive to light, and if they were, perhaps he became so accustomed to light (just as we do) that when the intensity of the light on him is changed he will react to it.

Once again the children designed and performed experiments and

Children need experiences that permit and encourage them to inquire into natural phenomena. (Photo courtesy Science Curriculum Improvement Study, University of California, Berkeley.)

secured data to let them test their hypotheses. They then designed a few other experiments with which they could verify their results. The unique opportunity an upper grade teacher has is that he can and should select investigations for his pupils that will allow and encourage them to "operate upon hypothetical propositions rather than being constrained to what he has experienced or what is before him."[6]

A teacher at any grade level does have one additional responsibility when teaching by inquiry which will influence his entire attitude toward the procedure and, therefore, also affect his pupils. That responsibility is related to what the teacher expects to happen in the classroom. If the teacher begins teaching by inquiry and expects the children in his class to discover something *new* that will be a contribution to knowledge, he is going to be vastly disappointed with inquiry. Discovering something new is *not* the reason for teaching by inquiry. The active involvement of children in the process of finding out "why," "where," "how long," "when," and so forth, is the reason that inquiry is valuable. *Learning goes on during the process and is not represented by the product of the inquiry.* Only through such

[6] Jerome S. Bruner, *The Process of Education* (Cambridge, Mass.: Harvard University Press, 1962), p. 37.

experiences as these will a child develop his rational powers and truly learn how to learn.

If the schools believe as the Education Policies Commission does—"No school fully achieves any pupil's goals in the relatively short time he spends in the classroom. The school seeks rather to equip the pupil to achieve them for himself,"[7]—then children must be given experiences that will lead them to identify problems, collect information, and make judgments about the solutions to those problems. Children will not develop such practical and intellectual characteristics if they learn and recite lessons. These educational outcomes will be achieved only if children are given experiences at their intellectual level which will allow them to begin to practice what we wish them to become proficient at doing. One final factor should be internalized by the teacher. If the child is led to make a genuine discovery, it may not be new to science but it will be new to him: "For if man's intellectual excellence is the most his own among his perfections, it is also the case that the most personal of all that he knows is that which he discovered for himself."[8]

Any teacher "worth his salt" by this time is probably asking himself and those around him where he is going to find a year's worth of investigative experiences. Is the teacher expected to develop such learning activities by himself? Certainly not! The teacher is expected to examine all the materials that are available and investigatory in nature and select from them those that best fit the characteristics and needs of his class. We shall return to a discussion of the materials available in Chapter 9.

In summary, then, a teacher discharges his responsibilities for providing what to investigate by:

1. Knowing the developmental characteristics of his pupils, and
2. Making careful selections from the available materials in order to provide the children proper *investigative* experiences.

Responsibility for Keeping the Investigation Going

If you have ever been in a group that is discussing an issue and no one can make a contribution, you realize the important role the teacher must play in an inquiry-centered classroom. Silence, which

[7] Educational Policies Commission, *The Central Purpose of American Education,* op. cit., p. 2. [See Appendix C.]
[8] Jerome S. Bruner, *On Knowing* (New York: Atheneum, 1965), p. 82. (Originally published by the Harvard University Press.)

results because no one knows where to begin investigating a problem or how to begin to interpret data that have been collected, can be embarrassing to children, and once a child has been embarrassed he is going to be more careful in the future about placing himself in a similar situation. We are, of course, saying that embarrassment can harm motivation, and one of the outstanding characteristics of the inquiry system of learning (when properly conducted) is its ability to bring about self-motivation. The child learns to accept success or failure not as reward or punishment but as information that will tell him how to adjust his investigative procedures in order to arrive at results he would interpret as satisfactory. If, however, the child cannot make a contribution to the discussion, he can become afraid of a future investigation before it begins. He is then in a poor position to profit motivationally or intellectually from an investigation. *The teacher* has the responsibility to prevent the child from having an experience that will harm his motivation or cause him to look upon the process of inquiry with distrust or even fear. When children look forward to an investigation as a time when they have fun and are constructive, the teacher can be sure that he has fulfilled his responsibilities of establishing a proper environment, providing topics to investigate which are not beyond the intellectual level of the child, and keeping the investigation under way in a positive manner. But what does a teacher do to keep an investigation progressing positively? There are several factors that form the answer to that question and they all basically revolve around the cardinal points of materials, clues, cues, and questions.

No learning by inquiry can take place unless the children have proper materials to work with. An extremely important role of the teacher, then, is to make certain that materials are available to conduct an investigation. If you want the children to determine whether or not different types of plants need different amounts of water, you need several different types of plants. If, for example, you wish children to investigate the geranium-artificial light problem mentioned earlier, you need geranium plants, a dark place in which to put the plant so that the only light it receives is artificial light, and an artificial light. Regardless of the situation the teacher and his pupils decide to investigate, the teacher has the responsibility for securing the necessary materials—this does not rule out teachers requesting children to bring specific items to school or accepting voluntary pupil-contributed materials. If chalkboard, chalk, and "good books" are substituted for actual experience with materials, you are asking children to construct mental abstractions. This the concrete operational child cannot do because abstractions cannot be directly verified. The child has no choice, therefore, but to memorize facts— we have already explored the futility of that procedure. In summary: *To keep an investigation going the teacher must supply the child with proper and sufficient materials.*

While the children are identifying the problem to investigate, performing the investigation, or interpreting the data that have been secured, there is no doubt that the most important role of the teacher is to ask many questions, making sure that they are asked in the proper manner.

Ask yourself why teachers ask questions and record your answer.

The first reason some teachers will give is that they ask questions to find out what the pupils know—that is a legitimate use of questions. The answers to such questions allow the teacher to adjust his teaching to accommodate the deficiencies or gross misunderstandings the children have, recover ground already explored, or completely change his teaching procedure. In all these cases, however, you will notice that the teacher is leading the learners to correct their own misunderstandings and/or learning deficiencies. *He is not using the question as a basis for telling the learners what they should know.* When teachers ask questions to find out what the children know in order that such information can be used to make them change their opinions and think as the teacher does, he is using questions improperly. (In fact that procedure is using questions as a forerunner to brainwashing.) Robert Karplus comments on the latter questioning technique thus:

> Teachers usually ask a question, . . . , to get an answer already formulated in their own minds or to make a point of their own choosing. Teachers rarely ask a question because they are really curious to know what the pupils think or believe or have observed.[9]

In other words, teachers too often want children to leave school knowing what they, the teachers, know. Teachers who use questions in this manner do not believe that the child can contribute to his own education. Such persons must, then, also believe that the child must be fully educated for his future when he leaves school, because if he cannot make a contribution to his own education while he is in school, he cannot be expected to have learned how to learn. Therefore, he

---

[9] Robert Karplus, "Science in the Elementary School," *New Developments in Elementary School Science—A Conference*, John W. Renner, Director, Oklahoma City, Frontiers of Science Foundation of Oklahoma, Inc., 1964, p. 10.

cannot continue to learn on his own after leaving school. This is an absurd position for a teacher to find himself in, and one that the Educational Policies Commission rejects. (See Appendix C.) But that is the position teachers assume as long as they insist on using questions to make a point which *they* wish to make and not to use the answers of the children to further child understanding. As Karplus has pointed out, this attitude of teachers toward questions is picked up by the children: "The pupils, of course, adapt quickly to this situation. After a few years in school, answering questions is for them more a mind-reading proposition than a matter of reasoning about the substance of a scientific problem."[10]

When a teacher asks "What do you think, Susan?" he must be very sure he is really asking Susan what she thinks and not, "What do you think I think, Susan?" This means that when Susan tells the teacher what she thinks, the teacher is obligated to accept Susan's answer cheerfully. If a teacher asks questions and then tells the child giving the answer, "No, that is wrong," or "That's not what I had in mind," the pupils will attempt to become, as Karplus said, "mind-readers" or they will completely withdraw and simply say "I don't know." If a child volunteers his best efforts in answering a question and they are rejected again and again, his ego is damaged, and in a short while he is not going to place his ego in jeopardy by responding to a question. Does this latter statement imply that teachers are obligated to accept all answers that children offer to questions? Our findings tell us that teachers should accept all honest answers to questions, and Karplus defends this position:

> . . . student's replies should be judged on their merit and not on the basis of conforming to the teacher's expectations. . . . One way of framing suitable questions is to address them to individual pupils, "What changes have you observed, John?" or "Do you think the objects interacted, Mary?". . . . The only incorrect answers to such questions would be very deliberate lies on the part of the pupils. As long as they are honest, their replies are automatically correct even if each child reports a different observation and none agrees with the teacher.[11]

We said earlier that when the teacher does not accept answers given by the children, ego damage is a distinct possibility. There is another, equally serious outcome that results from children attempting to read the teacher's mind or withdrawing from the learning situation—inquiry stops. When the learner begins to try to figure out what

10 Ibid., p. 10.
11 Ibid., p. 11.

Teachers must ask questions, and they must also accept the answers children give them.

the teacher wants, he stops inquiring into the topic being investigated. He has then stopped developing his rational powers and learning how to learn and has begun to "figure people out." In fostering the spirit of inquiry with questions, therefore, the teacher is obligated to accept those answers the children give him.

But what if the children are being led (by themselves) toward an erroneous concept? Earlier in this chapter we explained the value of teachers having children repeat an experiment using a different approach in order to get data from the second procedure which would disagree with the data obtained from the first. The same general principle applies here. After one child states his observations or opinions, whether they are acceptable or unacceptable (to the teacher), the teacher is obligated to poll the remainder (or a representative sample) of the class. In most cases when one child has observed something unacceptable or interpreted data erroneously, the observations and interpretations of his classmates will assist him in discovering *for himself* where he was incorrect. If that rare case occurs where the entire class gives unacceptable answers to a teacher-asked question, then, of course, the activity must be reexperienced. The teacher must be careful to impress on the learners the idea that the activity is being redone to verify their findings. In such a situation the teacher has obviously used questions to keep the learning environment conducive to investigation. Questions are a valuable aid, but they must be asked to find out what the children know, and their answers must be used by the teacher as information to enable him to determine the direction the class work should take. As soon as the teacher begins to use answers to questions as a basis for reward and punishment, he has harmed motivation and the spirit of inquiry in the classroom.

Often teachers use questions as a disciplinary measure. If the teacher is using a question to redirect the attention of a child from something nonproductive to something productive or to help him focus his attention, with the rest of the class, on the problem at hand, we would agree that a limited use of this technique can have a beneficial effect. If, however, the teacher uses questions to show the child (and the rest of the class) that he doesn't know something, has made an unacceptable interpretation of data, has improperly designed an experiment, or "hasn't studied," we condemn such uses of questions. The teacher that follows this procedure not only destroys the morale of the child he focuses on but also raises sincere doubts in the minds of the other children about the sincerity of the teacher when he says he wants them to explore, invent, discover, and freely express their findings. Questions can be used productively in a disciplinary way only if they are intended to focus (or redirect) the attention of children on the problem being considered.

How is a question asked? Perhaps the best way is to phrase the question as simply and directly as possible, to stop for just an instant and then call upon an individual child. Calling upon the child first and then asking the question is an invitation to the rest of the pupils to stop thinking about the specific question being asked. This will not always happen, but there exists that inherent danger. Sometimes teachers ask questions and then do not ask a specific child; this procedure leads the class to provide, and the teacher must then accept, a "gang" answer or chorus. While this procedure does stimulate the entire class to think about the question, gang answers could result in serious class-control problems. If the question is asked directly, and the teacher pauses—the entire class is stimulated to think. If an individual is then called upon, the possible loss of class control by the teacher is avoided.

One of the most important principles to remember in questioning is that the questions the teacher asks should not be trivial; they should be genuinely concerned with the problem being identified or the data being interpreted. The first question asked should be so directed that it starts the discussion about the most apparent aspects of the pending or completed investigation. A question such as "How much have your plants grown since the last watering?" is direct, to the point, and suggests a definite pupil action. The foregoing question is superior to "What effect has the water which we have been giving the plants had on them?" This question suggests that there should be some obvious effect that water has had on the plants (and there may be none) and also demands that the children begin to think in the abstract—an ability that elementary school-age children do not usually have. Questions, therefore, should be direct and to the point. Questions must also not be too broad in scope, but should let the child focus on a specific idea. "Name one property which your object has, Mike" is a superior question to "What properties does your object have, Mike?" Each question asked should let the learners uncover just a bit more of the concept being developed and, in most cases, small steps or "bites" are best for this. Questions, then, should be important, direct, specific, and when used sequentially should lead the children to the development of a concept.

There is another frame of reference from which teachers must evaluate their questioning techniques. When something is unknown to you, you ask questions. Furthermore, the understandings you subsequently develop about the unknown will very probably depend directly on the type and caliber of questions you ask and the responses you receive. Teachers can respond to a student's questions in two ways: (1) by providing him with a finite answer, or (2) by providing him with the motivation and ideas necessary to continue the inquiry himself. Giving a student a direct answer often supplies him with all the information he needs and thus inquiry and learning stop. On the other hand, responding to a question with another question or with an alternate suggestion about the investigation can stimulate the learner to continue thinking about the problem and thereby continue learning. Questions that focus the attention of the learner on a specific factor in the investigation or give him direct information are *convergent*. A convergent question tends to cause the student to look inward toward what has been done and not outward toward what might be done; in other words, it tends to terminate an investigation. Such questions encourage the learner to concentrate on retaining facts rather than using his head for something better, such as evaluating a suggestion from the teacher, analyzing what needs to be done to implement a thought triggered by a question from the teacher, or synthesizing data from an experiment and drawing inferences and generalizations therefrom.

Convergent questions can be used to advantage in inquiry-centered teaching *if* the teacher uses them to focus attention on a particular portion of an investigation with which the learner is having difficulty. If the learner is led to analyze his error through a series of convergent questions, he can correct it and move on to fitting that piece of information into the larger picture. Once the student is thinking in a convergent manner, however, the teacher has the responsibility for asking questions that will stimulate the student to think in a wider scope. This type of question is a *divergent* question.

Divergent questions invite the learner to think in a multiplicity of directions and to consider a number of possible explanations for the data collected. T. C. Chamberlin stated the ultimate use of divergent questions when he explained that an investigator should advance several hypotheses regarding the solution to a problem and not "fasten his affections unduly upon any one."[12] The best type of divergent question is, "What do you believe the best procedure is to collect information?" A typical convergent question often asked by teachers is, "Does the information you have support the idea we have been studying?" Convergent questions tell the learner that what is really important is not what he thinks or what his information tells him, but that the proper thing to believe is what he has been told. Divergent questions tell the learner that it is what *he* has to say that is important. If your purpose in the classroom is the transmission of information about a particular discipline, divergent questions are of little value because they tend to lead the learner away from what is and toward what might be. The principal purpose of asking divergent questions is to find out the direction of the learner's thinking and what he is thinking.

Just as no one can tell you exactly how to establish and maintain discipline in your classroom, no one can tell you precisely how to ask questions. At one point in our research, we asked a group of fifty experienced, inquiry-centered teachers to contribute their ideas on asking questions. We have summarized their responses on the following pages but have left to the reader application of their ideas to convergent or divergent questions. Each teacher was asked these six questions:

[12] T. C. Chamberlin, "The Method of Multiple Working Hypotheses," *Science* (May 1965), 754–761. First published in *Science* (February 1890).

1. Why do you ask questions?
   [Responses]
   a. To start the learner thinking.
   b. To see if the learner is thinking in the direction of the problem.
   c. To put the learner on a definite track if necessary.
   d. To invite learner participation.
   e. To see what the learners know about a particular problem before beginning an investigation.
   f. To create interest.
   g. To allow learners to develop confidence.
2. What do you expect from a question?
   [Responses]
   a. An honest reply.
   b. A response that leaves both the teacher and the student free to ask another question (thus questions that invite a Yes or No answer are of limited value).
   c. An opportunity for the student to ask himself a question.
3. What do you want a question to do to the learning situation?
   [Responses] The question should . . .
   a. free a student to ask questions.
   b. personally involve the learner.
   c. lead the learner or suggest to him.
   d. stimulate interaction among the learners.
   e. lead to further investigations.
4. What kind of question should be asked?
   [Responses]
   a. An important one.
   b. One to which the learner believes the answer is important.
   c. One that stimulates inquiry.
   d. A question devoted to one idea that is small enough to comprehend.
   e. A question that can be built on.
   f. A question that is not misleading.
   g. One that requires more than Yes or No.
   h. Use "why" questions sparingly, since they can be indefinite; instead of asking why something happened or is true, ask the student what evidence he can give that something happened or is true.
5. When do you ask a question?
   [Responses]
   a. When you want the learner to move on.
   b. When a learner's mind is wandering.
   c. To get learners back on the track or away from a dead end.
   d. To solicit problems and develop areas for investigation.
   e. To check the group's understanding.
   f. To stimulate group discussion.
   g. To improve a learner's self-image.
   h. To focus attention on the inquiry at its beginning.
   i. To see if a learner is ready to undertake an individual inquiry.
   j. To provide the teacher with the opportunity for conceptual invention.
   k. To initiate exploration.
   l. To begin discovery experiences.

m. To lead the learner toward another concept.
n. To find what the learner is doing and thinking.
6. How do you ask questions?
[Responses]
a. Ask for the attention of the class.
b. Ask with enthusiasm and genuine interest but easily and informally.
c. Ask the question and then select a respondent.
d. Encourage the students first to listen carefully to the question and then to volunteer answers.
e. Don't rush the student to respond.
f. Generally use volunteers to answer.

You know, of course, that all answers must be accepted. These six general, teacher-made categories provide you with the information to develop your own questioning techniques. We present them to you not as rules but as data on which to build your own solutions. In summary, *questions properly asked and the replies to them properly used are exceedingly important in teaching science by inquiry.*

Suppose a class cannot get an investigation designed or gets one under way and becomes hopelessly "stuck." What responsibilities does the teacher have here? The Educational Policies Commission states that the teacher has the responsibility of "selecting problems which are within his [the child's] grasp, providing clues and cues to their solution, suggesting alternative ways to think about them."[13] In other words, teachers have a definite responsibility to assist in keeping the children moving in their investigation. That statement does not mean that children are not allowed to follow an incorrect hypothesis or assumption. In fact, there are many times when young investigators will teach themselves much more by following an incorrect assumption than they will by being kept on the precise course by the teacher. Children should be permitted to follow that plan of investigation which seems logical *to them.* If that investigative pattern is not a fruitful one, that fact will most likely be discovered because the data produced do not make sense, or the investigation itself cannot be pushed to completion with the operational plan with which it was begun. In either case, such a situation clearly demonstrates the need for informed, adult assistance. The teacher needs to step into the investigation at this point and review with the children how they reached the point in the investigation at which they are. Often in such a review the children themselves will see where they had begun their search upon an incorrect assumption or wrong information. If not, the teacher needs to suggest to them an alternate way of thinking

[13] Educational Policies Commission, *The Central Purpose of American Education,* op. cit., p. 17. [See Appendix C.]

about the original problem that will ultimately lead them to a redesign of the investigation which they will be able to pursue to completion and that will provide them usable data. An alternate way of thinking about a problem is not telling children an answer—it is simply a method of refocusing their attention on the problem being considered.

A group of children was studying the ideas of skeletal structure by assembling skeletons of various animals. Upon receiving their particular package of bones the children carefully inspected them, began to assemble the skeleton and immediately became convinced that the skeleton was a rabbit (it was a cat skeleton). This assumption led them to consistently look for "ear bones" which they asserted must be long and wide. The entire project was hopelessly stalled because the children could not understand why they could not find the ear bones. Although the teacher could have told them that a rabbit's ears do not contain bones, he elected to suggest an alternate way of thinking about the skeleton. He asked the children why they thought their skeleton was that of a rabbit, and they replied that the bones of the back legs were shaped like a rabbit's back legs, and the skeleton was about the size that a rabbit's skeleton would be. Those are both good reasons, and the teacher used both in providing the children an alternate way of thinking about the skeleton. He asked the pupils what other animals were about the size of a rabbit, and they named several, among which was the cat. He then asked them if any of the animals they had just named might have back legs similar to a rabbit's. Before too long the children decided that a cat might. The teacher then said, "If your skeleton is that of a cat or any of the other animals you named rather than a rabbit, what kind of ear bones would you expect to find?" The children agreed they probably would not find any and began assembling the skeleton. Notice that the teacher did not in any way suggest that the pupils were wrong in their thinking about the ear bones of a rabbit. He simply provided an alternate way of thinking about the skeleton to assist the children in keeping the investigation moving.

Providing a clue and/or cue to the pupils who are stuck is a more direct process than suggesting alternate ways of thinking about a problem. Often the clue which is provided is very specific and germane to the investigation only at that particular point and at that particular time. For example, the teacher placed a mealworm in the middle of a 3 inch x 5 inch card and held the card above a table. The mealworm crawled off the edge of the card and fell to the table. The teacher asked the child if what he had just seen suggested anything to him about whether or not mealworms could see. The child answered,

"If the mealworm can see, he shouldn't have fallen off the card." The pupil was then asked what kind of clue his observation gave him about his belief that mealworms can see. (The child had previously stated that he believed they could see.) The pupil agreed that his observation did give him some ideas, but he would need to do more experiments to determine what the clue he had just received meant. Notice that the clue the teacher provided was one the child could observe, and not a verbal one. Clues that provide actual data for the children are the best (the child is concrete operational), but sometimes verbal clues and cues are the only ones that can be used. Teachers should not refuse to provide clues just because the clue is a verbal one. Teachers, then, do have a particular responsibility to keep an investigation going by providing alternate ways of thinking about a problem and clues to the solution of the problem when the investigation bogs down, or when it has followed an incorrect direction to a point from which it cannot progress. In summary: *Teachers must be ready to provide alternate ways of thinking about an investigation and clues to a problem's solution when using the inquiry method of teaching.*

In this chapter we have not mentioned the teacher's responsibility to evaluate continuously the progress in science of each child he is teaching and the effectiveness of the science program itself. This omission does not mean to imply that in science continuous evaluation of pupil and program is not a responsibility of the teacher. We firmly believe that evaluation is an extremely important part of an inquiry-centered science program—so important, in fact, that Chapter 10 is devoted entirely to it.

The roles of a teacher in an inquiry-centered science program are many. He is a selector of learning experiences and the instigator of a series of inquiry experiences as well as the person completely responsible for establishing an environment in which children will feel free to investigate and express themselves. He must be an astute listener to children so that he may ascertain how and when he must shift the emphasis on his teaching in order to maintain an atmosphere of investigation. At times, the teacher serves as a secretary to the group in recording and analyzing data, and the children must think of him as a fellow investigator rather than as an adult authority. The promotion of imagination and creativity is his job, but he must also be able to provide alternate ways of thinking about a problem and furnish clues in a manner that will not destroy that creativity. Perhaps his most important classroom responsibility in assisting children to develop their rational powers is the proper and accurate use of questions. *The teacher using the inquiry method is a guide to learning rather than an authority and a source of information.* Such a person should think of his role not as directly teaching the children but rather freeing them to learn by giving them the direction, guidance, and materials they need in the learning process. Is such a person a reality, or does he exist only in the wishful thoughts of science educators? Such a person is a reality (and they are quite plentiful), but before a prospective teacher can become an inquiry-centered teacher, he must know and respect children, the structure of the discipline of science, and the learning process. Because without learning there is not teaching, and there will most certainly be no learning (i.e., rational power development) if the teacher does not provide opportunities and motivation for learning rather than authoritarian reasons why children should learn. This latter statement implies (as we have shown several times in this chapter) that the pupil has an active, definite role to play in an inquiry-centered classroom. That role we shall examine in the next chapter.

8 | The Inquiry-Centered Classroom Environment

John Dewey characterized traditional education in this way:

> The main purpose or objective is to prepare the young for future responsibilities and for success in life, by means of acquisition of the organized bodies of information and prepared forms of skill which comprehend the material of instruction.[1]

Preparing a child for life after school is indeed an important and desirable task, and Dewey was not taking issue with that goal. What he was objecting to is the traditionalist viewpoint on education; that to be prepared for future responsibilities, boys and girls must first acquire organized bodies of information already known and develop skills already perfected. Here again neither the information already known nor the skills that have been perfected are what is objectionable; rather, the manner in which the traditionalist would have them used is what is being questioned. For example, from the traditionalist frame of reference the skill of taking a measurement is getting the answer—from the modern point of view, skill in measurement can be used constructively only when the pupils have identified why the measurements are beneficial, how measurements can be viewed from the standpoint of accuracy and variation, and what is necessary to take a measurement. Dewey's principal complaint is not with information or skills but with the *role of the learner* in acquiring the information and skills. To accept education as the traditionalists view it, the pupils must have the attitudes, says Dewey, of "docility, receptivity, and obedience."[2] With the possible exception of obedience, these characteristics are not the normal, natural traits of a child, and, there-

[1] John Dewey, *Experience and Education* (New York: Collier, 1963), p. 18. (Original copyright held by Kappa Delta Pi, 1938.)
[2] Ibid.

fore, the traditionalist form of education is unnatural for him. Dewey's concern was for the *child* rather than with the material to be learned or the skills to be developed. Has concern for the pupil assumed a different role in inquiry-centered classrooms? Let's examine that question.

The Inquiry-Centered Classroom

Starting with the classroom situation and working toward the learner is a completely deductive process; that is, we are reasoning from the general situation (classroom) to the particular case (the learner). Often deductive reasoning gives us insights into a perplexing situation which cannot be obtained in any other way, and inquiry-centered learning (and teaching) can be perplexing. We shall begin this discussion by asking what sort of situation an observer would expect to encounter if he walked into a classroom where science is being taught by the inquiry method. The most unique factor obvious to a visitor would be the absence of docility. Children would not be passively accepting what the teacher is telling them and/or directing them to do. If the observation is initiated at the beginning of the solution to a problem, procedures being designed by the children to carry out the investigation will be seen. Another factor about an inquiry-centered classroom which would be striking to a classroom visitor would be the role of guidance, secretary, material-supplier, questioner, and clue-giver the teacher occupies. In a classroom where science is taught by inquiry, you will find children carrying out investigations. They will use the library and reference sources (including the teacher) as such sources should be used; they will refer to them when specific information about a specific point is needed or when verification of a fact is desirable. The atmosphere of the classroom will be one that shouts, "We want to find out, but let *us* do it!" Isolating interesting problems, planning their solutions, carrying out those plans, and interpreting the data from experiments will be the principal activities in which the learners are engaged.

Desks arranged in neat, orderly rows, books carefully arranged on shelves, and all other such overt expressions of orderliness will not necessarily be present in an inquiry-centered classroom. Often the young investigators will find that they need to work together and must have a large space, which four of their desks could, if combined, provide. Children will, if left to their own devices, push desks together to provide work space, leave books open to the necessary page,

Children will rearrange classrooms to suit their needs if allowed to do so.

and in many other ways arrange a classroom for their convenience. Such children need to be questioned occasionally about whether or not the classroom arrangement they have designed is best for their work, and if the teacher causes the children to think about why they are rearranging the room, they will learn to consider carefully what the furniture and space needs are for their work before they begin to rearrange. Such responsibility does, of course, contribute to the development of the pupil's problem-solving abilities. We are not saying that a classroom in which inquiry teaching is done needs to be a focus of disorder, but we are saying that many times an orderly classroom must become temporarily disordered before it can be reordered in a way conducive to problem solving.

There are those in education who contend that a physically orderly classroom contributes to the mental orderliness of the pupils. No data are available to verify or refute such a belief, but we would advance the hypothesis that an environment of classroom orderliness is not directly related to the habits of mental orderliness the children develop. We are not opposed to a classroom that is physically orderly and in which children are required to put equipment away, straighten out desks, and throw away used paper and materials. These activities represent excellent experience for pupils and greatly contribute to the development of habits of personal neatness. Whether a person is working in a laboratory, a department store, maintaining a home, or supervising a community, personal neatness on the part of all concerned is an essential operating principle. The campaign against littering highways, for example, demonstrates that we have not been as successful in cultivating personal neatness responsibilities as we should. We do feel that physical order in the classroom is necessary, but it should be encouraged and fostered for reasons other than developing habits of mental orderliness.

There are times during an inquiry experience when a classroom visitor could wonder if habits of personal orderliness can be developed from the freedom of use of materials and movement which children must have in this scheme of learning. This, of course, depends on the teacher and the responsibility he assumes for developing in children acceptable attitudes toward personal neatness. Perhaps the "classroom-appearance" problem is best summarized thus: Orderliness and decorum should be present at the beginning of an inquiry experience and also at the end. There are, however, periods between these two reference points when orderliness must give way to other factors in the inquiry process which are momentarily more important.

For some reason, and no one seems to know why, the attitude has developed that the quiet classroom is the classroom in which learning is progressing most rapidly. Perhaps this attitude developed in the educational past when books, charts, films, filmstrips, slides, and all other types of educational materials and proper learning activities were so scarce that if the learner was to find out anything he had to listen to the teacher. If so, that attitude lost meaning with the invention of the printing press. Another notion about the quiet classroom that is sometimes advanced is that the children being quiet in the presence of the teacher shows respect. It may—but it may also show fear. In any case, there are occasions when administrators, school board members, and even parents judge the effectiveness of a teacher by how quiet he can keep the classroom. These persons seem to think that a quiet atmosphere is conducive and even essential to productive thinking; such is not the case.

If you wish to test the hypothesis that children must have a quiet atmosphere in order to be constructive and/or creative, walk onto a playground filled with children and listen to what is going on. Games are being invented, rules are being interpreted, and procedures for having fun are being created and/or adjusted. All of this is taking place in an atmosphere that would be described as anything but quiet! Creativity and quietness in children are not *necessarily* essential partners. Adults seem to feel that they need quiet and solitude to be creative; and many do. We would advance the hypothesis that *here is a case where an attempt is made to fit an adult frame of reference to a child, and the "fit" is none too good.* If certain children like to work in solitude and quietness, then, obviously, no attempt should be made to deprive them of that opportunity (we have not found many who desire this environment), but the majority of children are happiest, and most creative, and productive when they are left in the normal atmosphere of *their* classroom. We are not advocating a noisy classroom. What we are suggesting is that noise being made by a group of pupils involved in the planning of an experiment, carrying out that plan, or interpreting the results the experiment produced is inquiry-centered noise and essential to the process of inquiry. We would agree that unnecessary noise (yelling, foot stamping, desk pushing, etc.) is not necessary or desirable to the progress of the learning experience and can be very disturbing; in fact, such behavior is impolite to other children in the class and other classes within the school. Such behavior cannot be permitted, and, if it is, the teacher is allowing the children to develop irresponsible attitudes with respect to one person's responsibilities to another.

How can a teacher judge when the noise becomes excessive? You cannot be given an answer to that question because no two school buildings are alike and no two teachers have the same tolerance level for noise. Ask yourself if the noise is *productive* noise and if in that particular building it will disturb anyone. If the answer to the first criterion is No—that is, the noise is not productive—then you, as the teacher, should get the attention of the class and find out why. If the level of productive noise is disturbing other classes, you and the children need to determine an effective way to control it. Noise, as such, is not the hallmark of a good or poor investigation being carried on in the classroom—the deciding criterion is what is causing the noise or the lack of it.

A classroom in which science is taught by inquiry, then, has investigations in progress. But no investigation, whether conducted by a child or an adult, can be carried on from one location and in complete silence. Movement about the room by the pupils and a certain level of noise are inevitable, if not essential, because of the interchange of ideas among the children. (Remember, social interaction is an essential factor for learning.) If such an interchange is not going on, then there is a good possibility that the children are not receiving the benefit from the experience because one of the essential ingredients in any inquiry situation is for the investigators to try ideas, schemes, and hypotheses on one another. The classroom environment, as we said in Chapter 6, should be so maintained by the teacher that it encourages

Children can gather data from teacher demonstrations.

and nurtures investigation. The description of a classroom where inquiry is the primary concern was summed up nicely by Thier and Karplus in their statement that "the classroom must be reorganized so that it resembles a laboratory in which children can have actual experiences with natural phenomena."[3]

Ways of Involving Children with Science

So far in this book, we have discussed the nature of science, the broad functions of education, the general characteristics of children, the nature of inquiry, the specific experiences in science the pupil should have, and the part the teacher must play if the child is to profit from inquiry-centered learning. We have not as yet directly related the child, inquiry, and science; nor have we discussed the several ways a child can learn (or learn about) science and why, from all those various learning procedures, learning by inquiry is superior.

[3] Herbert D. Thier and Robert Karplus, "Science Teaching Is Becoming Literate," *Education Age*, 2, no. 3 (January–February 1966), 40–45.

Four principal procedures can be used to involve children in the study of science. The lowest level of pupil involvement consists of reading about or being told about the progress and products of the scientific enterprise. Beautifully illustrated science textbooks, films, filmstrips, encyclopedias, and all other manner of media which the child can use to "tell himself" or assist the teacher in telling him about science fall into this category of contributing to the minimal involvement of a child in science. When a school's science program relies completely on textbooks and other media (and if these materials are properly prepared), that program is probably making a greater contribution to the development of reading ability than it is to the development of scientific literacy. The second level of child involvement in the study of science is discussions among the pupils or between the pupils and the teacher about some scientific topic. This is, of course, social interaction. From the frame of reference of scientific literacy, however, both of the foregoing procedures are of minimal, if not questionable, value because they are completely verbal and, as such, are necessarily abstract. As we have previously said, requiring children to use abstractions in learning science is of very questionable value because, according to Piaget, the ability to think abstractly does not begin to develop until the formal operations stage, which begins, according to our data, late in high school. Seeing how these two levels of child involvement with science contribute very greatly to the development of a child's rational powers is difficult, and we have already shown that science can, if properly taught, make such a contribution.

The third level of pupil involvement occurs when the teacher demonstrates something to the pupils or the pupils demonstrate to each other. Children (and often adults) are very fond of using this method to lead a peer to see how to operate a gadget or perform a physical act; "Here, let me show you," is a common phrase heard on the playground or in the classroom. By this procedure the notion that the teacher (adult or child) wishes to teach moves from the level of a verbal abstraction to a concrete realism because "something" is being used on which the learner can focus his attention. This concrete something produces data that the learner can place in his cognitive structure and use to solve the problem facing him. Although this level of involvement is superior to the previous two and is a procedure that produces data, it provides the majority of the pupils with only a vicarious experience. Most of the learners do not actually produce the data they receive and, as such, the data are not truly their own. If the demonstration is done without comment from the demonstrator,

Children must do their own experimenting.

the data produced very closely approach being owned by the observer because what he has perceived he has obtained with his own powers of perception.

While the foregoing level of involvement can and often does approach the level of inquiry-centered science teaching, it cannot achieve the same goals the last and most ideal level of child involvement can. In the most effective method of involving the child with science, he is given the objects and/or materials with which he needs experience. He performs all the manipulations himself, makes his own observations, records his own data, and makes his own interpretations. He is, in other words, involved with exploration, invention, and discovery. The findings he makes are his own property; he is not dependent upon information and data supplied by others and which he only vicariously participated in gathering. The frame of reference from which he views the problem confronting him is an extremely realistic one because "he was there" himself. To achieve this latter stage of involvement the child must be allowed to do *his own experimenting*.

We have thoroughly endorsed inquiry-centered science teaching as an indispensable vehicle to the development of the ability to think. The last procedure of pupil involvement demonstrates how the learner must use the rational powers of imagination, analysis, synthesis, classification, comparison, and inference. These are the essence of the ability to think. There is, however, another valuable outcome from this complete involvement of the children.

Background and Future Learning

You have no doubt heard people use the phrase "I just don't have the background for that." What, exactly, are they saying? They are telling the listener that in their lives they have not had experience that makes them able to understand or appreciate the situation with which they are faced. If, for example, you were suddenly to find yourself in the middle of a classroom of children from a foreign country, you could not understand or appreciate what was taking place because perhaps the language being spoken would be unfamiliar to you. Unfamiliarity and lack of background are just additional ways of saying that you lack experience in or with a particular area. If you are the least bit unsure of the Piagetian concept of structure building explained in Chapter 3, it is suggested that you go back now and review it.

Experience provides us information that we use to construct for ourselves a conceptual framework about the discipline being investigated. This conceptual framework consists of the relationships that exist among all the various facts and principles encountered as well as an understanding of why these relationships exist. A meaningful conceptual framework of a discipline is an invaluable possession because it enables us to understand future information about the discipline under consideration. Put in another way, a conceptual framework permits us to maintain our equilibration when new information is received. Education can, through experience, build for the learner a cognitive structure that enables him to receive information and place it in his conceptual framework in a meaningful way. When a learner is able to do this, he has amplified that structure itself (by assimilation and accommodation) and has made it possible for himself to receive more complex material in the future. Notice, however, we emphasized that the learner must be the one to receive the information and place it in his own cognitive structure. *This cannot be done for him.* This means that he must determine how he is to place the new information in his conceptual framework and how he is to assimilate and accommodate the new information. Such a determination cannot be made if the learner has not had the experience (built a cognitive structure) necessary to enable him to find out how to make it. If, therefore, a learner is to know how to place information into his conceptual framework, he must have been faced at some time during his education (hopefully, constantly) with a mass of data from which he had to extract meaning and then relate that meaning to his own conceptual framework. This is, of course, another way to describe inquiry, and the type of elementary school science program we have been decribing can provide pupils with such experiences.

Complete involvement of the pupil in a learning situation in which, under the guidance of the teacher, he isolates the important factual outcomes, decides upon their relevance, and places them in his conceptual framework provides him with the experience necessary to teach him how to handle data and place their meaning in his conceptual framework. In the future, therefore, when a teacher is not present to provide guidance, a learner, who has had such an experience, will be able to continue to build his conceptual framework on his own. Building a cognitive structure of a discipline also provides a pupil with a substitute for accumulating large quantities of factual material. If an understanding of the structure of a discipline is discovered by the child, he has developed, for future use, a method of handling new information about that discipline; he has a structure upon which to place the new information and knows how to place it there. The same is true if a learner who has truly learned the structure of a discipline forgets a known item of information; he can utilize his understanding of the structure of the discipline to supply himself the needed information. As Phenix has said, "If one possesses the tools of inquiry, he is not in need of a large store of accumulated knowledge."[4]

Phenix has succinctly summarized what we have been saying. We would add to his statement that a self-developed understanding of the conceptual framework of a discipline greatly alleviates the need for an accumulation of information. Doctor Albert Szent-Györgyi expresses his feeling toward the accumulation of knowledge this way:

> I do not depreciate knowledge and I have worked long and hard to know something of all fields related to biology. But I have retained only what I need for an understanding, intuitive grasp, and in order to know in which books to find it.[5]

The scientist just quoted is saying that in order to operate effectively in our scientific society, the learner must develop a conceptual framework (intuitive grasp) in which to place all future learning experiences. There are many educators who firmly believe that a "good" book can form the basis for a science program. Dr. Szent-Györgyi has this to say about books:

> It is thought that . . . books are something the contents of which have to be crammed into our heads. I think the opposite is closer to the truth.

[4] Phil H. Phenix, *Realms of Meaning* (New York: McGraw-Hill, 1964), p. 333.
[5] Albert Szent-Györgyi, "Teaching and the Expanding Knowledge," *Science* (December 1964), 1278–1279. [See Appendix C.]

Books are here to keep the knowledge in while we use our heads for something better.[6]

We, like Dr. Szent-Györgyi, are not opposed to the scientific information or knowledge that our civilization has accumulated, but there is no possible hope of teaching a child all or even a small portion of the scientific information known today; it must, therefore, be kept in books. Furthermore, the facts of science, as they exist at the moment you are reading these words, stand an excellent chance of not being facts in a few years. Therefore, to teach children methods of securing and processing information and placing it in a conceptual framework seems the most efficient educational course to follow because "methods change much more slowly than do the results of applying them."[7]

Translating the foregoing directly into a strategy for teaching science tells us that we must confront the children in our classes with direct experiences involving phenomena from their environment which are at their intellectual level. They must, as first graders, be made aware of the many items to observe in their environment. That experience assists them in building a conceptual framework and will assist in their further cognitive development because every part of a conceptual framework which is added to their total cognitive structures assists them in expanding those cognitive structures. (Again, it is suggested that you correlate what is said here with the discussion in Chapter 3.) If we wish the learner to make sophisticated environmental observations at some future date, we must give him experiences that, in addition to developing his rational powers, will allow him to build a conceptual framework about his environment. If, for example, we feel the learner must ultimately be able to make refined measurements, he must be given the opportunity to build a conceptual framework about measurement by having meaningful experiences early in his educational experience. We, as teachers, have the responsibility to use, along with inquiry, those curriculum materials that will enable the learner to develop a conceptual framework of science. According to Thier and Karplus,

> children must be led to form a conceptual framework that permits them to perceive phenomena in a more meaningful way and to integrate their inferences into generalizations of greater value than they would form if left to their own devices.[8]

[6] Ibid.
[7] Phenix, op. cit., pp. 333–334.
[8] Thier and Karplus, op. cit., p. 40.

In Chapter 2 of this book, we isolated as the truly significant purposes for teaching elementary school science (1) to develop in the learner a command of the rational powers, (2) to develop in the student the ability and confidence to inquire, and (3) to develop an understanding of the changing nature of the environment in terms of matter, life, energy, and their interaction. Here we have encountered a way of achieving the third of our previously stated objectives—the development of understandings about the environment. Teaching an individual about his environment is a complex and long-term process; it cannot be done in the course of a few years of formal education. Introducing a pupil to his environment by inquiry, however, enables him to begin to develop a conceptual structure about the environment which will allow him to continue this development throughout his life. The development of this structure can be carried on simultaneously with the development of the learner's rational powers and the ability and confidence to inquire. The key element in this development is the teacher—he must select materials and learning experiences that will enable the learner to achieve both purposes. We shall return to the problem of curriculum selection in Chapter 9.

The Flexible Inquiry Classroom

Thirty fourth graders were being led toward the notion that a standard unit of measurement is necessary before those persons taking the measurements can discuss them. The children were given the diagrams of Long Lake and Round Lake, which you met in Chapter 5. They covered the two diagrams with lima beans and discovered that when the lakes were covered there was, among the 15 pairs of children, a variation of 20 beans. From those data they discovered that lima beans are not an especially satisfactory measuring standard. They then went on to complete the lesson (see pages 148–156 for the complete lesson). Several of the children, however, were fascinated with the notion that by just reaching into a sack and taking out a handful of lima beans you would get such a large variation in bean size. In fact, the children spent a good bit of time just commenting on the variation in the sizes of the beans and comparing specific beans. The pupils had obviously found something that interested them. The writer was a guest in the school that day and a few days later received the following in a letter from one of the pupils: "I found out what you mean when we placed the lima beans on the lake. Because when I got home we had some lima beans. So I put some on the lake. And when I was with you I had 45. And at home I had 38."[9] This child had discovered the concept of variation and it obviously fascinated her.

This child's letter illustrates another extremely important point about inquiry—it does not take place on a schedule. The children were told to keep the diagrams of Long Lake and Round Lake if they wished. The young scientist who wrote the letter profited greatly from keeping those diagrams; she went home and redid the experiment. Had the diagrams been collected at the end of the period, the discovery so pointedly described in Linda's letter would not have been made, and an important part of her conceptual structure of science would not have been added. This tells us that science materials must be available to the children whenever they have free time. If this practice is followed, children will not confine learning science to the science period. Anything that the children can take home, keep in their desks, or feel is their own stimulates them to continue their investigations by themselves. The foregoing letter is a prime example of that. Whenever a child begins to experiment and/or investigate on his own, he has begun to develop his conceptual framework of science by himself. He has, in other words, begun to learn how to learn, and that achievement is the ultimate goal of science education. All this can be the result of an inquiry-centered classroom, and a part of such a classroom is making materials and experiences available for the children during their "free time" and/or at home.

Allowing children to take materials home is an excellent way to begin an investigative study. We have discussed the work of children with mealworms earlier in this book. The investigation can be initiated very effectively by giving each of the children a small plastic bag, two mealworms, and some bran. The directions to the pupils are quite simple; they are to take the mealworms home, place them and the bran on a table, find out all they can about the way the organism acts, accurately record all their findings, and bring those findings back to classroom. The findings of the children can be listed on the chalkboard, and those that interest the children most can form the basis for the investigations the class will make. The teacher can allow the children to select those topics that they feel are most interesting to investigate and retain a record of the other findings in order to extend the investigations or simply to have a store of ideas to keep them moving.

The children, in the example cited, were allowed to keep their

[9] The writer of this letter is Miss Linda Vance, who was a fourth grader in the Monte Cassino school in Tulsa, Oklahoma, at the time the letter was written (January 21, 1966).

mealworms at home, and this permitted the teacher to provide home-work assignments that were purely investigative. At one point in the unit, the children hypothesized that a mealworm can see in the dark. Quite obviously that hypothesis cannot be tested in a well-lighted classroom. At a later point in the mealworm investigation, the problem of the organism's ability to hear arose. Here, again, the children believed they could provide more different types of noise at home than in the classroom. Procedures were designed, and the investigation was carried out as a homework assignment. Many of the pupils went far beyond gathering the information necessary to solve the particular problem being considered. They consistently brought back to the classroom information from their home-conducted investigations which further expanded the problem being considered, posed new problems, and allowed the pupils to refine future investigations. Using such homework activities represents the finest procedure a teacher can use to provide for individual differences. The parents of the children were most responsive to the type of work the children were doing, and several became involved in the investigation themselves. In summary, then, allowing children to take materials home is an excellent way to introduce an investigation, to make meaningful and productive homework assignments that are truly investigative in nature, to encourage the young investigator to extend the class-identified problem, and to provide, to a degree, for individual differences.

The classroom, if properly utilized as a laboratory, provides many opportunities for productive inquiries about the pupil's natural environment. The pupil's home can also provide facilities for initiation, and extensions of inquiry activities, many of which could not be done in the regular classroom because of time or other limitations. Still another much overlooked place where many successful inquiries can take place is the out-of-doors. Holt stated the case for the out-of-door classroom environment when he said, "We need to get kids out of school buildings, give them a chance to learn about the world at first hand."[10] Many inquiry activities can be done, at least in part, out of doors. Organism hunts to inquire concerning the number and variety of organisms living in the immediate area of the school or home are valuable experiences that can be gained only out of doors. These nature explorations allow children to develop and extend such concepts as variety of organisms, habitat, food web, interrelationship of organisms, population, community, and adaptation. These and many

[10] John Holt, "School Is Bad for Children," *Saturday Evening Post*, February 8, 1969.

other important concepts can be dealt with only superficially inside a building.

Here are some examples of types of out-of-doors activities. A group of fifth-grade students was taken to a grassy spot on the school playground where the teacher, with the help of two students, had pushed 200 toothpicks into the ground—50 red, 50 blue, 50 yellow, and 50 green. At the teacher's signal, the class began a visual search of the area for toothpicks. Time was called after a few minutes, and the toothpicks were taken to the classroom. The teacher made a histogram showing the total number of toothpicks of each color found. The class found 33 blue, 38 red, 7 yellow, and 3 green toothpicks. The children were led by the teacher into a discussion of the reasons for the different numbers of toothpicks found. They concluded that the more nearly an object blends into the surroundings, the more difficult it is to find visually. This activity provided a starting point for subsequent activities leading to the invention and use of the concepts of protective coloration and adaptation.[11]

A fourth-grade class had been working with the problem of describing the relative position of objects in their environment. In the classroom, they had learned to use reference objects, distance, and direction (above, below, right, left) in describing the relative position of various objects. The teacher then introduced the pupils to use of the compass face to determine the direction of objects. The class was then assigned the task of mapping the playground. Students in teams of two made the necessary measurements of distance and direction to each swing, slide, and other objects on the playground from the reference object they chose and then returned to the classroom to use the information in making maps. As the pupils made their maps and compared them with the maps made by others in the class, considerable variation was discovered in the distances between and representation of objects. Class discussions led to a standardization of measurement, scale, and symbols to be used.

Allowing upper elementary pupils to develop their own schemes to classify fossils, insects, leaves, or rocks they have collected is a very rewarding experience. Each of the different classification schemes developed can be examined by the class. Even the classification schemes can be classified; this is a beginning formal operational activity and one that sixth graders should meet.

---

[11] This idea for the toothpick activity came from an article by Dr. John E. Klimas, "Ecology, Why You Must Teach It," *The Grade Teacher* (January 1969), 93–127. Many other excellent outdoor activities which lead to the development of ecology-related concepts are discussed in this article.

There are numerous activities in which observational data dealing with the sun, moon, stars, and planets could be collected, organized, and interpreted. Weather could also provide a valuable and interesting source of data. In each of these activities, however, the focus should be on data collection, organization, and the search for regularities or patterns.

Teachers who do not extend their classroom to the out-of-doors place severe limitations on inquiry activities. Generally speaking the out-of-doors should be used as a laboratory in which information is collected. More often than not, the information collected out of doors will be organized, evaluated, and interpreted in the classroom. Not only does a teacher severely limit a pupil's immediate learning if he does not utilize the out-of-doors, but he also helps to establish an unhealthy attitude on the part of the pupil—the attitude that learning must take place inside a building, a school building.

The teacher's responsibilities in an inquiry-centered classroom were discussed in Chapter 7, and here we have explained the overall environment necessary to allow a teacher to discharge those responsibilities. There is, however, an inescapable responsibility which we (the authors of this book) have to teachers. That responsibility is to state what type of background and educational experience a teacher needs to be able to use inquiry in his classrooms. Thier and Karplus express their opinion concerning the necessary teacher education experiences thus:

> Teachers must develop the ability and desire to accept children's answers as evidence of their observation or understanding of the situation being examined. This change in the teacher's view of her role in the classroom will require major changes in the whole structure of pre-service and in-service teacher education in America. The real problem is not what education or science courses are taken by the prospective teacher, but instead it is the question of how these courses are conducted and organized. A prospective teacher who spends her pre-service career in situations conducted almost entirely on the first two or even the first three levels of involvement described for the pupil will not suddenly be transformed into an individual who can operate on the fourth level by the act of signing her first teaching contract.[12]

When teachers secure experiences such as those referred to by Thier and Karplus, have an understanding of children, and isolate curricula that will allow inquiry to be practiced, they will be able to establish a

---

[12] Thier and Karplus, op. cit., p. 44. The "levels of involvement" referred to here are exactly the same as what have been labeled in this chapter as the "principal procedures" for involving children in the study of science.

classroom environment for science and teach it in a manner that will allow the discipline to make the maximum contribution to the learner's rational powers and also allow pupils to develop an understanding of the structure of the discipline. The specific curricula that we feel will enable teachers to accomplish their goals are the subject of the next chapter.

9 | Curriculum Models

In order to implement what has been said in the first eight chapters of this book, teachers must have "tools" to work with. The "tools" of the teacher are the curricula he uses. Without activities for children to engage in, the central purpose of the school cannot be achieved, because one does not just think, he must think about something. The purpose of the curriculum, then, is to provide children with something to think about.

There are two distinct positions on what should be provided children to think about. One point of view is that the school should tell the child *exactly* what he should know, and the teacher's purpose is to make sure the child knows (probably has memorized) it—little necessity for much use of the rational powers there. The other school of thought about the construction of a curriculum is that the child should be provided investigations to complete, and what he knows when he finishes these investigations will depend on the data he got from the investigation and how he has interpreted those data. This latter point of view thoroughly embraces the position that the primary role of the school is to teach a child to think. Obviously we subscribe to the second position.

Describe the general principles on which a curriculum designed to achieve the central role of the school would be based. What are some of the obvious characteristics you would look for?

Often when curricula that are constructed along investigative lines are described, the listener hears "unstructured." Do not be so misled. An investigative curriculum can be and usually is very structured. Such structure is easy to introduce into a curriculum committed to investigation because you structure the thinking and activities of the children by the materials you place in the classroom. Do not feel that structure is undesirable. We take the position that structuring the classroom by the introduction of materials with which the learner can have exploration, invention, and discovery (inquiry) experiences is the proper role of the teacher and also provides an environment that promotes and encourages rational power development. If the teacher accepts only certain results and does not allow the children to explore materials and/or situations thoroughly, he has overstructured the classroom, and content-mastery outcomes have taken precedence over intellectual development.

Introducing curriculum structure into a classroom by using materials has great value in elementary school science—you can simultaneously introduce the process and content structure[1] of the discipline of science. Learning activities can be introduced which will allow the classroom work to move forward in a well-organized fashion and, simultaneously, the learner will be building a conceptual structure (just as Piaget used the term) of the discipline of science.

If you have observed carefully, you will have noticed that what has been referred to thus far are *learning activities*. We use that phrase to mean that the child actually interacts with the materials of science, discusses these concrete happenings with his peers and the teacher, and changes his cognitive structures in terms of his findings. There can be no doubt that reading can represent a learning activity. Much valuable learning can come from reading about things. There are, however, two primary factors that limit the use that should be made of reading in elementary school science.

First, reading about any object, event, and/or situation before having any kind of actual experience has to result in abstract thinking. Now the data presented in Chapter 3 and Appendix C clearly demonstrate that the children populating elementary schools are definitely concrete operational. This simply means that any mental operations the child is expected to do must be done in terms of the experience he has had. Reading about something actually experienced can be helpful. Reading in science books about such topics as atomic structure, the DNA molecule, and nuclear energy may be excellent reading experiences, but they are not contributing to the development of the child's conceptual framework of science. Reading does not permit a child to develop his concept of science in terms of the relationship

---

[1] Technically the use of the word "structure" here is different from the way it has been used to this point in the chapter. Here we mean what the organizing concepts of science are and how they are related to the processes of finding out. If this double use of structure bothers you, go back through what has been said so far and substitute "organize" for "structure" up to this use.

between process and content. He necessarily sees the content side only, because he has not been involved in the process. Elementary school science textbooks, therefore, cannot lead a child to develop a conceptual structure of the discipline of science; they primarily teach the skill of reading.

The second reason why reading is of limited value in teaching elementary school science has to do with evaluation (the topic of Chapter 10). Science, to make its maximum contribution to the intellectual development of a child, must be taught as a system of investigation that yields data that can be used to make inductive inferences. Evaluations, therefore, must be made, just as the teaching has been done. If the science program concentrates upon reading, there can be no investigation and, consequently, evaluations cannot be made of a child in terms of how proficient he is in science; he must be evaluated in terms of what he has read. Since science is not the area where the teacher grades on reading *skill*, the only other choice he has is to grade the child on how well the child remembers the content. That is, of course, grading on memorization (which *is not* science) and not upon the ability of a child to explain something in his world in terms of the information he has (which *is* science).

For the foregoing reasons, we find the elementary science textbook series of limited usefulness in constructing the science curriculum. Some of these textbook series have accompanying materials, but even then, too often the text *tells* the child the answer and does not allow him to develop an answer in terms of the data his investigation provides him. In selecting curriculum models to present to you, therefore, we found going to sources beyond textbooks necessary. We have selected three curriculum models: (1) the Science Curriculum Improvement Study (SCIS)[2], (2) the Elementary Science Study (ESS)[3], and (3) Science—A Process Approach (SAPA).[4] As you read about the curricula developed by these three groups, keep firmly in mind the concept of "model," which was discussed in Chapter 6. In that discussion the scientific model was presented as the result of utilizing all the available data about a certain unknown to construct an explanation of the unknown. Here, then, are three models that have been constructed about the unknown, labeled "the elementary science cur-

---

[2] Lawrence Hall of Science, University of California, Berkeley, Robert Karplus, Professor of Physics, Director. Materials published by Rand McNally & Company, Chicago.

[3] Education Development Center, 55 Chapel Street, Newton, Mass.

[4] American Association for the Advancement of Science, Washington, D.C. Materials published by the Xerox Corporation, New York.

riculum." As you study these models, keep firmly in mind the central purpose of education, the intellectual levels concept of Piaget, and the nature of the discipline of science.

Science Curriculum Improvement Study[5]

A child's elementary school years form a period of transition; in these years he moves away from a heavy dependence on concrete experiences and begins to use abstract ideas to interpret his observations. By investigating phenomena in the classroom, he continues the exploration of his environment he began in infancy, but in a more organized fashion. Ultimately he will use modern scientific concepts to create his own view of the world.

Change and diversity—in the weather, at the zoo, or elsewhere— always arouse our interest and attract attention. Children, curious about their surroundings, naturally seek to organize and catalog the diversity of animals, plants, and nonliving materials they discover. In this respect, they resemble scientists, who are devoted to understanding the basic conditions governing change. Through investigation, scientists advance the frontiers of knowledge. Similarly, children advance their thinking processes from the concrete to the abstract and develop a disciplined curiosity as they accumulate experiences and ideas. In other words, they become scientifically literate.

A person's scientific literacy results from his basic knowledge, investigative experience, and curiosity. In the SCIS program, these three factors are integrated, balanced, and developed through the children's involvement with major scientific concepts, key process-oriented concepts, and challenging problems for investigation.

Educators frequently distinguish among content, process, and attitude when they describe an educational program or evaluate its outcomes. The SCIS program combines these factors. Children are introduced to knowledge of scientific content through their experiences with diverse physical and biological materials. And, in the course of their investigations, they engage in observation, measurement, interpretation, prediction, experimentation, model building, and other processes.

The SCIS program helps children form positive attitudes toward science as they explore phenomena according to their own preconcep-

[5] The material found in this section has been taken and adapted, with permission, from Science Curriculum Improvement Study, *SCIS Sampler Guide*, Rand McNally & Company, Chicago, 1970.

tions. They learn to cope confidently with new and unexpected findings by sifting evidence and forming conclusions.

Central to modern science, and therefore also to the SCIS program, is the view that changes take place because objects interact in reproducible ways under similar conditions. Changes do not occur because they are preordained or because a "spirit" or other power within objects influences them capriciously. By interaction we refer to the relation among objects or organisms that do something to one another, thereby bringing about a change. For instance, when a magnet picks up a steel pin, we say that the magnet and the pin interact. The *observed change itself*, the pin jumping toward the magnet, is *evidence of interaction*. Children can easily observe and use such *evidence*. As they advance from a dependence on concrete experiences to the ability to think abstractly, children identify the conditions under which interaction occurs and predict its outcome.

The SCIS program utilizes four major scientific concepts to elaborate the interaction concept—matter, energy, organism, and ecosystem. Children's experiences and investigations in the physical-science sequence are based on the first two; the last two provide the framework of the life-science sequence.

Matter, perceived as the solid objects, liquids, and gases in the environment, is tangible. It interacts with human sense organs, and pieces of matter interact with each other. Material objects may be described and recognized by their color, shape, weight, texture, and other properties. As children investigate changes in objects during their work in the SCIS physical science program, they become aware of the diversity of interacting objects and of their properties.

The second major concept is energy—the inherent ability of an animal, a flashlight battery, or other system to bring about changes in the state of its surroundings or in itself. Some familiar sources of energy are the burning gas used to heat a kettle of water, the unwinding spring that operates a watch, and the discharging battery in a pocket radio. Each of these objects provides evidence that energy is present. The counterpart of an energy source is an energy receiver, and a very important natural process is the interaction between source and receiver that results in energy transfer.

The third concept is that of a living organism. An organism is an entire living individual, plant, or animal. It is composed of matter and can use the energy imparted by its food to build its body and be active. The organism concept therefore represents a fusion of the matter and energy concepts; but it is also broader than these, so it is identified and described separately.

As children observe living plants and animals in the classroom or outdoors, they become aware of the amazing diversity of organisms and the life cycles. They observe how plants and animals interact with one another and with the soil, atmosphere, and sun in the vast network of relations that constitute life. The focus of the SCIS life science program is the organism-environment relationship.

The study of life focused on organism-environment interaction leads to the ecosystem concept. Thinking about a forest may help you understand the ecosystem. A forest is more than an assemblage of trees. Living in the shade of the trees are shrubs, vines, herbs, ferns, mosses, and toadstools. In addition, the forest swarms with insects, birds, mammals, reptiles, and amphibians. A forest is all of these plants and animals living together. The animals depend on the plants for food and living conditions. The plants use sunlight, carbon dioxide, water, and minerals to make food to sustain themselves and other organisms in the forest. The interrelated plants, animals, sun, air, water, and soil constitute an ecosystem.

What you have read so far has probably led you to conclude that the SCIS is a content-centered program. We interpret it as being exactly that. You will also notice, however, that investigations the children perform have also been referred to several times. The SCIS program was constructed on the basic premise that the first task of the curriculum maker was to isolate that content which can be taught through investigation to preoperational and concrete operational children. But in addition to the scientific concepts just described the developers of the SCIS program believe that there are four process-oriented concepts—property, reference frame, system, and model—with which children should have experience if they are to develop scientific literacy. These concepts, together with others that relate to specific units, are at the heart of the processes of observing, describing, comparing, classifying, measuring, interpreting evidence, and experimenting.

The concept of property by which an object may be described or recognized has already been referred to. A property is any quality that enables you to compare objects. Properties also enable you to describe or compare concepts. For example, the term "climate" (hot, cold, temperate) summarizes the properties of weather in a specific region; and food production is a property of green plants.

Every description and comparison of natural or social phenomena reflects the observer's point of view or frame of reference. To the young child, who relates objects to himself rather than to others, the discovery of other frames of reference is a challenge.

In science, where the position (location) and motion of objects are important subjects of study, the reference-frame idea has been developed into the awesome relativity theory. Yet the basic concept, as included in the SCIS program, is simple—the position and motion of objects can be perceived, described, and recognized only with reference to other objects. When you say "The car is at the south end of the parking lot," you describe the location of the car relative to the parking lot. In this example, the parking lot and compass direction serve as a reference frame. However, when you say "The car is to your left," the listener's body serves as a reference frame. A child who considers several reference frames thereby overcomes the usual self-centered viewpoint.

The third process-oriented concept is that of a system, which SCIS defines as a group of related objects that make up a whole. It may include the battery and circuits that make up an operating pocket radio, or it may consist of a seed and the moist soil in which it is planted. The system concept stems from the realization that objects or organisms do not function in isolation but exist in a context while interacting with other objects or organisms.

A subsystem is part of another system. Thus, moist soil is itself a system comprised of clay, sand, water, and decayed matter. It is at the same time a subsystem of the seed-moist soil system. The seed, with its coat, embryo, and stored food, is another subsystem.

Sometimes it is hard to decide what to include when defining a system. Does the soil-seed system include the air that permeates the soil? Ordinarily children would not include air because moisture is usually the most important factor in germination. However, if a child were to deprive the soil-seed system of air, the result would make him aware of its importance to plant growth.

A system becomes a new system whenever matter is added to or removed from it. When nothing is added or removed a system retains its identity, even though it may change in form or appearance. When selecting a system, children focus their attention, organize their observations, and relate the whole system to its parts (objects or subsystems). They become skillful in tracing a system through a sequence of changes.

The fourth process-oriented concept is the scientific model, which was discussed in Chapter 6. The SCIS program explains why children should experience the models concept:

> Scientific models permit children to relate their present observations to the previous experiences with similar systems. Models satisfy the

children's need for thinking in concrete terms. Models also lead to predictions and new discoveries about the system being investigated.[6]

In order to implement the foregoing, and to adhere to the principle that children should have experiences with the physical and life sciences each year, the SCIS program consists of twelve units. The distribution of the various units throughout the six years of elementary school education is as follows.

	Physical science units	Life science units
First level	Material Objects	Organisms
Second level	Interaction and Systems	Life Cycles
Third level	Subsystems and Variables	Populations
Fourth level	Relative Position and Motion	Environments
Fifth level	Energy Sources	Communities
Sixth level	Models: Electric and Magnetic Interaction	Ecosystems

The first level[7]

Material Objects. In this unit children study common objects and special materials and describe them by their properties, such as color, shape, texture, hardness, and weight. Properties are studied by the children as they observe, manipulate, compare, and even change the form or appearance of objects. As they compare properties and recognize the differences among similarly shaped pieces of aluminum, brass, lead, steel, pine, walnut, and acrylic, children assimilate the concept of *material.* Property comparison also leads children to the concept of *serial ordering.*

The pupils also investigate the properties of solid, liquid, and gaseous materials. Each child has many opportunities to apply what he has learned about material objects, their similarities and differences, the *changes* that may be brought about, and the need for observable *evidence* to support his conclusions. Near the conclusion of the unit, the children are introduced to simple experimentation. Experiments are done with floating and sinking objects, and air. Since most children have entered the concrete operational state by late in their first year of school, simple experimentation is possible because they recognize states in a transformation. Piaget has isolated this as a trait of a concrete operational thinker (see Chapter 3).

[6] Ibid., p. 9.

[7] Much of the material found in the descriptions of the units, appeared in John W. Renner and Don G. Stafford, "Elementary School Science," *BIOS* (December 1970), 162–172.

Sorting, classifying, comparing, and serial ordering are all experienced in Material Objects. *(Photo courtesy Science Curriculum Improvement Study, University of California, Berkeley.)*

Organisms. Children become familiar with some of the requirements for life as they set out seeds and watch the growth of plants. This experience is extended when the class builds aquaria with water plants, fish, and snails. Three natural events occurring in the aquaria are observed and discussed: *birth* of guppies and appearance of snail eggs, *growth* of guppies and snails, and *death* of organisms.

When they explore the school yard, nearby park, or nature area, children discover plants and animals living outside the classroom. The pupils are led to the concept of *habitat* as they compare these land organisms with those living in the aquaria.

After a few weeks, the algae in some of the aquaria increase in sufficient numbers to make the water green. The children usually notice this change and sometimes ask about its cause. Through a series of experiments and observations they recognize the presence of tiny green plants that are called algae. Children may then find evidence that algae are eaten by *Daphnia*. When they discover that guppies feed on *Daphnia*, the children can use this series of observations as the basis for understanding the concept of a *food web* depicting feeding relationships among organisms.

Detritus, the black material accumulating on the sand in aquaria after a few weeks, is a combination of feces and dead plants and animals. Children infer, as they compare seeds grown in sand with and without detritus, that it acts as a fertilizer, enhancing plant growth.

Each experience with living organisms should increase the child's awareness of differences between living organisms and nonliving objects.

The second level

The units studied in the second year are entitled *Interaction and Systems* and *Life Cycles*. In both units the theme is change, which is observed as *evidence* of interaction or of the development of a plant or animal. The two units, therefore, require children to add the mental process of interpreting evidence to the observational skills they developed in the first year. As with the first year units, these two units can be taught in either order or simultaneously. Simultaneous use of the units is very convenient because during the *Life Cycles* unit there are often periods of time when the living systems are static or growth is not obvious. During these times, activities from *Interaction and Systems* can be profitably integrated.

Interaction and Systems. The central concept of the entire SCIS program, *interaction*, is introduced in this unit. The children's work with objects and organisms in the first year has given them the background necessary for understanding the interaction relationship. In later units, the program will emphasize the application and refinement of the interaction concept as children investigate biological, chemical, electrical, magnetic, thermal, and mechanical phenomena.

The first two parts of this unit are devoted to the interaction and systems concepts, respectively. The idea that a change may often be interpreted as evidence of interaction (for example, when photographic paper turns dark on exposure to sunlight) is explained. The remainder of the unit is divided into four parts in which the children investigate interactions and systems, pulley systems, dissolving (copper chloride, aluminum), interaction-at-a-distance (interaction without the objects touching, as in magnetism), and electric circuits. The sequence of these investigations can be altered to suit the teacher's preference. Throughout children observe and interpret evidence of interaction.

Scientific concepts are developed in the unit, as are the children's skills in (1) manipulating experimental equipment, (2) reporting observations, and (3) recording observations during experiments.

Life Cycles. The investigation of ecosystems begun in *Organisms* is continued in *Life Cycles.* The unit, however, focuses on individual organisms, which alone show the characteristics of the phenomenon called "life." At this time the interrelationships and interdependencies within the ecosystem have secondary importance.

Each kind of plant and animal has its own life cycles. By studying the life cycles of selected plants and animals, children observe the characteristics of living organisms. Seeds are planted and then germination observed. Plants are cared for until they reach maturity, produce flowers, and form a new generation of seeds. The fruit fly, frog, and mealworm are observed while they metamorphose. As one generation of organisms produces another, children are led to consider biotic potential (see definition, p. 135) and the effects of reproduction and death on a population. Finally, when some of the similarities and differences between plants and animals have been considered, and children have defined the two categories on the basis of their own observations, they proceed to the more general question, "What is alive?" With each experience, a child's awareness of the differences between living and nonliving objects should increase.

The third level

Subsystems and Variables. The subsystems concept is introduced to give the children a grouping of objects intermediate between a single object and an entire system. The grains of sand in a mixture of sand, salt, and baking soda, the salt in a salt solution, the Freon in a bag interacting with water, or the arm and rivets in a whirlybird system are all examples of subsystems.

As the children experiment with solid and liquid materials, they use the techniques of sifting to separate solid powders and of filtering to separate an undissolved solid from a liquid. At the same time they recognize that dissolved solids in solutions cannot be separated by filtering. Instead, the presence of dissolved solids may be identified by schlieren or by a residue that remains after the liquid evaporates. There are further experiences with the liquid Freon, a material that not only evaporates quickly at room temperature but condenses to a liquid form when cooled with ice. The work with solutions and with Freon serve to deepen the children's awareness of the principle of conservation of matter, *even though this is not stated explicitly in the unit.* The technique of using a histogram to compare data is introduced when the children take temperature readings during the melting of ice and interpret their measurements.

In the last part of this unit, children investigate the whirlybird (a rotating propellerlike device that is powered by a taut rubber band) and discover that its operation depends on many factors they can control and on a few they cannot. The *variable* concept helps them to identify and investigate factors influencing the motion of the whirlybird arm, including adding weights in the form of rivets to both sides.

Populations. In this unit attention is directed toward populations of organisms rather than toward individual plants and animals. Children observe the growth, eventual leveling off, and decline of isolated populations of *Daphnia*, aphids, and fruit flies. They relate increased population sizes to reproduction, and population decline to death.

The children build aquaria and terraria in which several populations live together. The aquaria contain populations of *Daphnia*, hydra, snails, algae, duckweed, and *Anacharis*. The terraria contain grass, clover, crickets, and chameleons. By observing the interacting populations in the aquaria and terraria, the children gain some understanding of the relationships among populations in nature. For example, the children observe that hydra eat *Daphnia*, with the result that the *Daphnia* population declines while the hydra population may increase. In the terraria, the children observe that crickets eat grass and clover and that when chameleons are added to the terraria they eat the crickets. Thus, the grass and clover populations are reduced, and the cricket population is eventually wiped out.

The fourth level

Relative Position and Motion. In this unit, activities dealing specifically with spatial relationships are introduced into the SCIS program. The investigations enhance the children's abilities to think critically, interpret evidence, and work independently. These are process objectives for the entire SCIS program. Children use *reference frames* to describe the position and motion of objects in their everyday environment.

Early in the unit, the artificial observer Mr. O serves the children as a *reference object* for describing relative position. Later they are introduced to *polar* and *rectangular coordinates* for a more exact description of *relative position and motion*. The children must apply the reference-frame concept in many activities, such as playing classroom games to locate objects, solving puzzles that require matching of relative positions, and surveying the school playground with a simple transit. The investigations in the last part, dealing with the

Mr. O helps children understand basic relativity when studying Relative Position and Motion. *(Photo courtesy Science Curriculum Improvement Study, University of California, Berkeley.)*

motion and tracks of rolling and interacting steel balls, relate the ideas and techniques developed in early parts of this unit to the matter, interactions, and energy concepts of the physical-science sequence.

Environments. The terraria that children design and build at the beginning of the unit reflect their preconceptions regarding the needs of organisms. As a result, there is a wide disparity in the growth and survival of the organisms living in the terraria, and these differences can be correlated with variations in *environmental factors* such as temperature, amount of water, and intensity of light. The term *environment* is defined as the sum total of all the environmental factors affecting an organism.

Afterward, the children seek to determine the responses of individual kinds of animals and plants to variations in the environmental factors. On the basis of experiments with isopods in a runway with graded temperature, the concepts of a temperature *range* and of an *optimum range* for that animal are introduced. In additional experiments, the children attempt to determine optimum ranges of other environmental factors for snails, mealworms, beans, grass, and clover. Before the unit is concluded, the children again construct terraria, but now they use their data on optimum ranges to plant a more favorable environment for their organisms.

The fifth level

The conceptual development of the SCIS program continues as examples of energy transfer are introduced in the physical science unit *Energy Sources* and of food transfer (the organic equivalent of energy) in the life-science unit *Communities*.

Energy Sources. During the fifth year, the pupils continue their study of matter and energy in the *Energy Sources* unit and also extend their skills in conducting scientific investigations. Their attention is focused on the energy transformations that accompany the interaction of matter in solid, liquid, and gaseous forms. The children's qualitative descriptions of energy transfer from a source to a receiver prepare them for later quantitative investigations of energy exchange.

The introductory investigations employing rolling spheres and paper airplanes are used to review interaction, variables, and other concepts with which the children have become familiar. These experiences and work with rotoplanes (propeller-driven rotating platforms) provide background for the invention of *energy transfer* and the identification of *energy sources* and *energy receivers*.

The children apply the new concepts to situations in which motion or temperature change provide evidence of energy transfer. They experiment with (1) stopper poppers, in which compressed air serves as energy source; (2) spheres rolling down ramps and colliding with a movable target, in which the rolling spheres serve as energy source; (3) the dissolving of sodium thiosulfate or magnesium sulfate, in which the water or the solid material acts as energy source; and (4) the melting of ice, in which the ice serves as energy receiver.

Communities. In this unit pupils investigate the food relations within a community of plants and animals. They experiment with germinating plants, discovering that food stored in cotyledons is consumed; however, another source of food, photosynthesis, supports the plant's growth.

The children observe the feeding behavior of animals in terriara containing various plants and animals. They identify the food chains and infer that photosynthesis in green plants not only supplies food for the plants but indirectly also for the animals in the community. The children count the large number of wheat seeds eaten by crickets, and the few crickets eaten by a single frog. On the basis of these data, the food pyramid is introduced.

When an animal or plant in the terrarium dies, the children place the dead organisms in a vial and cover them with moist soil. They observe the organisms' gradual decomposition along with the appearance of mold or an unpleasant odor. The children are told that organisms that satisfy their energy needs by decomposing the bodies of dead plants and animals are bacteria and molds.

The transfer of food through a community is illustrated by means of a chart showing the food relations among plants, animals, bacteria, and molds. The plants are identified as *producers*, the animals as *consumers*, and the molds and bacteria as *decomposers*. The inter-acting producers, consumers, and decomposers in a given area consti-tute the community.

The sixth level

The last year of the SCIS program contains both a climax and a new beginning. The study of *Ecosystems* in the life-science sequence integrates all the preceding units in both physical and life sciences as the young investigators study the exchange of matter and energy between organisms and their environment. The physical science unit, *Models: Electric and Magnetic Interactions*, introduces the concept of the scientific model and thereby opens a new level of data interpreta-tion and hypothesis making.

Ecosystems. Through the investigations in the *Ecosystems* unit children become aware of the roles played by oxygen, carbon dioxide, and water in the maintenance of life. When this understanding is combined with the habitat, populations, community, and other con-cepts introduced in the SCIS life-science sequence, the term *ecosystem* acquires its full meaning.

Initially, the children review the ideas introduced in the five earlier units by building a composite terrarium-aquarium. The organisms living in the containers represent plants, plant eaters, and animal eaters—organisms that flourish under varying environmental condi-tions. The *ecosystem* is defined as the system composed of a com-munity of organisms interacting with its environment.

After they observe water droplets on the inside of the terraria-aquaria, the children clarify the role of water in an ecosystem. The *water cycle* refers to the succession of evaporation and condensation of water.

The pupils study the carbon dioxide-oxygen exchange between organisms and their environment. They test their own preconceptions about oxygen and carbon dioxide when they compare the gases formed by plants exposed to light and to the dark, by animals living in a community with plants and animals in isolation. The production and consumption of the two gases are described as the *carbon dioxide-oxygen cycle*.

Models: Electric and Magnetic Interaction. The activities in the *Models* unit are directed toward increasing the children's under-standing of electrical and magnetic phenomena at the levels of concrete experiences and of abstract thought.

Children review some of their work in the *Interaction and Systems*

Children invent models to explain their data in the SCIS unit Models: Electric and Magnetic Interaction. *(Photo courtesy Science Curriculum Improvement Study, University of California, Berkeley.)*

and *Subsystems and Variables* units. Next, children explore the circuits' energy sources, constructing a battery (or electrochemical cell) to operate light bulbs and other circuit elements. Finally, the models concept is introduced in connection with mechanical and electrical "mystery systems." The pupils must explain the systems in terms of assumed objects that cannot be seen directly.

The second part of the unit is devoted to magnetism and various models, such as the magnetic field and the magnetic poles. In Part Three the children investigate more complicated electric circuits, and the *electric current* model is introduced to unify their theories. The distinction between *series* and *parallel* electric-circuit connections can be used for predicting the operation of light bulbs and other circuit elements if a consistent model for electric current has been chosen. In the concluding activities, electric energy sources and the chemical processes related to electric current flow are considered again.

The teaching method

The SCIS curriculum model employs a consistent teaching strategy throughout each unit. The children are provided materials which they are allowed to interact with in their own way; they are, in other words, allowed to explore the materials thoroughly and completely. The data from those explorations allow the teacher (and/or children) to invent concepts that can be used to explain what has been seen or to develop models.

After the child has a newly invented concept, he can now begin to ask himself many things about it. Finding items of information about the new conceptual invention is, of course, discovery. Discovery is, therefore, only a part of the teaching method used by the SCIS program.

You might be tempted to think that the information the SCIS units provides children could be told to them in much less time than using the units. You are, of course, correct; *but* the purpose of the SCIS units is *not* to transmit information (even though the children do gather much information). Rather, their purpose is to achieve the educational objectives that have already been discussed. The SCIS program does not believe that transmitting scientific information to a child is educating him in that discipline; they believe, as the units demonstrate, that educating a child in science is providing him experiences that will permit him to learn how to learn. Does the SCIS program represent good science? Let's measure it against four well-recognized standards.

First, and very important, the activities of the program should be recognizable as science by a practicing scientist. Since the major purpose of the scientist is to understand how the world works, to be recognizable as science by a practicing scientist the activities of the program must be of such a nature that the pupils are pursuing this end. Fundamental to the SCIS program are actual explorations of natural phenomena using a problem-solving approach.

Second, the program should reflect the cumulative nature of science in a sense that there is a continual building upon past learnings about nature. A collection of facts, no matter how vast, provides little real understanding of natural phenomena. The information and understandings gained by the pupil during his explorations in SCIS activities are the basis for conceptual inventions, and, in turn, provide a frame of reference for later explorations. Each concept is interrelated with others into a conceptual framework, which is an essential part of the science program. It provides a dynamic frame of reference into which new discoveries are incorporated and from which information or ideas are drawn. To use Piaget's notion, this program changes the child's mental structure, thereby increasing his abilities to use assimilation and accommodation. The SCIS sequence of topics Level 1 through Level 6 in both physical and life science given previously reflects the cumulative conceptual hierarchy of the program. Instead of an accumulation of facts to be remembered (many of which are no longer facts after a decade), the SCIS program develops a conceptual foundation which the pupil can build on for many years.

Third, from the point of view of the Educational Policies Commission, the substantive knowledge that pupils should learn should be chosen on the basis of

(a) The potential of the knowledge for the development of rational powers; and
(b) The relative importance of the knowledge in the life of the pupil and society.[8]

The method of inquiry used by the SCIS program not only allows but encourages the use of the various rational powers essential to logical thinking. In addition, the concepts developed in the physical science program (property, interaction, system, relativity, etc.) are essential to the collection, organization, and interpretation of information in other areas of knowledge as well. And, since the unifying theme of the entire science program is the ecosystem, one can readily see during this period of rapid environmental deterioration the importance of this to the life of the pupil and society.

Fourth, and very important, the science program must help each pupil achieve the *spirit of science* described by the Educational Policies Commission as "The spirit of rational inquiry, driven by a belief in its efficacy and by restless curiosity."[9] This spirit, the driving force behind successful practicing scientists, cannot be taught directly but must arise through successful inquiry experiences of the pupil. Is the SCIS program good science? The answer is, it is not only good science, but very good education!

Keep in mind that the group developing the SCIS model structured the work of the children by electing to lead them toward developing conceptual structures about matter, energy, organism, and ecosystems. They also elected to use exploration, invention, and discovery (inquiry)—the natural way of learning—to lead children to develop these structures. The materials were developed according to the intellectual model of Piaget. In other words, the SCIS model permits and encourages children to learn within a structured system, but not all children are expected to do or learn the same things.

[8] Educational Policies Commission, *The Central Purpose of American Education* (Washington, D.C.: NEA, 1961), p. 19. [See Appendix C.]
[9] Educational Policies Commission, *Education and the Spirit of Science* (Washington, D.C.: NEA, 1966), p. 1.

Elementary Science Study[10]

Your frame of reference for discussing this curriculum model can best be established by quoting directly from the ESS group itself.

> No group—ESS or any other—can design a single curriculum which will be suitable for the enormous variety of schools and school systems in this country and elsewhere. Planning a curriculum involves decisions which should be made only with knowledge about particular adults and children: their educational goals, their financial resources, and the circumstances in which they live and work. Those people whom the curriculum affects should be responsible for its shape and substance.[11]

This curriculum model is nearly a no-model model. The ESS group has simply said that there is no content that they feel should have precedence over any other. They explain their content frame of reference thus: "we have not proceeded primarily from theories about the structure of Science or from a particular conceptual scheme of learning."[12] Not only, then, did the ESS group not operate from a content structure they wished to teach children (as the SCIS group did), but they were not at all concerned about using a model of how children learned. How, then, did the ESS group construct its curriculum? ". . . we relied upon taking what we thought were good scientific activities into classrooms to see how they worked with children. We have tried to find out what . . . six-year-olds, and nine- and ten- and thirteen-year-olds find interesting to explore."[13] The ESS took many kinds of materials into many different kinds of classrooms, watched what the children did, listened to them very carefully, and made decisions on the basis of what seemed to interest both the children and the teachers. On the bases of those data, the ESS group developed ideas about units and put them into teacher's guides, films, film loops, equipment, and printed materials that would assist a teacher in leading children to become involved with the ideas being taught. All materials developed were subjected to vigorous classroom testing.

The no-model ESS curriculum model can best be characterized as a series of classroom resources which a school can use to develop its own curriculum. Each school must decide upon where an ESS unit is to be taught, or serious overlapping could occur, and the antimotiva-

---

[10] The material in this section has been taken and adapted, with permission, from *A Working Guide to the Elementary Science Study*, Education Development Center, 55 Chapel Street, Newton, Mass. 1971.

[11] Ibid., p. 4.

[12] Ibid., p. 2.

[13] Ibid.

Suggested Grade Levels for ESS Units

UNITS	K	1	2	3	4	5	6	7	8	9
Light and Shadows	▨	▨	▨	▨						
Match and Measure	▨	▨	▨	▨						
Printing	▨	▨	▨	▨						
Animals in the Classroom	▨	▨	▨	▨	▨					
The Life of Beans and Peas	▨	▨	▨	▨	▨					
Mobiles	▨	▨	▨	▨	▨					
Butterflies	▨	▨	▨	▨	▨	▨				
Eggs and Tadpoles	▨	▨	▨	▨	▨					
Geo Blocks	▨	▨	▨	▨	▨	▨	▨	▨	▨	▨
Pattern Blocks	▨	▨	▨	▨	▨	▨	▨	▨	▨	▨
Attribute Games and Problems	▨	▨	▨	▨	▨	▨	▨	▨	▨	
Tangrams	▨	▨	▨	▨	▨	▨	▨	▨	▨	▨
Musical Instrument Recipe Book	▨	▨	▨	▨	▨	▨	▨	▨	▨	▨
Growing Seeds	▨	▨	▨	▨						
Spinning Tables		▨	▨							
Brine Shrimp		▨	▨	▨	▨					
Changes		▨	▨	▨	▨					
Mirror Cards		▨	▨	▨	▨	▨	▨	▨	▨	▨
Primary Balancing	▨	▨	▨	▨						
Sand			▨	▨						
Structures			▨	▨	▨	▨	▨			
Sink or Float			▨	▨	▨	▨	▨	▨		
Clay Boats			▨	▨	▨	▨	▨	▨		
Drops, Streams, and Containers				▨	▨					
Mystery Powders				▨	▨					
Ice Cubes				▨	▨	▨				
Colored Solutions				▨	▨	▨	▨			
Rocks and Charts				▨	▨	▨	▨			
Pond Water		▨	▨	▨	▨	▨	▨	▨		
Starting from Seeds			▨	▨	▨	▨	▨	▨		
Where Is The Moon?			▨	▨	▨	▨	▨	▨		
Mosquitoes				▨	▨	▨	▨	▨	▨	▨
Whistles and Strings			▨	▨	▨	▨	▨			
Animal Activity					▨	▨	▨			
Batteries and Bulbs			▨	▨	▨	▨	▨			
Bones					▨	▨	▨			
Budding Twigs					▨	▨	▨			
Crayfish					▨	▨	▨			
Earthworms					▨	▨	▨			
Optics					▨	▨	▨			
Small Things					▨	▨	▨			
Tracks					▨	▨	▨			
Microgardening					▨	▨	▨	▨	▨	▨
Behavior of Mealworms					▨	▨	▨	▨	▨	▨
Peas and Particles					▨	▨	▨	▨	▨	▨
Pendulums					▨	▨	▨	▨	▨	▨
Senior Balancing					▨	▨	▨	▨	▨	
Stream Tables					▨	▨	▨	▨	▨	▨
Water Flow					▨	▨	▨	▨	▨	▨
Heating and Cooling						▨	▨	▨		
Mapping						▨	▨	▨		
Balloons and Gases						▨	▨	▨	▨	▨
Batteries and Bulbs II						▨	▨	▨	▨	
Daytime Astronomy						▨	▨	▨	▨	
Gases and "Airs"						▨	▨	▨	▨	
Kitchen Physics							▨	▨	▨	▨

Figure N. (SOURCE: *"A Working Guide to the Elementary Science Study,"*
Education Development Center, 55 Chapel Street, Newton, Mass., 1971, p. 7.)

tional "We-had-that-last-year" syndrome will appear. To assist a school in preparing its science curriculum model, the ESS group has provided data about where they have found each unit to be successful. Those data on all 56 ESS units are shown in Figure N. The black line in the chart indicates the range of grades for which the unit is primarily intended. The gray line shows those grades in which the entire unit or separate activities from it have been successfully adapted and used.

The ESS program, then, requires that the teacher thoroughly understand his educational purpose and the conceptual structure of science he wants to teach. He then selects from the 56 units available what his curriculum should be. If you carefully examine Figure N, you will see that the teacher can easily have a balance among life, physical, and earth science. Furthermore, all types of content are available for all grade levels.

After selecting units, how does the teacher use them in his classroom? The ESS group describes the implementation of its units as follows:

> ESS units will be most effective in classrooms where inquiry is encouraged: where teachers are able and willing to listen more than to talk, to observe more than to show, and to help their students to progress in their work without engineering its precise direction. Students will need their teachers to help them observe carefully, ask questions, design experiments, and assess the results of their work. To do those things without telling or directing too much requires a restraint that is born of self-confidence, as well as confidence in, and respect for, children. We have seen our materials reinforce these qualities in teachers. *We have also learned that in the long run these qualities are more important to the teaching of ESS units than is a substantive knowledge of science.*[14]

The exploration-invention-discovery phases of inquiry fit the ESS units. Some units are nearly all exploration (*Sand*, for example), others require a good bit of invention (*Kitchen Physics*, for example), and others are rich with opportunities for discovery (*Peas and Particles*, for example). We have had considerable experience with the ESS group and their units, and that experience has led us to conclude that these materials (and those developing them) show a concern and opportunity for intellectual development in children. One factor the teacher using the material must be constantly aware of is the match between the children's intellectual level and the materials. The ESS group did not overtly match its units to an intellectual development

[14] Ibid., p. 3. (Italics added.)

model as the SCIS group nearly always did. But the discrepancies are not as great as might be imagined because of the empirical manner in which the units were matched to children through extensive classroom testing. Keep in mind that if the science program is to develop an overall conceptual structure of science, *the teacher* (or curriculum constructor) must build that into the program through the units he selects. The ESS group did not ensure that outcome for the teacher as the SCIS group did.

The group developing these materials was genuinely concerned with how a school system would begin to implement them. Because of the nonsequential nature of the ESS units, a teacher and/or school could begin utilizing them on a limited scale. In fact, this recommendation has been made by the ESS group. "We urge any teacher, science supervisor, or principal who is eager to adopt an ESS inquiry science program to become experienced with ESS units on a limited scale before investing in a quantity of units and equipment or commiting himself to an extensive adoption."[15]

Describing each of the 56 ESS units as we did the 12 SCIS units is not possible here. What follows are descriptions[16] of several of the ESS units.

1. *Animal Activity*—Grades 4 to 6. This unit introduces children to several techniques for observing and measuring the activity of mice, gerbils, or other small animals. Using an exercise wheel coupled to a counter which records the number of times the wheel turns, children gather data on the activity of animals under varying conditions. They can test the effect on an animal's liveliness of such factors as diet, age, size of cage, time of day, and noise.

The student booklet, *Experiments on Animal Activity*, gives accounts of several ingenious experiments performed by biologists investigating the activity of mammals. The case studies make good starting points for discussions and can help children to see the possible value and interest of their own investigations to others. The unit is best taught on a flexible schedule. The study generally extends over a period of two months. Since most experiments take many days to complete, only a few minutes may be needed for the unit each day. Informal work with small groups has been most effective.

2. *Balloons and Gases*—Grades 5 to 8. This unit gives children an opportunity to prepare and collect gases and to discover some of their properties. Preliminary work is done with acids and bases and a

[15] Ibid., p. 4.
[16] All descriptions have been taken and adapted from *A Working Guide to the Elementary Science Study,* op. cit., pp. 10–63.

colored indicator, bromothymol blue. Students generate a number of common gases and conduct tests that enable them to distinguish between the gases. The Teacher's Guide contains recipes for making "mystery gases" that students can generate and attempt to identify on the basis of their previous experience. The chemical reactions by which the gases are produced offer interesting avenues for further study.

3. *Batteries and Bulbs*—Grades 4 to 6. The activities included represent an introduction to the study of electricity and magnetism. Each child makes experiments with his own simple equipment (flashlight batteries, small bulbs, various kinds of wire, compasses, magnets). Children investigate such things as ways to light several bulbs with one battery, what happens when more than one battery is used, what is inside a battery, and how a bulb works. The materials are simple but sufficient for investigations at almost any level of complexity.

4. *Behavior of Mealworms*—Primarily for Grade 6. This unit stimulates children to ask questions about the observable behavior of an unfamiliar animal and then directs them to ways of finding the answers for themselves. As children observe and experiment, they learn some things about the process of scientific inquiry while they gather information about the sensory perception of the mealworm. The primary objective of the unit is to help children learn how to carry on an investigation.

Mealworms are convenient subjects for animal behavior experiments. They exhibit reasonably consistent and definite behavior, they require practically no care, and they can be purchased very inexpensively from a number of sources.

5. *Changes*—Grades 1 to 4. In this unit, children observe spontaneous changes—those caused by bacteria or molds, as well as some, such as rusting and melting, which are not due to life processes. They make up lists of things that they think will or will not change and then proceed to bring these things into class to verify their predictions. During the course of several weeks, food becomes garbage, wet metals rust, liquid becomes cloudy, maggots may appear, and rocks remain rocks. From the nature and timing of these processes, the children develop their own sense of biological and physical change.

6. *Daytime Astronomy*—Grades 5 to 8. This unit is built around children's observations of the shadows the sun casts on the earth at different times of the day and throughout the year. Children become familiar with the apparent motion of the sun by recording changes in the length and direction of the sun's shadows. The resulting "shadow-clocks" are used for telling time, for finding directions, and for

developing theories about the movement and relative position of the earth and sun. Working with globes indoors and outdoors, children can investigate conditions that occur all over the real world. An earth-moon scale model allows them to simulate the role that sunlight plays in phases and eclipses.

7. *Gases and "Airs"*—Grades 5 to 8.   A closed plastic tube is placed over a candle sitting in a trough of water. The candle goes out and the water rises in the tube. What makes the water rise? Why does the flame go out? How does a gas behave? What is air? Are there different airs? What happens to steel wool or bean sprouts when they sit in air? These questions, and the many others that students ask, are starting points for explorations that can help children to develop their own notions about what air is and how it behaves.

The equipment in the kit is complex enough for students to explore many dimensions of the questions that come up. The Teacher's Guide gives background for some of the experiments and suggests several ways the unit can be taught. The film loops provide help with experimental techniques and show some interesting experiments.

8. *Growing Seeds*—Grades K to 3.   This unit combines for young children the pleasure of nurturing plants with opportunities to seek answers to questions raised by the germination and growth of seeds. Children plant a collection of seeds and non-seeds to see which ones grow. "What happens to a seed after it has been underground for a few days?" "What does the seed look like inside?" "What happens if you plant it right at the bottom of the box?" Answers can be sought from the materials at hand.

Eventually each child follows the growth of his plant and cuts a strip of paper each day to show its height. Later he pastes his strips on a larger sheet of paper to make a picture of the plant's growth. Children find that the strips can tell them a great deal about the way their plants grew.

9. *Kitchen Physics*—Grades 6 and 7.   This unit introduces children to some properties of common liquids—how fast they flow through various-sized openings; how they fall and break up; how they heap up, are absorbed, evaporate, or attract and repel one another. Children measure the height of liquid columns with paper strips, which can be arranged to make a graph. They collect data, which they can analyze, discuss, and use to explain experimental results. They assemble and use a simple balance and then modify it for use as a tensiometer.

10. *The Life of Beans and Peas*—Grades K to 4.   Bean and pea plants are hardy enough to grow to maturity even under the variable

conditions of most classrooms. In this unit, children plant seeds and tend them. Eventually the seeds germinate and plants grow to maturity, flower, and produce pods containing new seeds to be planted. Each succeeding generation of beans and peas gives children a fresh opportunity to look closely at the sequence of events in the lives of those common plants and to gain a sense of the complete life cycle.

The Guide suggests questions that may interest the children and stimulate them to design their own experiments. There is also information on the practical care of the plants, to help keep them healthy in the classroom.

11. *Microgardening*—Grades 4 to 7. This unit deals with the growth of a microorganism: mold. The children sort out variables that influence the growth of mold and devise experiments to test for these factors. In doing so, they not only become aware of the diversity of color, texture, and structure of molds, but also become familiar with some basic scientific procedures.

Students are introduced to pure cultures and sterile techniques and become involved in problems that permit them to retrace the reasoning of some of the great pioneers in medicine, agriculture, microbiology, and food technology.

12. *Musical Instrument Recipe Book*—Grades K to adult. Making musical instruments combines craftsmanship with an exploration of the physical properties of devices that produce sound. There is great satisfaction to be derived from building an instrument that is pleasing and that works. This resource book contains illustrated instructions for making over twenty stringed, wind, and percussion instruments from inexpensive, readily available materials. It can be used as a construction manual and as a source of ideas for building original instruments.

Instrument making brings together many curriculum areas—science, crafts, social studies, and music. An instrument-making project can also yield a variety of instruments for classroom use at little cost.

13. *Mystery Powders*—Grades 3 and 4. Children investigate some properties of common household substances and ways of detecting their presence in a mixture. At first they try to identify the powders by smelling and feeling them and comparing them with known substances. Children find that some powders react in particular ways when they test them further with heat, iodine, and vinegar. They then use the techniques they have devised to try to determine the presence of individual powders when two or more are mixed together.

The powders are safe for children to handle and to taste, and are inexpensively obtained from grocery, drug, and hardware stores.

14. *Peas and Particles*—Grades 4 to 6. This is a unit on large numbers and estimation. Children deal with numbers informally, devising ways to estimate and approximate large amounts, sizes, and distances.

At first youngsters estimate large numbers of peas, marbles, or other objects in jars. In the process, they develop a variety of counting methods which can be compared and refined. The numbers generated by their estimations can also be the basis for discussions of the usefulness of approximate numbers, "rounding off" numbers, and so forth. Later the children apply similar strategies to problems of their own choosing.

The activities give children experience with numbers and counts as we often meet them in newspapers, budgets, surveys, and other areas of everyday life, rather than as exact figures in textbook problems.

15. *Pond Water*—Grades 1 to 7. The fantastic variety of life in a pond can serve as the basis of an almost endless study. *Pond Water* has three main components: a field trip to a pond, classroom observation of the water and mud brought back, and experimentation. The Teacher's Guide suggests ways of dealing with the problem of "which animals are the same" and offers a number of questions that have interested children.

A set of cards contains information on aquarium building, keeping animals alive, and making slides, as well as identification of a few of the most common animals, culture information, and suggested experiments.

16. *Rocks and Charts*—Grades 3 to 6. Children are natural collectors, and rocks are among the things they like best to collect. *Rocks and Charts* offers ways for teachers to help children carry their interest further by engaging them in the classification of some common minerals. Children are encouraged to look closely at the characteristics of rocks (and other things), to establish their own ways of comparing objects, to agree upon common standards for identifying and classifying things, and to find greater possibilities in their own collections. Chart making assists children further in focusing attention on the minerals themselves and on the need for standards in talking about them.

The Guide contains suggestions for many activities in the form of questions a teacher might pose to the children. It also includes suggestions for organizing a classroom so that small groups of children can pursue different activities at the same time.

Small Things is an interesting ESS unit.

The sand comes in various grain sizes, each a distinct color to encourage sorting activities. The brilliant hues inspire some children to make sand paintings, colored patterns, jewelry, and sculpture.

17. *Small Things*—Grades 4 to 6. This unit is an introduction to the microscopic world, the instruments needed to make it accessible, and the appearance and structure of minute living and nonliving things.

Children begin exploring magnification with water drops and hand lenses. They become acquainted with their own microscopes, and gradually improve their slide-making techniques while working with many things they wish to examine. Students look closely at such things as an onion, their own cheek cells, and, finally, single-celled animals. Examination of the cell structure in living things leads to a search for similar structure in nonliving substances.

18. *Structures*—Grades 2 to 6. Children love to build. *Structures* gives them a chance to develop some trial-and-error problem-solving techniques as well as to explore the relationship between the materials used in construction and the structural and aesthetic design of the objects that can be built with them.

Some of the materials used for building are paper, index cards, straws, modeling clay, wood scraps, Tri-Wall, cardboard, and spaghetti.

Activities in the Guide include making clay towers, building with straws and pins, designing scale model communities, large-scale construction with wood or Tri-Wall, and many others.

19. *Whistles and Strings*—Grades 3 to 6. Working with materials that produce sounds of definite pitch—such as stiff and flexible plastic tubing, straws, and different kinds of string—children explore the relationships between objects and the sounds they make. By altering and combining these and other materials, they investigate the physical conditions necessary to produce sounds and to change the pitch, volume, and tone quality of sounds. They construct sound-making contraptions for experiments and make simple musical instruments. Some children compose music for their instruments and play music together.

Whistles and Strings has been used as a science activity and as a combined music-science project.

The foregoing units, as well as those listed in Figure N, can be forged into an inquiry science program that will lead children to achieve the purposes of elementary school science outlined in this book. We have seen it happen. Keep in mind that the ESS units must be looked upon as a reservoir of material from which to construct a program—the SCIS materials constitute a sequential program.

Science—A Process Approach[17]

This inquiry-oriented elementary school science program has as its foundation the belief that an understanding of the scientific approach to gaining knowledge of the world is fundamental to the general education of a child. In order to assist children in securing this essential element of their education, they are provided experiences that result in a cumulative and continually increasing degree of understanding of, and capability in, the process of science. The group who developed the SAPA program describe the processes of science as those things a scientist does as he investigates. The processes of science can also be thought of as ways of processing information. There are thirteen processes emphasized in SAPA and those processes are

[17] The material in this section has been taken and adapted from *Commentary for Teachers of Science—A Process Approach* (1970), a publication of the American Association for the Advancement of Science, Washington, D.C.

spread throughout the seven levels of the program that are traditionally but not necessarily taught from kindergarten through grade six. During the primary grades children conduct investigations that utilize the processes of observing, using space/time relationships, classifying, using numbers, measuring, communicating, predicting, and inferring. According to the SAPA group the foregoing are the basic processes and provide the foundation for the integrated processes that are emphasized in the intermediate grades. The integrated processes are controlling variables, interpreting data, formulating hypotheses, defining operationally, and experimenting. The processes on which the SAPA program is based are defined and used as follows:[18]

1. *Observing.* Beginning with identifying objects and object-properties, this sequence proceeds to the identification of changes in various physical systems, the making of controlled observations, and the ordering of a series of observations.
2. *Classifying.* Development begins with simple classifications of various physical and biological systems and progresses through multistage classifications, their coding and tabulation.
3. *Using Numbers.* This sequence begins with identifying sets and their members, and progresses through ordering, counting, adding, multiplying, dividing, finding averages, using decimals, and powers of ten. Exercises in number-using are introduced before they are needed to support exercises in the other processes.
4. *Measuring.* Beginning with the identification and ordering of lengths, development in this process proceeds with the demonstration of rules for measurement of length, area, volume, weight, temperature, force, speed, and a number of derived measures applicable to specific physical and biological systems.
5. *Using space-time relationships.* This sequence begins with the identification of shapes, movement, and direction. It continues with the learning of rules applicable to straight and curved paths, directions at an angle, changes in position, and determinations of linear and angular speeds.
6. *Communicating.* Development in this category begins with bar graph descriptions of simple phenomena, and proceeds through describing a variety of physical objects and systems, and the changes in them, to the construction of graphs and diagrams for observed results of experiments.
7. *Predicting.* For this process, the developmental sequence progresses from interpolation and extrapolation in graphically presented data to the formulation of methods for testing predictions.
8. *Inferring.* Initially, the idea is developed that inferences differ from observations. As development proceeds, inferences are constructed for observations of physical and biological phenomena, and situations are constructed to test inferences drawn from hypotheses.

[18] Ibid., *Purposes, Accomplishment, Expectations*, pp. 5–7.

9. *Defining operationally.* Beginning with the distinction between definitions which are operational and those which are not, this developmental sequence proceeds to the point where the child constructs operational definitions in problems that are new to him.
10. *Formulating hypotheses.* At the start of this sequence, the child distinguishes hypotheses from inferences, observations, and predictions. Development is continued to the stage of constructing hypotheses and demonstrating tests of hypotheses.
11. *Interpreting data.* This sequence begins with descriptions of graphic data and inferences based upon them, and progresses to constructing equations to represent data, relating data to statements of hypotheses, and making generalizations supported by experimental findings.
12. *Controlling variables.* The developmental sequence for this "integrated" process begins with identification of manipulated and responding (independent and dependent) variables in a description or demonstration of an experiment. Development proceeds to the level at which the student, being given a problem, inference, or hypothesis, actually conducts an experiment, identifying the variables, and describing how variables are controlled.
13. *Experimenting.* This is the capstone of the "integrated" processes. It is developed through a continuation of the sequence for controlling variables, and includes the interpretation of accounts of scientific experiments, as well as the activities of stating problems, constructing hypotheses, and carrying out experimental procedures.

The general conceptual framework of the SAPA model is built around the physical, biological, and behavioral sciences and mathematics. The concepts[19] the program leads children to develop are:
1. Physical sciences
    a. Solids and liquids and their properties
    b. Gases and their properties
    c. Changes in properties
    d. Temperature and heat
    e. Force and motion
2. Biological sciences
    a. Observing and describing living things
    b. Modes of living and behavior of animals
    c. Human behavior and physiology
    d. Microbiology
    e. Seeds, seed germination, and plant growth
3. Mathematical topics
    a. Numbers and number notation
    b. Measurement
    c. Graphing

---

[19] For a detailed discussion of these concepts, see Appendix A. You are urged to read this material before going on.

d. Probability
e. Geometric topics

Each of the seven years of the SAPA program is guided by a carefully developed set of behavioral objectives. Those objectives clearly state what an individual child is expected to be able to do when he has successfully completed an exercise or a unit. The attainment of these objectives can be demonstrated by the child because he can do specific things that can be observed. Examples of behavioral objectives which the SAPA program leads children to achieve follow.

1. The child should be able to *identify* the following three-dimensional shapes: sphere, cube, cylinder, pyramid, and cone.
2. The child should be able to *distinguish* between statements that are observations and those that are explanations of observations, and *identify* the explanations as inferences.
3. The child should be able to *construct* an inference to explain the movement of liquid out of an inverted container when air moves into it.
4. The child should be able to *describe* and *demonstrate* that the farther an object is located from the center of a revolving disc, the greater its linear speed, although its rate of revolution is the same.
5. The child should be able to *construct* predictions from a graph about water loss from plants over a given period of time.[20]

Earlier the thirteen processes that the SAPA model is constructed around and the content that was selected to lead children to develop facility with those processes were listed. The SAPA group then matched processes and content necessary to learn them with the *intellectual* maturity of children in grades K–6. Each of the content topics was treated at several grade levels. The concept of magnetism, for example, is first met in Part B[21] (first grade) by the children observing the magnet's properties. Magnetism next appears as a principal topic in Part D when the children make observations on magnetic poles. In Part F the concept of magnetism furnishes the content for a data interpretation experience; the children study magnetic fields particularly with reference to the earth. The content conceptual structure of science is included in the SAPA model, but the child does not

[20] Commission on Science Education, *Commentary for Teachers of Science—A Process Approach* (Washington, D.C.: American Association for the Advancement of Science, 1970), p. 22.
[21] The SAPA program is keyed to educational levels. In implementing the program, the following coding system may be used: Part A—Kindergarten; Part B—First Grade; Part C—Second Grade; Part D—Third Grade; Part E—Fourth Grade; Part F—Fifth Grade; Part G—Sixth Grade. There is increasing experimentation with other distributions.

develop an entire concept at one grade level. In the SCIS model, for example, the concept of biological community is the topic for the fifth year; that experience requires some prior work but, in general, the community concept is taught in the fifth year. In the ESS model, each unit represents a concept, and if the concepts are to be tied together, the teacher must do it. So here you see three diverse points of view regarding how the content of elementary science should be handled, while all three curriculum models are designed to meet the same basic set of purposes; that is, the purposes this book has described.

In order to give a general notion of the manner in which the SAPA curriculum model is constructed, the processes taught and content used to teach them from Part D are listed below. The number in parentheses following each process indicates how many lessons, including the Part D one, have been taught up to this point of the program.

Inferring (3)—Observations and inferences
Inferring (4)—Tracks and traces
Predicting (3)—Describing the motion of a bouncing ball
Using numbers (10)—Dividing to find rates and means
Inferring (5)—The displacement of water by air
Measuring (13)—Describing the motion of a revolving phonograph
  record
Measuring (14)—Measuring drop by drop
Using numbers (11)—Metersticks, money and decimals
Communicating (10)—Using maps
Communicating (11)—Describing location
Measuring (15)—Measuring evaporation of water
Inferring (6)—Loss of water from plants
Predicting (4)—The suffocating candle
Observing (16)—Magnetic poles
Using space/time relationships (14)—Rate of change of position
Measuring (16)—Describing and representing forces
Observing (17)—Observing growth from seeds
Communicating (12)—Reporting an investigation in writing
Using space/time relationships (15)—Two-dimensional
  representation of spatial figures
Classifying (10)—Using punch cards to record a classification
Using space/time relationships (16)—Relative position and motion
Observing (18)—Observing falling objects

Each of the seven parts of the SAPA model has its own unique distribution of content and processes as shown in Part D. You will also observe that some of the processes have been used many times before; observing, for example, has been used fifteen times in Parts A, B, and C, while inferring has been used only twice. That content distribution clearly demonstrates an emphasis on continuity of process skill development. There is also continuity in the content, but it is not as tightly structured as is the process continuity. Quite evidently, to achieve the process skill development that the SAPA model outlines, exploration, invention, and discovery (inquiry) must be used in the classroom.

A Comparison

As was said earlier, the three curriculum models presented here all lead children toward the same purposes and those purposes are those subscribed to in this book. There are, however, differences among the three models.

The SCIS model is a content-centered model that utilizes the natural interests and intellectual abilities of the children to teach them the conceptual structure of science as well as the processes they need from time to time to uncover that structure for themselves. The SAPA model devotes its attention to teaching the processes the scientist uses as he investigates, and utilizes that content which interests children and which allows the processes to be taught. A conceptual structure of science emerges, but it is not as clear-cut and evident as that from the SCIS model. On the other hand, the process-structure that emerges from the SCIS model is not as evident as that from the SAPA model. The ESS model utilizes those topics they have found of interest and that can be taught to children. The conceptual structure of science must be put into the program by the teacher through his selection of units. The ESS units can be taught only by utilizing the complete involvement of the child in the processes of finding out. Neither the conceptual structure of science nor its process structure is as evident in the ESS model as in the other two. The selection of a model can only be governed by the purposes children are being led to achieve.

In all three models, however, there are four threads of continuity that can be extracted and utilized to blueprint a generalizable curriculum model. In all three models the children focus their attention upon a *concrete object, event, and/or situation* that can be studied in a concrete way. The utilization of abstraction as the focus of investigation does not exist. This reflects the concern of each model for the intellectual level of the learner.

Each of the models leads the children through an *investigation* of the object given him. That investigation produces *data* the learner is led to *interpret*. In other words, the generalizable curriculum model which can be used with any type of learning materials must reflect *objects, investigation, data gathering,* and *interpretation.* When an elementary school curriculum reflects those traits it is aimed toward the educational purposes outlined earlier. Quite evidently, the teacher controls the content conceptual structure he is teaching by the objects, events, and/or situation he selects for the children to study. In our opinion, that is the proper role of the teacher. If he utilizes exploration, invention, and discovery, the process structure *must* evolve through the interaction that takes place between him and the children.

Take an object and construct a learning situation utilizing the generalizable curriculums model.

Science and the Prereader

Can the prereader inquire about his environment? The answer to this question is emphatically Yes! Not only can he do inquiries but unless parents or teachers restrain him, he will continually inquire. Holt, in his article *School Is Bad for Children,* said that "almost every child, on the first day he sets foot in a school building, is smarter, more curious, less afraid of what he doesn't know, better at finding and figuring things out, more confident, resourceful, persistent and independent than he will ever be again in his schooling."[22]

It must be emphasized, however, that the teacher must take into account the limitations of the child's thinking ability when selecting what inquiries are to be done. The science program for the prereader should attempt to develop mental tools that will increase the pupil's range of explorations of his environment, and improve his ability to communicate to others the discoveries he makes during his explorations. There exists considerable research evidence that certain types of activities (describing, grouping, comparing, etc.) enhances progress in reading and arithmetic in first grade.[23] The prereader science program should focus on activities relating to key words of *observation* and *communication.*

First, because observation (looking, manipulating, touching, sniff-

---

[22] John Holt, "School Is Bad for Children," *Saturday Evening Post,* February 8, 1969.

[23] Donald G. Stafford, *An Evaluation of the Science Curriculum Improvement Study (SCIS) Material Objects Unit at Kindergarten Level* (Washington, D.C.: U.S. Dept. of Health, Education, and Welfare, Bureau of Research, 1971).

ing, poking, squeezing, stretching, etc.) is an activity in which prereaders can participate very effectively. It is also the most fundamental activity in science. Facts, the working material of the scientists, are simply descriptions of observations.

Second, because observation is an essential aspect of communication and/or learning. One child gains new insights or information by observing another child interacting with an object or a group of objects. Frequently heard expressions from 5-year-olds are, "Show me how you did that!" "Now let me see if I can do it." "Here, let me show you."

Even though the children cannot read or write, they can report their observations verbally to the teacher and other children. The prereader should be encouraged to report orally since in doing so he begins to develop the ability to mentally transform an observation into language. Early experience in verbally describing objects and changes that take place in them will help children to develop the ability to report accurately what they observe when studying natural phenomena.[24]

The inquiry cycle for prereaders should not strongly emphasize the "invention" step. The teacher might simply begin using a word such as "object" or "property" in his discussion with children as they describe a piece of matter. The children begin to develop an understanding of the concept as they observe the association of the word symbol with the piece of matter. The teacher can determine the level of understanding of the concept by the willingness and ability of the pupil to use it in a new situation, either in action or to describe an action verbally.

Most of the time in a prereader science class should probably be spent in simple explorations and teacher-child discussions on a one-to-one basis of these explorations. Hawkins, former director of ESS says, "There is a time, much greater than commonly allowed, which should be devoted to free and unguided exploratory work (call it play if you wish; I call it work). Children are given materials and equipment—*things*—and are allowed to construct, test, probe, and experiment without superimposed questions or instructions. I call this . . . messing about' ".[25]

The Elementary Science Study has produced a variety of units which lend themselves very well to the "messing about" type of

24 Robert Karplus, *Teacher's Manual for SCIS Kindergarten Program*, Trial Edition (Berkeley: University of California, 1964), p. 5.

25 David Hawkins, "Messing About in Science," *Science and Children*, 2, 5 (February 1965).

activities for prereaders and toward the accomplishment of the goals of observation and communication. Some of these are *Geo-blocks, Pattern Blocks, Tangrams, Mirror cards,* and *Attribute games.* These units can be used individually in any order and, within each unit, there is little or no sequence that must be followed.

The following two activities demonstrate learning experiences of this nature.

ACTIVITY I[26]

Materials

1 set of Geo-blocks per 6 pupils (Geo-blocks range in size from half-inch cubes to 2″ x 2″ x 4″ oblong)

Teaching Suggestions

a. Simply allow the children to unhurriedly explore the blocks comparing shapes, sizes, textures, etc.
b. When the children appear to have satisfied their appetites for simple explorations, suggest that they build a tower, a house, a city, a ramp or some other structure. Let children describe their structures to others.
c. Select one of the 2″ x 2″ x 4″ blocks as a model. Ask children to see how many ways they can make a block the same size and shape of the model using more than one piece.
d. Ask a group of pupils to sort the blocks into groups that seem to belong together.

The teacher might introduce the shapes of various faces of the blocks by simply referring to the faces by name again and again as the opportunity arises.

ACTIVITY II[27]

Materials

1 set of Pattern Blocks for 6 children (Pattern Blocks consist of wooden blocks of the geometric shapes triangle, square, diamond, trapezoid and hexagons which come in the colors red, natural, blue, green, and orange).

[26] Elementary Science Study, *Teacher's Guide for Geo-Blocks* (New York: McGraw-Hill, 1969), pp. 1–8.
[27] Elementary Science Study, *Teacher's Guide for Pattern Blocks* (New York: McGraw-Hill, 1970), pp. 8, 9, 10.

Teaching Suggestions

Generally speaking, if a child or group is engaged in an ongoing activity, he/they should not be interrupted to get everyone to work on a topic of the teacher's choice. The following are questions which might initiate activities.

a. *Making Pictures and Things*
   Can you build with the blocks?
   Can you make pictures?
   Can you make animals?
   Can you make a bridge? ——a train? ——a fence? ——a plane?
   Can you make anyone of the things you made, but bigger?——
   Smaller?
b. *Making "Floors"*
   Can you make a floor with just triangles? ——hexagons? ——
   diamonds? ——squares? ——trapezoids?
   Can you make a design for a floor of diamonds and triangles?
   ——Hexagons, diamonds and trapezoids?
c. Make a square from squares.
   Make a triangle from triangles.

There is an almost endless series of activities which can be done with *Pattern Blocks.* Many of these activities challenge upper elementary children as well as prereaders.

Activity III illustrates an informal activity that can extend over a period of several weeks. This activity allows the child to observe and discuss changes.

ACTIVITY III[28]

Observing an Animal

The observation of an animal is a valuable experience for kindergarten children. Any animal which has come to visit your classroom can be used for this activity. Sometimes the observation will extend over a short period of time as when children bring a pet kitten or rabbit to school for the day. Other animals can be observed over a longer period of time since you have provided a habitat for them in the classroom. Fish, turtles, caterpillars, hamsters, mice, and other animals fall into this category. Whether the animal is visiting for the day or will become a "resident" of the classroom, the activity should consist of at

[28] Reprinted with permission from *Teacher's Manual for SCIS Kindergarten Program*—Part I, Trial Edition, pp. 26–27, written and published by the Science Curriculum Improvement Study. Copyright 1964 by the Regents of the University of California.

least two parts. First the children should be given ample opportunity to watch the animal as it carries out various life functions such as walking, crawling, sleeping, and if possible, eating. This part of the observation should be quite informal and the children should be allowed to spend as much time as they like watching the animal. The second part of the activity involves the discussion by the children of what they have observed. At times, the children should do this on their own. At other times you should lead the discussion. This discussion is considered an aspect of the observation since any controversies or misunderstandings should be resolved not by the word of an authority but by further guided observations.

The Science Curriculum Improvement Study's first year unit *Material Objects*[29] also provides a variety of experiences for use with the prereader. These activities have been experimentally tested with 5-year-olds in kindergarten.[30] Findings of the research supported by the U.S. Office of Education indicate that 5-year-olds not only can participate successfully in the activities but that they also enjoy doing so. The activities of the *Material Objects* unit are sequential but allow the teacher considerable flexibility. The following activity illustrates the approach used in *Material Objects*.

ACTIVITY IV[31]

Teaching Materials

Objects in the classroom
Chart paper provided by the teacher

Teaching Suggestions

Your first lesson on material objects will be rather informal. Present classroom objects such as chalkboard erasers, books, chairs, and goldfish, and ask the children to tell you about them. Use the term *object* in your discussion.

As the children talk about an object, they will describe its uses as well as its properties (shape, color, texture). Accept statements related to use, but encourage your pupils to concentrate on properties. In your class

[29] *Material Objects Teacher's Guide* by the Science Curriculum Improvement Study, published by Rand McNally & Company, Chicago. Copyright 1970 by the Regents of the University of California.
[30] Stafford, op. cit.
[31] *Material Objects Teacher's Guide*, op. cit., pp. 24–25.

discussion employ statements and questions such as, "Yes, we use the chalk to write. How would you describe a piece of chalk to someone who has never seen one?" Spend only a short time on any single object. Some children may have difficulty describing many properties of a single object. They will then resort to describing its function.

"Properties of Objects" chart. Make a chart headed "Properties of Objects" to help your students develop a working vocabulary. Add words to it only after they have been discussed in class. Make no attempt at this time to formally define the word *object*. For the present, the definition is implied when you refer to a concrete classroom object. Use the word *property* when you discuss the children's answers to such questions as, "What is the color of this object?" "Is this object rough or smooth?" or "What is the shape of this object?" For example, you might say, "White and smooth are properties of this piece of chalk," to encourage children to think about properties. Later on, they should begin to use the word *property* as the objects are described.

Give the children opportunities to choose and describe objects in the classroom. Use one or more of the simple "object games" outlined below or make up others that seem appropriate.

Object games in the classroom. For variety, play object games with small groups of children while others are doing individual work.

Game 1. A child chosen as the leader whispers to you the name of an object in the room. The leader then tells the class in which part of the room (front, back, near a window) the object is located. He gives the class clues about the object (its properties) without revealing its name. After each clue has been given, the rest of the class should guess what object the leader has selected. You will find it best to allow only one or two guesses after each clue and to permit a single child to make only one guess for each object chosen. This technique will encourage children to concentrate on the clues instead of simply guessing at random. The first pupil to guess the object correctly becomes the next leader.

Game 2. The teacher or leader holds up an object. Only those children who correctly name a property of the object may stand up. Count the standing pupils to show how many properties were named.

Game 3. "Pocket Object" is played with a group of boys. Each boy removes all but one object from one of his pockets. Then, while holding his hand on the object, he gives clues to the rest of the group. The first child to correctly name the object has the next turn. A child is allowed only one guess in each round.

Facts and the Curriculum

The curriculum models that have been described here, and the generalizable model, are apparently not too concerned with the usual facts of science nor that children remember them. How important is the acquisition of factual information in the science program of the elementary school? Robert M. Hutchins, in an article in the *Saturday Review of Literature*, expressed his feeling about the importance of facts:

> Almost every fact I was taught from the first grade through law school is no longer a fact. Almost every tendency that was proclaimed has failed to materialize. The facts and tendencies of today are those that nobody foresaw fifty years ago. . . . I am especially embarrassed by the facts and tendencies I proclaimed myself. I can only hope that students in Yale law school have forgotten what I taught them. The courts have overruled and the legislature repealed most of what I knew.[32]

Hutchins is saying that facts are really not too important *as end products* in the educational process. The facts that a child is taught today have an excellent chance of not being facts in the not-too-distant future. If, says Hutchins, an educational system concentrates only on the teaching of factual information, there is little left when courts overrule, legislatures repeal, or new data are found to alter those facts taught. What, then, in Hutchins' opinion are the criteria that should guide the formulation of the curriculum? He states his beliefs this way: "The special function of our educational institution is to supply the intellectual tools, the intellectual discipline, and the intellectual framework necessary to understand the new problems we shall face."[33] Hutchins' "intellectual tools" we interpret to mean the rational powers of the free mind. From these quotes, as well as from what has been said in the previous chapters, we can conclude that of the three criteria listed for judging the content of elementary school science, the first one (the content selected must have the potential of leading the learner to develop his rational powers) is the most important.

Are we saying facts are unimportant? Certainly not! In working with science at any level, facts are important. When Pasteur, for example, began his search for data that would allow him to discover why wine spoiled, he asked himself factual questions and his investigation produced factual answers. The facts that solved his problem were his end point. But educating a child means that he must be provided the intellectual framework (already possessed by Pasteur) in which he will learn *how* to isolate and use the facts he is dealing with.

[32] Robert M. Hutchins, "Are We Educating Our Children for the Wrong Future?" *Saturday Review of Literature*, September 11, 1965, p. 66.
[33] Ibid., p. 83.

In order to provide the child with the necessary intellectual framework (structure of the discipline), he must have experience in isolating and using facts and not just in learning them. The elementary school science curriculum must give children the opportunity to find facts, experiment and hypothesize with them, and verify them. Facts are the medium through which the learner has experience, but that experience must consist in working with them rather than memorizing them. Contrary to what many practicing teachers believe, a child does not necessarily understand science when he can recite great amounts of factual information, but he has acquired a degree of sophistication in science when he has the ability to use facts in the solution of a problem.

The group developing the SAPA program commented especially about the importance of facts by asking and answering this question.

What is the Place of the Content (Facts) of Science in This
Process-Oriented Program?
Certainly you cannot teach scientific processes without using some
content. Much science content is included in *Science—A Process*
Approach, but the emphasis is on the processes. In order to attain
competence in the processes of science, children deal with such topics
as plants, animals, energy, light, temperature, heat, solids, liquids, gases,
life cycles, electricity, magnetic fields, motion, falling bodies, forces, the
sun's motion, and many others. The children become very interested in
and curious about the topic they are studying even though the primary
objective of the instruction is for them to acquire new competencies in
the processes of science. Many will pursue their aroused interest through
additional tests and investigations and through reading.[34]

One of the tasks that every teacher faces is evaluation of the curriculum, the children, and himself. One point of view holds that the primary responsibility of the teacher is to evaluate the content a child retains. In other words, a child's educational progress depends solely on his memory. We do not accept that point of view. There are many more important factors for the teacher to concentrate on. The first evaluation responsibility of the teacher is to decide upon the effectiveness of his curriculum in relation to his purposes. Then, the teacher should constantly evaluate himself. How does he accomplish all of this? Evaluation is the subject of Chapter 10.

[34] Commission on Science Education, *Commentary for Teachers of Science—A Process Approach* (Washington, D.C.: American Association for the Advancement of Science, 1970), p. 11.

10 | *Evaluation in Science Education*

When evaluation is mentioned in connection with the educational enterprise, different meanings are immediately focused on by different people. To most students evaluation means grades and examination, and that is also certainly one of the meanings teachers focus on. Teachers, however, also think of evaluation in terms of the appropriateness of materials and the overall structure of the course they are teaching with respect to how accurately the particular science they are teaching is portrayed. Not infrequently teachers also think of evaluation as how well the course and its materials fit the particular students they are teaching. That is an extremely fine use of evaluation and one that every teacher should continuously perform.

The most significant use of evaluation in any field is how well what was to be done has been done. An auto mechanic, for example, evaluates his work by asking himself how well an engine runs after he finishes with it; a tailor asks himself how well a garment fits his client; a physician evaluates his efforts by how completely his patient is restored to physical and/or mental health, and a lawyer by how adequately his client has been treated. In all cases, the evaluator has some objective he judges his performance by. The mechanic compares the functioning of a newly repaired engine to, perhaps, a new one and thus makes allowances for the materials, that is, the old engine he is working with. The physician must judge his performance by the age and initial condition of his patient, and so on. In short, anyone must evaluate his work in terms of what he began to do; that is, his objectives. The results of that evaluation can be used not only to judge the effectiveness of what has been done but also to furnish feedback to the person doing the job which will allow him to adjust the manner in which he discharges his responsibilities.

The foregoing, when applied to teaching, means that every teacher has three distinct evaluations to make. He must

1. evaluate pupil performance,
2. evaluate the programs he is using, and
3. evaluate his own performance as a classroom teacher.

In making those three evaluations, the teacher must, as does any person doing a job, use some evaluative criteria. Those criteria for a teacher are the objectives of the field in which he is teaching. The three objectives of science teaching were discussed in Chapter 2. Those objectives are to develop in each student

1. a command of the rational powers.
2. the ability and confidence to inquire.
3. an understanding of the changing nature of the environment in terms of matter, life, energy, and their interactions.

The teacher must translate the content of the particular discipline being taught into evaluative tools that he can use to judge student performance, the programs used, and his own effectiveness in terms of these three general objectives. Any other objectives that might be constructed for a particular subject must lead directly to the three general objectives of science education. If, for example, a fifth-grade teacher lists as an objective the ability to explain the process of energy transfer, he must be able to trace the importance of that ability to the three general objectives. Such an objective would certainly require that a student analyze and synthesize (two of the rational powers) and inquire into the relationships and interactions among matter. In judging a student's understanding of energy transfer, his abilities to analyze, to synthesize, and to see interactions can be evaluated. However, the information he might use to answer a question might as easily come from rote memory as from his ability to analyze, to synthesize, and to see relationships *if* the evaluative tool —the questions asked—permit him to do so. Teachers must be able to perform evaluations that distinguish between rote memory and functional understanding. The latter leads to the achievement of objectives; the former does not.

Evaluating Pupils

The evaluation program of the elementary school should be designed primarily for guidance purposes. The teacher is not free to say No to the request of any pupil for opportunities to learn more about science; he can only inquire, "For what types of learning experiences is the pupil ready?"

The more specific purposes served by the evaluation of pupil progress in science education may be stated as follows:

1. Evaluation motivates the learning of science by providing pupils with information concerning their own progress in developing concepts, in using scientific procedures in problem solving, and in becoming increasingly self-directing. Manolakes has called attention to this purpose of evaluation: "The process of taking stock is crucial to learning, and no child should go home at the end of the day without a clear understanding of what he has accomplished and what still remains to be done."[1]

2. Evaluation provides the teacher with evidence of how well he has taught; it suggests alterations in methods and materials that need to be made in order to teach more effectively in the future.

3. Evaluation provides the basis for reports to parents, and thus fosters home-school cooperation in the interest of better educational opportunities for children.

4. A sound program of evaluation enables teachers to answer criticisms of the school program. It also promotes a better understanding of the objectives of the science program and the extent to which the objectives are being achieved.

Although it is recognized that the program for evaluating pupil progress in science education should be developed cooperatively by the local school staff, some general principles for developing the program may be useful.

The evaluation program should be comprehensive

Because all phases of child development are interrelated, the teacher needs information about the social and attitudinal development of pupils as well as their academic progress. All too frequently in the past, evaluation has been confined to that which is most easily measured. Although measurement is an important phase of evaluation, it does not constitute the entire program. Measurement is concerned with the quantitative aspects of pupil progress, whereas evaluation is concerned with both the quantitative and the qualitative aspects. Achievement tests have, in the past, been too much concerned with recall of isolated bits of information about science. The new elementary school science program requires more emphasis on evalua-

---

[1] George Manolakes, *The Elementary School We Need* (Washington, D.C.: Association for Supervision and Curriculum Development, 1965), p. 11.

Figure 10–1. "Our Science Class." (Reprinted with permission from
Interaction and Systems Evaluation Supplement, *Trial Edition, p. 7, written*
and published by the Science Curriculum Improvement Study. Copyright ©
1971 by The Regents of the University of California.)

tion instruments and procedures designed to reveal pupil progress in
understanding, in concept development, in attitudes, and in behavior.

Some instruments have been designed to measure important attitudinal and behavioral changes. Figure 10–1 is an instrument designed to help the teacher gain understanding of how the pupils view
the science class. How the pupils perceive the class activities could
cause a teacher to continue or modify his approach in the classroom.

Figure 10–2. "Faces." (Reprinted with permission from Interaction and Systems Evaluation Supplement, *Trial Edition, p. 8, written and published by the Science Curriculum Improvement Study. Copyright © 1971 by The Regents of the University of California.)*

An instrument like this should be used several times during the year. A teacher can also use this instrument to determine the kinds of activities pupils like best by asking them to cross out the activity they like least and encircle the one they like best, or rate the activities in the order they like them from best to least. Figure 10–2 can be used to help the teacher determine how pupils feel about various activities. Collecting this information on the activities over a period of time enables the teacher to isolate those that are liked best by the children; those are probably the most productive.

Other attitudinal and behavioral evaluations can be made by direct observation by the teacher. The Science Curriculum Improvement Study group has identified for purposes of evaluation four attitude areas that are a part of scientific literacy, as well as various behaviors, which may be observed, that are associated with the areas. These are as follows:[2]

[2] Reprinted with permission from *Interaction and Systems Evaluation Supplement,* Trial Edition, p. 17, written and published by the Science Curriculum Improvement Study. Copyright © 1971 by the Regents of the University of California.

(a) *Curiosity or Interest*
manipulates new equipment
participates actively in experiments
observes objects and events intently
asks questions about objects or events
asks for materials to extend investigations at school or at home
(b) *Inventiveness*
uses equipment in unusual and constructive ways
suggests new experiments
volunteers solutions to problems
(c) *Independent or Critical Thinking*
expresses his own ideas
listens to the ideas of others
predicts the outcome of an experiment
uses evidence to support his conclusions
evaluates evidence presented by children
changes his ideas in response to evidence
(d) *Persistence*
continues to investigate materials after their novelty has worn off
completes an activity even though other children finish earlier
records observations or data spontaneously
repeats an experiment in spite of apparent failure

Written work in pupil evaluation

Another common pupil-evaluation practice that can be used by teachers in upper elementary school if done correctly is written work that is "handed in." The teacher in assigning such work makes the assumption (often valid) that by performing the assigned task the student will move closer to achieving the course objectives. Written work cannot be justified on any other basis. Requiring students to do written "busywork" is beneath comment, and the same is true for work assigned as a disciplinary measure. When a teacher assigns extra experiments to do or questions to answer as punishment, he is using the content vehicle that can lead students to achieve the objectives of science education in a manner that will eventually convince them that the principal purpose of the content is to discipline their social behavior. This is hardly a student attitude that will lead to achieving the ability and confidence to inquire.

Work that is given to the teacher for evaluation without the student being present and written examinations comprise the majority of the evaluation category of written work. From our frame of reference daily written assignments and examinations must (and do) reflect the teaching and learning philosophies of the teacher. If the teacher is leading students to learn by inquiry, then he must evaluate the ability of the student to inquire and utilize the results of that inquiry. There is probably no action of a teacher which reflects his basic beliefs about teaching and learning as accurately as the written work he assigns his classes. If he purports to believe in inquiry and evaluates his students upon their abilities to accumulate and memorize factual detail no one, *and most of all his students*, will take him seriously. Written work, whether out-of-class assignments, reports of experiments and/or investigation, or examinations, which is intended to evaluate the results of an inquiry-centered learning experience must reflect such characteristics of inquiry. *That is, the written work must require the learner to classify, analyze, evaluate, interpret, synthesize, predict, or generalize.*

The exercise shown in Figure O is an example of the type of written work problem a fifth- or sixth-grade pupil might do. Notice that the pupil is given data to sift through, evaluate as to relevance, classify into some pattern (or decide a pattern does not exist), and synthesize some relationship, and make predictions.

Imagine that you are one of thirty-five students who were each given a mimosa leaf. —leaflets
You were asked to count the leaflets on each leaf and record the number on the chalkboard at the front of the room. Here are the 35 values:

> 18, 22, 16, 20, 24, 26, 20, 18, 18,
> 16, 20, 22, 21, 18, 20, 20, 18, 22,
> 26, 16, 18, 20, 18, 18, 20, 22, 16,
> 14, 18, 20, 16, 18, 18, 22, 18.

(1) State some general patterns from the data.
(2) Organize the data into a histogram or some other classification scheme.
(3) What predictions about mimosa leaves could you make based on the patterns you have isolated?
(4) How would you test your predictions?

Figure O.

Now, you can write a similar exercise!

Study both your exercise and the one provided here and decide whether or not they evaluate observable, measurable aspects of student behavior. Some additional guidelines that can be used in writing an exercise for pupils in a class are:

1. *Does the written work assigned allow—in fact, encourage—the learner to utilize the results of previous investigation?*

One of the basic axioms of learning is that we learn many "things" in terms of what we already know. Written work can provide the learner the opportunity to relate what he is presently doing to what he has already done; this experience can perhaps disequilibrate him and enlarge his concept of the environment. If a student is expected to relate (synthesize) the results of two investigations, he should be reminded of the past investigation; that is, you are not evaluating his memory to remember the previous results.

2. *Does the written work lead the learner toward discovering a new investigation that needs to be done?*

Written work that satisfies this criterion is open ended (divergent); anything less is convergent. Summaries are convergent and a "list-the-properties" type of question is also convergent. Occasionally you need to use those kinds of questions, just to sharply focus the attention of the student upon a specific. Do not delude yourself that any rational powers are being developed (except perhaps recall) while you are focusing the attention of the class. But when the learner sees the next step that needs to be taken, he is being led in a divergent path. That path will encourage him to enlarge his scope of content understanding and provide him a natural opportunity to develop his rational powers.

3. *Does the required written work provide the learner the opportunity to make his own interpretations of "things" as he sees them; that is, is he provided an opportunity to use his imagination?*

There is no doubt that use of the imagination is at the heart of creative thinking and is the natural outgrowth of the use by the learner of analysis, evaluation, synthesis, and the other rational powers. We believe, however, that if the student is not provided the opportunity *and encouraged* to utilize the rational power of imagination that he will most likely not make the trip. There is much evidence that suggests that the normal educational establishment does not encourage such trips. (See Charles Silberman, *Crisis in Education*, Random House, New York, 1970.) Written work can provide part of the stimulus necessary to start the imagination and also provide the teacher a measure of how the activities of his class are changing that behavior. Consider this exercise.

One of man's qualities, or attributes, which sets him apart from other living creatures is strong hands with opposable thumbs; that is, the thumb can push against the fingers of the same hand.
a. What kinds of things does this allow man to do better than other animals?

b. List a special attribute of some other animal that allows him to do things that man cannot do as well.

c. Can you think of a special attribute which some animal has that makes him especially suited to live at certain places on the earth?

4. *Does written work allow the learner to work at his own level rather than at some level that is nebulous to him?*

This evaluative criterion needs to be consciously applied by the teacher to his *expectations* of the student. If permitted, students will work at their level and, in most cases, make a conscious effort to produce their best work. If the teacher consistently tells the learner that his written efforts are not acceptable, that written work is harmful. In Chapter 3 the developmental levels concept of Piaget was introduced. Knowing where your students stand in the developmental scheme will give you a frame of reference for what you can expect from them. Do not expect a concrete operational learner to do formal operational work. Written work provides the teacher the opportunity to watch the intellectual levels of students grow, but he must evaluate written work from a level of proper expectations and not from some absolute standard that reflects content mastery (often memorization).

Preparing and Scoring Written Work. You have no doubt concluded that preparing written work such as that suggested by the foregoing five criteria can be an exacting task. Nor will the questions and exercises you prepare necessarily be exactly on target the first time you use them. If you evaluate the response of the pupil, you will find much guidance there to assist you in increasing the quality of written exercises. The length of sentences used, the language employed, and the specific details given and asked for are all factors that influence the quality of your evaluative instruments.

The phrase "written work" has been used here without reference to whether the exercise was a developmental exercise used in a daily class situation or in an examination. When examinations are focused on, there are many types of questions which can be used. True and false, multiple choice, matching, and essay questions are the major types of examination questions generally used. There are many specific factors which, if properly utilized, will increase the quality, validity, and educational soundness of your examination questions. Discussing those specific factors is not within the scope of this book. Many excellent books have been written on test construction. You are urged to consult such a reference.

If the essay-type question is utilized either as a test item or in a daily class situation, and employs the five criteria discussed here, not many are necessary to gain an impression of how the student is growing intellectually. We believe that using only a few such questions frequently provides a better overview of the students' progress than does giving a long list of such questions at one time. When a learner is dealing with only a few questions, he does not feel the pressure of hurrying through one in order to respond to them all and finish the written work. Since this procedure limits the samples of the course which can be evaluated, the questions must be carefully constructed in order to determine the progress the learner is making toward the objective of the course and science education.

When completely objective-type written work is used, scoring is no problem—the student's response is either right or wrong. Only in the teacher and the student dialogue about the answer can the teacher gain an insight into the logic that went into selecting the response that was made. It is for the foregoing reason that we do not feel that the evaluation of a student's progress should be made *only* on the basis of objective written work. Carefully constructed objective examinations that adhere to the previously given five criteria have a place in evaluation but need to be used in conjunction with (though not necessarily at the same time) essay-type written work. Such written work can be from a daily class situation or an examination. Essay-type written work allows the teacher to catch and evaluate the logic that went into the student's response. In scoring such written work the only defensible criterion to use is the logic and inductive inference the student used. If the answer is given the greatest share of the weight in determining the student's performance, the teacher has contradicted the basic tenet of inquiry; he has judged the student upon some predetermined absolute standard and not on the student's ability to make an inductive inference. If the teacher is guilty of this breach of inquiry, the pupils in his classes will soon learn that getting the approved answer is the important thing. If that happens, leading learners to achieve the objectives of science education will become an impossibility.

Semiformal pupil interview in evaluation

The term *semiformal* is used to distinguish between this type of evaluation and the informal interview that is conducted on a day-to-day basis as the teacher interacts with individuals or small groups in a class during a regular activity. During the semiformal interview, the teacher should have some predetermined tasks and questions with which the pupil interacts. This type of evaluation can not be done very often for each pupil, but it can provide the teacher and pupil

Much valuable evaluation can be made in the semiformal pupil interview.

very valuable insight concerning the pupil's understanding of concepts or his mastery of process skills.

Following is an example of an interview instrument that could be used to evaluate process skills.

Process Definitions[3]

The following definitions have been constructed to identify the processes which the tasks have been designed to assess. The reader must understand that each definition is specific to the process as it is used in this instrument.

Observing. The process through which information is obtained, either directly or indirectly, with the intent of understanding more about an object or situation. This process is based on the utilization of the five senses—seeing, touching, hearing, smelling, and tasting, either partially or in totality in any specific situation.

Classifying. The process of mentally or physically placing objects in groups which have systematic relationships. These relationships can occur among the objects of a specific group and among or between groups.

Measuring. The process of obtaining the dimensions of an object by

[3] M. C. Weber, "The Influence of the Science Curriculum Improvement Study on the Learner's Operational Utilization of Science Processes." Unpublished doctoral dissertation. University of Oklahoma, 1971, pp. 64–76. Reprinted with permission of the author.

comparing the object to a standard unit. Any selected unit can serve as this standard.

Experimenting. The process of recognizing and controlling variables while doing something in an attempt to solve a problem. The problem can be externally designed and presented to the experimenter or the problem can be structured internally by the experimenter.

Interpreting. The process of searching for a meaningful understanding in accumulated data with the intent of utilizing the understanding in answering questions relative to the data.

Predicting. The process of foretelling the behavior of an event from the available data which is currently at hand.

Process—Observing

Task 1. Nos. 1–0 and 2–0.

Materials:	A piece of clear, transparent plastic 8½ x 5¼ inches.
Administrative procedure:	Give the plastic to the child.
Instructions to the child:	Describe this object.
Score.	1 0. Place a check in the acceptable[4] column if four properties are given.
	2–0. Place a check in the acceptable column if eight or more properties are given.

Task 2. Nos. 3–0 and 4–0.

Materials:	Ten pieces of chalk, four marbles, three ping pong balls, five dominoes, three wooden cubes, four nails, two identical boxes (cigar).
Administrative procedure:	One of the empty boxes is sealed with three pieces of chalk in it. Place this box in front of the child. Place the objects and the other empty, opened box in front of the child.

[4] Dr. Weber suggests that the test administrator score each response as acceptable or unacceptable. He used a sheet that listed 34 divisions, with space to check acceptable or unacceptable for each division.

Instructions to the child: What is in this sealed box? (The administrator will just point to the sealed box.)

Score: 3–0. Place a check in the acceptable column if the child manipulates the sealed box before he attempts to make the identification.

4–0. Place a check in the acceptable column if the child attempts to use the empty box and the objects to identify what is in the sealed box.

Task 3. Nos. 5–0 and 6–0.

Materials: Magnifier, ruler, a piece of string, two sea shells (different), a spring balance.

Administrative procedure: Give the materials to the child.

Instructions to the child: Tell how these two shells are different.

Score: 5–0. Place a check in the acceptable column if the child gives four qualitative differences (non-measured, non-numbered).

6–0. Place a check in the acceptable column if the child gives two quantitative differences (measured, numbered).

Process—Classifying

Task 4. Nos. 7–C and 8–C.

Materials: A collection of the following objects: two nails, one plastic spoon, 4 x 4 inch aluminum foil, four marbles, one thumb tack, one wooden pencil, one index card (3 x 5 inches).

Administrative procedure: Give the collection of objects to the child.

Instructions to the child: Place these objects in groups so that the objects in each group are alike in some way and tell how they are alike.

Score: 7–C. Place a check in the acceptable column if the child places all the objects in logical groups.

8–C. Place a check in the acceptable column if the child properly identifies the characteristic of each group.

Task 5. Nos. 9–C and 10–C.

Materials: Cards cut in these designs: six red diamonds, six blue diamonds, six yellow diamonds, six red circles, six blue circles, six yellow circles, six red rectangles, six blue rectangles, six yellow rectangles.

Administrative procedure: The cards will be placed in a pile in front of the child and the administrator will begin and control the initial part of the activity. With the appropriate instructions he will give a set of two cards to the child and then give a set of two cards to himself. The administrator will do this for a total of three moves. The following pattern will be followed:

	To Child	To Administrator
1st move	R ◇Y	R ◇B
2nd move	B R	Y Y
3rd move	Y B	R R

After the administrator has completed the third move, the child will be asked to select from the card pile, two cards for himself and two cards for the administrator.

Instructions to the child: I am going to give you two cards and then give myself two cards. I will do this in a special way. Here is your first pair of cards and here is my first pair of cards. Here is your next pair and here is my next pair. Here is

your third pair and here is my third
pair. Now, you give yourself two cards
and then give me two cards. Do this
in the same special way which I did.

Score: 9–C. Place a check in the acceptable
          column if the child gives himself
          either two of the same shape
          or two of a different color.

          10–C. Place a check in the acceptable
          column if the child gives the
          the administrator two of the
          same color.

Process—Measuring

Task 6.   Nos. 11–M and 12–M.

Materials: A collection of the following: a strip
              of paper two inches by one-half inch,
              a marble, a nail, a button and twelve
              beans, and a 3 x 5 inch card. (No
              ruler.)

Administrative procedure: Give the collection to the child. After
                             he examines them, give him the 3 x 5
                             card.

Instructions to the child: Measure the length of this card.

Score: 11–M. Place a check in the acceptable
          column if the child attempts to
          use any of the objects to
          measure the card's length.

          12–M. Place a check in the acceptable
          column if the child actually
          gives a measurement. Example
          — 3½ nails long.

Task 7.   Nos. 13–M and 14–M.

Materials: Tripod support, stiff wire, a rubber
              band, a sheet of graph paper, ½ oz.
              fishing weights, and a large nut (a
              threaded head of a bolt).

Administrative procedure: Give the objects to the child and then
                             hand him the nut.

Instructions to the child: What is the weight of this object? Use any of these objects if you want to. These fishing weights weigh ½ oz. each.

Score: 13–M. Place a check in the acceptable column if the child attempts to calibrate the rubber band stretch with the ½ oz. weights.

14–M. Place a check in the acceptable column if the child gives the weight of the nut as between 2–4 ounces.

Task 8. Nos. 15–M and 16–M.

Materials: Four 3 x 5 inch blank index cards with one each painted red, yellow, blue, and green, a small metric-scale ruler.

Administrative procedure: The four cards must be of identical length but each painted a different color. The metric ruler should be in the 160 mm class or larger.

Instructions to the child: Measure these cards and determine how many little marks each card is long and how many little marks each card is wide.

Score: 15–M. Place a check in the acceptable column if the child gives the length of each card as identical — 127 marks.

16–M. Place a check in the acceptable column if the child gives the width of each card as identical — 76 marks.

Process—Experimenting

Task 9. Nos. 17–E and 18–E.

Materials: Solutions of salt water (A), water with phenolphthalein (B), and distilled water (C). The following dry powders:

lead nitrate (1), calcium oxide (2), and sodium chloride (3). Straws to serve as droppers and scoops. Wax paper on which to mix. Powder papers and small paper cups to hold the liquids.

Administrative procedure: The solutions and the powders must be prepared before the test administration. Give the child about 25 ml of each solution and 5 grams of each powder. Also, a sheet of wax paper should be given for the mixing. The straws, cups, and powder papers should be discarded after each child is tested. In placing the materials before the child, make it a point not to order them, i.e., 1, 2, and 3 or A, B, and C.

Instructions to the child: A red color will be formed when one of these liquids and one of these powders are mixed. Find which two will give the color.

Score: 17–E. Place a check in the acceptable column if the child approaches the task in a systematic manner, i.e., put powder 1 in liquid A, B, C, etc.

18–E. Place a check in the acceptable column if the child finds powder 2 and liquid B will give the red color.

Task 10.   Nos. 19–E and 20–E.

Materials: A piece of cotton material (3 x 10 inches), a piece of knit material (3 x 10 inches), four containers, a source of time measurement, a ruler, and water.

Administrative procedure: The materials are given to the child.

Instructions to the child: Which of these pieces of cloth will soak up water faster? Tell what you would do in finding out.

Score: 19–E. Place a check in the acceptable column if the child gives *two* of the following:

___Put the same length of each cloth in water.

___Keep them in the water for the same length of time.

___See how far the water moves on each cloth.

___Use water of the same temperature.

___Use same amount of water.

Instructions to the child: Go ahead and see if the cloth you selected does soak up water faster.

Score: 20–E. Place a check in the acceptable column if the child approaches the task in a systematic manner, i.e., controls the variables as he listed in 19–E.

Task 11.   Nos. 21–E and 22–E.

Materials: Ruler, string, scissors, support stand, wire, washers, three lenses, three index cards, three rubber stoppers, and three marbles.

Administrative procedure: The collection of materials is given to the child. The objective is to see whether the child can utilize them in some experimental design.

Instructions to the child: Here are some things. Use them and work an experiment of some kind. Do anything you wish. I will be asking you some questions about your experiment in five minutes or before if you finish your experiment.

Score: 21–E. Place a check in the acceptable column if the child does *all* the following:

___Identifies an experimental problem. (What is the name of your experiment?)

___Sets up the materials in an

attempt to solve the problem. (What did you do in your experiment?)

___Shows a concern for the necessity of controlling the variables.

22–E. Place a check in the acceptable column if the child does *all* the following:

___Attempts to hold some variables constant.

___Actually arrives at some data.

___Offers a possible solution based on his data.

Process—Interpreting

Task 12.   Nos. 23–I and 24–I.

Materials: Four microscope slides and four water solutions of sodium chloride for each child.

Administrative procedure: The day before the task, the four slides must be prepared to insure the water will be evaporated.

Slide	Liquid	Water	Sodium Chloride
A	A	250 ml	1 tsp.
B	B	250 ml	5 tsp.
C	C	250 ml	3 tsp.
D	D	250 ml	10 tsp.

Instructions to the child: These liquids were made by putting salt in water. Each bottle has a different amount of salt. These glass slides were prepared by placing a drop of liquid on the glass. The letter on the glass slide tells which bottle of liquid it came from. Which liquid has the most salt in it?

Score: 23–I. Place a check in the acceptable column if the child attempts to correlate the amount of salt on the slide with the liquids.

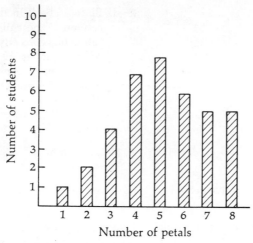

Figure P.

24–I. Place a check in the acceptable column if the child determines liquid D has the most salt.

Task 13.   Nos. 25–I and 26–I.

Materials: See attached graph [Figure P].

Administrative procedure: Give the graph to the child.

Instructions to the child: After a windstorm, a science class went out to a flower patch to see how much the flowers were damaged. Each child picked one flower and counted the petals which the flower still had. They made a graph showing the number of petals which the flowers had. (Give the graph to the child.) I will ask you some questions.

Score: 25–I. Place a check in the acceptable column if the child answers the following correctly:
___What is the smallest number of petals in any flower? Ans. (1).
___What was the number of petals which was most often found on the flowers? Ans. (5).

26–I. Place a check in the acceptable column if the child answers the following correctly:

___What number of flowers had seven petals? Ans. (5).

___How many students are in the class? Ans. (38).

Task 14.   Nos. 27–I and 28–I.

Materials: A 100 ml graduated cylinder, six marbles, and water.

Administrative procedure: Give the materials to the child with the cylinder filled to the 50 ml mark.

Instructions to the child: When you place these marbles in the water, the water level will rise. Put these marbles in the water, two at a time and write down how many marks the water level rises each time. Do this until all six marbles are in the water. I will ask you some questions when you finish.

Score: 27–I. Place a check in the acceptable column if the child answers correctly from his data this question—Does the water level rise the same amount each time two marbles are placed in the water?

28–I. Place a check in the acceptable column if the child answers correctly from his data this question—How many marks would the water level rise if just three marbles are added to the water?

Process—Predicting

Task 15.   Nos. 29–P and 30–P.

Materials: A rubber band, a small piece of stiff wire, a support stand, a ruler, graph paper, and four washers.

Administrative procedure: Give the materials to the child.

Instructions to the child: You have four washers here. How far will eight washers stretch this rubber band? I will ask you to tell how you found out.

Score: 29–P. Place a check in the acceptable column if the child determines how far the four washers will stretch the rubber band.

30–P. Place a check in the acceptable column if the child gives an answer for the stretch of eight washers as based on his data.

Instructions to the child: How did you find out?

Task 16. Nos. 31–P and 32–P.

Materials: A pendulum and support, a ruler, and a timer or watch for administration.

Administrative procedure: The pendulum is set up and its nature explained to the child. The administrator will adjust the pendulum's length at 20 inches. The child will count the swings for one-half minute. The pendulum will then be adjusted to 10 inches and the child will again count the swings for one-half minute. The administrator will do the timing.

Instructions to the child: How many swings will the pendulum make in one-half minute if we were to shorten the length to five inches?

Score: 31–P. Place a check in the acceptable column if the child makes a prediction based on his data from both the 20 inch and 10 inch lengths.

Say to the child: Will you now check how accurate your answer was to the five inch pendulum length?

Score: 32–P. Place a check in the acceptable column if the child shortens the pendulum length to five inches and counts the swings in one-half minute.

Task 17. Nos. 33–P and 34–P.

Materials: Three different kinds of rubber balls (different in diameter, color, etc.).

Administrative procedure: The three balls are given to the child.

Instructions to the child: Here are three rubber balls. You can do anything with them that you wish except bounce them. Decide which one will bounce higher when dropped from the same height.

Score: 33–P. Place a check in the acceptable column if the child manipulates the three rubber balls to obtain data of some kind from which his prediction was made.

34–P. Place a check in the acceptable column if the child makes an accurate prediction based on his data.

Evaluation of pupil progress should be continuous

Too frequently, in the past, evaluation of pupil progress has been regarded as something that happens after pupils have completed a given science assignment or project—as something that takes place at stated intervals, such as the end of a six-week period. It is obvious that evaluation of the type we have been discussing must be viewed as a continuing activity that is an integral part of the teaching-learning process rather than as an aftermath. To make a continuous evaluation meaningful, records must be maintained that will allow not only the teacher but the child and parent to understand what progress is being made. Examples of such records are graphs, diaries, checklists, individual and group profiles, teacher-pupil conferences, written work, and formal and informal observations of student behavior.

Evaluation of pupil progress should be a cooperative process

Learning to evaluate his own progress toward clearly defined goals is a vital phase of the child's education. Failure to develop in the child

Evaluation is a cooperative process.

both the desire and the ability to share in the evaluation of his own progress has unfortunate consequences. Evaluation can become a form of threat or coercion, and the temptation to try to deceive the teacher by cheating on examinations is great.

On the other hand, cooperative evaluation is rewarding to the individual pupil because it provides a means of gaining insight into his strengths and weaknesses and indicates what steps need to be taken to accomplish the goals he is pursuing.

To use the evaluative procedures we have suggested, your grade book must be a looseleaf notebook. Perhaps the first page will be a class profile sheet that allows you to see at a glance how the class is progressing toward the goals you established. Following this page in some order will be the individual pupil records. Each pupil might have profile sheets indicating his progress in concept, process, and attitude objectives. The entries on the sheets will come from informal observation, semiformal interview sessions, written work including examinations, and pencil and paper instruments designed to measure perception of the classroom activity or activity-type preference.

Is this type of evaluation subjective? Definitely! But who is better qualified to make a subjective evaluation than the teacher who is with the class over a long period of time and knows not only the children but his objectives. The teacher, as a professional, must be willing to rely to a great degree on his subjective evaluation and he must have collected evidence on which to base his judgments.

Standardized achievement tests

Many school systems rely heavily on end-of-year standardized achievement tests to determine how well the pupils have learned science. Achievement tests might be useful if, and only if, the test measures achievement of the objectives you were trying to accomplish. The achievement test can at best do only a very limited job of determining overall achievement—and, if the achievement test does not measure what you were trying to achieve, it is only an expensive exercise.

Evaluating Elementary School Science Curricula[5]

Today's elementary schools may lack many of the features, facilities, and opportunities the modern educator would like to see in them, but after reading Chapter 9, you will no doubt agree that they do *not* lack science curricula to select from. But how does one know which curriculum to select? The answer to the foregoing question is—it depends upon the purposes for which a particular subject is taught.

As we have stated previously, we believe that elementary school science should permit and encourage every child to develop—

1. the ability and confidence to inquire.
2. a command of the ten rational powers.
3. an understanding of the changing nature of the environment in terms of matter, life, energy, and their interactions.

What follows is a set of criteria which can be specifically used to evaluate an elementary school science curriculum to determine whether or not it can lead children to achieve the foregoing purposes.

Before using the criteria, there are a few basic ground rules which we feel are important enough to explain. You will observe that each criterion is written in the form of a question which must be answered Yes, No, or Information to determine not available. This technique was used deliberately because we believe that any evaluation instru-

[5] The material in this section is based on "Evaluating Elementary School Science Curricula," Kenneth Absher, Larry A. Darbison, Kay Giesentanner, Bari J. Herbert, Mrs. Richard Hutton, Anton E. Lawson, John W. Renner, Mrs. Tom Ridgway, Janet S. Stewart, and George C. Worth, in *Science and Children* (December 1972), pp. 12–15.

ment should yield definite information. The criteria are mutually independent; just because one is answered negatively does not invalidate all the criteria following it. Furthermore, your evaluation does not need to achieve only affirmative answers to decide to use a given program and/or unit. The criteria were designed to provide information that can be used to allow you to make science-curriculum decisions.

1. Does the unit emphasize the processes of science as well as the information acquired?

Teach science as science is, and science is process.

2. Are the students actively involved?
   a. Do the pupils do their own investigations?
   b. Do the pupils gather their own data?
   c. Are the pupils encouraged to perform experiments on their own?
   d. Are pupils led to form hypotheses?
   e. Is the primary responsibility for data interpretation and evaluation left to the pupils?

3. Do the learning activities allow use and potential development of the rational powers?

The central purpose of American education as stated by the Educational Policies Commission in 1961 is to develop the ten rational powers, which they described as "the essence of the ability to think."[6] The learning activities of the program under consideration should include activities in which the use and development of these powers is demanded. In looking through the programs, examples of these activities should be apparent; classification of bottle caps, buttons, seeds, animals or plants should be required. There should be evidence of the students being called upon to imagine, experiment, synthesize hypotheses, and analyze and evaluate data the experiments produce. Also instances of students comparing things such as animals, rocks, or any other variety of materials or data should be apparent. Students should be encouraged to generalize from their classroom experiences and experiments to out-of-class experience in order to discover the important relationships.

Because of the nature of the processes of science if you are able to answer Yes to question number one, in most cases, you will be impelled to answer Yes to question number three.

4. Does the program fit the developmental level of the child?

The developmental level concept based on Jean Piaget's model of learning has been thoroughly discussed in Chapter 3.

[6] Educational Policies Commission, *The Central Purpose of American Education* (Washington, D.C.: NEA, 1961), p. 5. [See Appendix C.]

5. Does the unit contain a variety of *materials* which appear to interest the child?

Children should be given *concrete* objects which they can handle and experiment with. These materials allow the children to be involved as they analyze, compare, and otherwise develop their rational thinking.

6. Does the unit contain a variety of *activities* which appear to interest the child?

Activities that interest the child will greatly increase the frequency and consistency with which his needs are met as he participates in the learning experience. (Read → as "lead(s) to.")

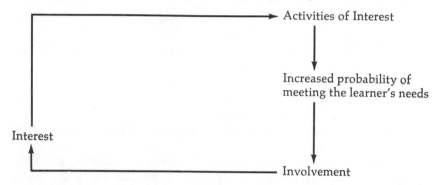

7. Do the teacher's guides explain purpose and methodology?

The nature of any guide is that it provides a skeletal outline of *what* is to be achieved and *how* those achievements are to be accomplished. A useful guide would include stated objectives with sample exercises discussed and related activities given. Consequently, a useful teacher's guide must explain the what (purpose) and the how (methodology).

8. Does the entire program have a conceptual framework?

A conceptual framework is an expandible reference model (i.e., organizational scheme) which allows the learner to place and evaluate new information. We believe that a science program with a conceptual framework has a dimension that one lacking it does not have. That dimension adds depth to the program and allows the child to develop a structure in which to categorize ideas, concepts, and experiences. A conceptual framework gives direction to the ideas taught in the program and certainly gives the teacher added confidence in the materials and methods being used.

9. Does the program reflect the structure of the discipline?[7]

So many programs in the past and even today fall far short of the

---

[7] For an extensive discussion of the phrase "structure of the discipline" see Jerome S. Bruner, *The Process of Education* (Cambridge, Mass.: Harvard University Press, 1962), chap. 2.

real goal of science education, and that is to teach science. Science can and should be taught to help students think, solve problems, and become confident, but for a program to be truly successful it must remain true to the discipline. By this we mean it must teach the underlying concepts of the field and not trivial items of passing interest upon which so much of certain science textbooks are based. (See purpose number three stated in the introduction to this section.) Only in this way will the student become aware of the simplicity and organization which form the basis of any field of science.

10. Are the concepts each unit purports to develop clearly stated?

Since the teacher must have definite objectives in mind when selecting a science program, clear statements of the concepts of each unit will facilitate the selection process. In the teaching process, having the concepts of each unit clearly stated will allow the teacher to set goals and arrange priorities in order to utilize the unit to lead children to develop the basic concepts of the unit.

11. Does the program encourage the teacher to accept all sincere student answers as valuable?

A student's answer is always valuable even if his answer isn't "correct." That incorrect answer may lead to more questions and the teacher can guide (by questioning or by the children experimenting) the pupil to conclusions supported by evidence. In this way, the child learns by doing. The material provided for the teacher should give clues for questioning and suggestions for leading the children to experimenting rather than outlining specific facts to be mastered.

12. Is the unit flexible enough to be adapted to the needs and interests of a particular class?

The unit should allow rearrangement, expansion, condensation, tangent activities, and individual projects. The teacher should be encouraged to use his discretion in order to create the most dynamic learning situations and experiences for each individual child and the distinct (unique) class he is teaching. If the units are structured too formally or rigidly to allow them to maintain their effectiveness after necessary alterations are made, then it is not flexible enough to be adapted.

13. Can a child with limited reading ability succeed in the program?

Reading is extremely important, but achievement in science should not be dependent upon it.

14. Are the teaching and resource materials carefully integrated into the program?

If films, slides, or recordings are to be used with a lesson, the teacher needs to know what purpose these materials serve. Are they included to demonstrate something that can't be done by the class, or would be difficult to do successfully? Is it something that is needed at a particular time to make the lesson meaningful, or to allow the class to proceed with better understanding? Is the time that the material should be used for maximum effectiveness specified, or are the materials to be used at any convenient time? If the material has value, then there is a best time for it to be used, and the teacher needs to know when that time is.

15. Is a format provided which allows the teacher to set up and teach each unit smoothly?

16. Is the cost, construction, mobility, durability, and availability of materials reasonable and practical?

Whether or not the cost of a science program is reasonable and practical will be determined largely by the ability and willingness of the school to finance it. If the program requires the use of consumable items such as chemicals, seeds, and special solutions, their cost and availability must be considered. If the items are not common ones the students can bring from home or that can be obtained locally, the price of the program is affected. With any elementary program the teacher, with a minimum of difficulty, should be able to handle and move from place to place the materials that will be used.

Do not attempt to produce some numerical score using these criteria (although that could be done). Rather, after you have used the criteria on a particular science program, look at *which* of the criteria you have answered positively and which negatively. Then consult the purposes you have stated for teaching science. Only when you compare *your* purposes and the answers *you* gave to each criterion while evaluating a particular program will you know which No and Yes answers are most important to *you*. No one can evaluate a curriculum for you; that's your job. The foregoing criteria can help you focus your attention on those aspects of a curriculum that are important to you.

Evaluating Teachers

There is probably no more inexact evaluation that can be made than that of teacher effectiveness. The literature of education contains the reports of many studies that have attempted to assess the value of teacher behavior in a classroom. Those studies will not be reviewed here, but if you are interested you are urged to investigate the literature. We believe that *teacher performance in the classroom should be evaluated in terms of what is done to further the accomplishment of the objectives of science education.* In other words, what specific, overt behaviors will be used by a teacher who is using inquiry?

1. *He listens to the students.*

An inquiry-centered teacher listens to what the students have to say about an investigation or problem and utilizes their contributions in carrying the classroom activities forward. Utilizing the learner's contributions to the problem being considered establishes rapport, but it does much more; it tells the students that they, as well as the teacher, have a responsibility in carrying out the learning activities. A teacher who listens tells the learners that what they have to say is a valuable part of the investigation being conducted; that teacher behavior greatly contributes to developing student confidence to inquire.

2. *He accepts the results of an investigation which the student gets.*

Too many times teachers will accept only experimental results that constitute the "right" answers. If a learner has honestly done an experiment and honestly contributes his results to the class discussion, the teacher has the responsibility of accepting those results. What do you do if the results are completely unacceptable to science? Suggest other investigations that represent different ways of solving the same problem. The second investigation will probably produce results contradictory to the first. Now the student must make a decision regarding which set of results he must accept and he will probably decide that one of the investigations (perhaps both) must be done again. If you had rejected his first set of results, he would have simply tried to outguess you as to what results you would accept.

3. *An inquiry-centered teacher's questions will focus the students' attention on specific points in the investigation.*

Of extreme importance is the fact that questions are asked to find out what the students are thinking. Too many questions asked by teachers are simply "Can-you-guess-what-I'm-thinking" type questions. When the learner gives an honest reply, it must be accepted, and if that response is one that could lead him astray, he should be asked another question that will demand and/or allow him to refocus his attention.

4. *He is a guide for students during an investigation.*

He asks questions, provides clues and cues to those frustrated and/or on dead center, recommends reference books to consult and other investigations to perform, suggests alternate ways of thinking about a problem, challenges results, and provides materials needed.

5. *For a year's work, he is more concerned with the type and quality of investigations that are done than with the number completed.*

The "we-must-finish-the-book" attitude has no place in a classroom that is concerned with achieving the objectives of science education.

6. *A teacher who believes that learning occurs by student involvement will utilize the full exploration-invention-discovery sequence of inquiry as it was discussed in Chapter 4.*

Many teachers who encounter the exploration-invention-discovery sequence will immediately remark that they allow students to gather information from many sources, provide the student with a textbook that gives him information, and tell him much information. They conclude that they are using inquiry, and so they are—*partly*. They are no doubt providing their students with excellent opportunities to explore the area they are working in very thoroughly because exploration is the gathering of information. But for many teachers the inquiry sequence stops right there. The accumulated information has become their goal. They do not engage in, nor do they permit and/or encourage their students to engage in, conceptual invention. Furthermore, the idea of sending students into a laboratory situation to discover all they can about a newly acquired concept is foreign to them. The teacher who uses inquiry in an incomplete way also uses the laboratory in an incomplete way—he sends students there to accumulate information; that is, to explore again. We believe that much of what today is called science teaching is only exploration and that alone, as important as it is, will not lead students to achieve the objectives of science education. Even the most traditional of teachers, however, has taken the first step toward inquiry; he has allowed students to explore a given problem and/or area of science. When all teachers utilize the full sequence of exploration, invention, and discovery, science teaching will have begun to lead students toward achieving the goals of science education and the general goal of all education—the development of the ability to think.

11 | The Future

Writing a chapter entitled "The Future" for a book on inquiry-centered science teaching is nearly a paradox, because the future of science teaching cannot be predicted with any data that were scientifically collected. In fact, since there are so many poorly understood sociological and political factors involved in our educational programs, the future can hardly be predicted at all. Perhaps it is better that way. When we titled this chapter "The Future" we had in mind the work that still lies ahead of us in making science teaching truly scientific and intellectually centered and not an exercise in transmitting a few facts about science, a lot of facts about technology, and a few disconnected, and in many cases erroneous, tales about the history of science. We feel that at the beginning of the 1970s science teaching has a good start. For the next few pages we will comment upon those emerging ideas which we believe will represent the most fruitful ones to concentrate on during the ensuing years. As you read the next few pages bear in mind that we are not stating any answers—just questions and hypotheses. Perhaps the next few pages should be entitled "Thinking out loud—with a pencil!"

Piaget and Science Teaching

The results, and the interpretation of those results, of the researches of Jean Piaget have a great deal to say to the science teacher which we do not feel has as yet been heard by that group. Pupils in the elementary school are entering into a state of concrete operations during which logical operations must deal with immediate present reality. Learners some time between the ages of 11 and 15, according to Piaget, enter the stage characterized as formal operational. Bruner has described formal operations as "the child's intellectual activity seems to be based upon an ability to operate on hypothetical proposition rather than being constrained to what he has experienced or what is before him."[1]

Think about some of the topics that are introduced in many elementary school science courses in the primary grades. We refer to such topics as atoms and molecules, the solar system, conservation of mass and energy, and genetics. Most assuredly each one of the foregoing topics represents a hypothetical proposition. In fact much of what is today presented in conventional elementary school science could be characterized as highly abstract hypothetical propositions. As a matter of fact, these topics are too abstract for most present-day secondary school students to deal with effectively, with understanding. At one time, we were tempted to think what a fortunate circumstance; students were entering formal operational stage by age 11 and were quite well advanced by 15 years of age. This meant that science that deals with hypothetical propositions and quite abstract concepts could be dealt with in upper elementary and junior high school. We no longer believe, however, that even the majority of secondary school students are formal operational. Our own research (see Appendix A) has shown us that when you present a junior high school student with two identically sized and shaped cylinders of different weights, the majority of them believe the heavier one will push a water level up more than the lighter one (conservation of volume). When secondary school students in grades 7 through 12 are given a simple pendulum to experiment with, well over 70 percent of them cannot separate the variables of weight and length and then exclude weight as a relevant factor to the pendulum's motion. If they cannot think about their thinking to a degree that will let them solve such problems as the foregoing, how can we expect them to separate one theory from another and exclude one in favor of the other, or understand the relationships between laws, theories, and facts. How can we expect such students to make mental-operational models to explain regularities in nature? Karplus and Peterson[2] demonstrated that secondary school students do not have a concept of the simple, but abstract, ratio! Imagine what you do to all phases of secondary science teaching if you eliminate all concepts more abstract than the ratio! Even more important, if the majority of secondary school stu-

---

[1] Jerome S. Bruner, *The Process of Education* (New York: Random House Vintage Books, 1960), p. 37.

[2] Robert Karplus and Rita W. Peterson, "Intellectual Development Beyond Elementary School II: Ratio, A Survey," *School Science and Mathematics* (December 1970), 813–820.

Table 11–1

Age—months	Sample size	Conservation of					
		Number	Solid amount	Liquid amount	Length	Area	Weight
60–64	12	3	2	2		1	1
65–68	12	7	2		2	2	3
69–72	12	6	3	4	1	2	1
73–76	12	8	7	7	3	6	3
77–80	12	8	5	5	3	2	6
81–84	12	9	5	5		3	5
85–88	12	11	11	9	6	9	10
89–92	12	11	9	11	9	8	11
93–96	12	9	9	8	7	6	8
97–100	12	12	12	11	9	8	11
101–104	12	12	11	8	5	7	8
105–108	12	11	9	9	7	8	10
109–112	12	11	10	10	7	7	6
113–116	12	11	11	10	7	7	7
117–120	12	12	12	10	7	6	9
121–124	12	9	12	11	7	8	9
125–128	12	11	11	10	9	7	11
129–132	12	12	11	11	12	10	10
133–136	12	12	12	12	8	7	12
137–140	12	12	10	10	10	10	12
141–144	12	12	12	12	12	12	12

SOURCE: John W. Renner, Judith Brock, Sue Heath, Mildred Laughlin, and Jo Stevens, "Piaget Is Practical," *Science and Children* (October 1971), p. 23.

These data were gathered by a group of experienced test administrators, all of whom cannot be acknowledged. The authors are especially grateful, however, to Jo Stevens, Judith Brock, Mildred Laughlin, and Sue Heath, Kennedy Elementary School, Norman, Oklahoma.

dents is not formal operational, then we can be sure that very few of the upper elementary school pupils possess this level of development. In fact, a sample of 252 children drawn from the Norman, Oklahoma, Public Schools tested on six Piaget Conservation tasks shows inconsistencies in children's ability to conserve length, area, and weight until almost 11 years of age.[3] Table 11–1 shows the change of con-

[3] John W. Renner, Judith Brock, Sue Heath, Mildred Laughlin, and Jo Stevens, "Piaget Is Practical," *Science and Children* (October 1971), pp. 23–24.

servation ability with age in the sample. Since the ability to conserve is perhaps the most widely used indicator of the extent to which a child has entered the stage of concrete operations, students at the sixth grade level have apparently just entered fully into the concrete operational stage.

Karplus and Peterson stated there is a "serious gap" between the curricula we are using and the reasoning abilities of the students. The foregoing examples clearly demonstrate the validity of that statement. What is to be done? Two closely associated things we propose will come about in the future.

First, curriculum planners will, because of the levels concept of Piaget's theory, put more emphasis on a coordinated, articulate K–12 science program. At present most school systems have three disconnected levels of science—elementary, intermediate, and senior high school—with little if any attempt or desire on the part of the teachers at the three levels to participate in the overall planning of the total science program. Science coordinators have helped the situation somewhat, but there is a long road ahead before a truly coordinated K–12 program emerges. Second, as a result of the attempts of science teachers to coordinate a K–12 science program, the need to establish specific objectives for each level will arise. One such objective for elementary school science could and should be to actuate the beginning level of hypothetical thinking (formal operations) by the end of the elementary school program. Research needs to be conducted in the near future to determine just what kinds of experiences are needed in elementary school—experiences which the research of Karplus and Peterson indicates that pupils are not getting now—to actuate the level of formal operations. The formal operational level of thinking could be nourished by the intermediate and junior high school science programs and used in the senior high program to make science and other programs meaningful. Other specific objectives for each level of the K–12 science program will arise naturally in the planning when the Piaget levels concept is used.

Teaching Methods and Inquiry

The teaching structure that has been presented to you in this book is based on the exploration-invention-discovery sequence. That sequence has been presented as inquiry, and inquiry has been presented not as *a* method for science teaching but as *the* method. Certain pro-

Children of today will have to solve problems that haven't been identified using techniques that have not yet been invented. An inquiry science problem can assist a child in developing his creativity.

cedures or techniques such as discussion, questioning, demonstration and even short lectures in upper elementary have a definite place in the teaching method. We take the position, however, that exploration, invention, and discovery are the three phases of *learning* by inquiry —everything that is learned is learned that way. The above-mentioned techniques are simply employed as a part of one of these three phases. A short lecture, for example, can be used effectively in setting the stage for an exploration and is the principal technique for invention. During and following the exploration phase and during the discovery phase the teacher-pupil and/or small group discussions and questioning are especially fruitful. Demonstrations can be used effectively during the invention and discovery phases. One must keep in mind, however, that lecture, demonstration, questioning, discussion, and others are only techniques that enable one or all three phases of inquiry to move forward.

We predict that in the future all science teachers will come to look at teaching and inquiry as synonyms and when they do, then the methods-phases-techniques concept will make sense to them. When that happens science education can begin to make its maximum and natural contribution to the central role of the school, namely the development of the ability to think.

Diagramatically our scheme looks like this:

Teaching Method   Inquiry

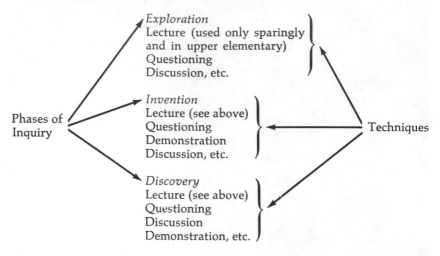

Phases of Inquiry

Exploration
Lecture (used only sparingly
and in upper elementary)
Questioning
Discussion, etc.

Invention
Lecture (see above)
Questioning
Demonstration
Discussion, etc.

Discovery
Lecture (see above)
Questioning
Discussion
Demonstration, etc.

Techniques

The Spirit of Science

The future of science in the elementary school depends on only one person—you, the classroom teacher. If you elect to follow a course of action which introduces children to the factual side of science only, its future in the elementary school classrooms in this country is very bleak. From such an experience children will conclude that science is a static body of information which "the books" spell out for them and which they are expected "to know." These kinds of experiences will convince children that science is not really for them, and the really exciting aspects of learning are found in other fields. If, however, you provide an educational environment for your pupils from which they learn that science is concerned with investigations and those investigations demand that a person apply his mind to the problem and continue to maintain that contact until the problem is solved, he will learn that science is a stimulating, productive enterprise he enjoys. In other words, if children meet science as a dynamic enterprise—one in which they can participate, and through participation develop the "spirit of science,"—its future in the elementary school is bright.[4] There are, we believe, several good reasons why the future of elementary school science must be kept bright.

[4] The "spirit of science" is defined by the Educational Policies Commission of the National Education Association in the bulletin, *Education and the Spirit of Science*, published 1966, as follows: "The Spirit of rational inquiry, driven by a belief in its efficacy and by restless curiosity." p. 1.

Teaching the Structure of Science

The citizen of tomorrow will encounter many problems, old and new, with which he will be unable to cope because today's schools cannot possibly provide the learner with specific information about the problems or specific techniques for solving them. By the time the learner is in a position outside the school to put to use the information and techniques he acquired in school, the chances are quite good that the techniques needed to solve the problems will have changed and the information he has will be obsolete or false. Our educational institutions are operating in an era when information is being produced so rapidly that even the specialists in any given field of science can barely keep abreast of the current developments. That staggering fact certainly tells us that we cannot expect our elementary schools to be teaching the latest factual information in science. But even if it were possible for a school to convey to its pupils—at the proper educational level—the latest in biophysics, space chemistry, and bionics, such a procedure would be educationally unsound.

Before such advanced notions as DNA, the language of computers, and spectroscopy can be used by a learner, he has to possess a background (a structure) that will enable him to understand and appreciate such ideas. Not too many years ago the proper background for understanding that advanced notion of science was thought to be the accumulation of all the information about a particular topic which could be amassed. We have learned that such educational experiences do not guarantee that a learner will be able to cope with advanced ideas in the future. Such heavy doses of factual content, often "learned" by rote memory, do not build for the individual a conceptual structure of the discipline of science. They only provide him with an encyclopedic knowledge and if the new information does not fit the specific part of the encyclopedia with which he is familiar—he does not know what to do with it.

A conceptual framework of a discipline is constructed only by providing the child with experiences in which he encounters the relationships that exist among things and which provide him a way of looking at various things. A conceptual structure of a discipline, in other words, is built only when the pupil has the opportunity to learn *how* to look at a given item of information as well as having the opportunity to look at the information. If we consistently provide children with experiences in science which lead them to understand that science is investigation and that they must base their generalizations upon what they have observed, measured, and otherwise found, we will have provided them with a conceptual framework. That framework will enable the learner to understand what he encounters in the future. The finest intellectual development of the future, which must be forthcoming in the elementary-science experience of pupils, must provide them with experiences that will allow them to build a conceptual framework of science that has been derived more from *how* the subject matter is encountered than it is from what is encountered.

Such a development in our educational system would have profound effect upon this country and the world. The inhabitants of the planet Earth, and particularly in the United States, are richly endowed with the ability "to do" something. We have all kinds of "doers." There is much evidence all around us which can be easily used to convince ourselves of that. The nearly astronomical rise in our gross national product since World War II, the tremendous technology that has been developed for the exploration of space, and the advances that have been made in conquering diseases are but a few of the pieces of concrete evidence which can be used to support the hypothesis that the world is quite well-populated with persons who have the ability to do at least one thing. Our success as doers will most certainly result in a shorter and shorter workweek for those who have the ability to do. Is this bad for a society to have found itself populated with persons who have the ability to do something? Possibly, yes. If those who have ability to do have not also developed the ability to understand the consequences of their "doings," then there exists the inherent danger that the entire culture could suffer from too much "doing." Man learned, for example, that the vast timber resources of early America represented untold wealth if he could but get the timber cut and to an eagerly awaiting market. When the rush to cut and market timber began, the doer developed techniques to bring about this action which were fantastically efficient. Before too long, however, the effects of too much doing began to show on the face of the earth. Only then did the doer start to develop understandings about the results of his doings.

When a culture is populated with those who can do and also understand something, there has been an effort made by that culture to improve the situation. Some agencies or persons within that culture have, for all, assumed the responsibility of assuring that those who can do also understand. Furthermore, this is a long-term development —not one that can be decided on today with the results delivered tomorrow. If our culture is going to be populated with those who can understand as well as do, the schools must immediately assume responsibilities that they are now only moderately accepting. There are many persons teaching in the schools today who firmly believe that their most important responsibility is communicating information to children. That is merely making doers out of children because having only information is what produces doers. When the school assumes the task of letting its pupils identify problems, design procedures for solving them, assess the results of those procedures, and put into practice results that are promising, it will be assisting the learner in not only developing his ability to do but also his ability to understand. The schools will be assisting the learners to develop the rational powers of their minds, and we have already seen that elementary school science represents a natural vehicle to foster that development.

There also exists within our culture a technique for transmitting information which, if used wisely, can greatly assist in the intellectual development of today's pupils. If, however, that technique is not correctly used, it can possibly do great harm to the educational enterprise of this country. The technique of which we speak is "programmed methods of instruction." Those persons who firmly believe that the principal role of our schools is the transmission of information see in programmed teaching the opportunity to present in a rather succinct, efficient manner that information which they believe the learner should know, and they are right. There is no doubt that there are many tasks that can be done much more effectively by programmed instruction than by one teacher working with a group of 25 to 35 children. We, as educators, must immediately begin to assist the programming enthusiasts in finding those tasks and designing programs that can be effective in teaching them. We are not opposed to programmed learning per se. (Remember, *social interaction* is one of the factors necessary for developing rational powers.) Unless classroom learning experiences that require the interchange that can come only from a teacher working with students are designed and implemented, there is a very great possibility that programmed instruction will take over the bulk of the education provided for children. This would, in our opinion, be providing our culture with more citizens with the ability to do and fewer with the ability to understand.

If we assist the programmers in finding the proper place in the educational enterprise for programmed learning, it can be an invaluable tool to our schools. We see that place as being supportive to the inquiry-centered classroom—but certainly not replacing that environment. The curricula of elementary school science will, in the future, demonstrate the type of educational experience a child must have to develop his rational powers. In fact, the curricula that can and will do this are now in their beginning stages, and were described in Chapter 9. From such curricula, the proper utilization of programmed instruction will emerge which will allow this teaching-learning technique to efficiently serve its principal purpose (the transmission of information) and the central purpose of education (the development of the learner's rational powers). This event will take place in elementary school science, however, only if modern curricula and classroom methodology are adopted into the classrooms of today's elementary schools.

The Need for Scientific Literacy in the Future

Perhaps the greatest understatement that can be made about science and the future is to proclaim that we are living in a scientific age! In fact, the age we are living in is nearly a "superscientific and technological" one. Our very existence depends not on one or two developments of science and/or technology but upon so many that comprehending even a portion of them is difficult. When a democratic culture depends upon science and technology for its existence, the members of that culture will ultimately be called upon to make decisions about the direction they want their society to take. It is impossible for a citizen to make an intelligent judgment relative to the direction he wishes his government to move unless he possesses information and *knows how to interpret it.*

The supplying of an individual with information enough to last him a lifetime while he is in school is an absurd goal for an educational institution to follow. When the learner needs to use that information he will have forgotten it, or it will be (as we have previously said) obsolete. Those facts leave little choice for what the school can do to assist tomorrow's citizen in becoming scientifically literate; they must teach him how to interpret the information he will encounter in the future. This suggests that learners must have experiences in isolating and interpreting information while they are in school. In addition, educational experiences such as this are the "heart and soul" of learning the structure of a discipline. Thus, when a teacher provides inquiry experiences in science for a learner, that pupil is being provided not only with the opportunity to increase his ability to interpret information, he is also building a conceptual framework of the discipline of science. The cultivation of these understandings will allow the learner to develop the scientific literacy he will need to function in solving the problems that do and will continue to face our culture. Surely one of the most accute problems which tomorrow's voters (today's elementary school pupils) will be called upon to face is the problem of overpopulation.

Biologist Paul Ehrlich tells us that the population of the world did not reach 500 million persons until "about 1650."[5] By 1850 that population had doubled and by 1930 it had doubled again. The population of the earth, according to Ehrlich, is now approximately three billion; or, whereas it took 80 years (1850 to 1930) to place a billion persons on earth, the last billion arrived in a short 35 years. We are now at a point, says Ehrlich, where "our current doubling time seems to be about 37 years, but the time for doubling to occur is still diminished, pushing our rate of growth ever upward."[6] Here, then, is certainly a problem with which tomorrow's citizens are going to be faced: how to curtail the serious population growth that could ultimately result in "120 persons per square yard of the earth's surface."[7]

What are the possible solutions to a problem such as this? The hypothetical solutions involve such diverse elements as altering the tax structure, rigidly controlling the birthrate, the establishment of a policy-making group in the biological sciences, changing our moral codes, and designing unbelievable facilities to house the billions of persons who will inhabit the earth. Most certainly, if tomorrow's citizen is going to be expected to assist intelligently in the solution of such problems, he must have a conceptual structure of the discipline of science which will allow him to properly handle information about the problem and its proposed solution. To do this adequately, today's elementary school child certainly must have the ability to interpret that information after he has received it.

If the members of our society are going to have such understandings, the schools must provide children with the experiences necessary to develop them. Furthermore, we cannot rely upon the secondary schools and colleges to do this job. By the time a future voter enrolls in the junior high school, his mental habits are fairly well determined. Anything that can be done at this late date will be largely a partial restructuring of how the pupil views a problem and will be, at best, inefficient. The elementary schools of today must implement curricula in science (as well as other subjects) which will provide pupils with a conceptual structure of the discipline and with the intellectual development (the maturation of his rational powers) in order that he

[5] Paul Ehrlich, "The Biological Revolution," *Stanford Review* (September–October 1965), 20–48.

[6] Ibid., p. 22.

[7] Ibid.

might be able to assist in solving the problems that will confront our culture in the immediate future.

The Elementary School Science Curriculum of the Future

The concept of the school, which is held by the majority of the citizens of this country, and their concept of curriculum are synonymous. The general public believes that schools exist to teach "something" and that something they understand to be the curriculum. To a large degree the public is correct. Schools do exist to teach something. If we assign a rather divergent scope of activities to that something, then the views of the professionals and the public become one. The professional's view of curriculum, however, includes not only the specific topics the learner will encounter but also all the various activities in which he participates while encountering those specifics. Keeping before us the idea that curriculum involves not only the "what" to be encountered but also the "how" it is to be met, is the unique responsibility of the educator. He must be the person who has the ability and courage to view the curricula that children experience, not only from the point of view of what is taught and how it is taught, but from the frame of reference of what should be taught and how it should be taught. The only person in a given classroom whose responsibility it is to resist the introduction of improper educational experiences for children is the *teacher*. He can, however, be much more effective in making those decisions if he has the support of his school administrator. Pressures from the community and the nation with respect to what the elementary school science curriculum should contain must be accepted, evaluated, and acted upon by you, the classroom teacher. For many years such pressures were very difficult to reject because the existing curriculum for elementary school science did little more than give the children experience in reading and, therefore, there was no logical defense against community, state, and national curriculum pressures. That void in the elementary school curriculum is rapidly being filled, however, by national curriculum-development groups. At the present moment there are in existence curricula that will allow a teacher to develop such an attractive and efficient science program that the pressures from outside the school to adopt a "pet idea" of some group can be effectively neutralized. We do not mean to infer that offers of suggestions, guidance, and assistance from the community should be ignored. But, if an effective science program is under way, the attention it draws will motivate interested citizens to assist what is being done rather than attempt to introduce something different.

In order for a teacher to select his classroom curriculum, he must first know what is available. Every teacher must, therefore, keep abreast of the curriculum developments going on in science education. Professional periodicals, meetings, colleagues, and the science consultant of the system are the most important sources for keeping informed about the frontiers of science education. The services of a science consultant are consistently being made available to teachers by more and more school systems. Schools are realizing that each teacher cannot plan his own program independently of the other teachers in the system. To have the learner develop a conceptual structure of science in which each year's experience will use the previous year's learnings and demand the succeeding year's, demonstrates that the program must have someone who is coordinating all parts, testing the effectiveness of new ideas, and replacing portions of the program when necessary. This "someone" also can assist the teacher in introducing new ideas, trying new materials, or even using different and/or novel teaching techniques. Such a person is a science consultant. As school systems develop a complete understanding of what science contributes to the intellectual development of a child, the services of a science consultant will become more and more available to teachers and, of course, the improvement that results from those services will ultimately benefit the children. The primary function of the science consultant will be (and is) to assist the teachers in surveying the curricula available, selecting what is appropriate for a given school in a particular educational system in a certain geographical location, and implementing that selection.[8]

Will enough and different curricula be available so the consultant and teachers will have sufficient choices? The trend is most certainly in that direction. As we have previously stated, the national curriculum groups have produced a great variety and a considerable quantity of materials for elementary school science. At least two types of programs are available which will make the building of an integrated science program for the elementary schools feasible. Those two types of programs are the "sequential" and the "unit" plans. When a sequential program is adopted, the entire "package" should be implemented. In adopting such a program it is necessary that its purposes

[8] For a rather comprehensive treatment of the productive relationship which should exist between a teacher and a consultant see Kenneth G. George, *How to Utilize the Services of a Science Consultant* (Washington, D.C.: National Science Teachers Association, 1965).

be understood because most such sequential programs are devoted to a set of purposes for elementary school science for which they faithfully produce materials to accomplish. The adopting of such a sequential program is very advantageous in many ways; for example, the problem of coordination is minimized, the introduction of a new teacher to the system by the science consultant and other teachers in the program is facilitated, and the materials problem follows the same pattern each year. There remains, however, the first hurdle that must be crossed in adopting a sequential program—its purposes and the purposes the school wishes the pupils to achieve through the study of science must be in harmony. The purposes of the newly developed sequential programs are in agreement with the purposes that have been emphasized in this book.

There have been developed by some curriculum development groups, plans of study in elementary school science which conform to the accepted definition of a unit—a major understanding. Each of these units leads the child through an investigation of a given topic in some depth. The teacher and consultant are left with the decision of putting these units together into a teaching pattern. There is a degree of flexibility in this scheme of curriculum development which is not found in the sequential approach. There can be, however, serious lack of continuity that occurs automatically with the sequential plan. The unit plan has specific objectives for each unit, and these must be completely accepted before any unit can be used in the classroom. While, in general, the units have different specific objectives the overall purposes of the units developed by each development project are in complete harmony with purposes we have suggested for elementary school science.

There now exists adequate curricula from which a teacher and his consultant can select those experiences that are needed to implement the established purposes of elementary school science education. This development will give the elementary school teacher a degree of freedom he has not had in the past.

One trend which is developing and which seems to have a firm basis for its appearance is the disappearance of a textbook that provides the children with information. In place of the textbook the recent science curriculum developments are providing the learner with a work sheet and/or manual which he uses to collect data. These data are then used by the child when the class discusses its findings. The pupil has before him during the discussion what he felt about a certain object, event, or property and has an opportunity to compare his observations and thinking with his peers.

Throughout this book we have emphasized the elementary school science curriculum developments which national study groups have produced. We are fully aware, and so should you be, that such programs represent a type of pressure on the teacher from a national level. These curriculum innovations have been supported by such prestigious groups as the National Science Foundation, the United States Office of Education, and private foundations. These curricula have, however, an extremely important factor in their favor; they have all been developed with the assistance of elementary school teachers, as well as scientists. Furthermore, all of these plans of study in science have been evaluated for their classroom usability *by teaching them to children.* The children, in other words, have been the principal evaluators of these curricula.

Will such elementary school science curriculum-development groups continue to be necessary in the future? This is, of course, a difficult question to answer, but based on what is currently being produced by other curriculum sources, the answer, it seems likely, is that there will be a need for national curriculum groups to continue to function. If in the future, curriculum-development schemes are devised by individuals and/or private groups, then the need for such massive curriculum efforts may pass out of existence. Judging by what is occurring at the present writing, however, these national curriculum-development groups will continue to have a place on the scene of American education.

Teaching science by the inquiry approach is not easy. It requires the dedication of the classroom teacher, the support of the school's administration, and courage for a school to do what is best for the children in order to develop their rational powers—their ability to think—as well as increase the complexity with which they think. A program in elementary school science which will accomplish all of the goals outlined in this book will require a considerable amount of time to plan and implement. But the program's goal will not be accomplished unless teachers and administrators select a starting point. So, as John F. Kennedy said in his 1961 inaugural address, "Let us begin!"

APPENDIXES

A | Research in Formal Operations[*]

The problem which we set out to solve was simply this[1]: at which of the intellectual levels of Piaget are the students in Oklahoma's secondary school (grades 7–12) operating. We divided the state of Oklahoma into several sections, based upon the type of activity the citizens used to support themselves—agriculture, mining, industrial, etc. We also took cognizance of the rural-urban-ghetto concentrations of population. After the several sections of the state had been identified, schools were randomly selected from them and students were randomly selected from each school. All the interviews in a particular school were completed at the same time; the interviewing was done between September 1, 1970 and March 1, 1971. Because the participating schools were promised anonymity, they will not be listed here.

The decision was made to first establish that every student interviewed was at least concrete operational. The conservation of solid amount and conservation of weight were selected for the purpose. The first of these conservations is normally accomplished at about 7 years of age[2] (see Table 3–1, Chapter 3). The conservation of weight is not accomplished, according to Piaget,[3] until about 10 years of

[*] From *Teaching Science in the Secondary School* by John W. Renner and Don G. Stafford. Copyright © 1972 by John W. Renner and Don G. Stafford. By permission of Harper & Row, Publishers, Inc.

[1] Formulating the procedures for this project and gathering the data represented a tremendous amount of work. We are grateful to the schools for their cooperation, and especially grateful to Dr. Joe McKinnon, Larry McKinney, Mrs. Martha Nell Dodson, and Mrs. Jill De Spain who interviewed many students.

[2] Jean Piaget and Barbel Inhelder, *The Psychology of the Child* (New York: Basic Books, 1969), p. 99.

[3] Jean Piaget, *The Psychology of Intelligence* (Totowa, N.J.: Littlefield, Adams, 1966), p. 147.

age; compare that statement with the data given in Table 3–1. Our reasoning was that those two tasks would span a wide enough age range to enable us to establish concrete operations at varying levels.

The conservation of volume appears, according to Piaget,[4] at between 11 and 12 years of age and indicates the entry into the formal operations period. Two tasks were selected from those suggested by Piaget and Inhelder[5] for determining the ability of a student to think formally: the elimination of contradictions and the principle of exclusion (see Chapter 3). These were selected because they embrace elements of all the other tasks suggested by Piaget and Inhelder[6] and because they are efficient to administer. The results we obtained have led us to believe that the reciprocal implications task should probably have been substituted for the elimination of contradiction. What follows is a description of how each of the tasks was administered and scored. The total number of students interviewed was 588.

1. The conservation of solid amount

The student was allowed to work with two balls of clay until he was convinced each ball contained the same amount. The examiner then distorted one of the balls, and the student was asked if the distorted clay or the clay ball contained more, or if each contained the same amount. The task was administered to establish if the student was concrete operational. If he successfully completed the task, he was rated IIA and given one point. Piaget has stated that the child learns to solve this problem at about 7 or 8 years of age.[7]

2. The conservation of weight

Piaget believes that this ability is developed at 9 or 10 years.[8] The student was given two balls of clay and allowed to work with them until he believed their weights were the same. The examiner then distorted one of the balls and asked the student to tell him (without picking up the clay) which portion of clay weighed more, or if they weighed the same. A correct response placed the student in Class IIB and yielded him two points.

[4] Ibid.
[5] Barbel Inhelder and Jean Piaget, *The Growth of Logical Thinking from Childhood to Adolescence* (New York: Basic Books, 1958), chaps. 1–5.
[6] Ibid.
[7] Piaget and Inhelder, op. cit., p. 99.
[8] Ibid.

3. The conservation of volume

Piaget has stated that this ability is developed at 11 or 12 years of age.[9] The student was presented with two identical containers containing equal amounts of water and allowed to work with the volumes until he had convinced himself the amounts were equal. He was then asked if the distorted ball of clay (from task 2) would push the water level up more, if the nondistorted ball would push the level up more, or if the two amounts of clay would push the levels up equally. Successful completion of the task confirmed the student's level at IIB, and he was given two points.

4. Conservation of volume using two identically shaped cylinders of different weights

The third task used objects of equal weights and different shapes. This task appeals to the nonconserver of volume who had successfully completed task 2 by centering his attention on weight and believing that the levels of the liquid would rise equally because the objects weighed the same. In the task the student was given two metal cylinders of exactly the same size, but with very obvious difference in their weights. All the foregoing properties of the cylinders were pointed out to the student. He was next presented with two identical cylinders partially filled with water and allowed to adjust the levels until he was convinced that each tube contained *exactly* the same amount of water. The student was then asked if the heavy cylinder would push the water level up more, if the lighter cylinder would push the level up more, or if the cylinder would push the levels up the same. Successful completion of the task placed the student in class IIIA and he was awarded three points. If he predicted incorrectly and then explained the event after he saw it, he was classified as IIB and awarded two points.

5. The elimination of contradictions[10]

The student was presented with a small container of water and two wooden blocks. One block was large and heavy and would float; the other block was small and light but sank. The student was asked to predict which block would sink and which would float, or if the blocks would both sink or both float. The prediction was merely a device to involve the examinee in the problem, and no points were

[9] Ibid.
[10] Inhelder and Piaget, op. cit., pp. 20–45.

awarded for a correct prediction. If the student recognized that a rule probably existed to explain what he saw and that the explanation involved both the weight of the blocks and their volumes, he was ranked IIB and awarded two points. If the student recognized that the explanation involved the relationship of the volume and weight of the block to an equivalent volume and weight of water, he was rated IIIA and given three points. When the examinee could identify all the variables, order them, derive an hypothesis, test it, and state the results in a logical fashion, he was rated as completely formal operational, IIIB, and awarded four points.

6. The exclusion of irrelevant variables[11]

The examinee was presented a pendulum whose length could be easily changed and three different-sized weights which could be used for the pendulum bob. He was told to do as many experiments as he needed to, using many different lengths of string and all the various size weights, until he could explain what he needed to do to make the pendulums go fast or slow. The variables of string, angle, and push were also usually pointed out to the student. If the examinee recognized that length was the only relevant variable, i.e., if he excluded length, push, and angle, he was rated IIB and awarded two points. If he not only excluded the irrelevant variables but hypothesized a solution to the problem and demonstrated his solution, he was rated IIIA and given three points. If the student could state a general rule about pendulums in such a way that it could be tested, he was scored IIIB and awarded four points.

Table A–1 gives the sample size and the distribution of scores by grade level. Those receiving a score of 5 or below are preoperational. One wonders how eight such people reached senior high school (grades 10–12). There are many combinations of scores which would result in a total score of between 6 and 11 and not include a single IIIA rating. That group was rated purely concrete operational. By successfully completing all tasks through the second conservation of volume and scoring IIIA on the two remaining tasks, a score of 14 was reached. We felt that was the minimum achievement necessary to be called formal operational. That left scores 12 and 13 unaccounted for. This group demonstrated more intellectual development than the group scoring 11 and below, so they were more than concrete operational. Still they were not formal. We called them post-concrete operational.

[11] Ibid., pp. 67–79.

Table A–1

Score	7	8	9	10	11	12	Totals
				Grade			
0–5	5	3	4	4	3	1	20
6	8	5	5	6	5	3	32
7	11	20	10	9	6	10	66
8	23	16	12	19	16	3	89
9	13	13	12	9	14	15	76
10	15	20	19	11	13	19	97
11	5	7	16	11	11	13	63
12	8	9	4	10	13	6	50
13	5	9	3	5	6	9	37
14	2	3	6	5	4	6	26
15	0	1	1	3	5	8	18
16	1	2	2	2	3	4	14
	$n = 96$	$n = 108$	$n = 94$	$n = 94$	$n = 99$	$n = 97$	$n = 588$

Table A–2

Score	Classification	Number of students
0–5	Preoperational	20
6–11	Concrete operational	423
12–13	Post-concrete operational	87
14–16	Formal operational	58

Using the foregoing grouping procedures, the data in Table A–1 can be reduced as shown in Table A–2. Of the 58 formal operational group only the group scoring 16 could be called fully formal operational. That number is 14 of 588—2.2 percent! Equally important is the size of the purely concrete operational group! 423 of 588—72 percent. When the preoperational group is added to the concrete operational group, this latter percentage becomes 75.3. In other words, 75.3 percent of the students in the secondary schools are still, at best, concrete operational—a stage of intellectual development which Piaget's data has told him children begin to leave about 11 years of age and which they have fully left by age 15. The students interviewed were between 12 and 19 years of age.

Table A–3 gives a distribution of students scoring 11 or less on the six tasks; this enables you to ascertain where the non-formal operational thinkers are in the secondary school.

Table A–3

Grade	Sample size	Number scoring 11 or less	Percentage of the sample
7	96	80	83
8	108	83	77
9	94	77	82
10	94	68	73
11	99	70	71
12	97	64	66

Table A–4

Grade	Mean	Mean gain
7	9.07	—
8	9.45	0.38
9	9.66	0.21
10	9.72	0.06
11	9.95	0.23
12	10.74	0.79

Table A–4 shows one last piece of information, which perhaps will allow you to make some judgments about where the movement toward formal operation is taking place. The Mean Gain column in Table A–4 should be interpreted as mean gain within a grade—i.e., 0.38 means that from the seventh grade to the eighth grade the average gain per child was that much. The means column is simply the arithmetic average score per grade. We believe that because no grade mean is above 11, what is being done in grades K–12 to promote formal operational development needs to be examined.

The Research Results and Science Teaching

The data shown in Table A–3 have some commanding implications for science teaching. Consider graders 7, 8, and 9. No less than 77 percent of any group you will face is concrete operational, and in order for those students to profit educationally and intellectually from school, they *must* (not should, *must*) be interacting with concrete objects, events, and situations. In science that means that the course must be centered around the laboratory and *not* around a textbook.

Courses like those described in Chapter 7 (for example, IPS and TSM) are the types this group needs to enable them to profit intellectually. These results speak very clearly to administrators, those designing buildings, and the budget makers. To say that a junior high school science program exists without a laboratory is to say that a program exists which is nonprofitable to the learners (furthermore, it does not represent science). If any learner gains accrue from a nonlaboratory junior high school science program, they are gains in reading skill and vocabulary. The foregoing statements need to be carefully considered when junior high school science programs are being evaluated. The research cited here supports our position and, to our knowledge, no research evidence exists to refute that position.

Consider the data shown in Table A–3 for grades 10, 11, and 12. Here again, the students need the concrete experience of working with the laboratory. This is particularly true at the tenth-grade level, where biology has traditionally been taught and most of that population enrolls in it. Any teacher facing a biology class can be nearly certain that about 70 percent of those present are concrete operational thinkers. Now consider such concepts as the DNA molecule, gene mutations, and the chemical basis of life. From our perspective, such topics and concrete operational learners are grossly incompatible. For about 27 percent of the learners such topics are not possible but probably represent the exact type of subject matter needed.

Theories of ionization, particle versus the wave theory of light, the mathematical structure of relativity, molecular orbital theories, the relationship between bright-line spectra and the energy levels of electrons in an atom, and electronegativity all represent topics which are generally found in high school physics and chemistry courses. Obviously they are abstractions which require formal operational thinking. Now look at the data in Table A–3 for grades 11 and 12. Not too many formal operational thinkers are found there. True, physics and chemistry are not studied by a typical sample of grades 11 and 12. Teaching experience with those subjects at levels cited leads us to infer that the percentage of formal operational thinkers in these grades is probably much higher than the data in Table A–3 show. Even if the percentages of formal operational thinkers were increased by 50 percent over those found in our sample, that would not tell us that those enrolled in physics and chemistry are all formal operational. If, however, the subject matter of those two courses is carefully analyzed, most of it will be found to be suitable only for the formal operational thinker. Acceleration, for example, is a rate of change. That is a mental operation on a mental operation—exactly as formal operations are defined. Perhaps we should simply urge chemistry and physics teachers to determine where students are in their intellectual development spiral.

Testing the Evaluation Techniques

As was explained earlier, we adopted certain of the techniques designed and utilized by Piaget and Inhelder to isolate the formal operational thinker. The question that always plagues an investigator when he uses techniques designed by another is: Do those techniques really measure what they purport to measure? Stated in terms of this study, the question would be: Do the conservation of volume, the elimination of contradictions, and the exclusion tasks actually isolate the formal thinker? We had to know.

We were reminded that Piaget had described the formal operational person as "an individual who thinks beyond the present and forms theories about everything, delighting especially in consideration of that which is not."[12] This individual, then, can form theories or define axioms and then reason without regard to reality. He can fantasize, but his fantasy is always legitimately anchored in logic, although that logic need not be connected with reality. He can, in other words, reason with the "If . . . , then . . . , therefore . . ." construct.

Our attention was then directed to the many fields in which thinking with the foregoing construct represents the field itself. Bruner defines this type of intellectual operation as being "the stock in trade of the logician, the scientist or the abstract thinker."[13] Here, then, represented the population from which we could draw to test the validity of the Piagetian tasks we were using. The field of science was immediately ruled out as a possible group to use, for obvious reasons; the tasks were too closely allied to science in general and physics in particular. For similar reasons the field of mathematics was also excluded. The population available to us of those engaged in the pursuit of pure logic was not large enough to afford an adequate test population. We were then reminded that the "If . . . , then . . . , therefore . . ." construct was also the stock in the trade of the lawyer. He must always find the *if*, apply it to the *then*, and arrive at the *therefore*. All of this must be done in the abstract. We had located our test population—law students! In order to survive in the study of law, they have to think mainly on an abstract level. The question remained

[12] Piaget, *Psychology of Intelligence*, op. cit., p. 148.
[13] Jerome S. Bruner, *The Process of Education* (New York: Random House Vintage Books, 1960), p. 37.

Table A–5

Task	Score			
	IIA	IIB	IIIA	IIIB
Conservation of volume using clay	7	37		
Elimination of contradictions		6	15	23
Exclusion	6	7	12	19
$n = 44$				

as to whether or not our tasks would show them to be formal operational.

The aid of two law schools was enlisted. One had a complete resident population, and the other had a predominantly working, night-school population. We randomly sampled the first and third year classes (a total of 44 students) on the conservation of volume, the elimination of contradictions, and the exclusion principle. The results are shown in Table A–5. The scores (IIA, IIB, IIIA, IIIB) shown on the top horizontal have the same meaning as before. You will remember that the highest score possible on the conservation of volume using clay was IIB. The number in each cell of Table A–5 reflects the number of law students who achieved that particular score.

Interpreting the data in Table A–5 is essential to making statements about the validity of the tasks to isolate formal operational thinkers. You will notice that 37 of 44 (84 percent) scored the maximum on the first task. Furthermore, the IIIB cells contain the greatest numbers of any for tasks 2 and 3. In other words, there were more IIIB thinkers (completely formal operational) in our sample than any other level. With that thought, we agreed that anyone who reached IIIA and IIIB would be called formal operational. Using that criterion, 38 of 44 (86.5 percent) of the sample are formal operational on the elimination of contradictions, and 31 of 44 (71 percent) reached formal operations on the exclusion task. Since these two tasks both isolate formal thinkers, the data from both cells could be combined to give a general notion of their ability to isolate the formal thinker. When that is done (69 + 88), a percentage achievement of the law students tested is 78.5 percent. If the data from the conservation of volume are added (106 + 132), a percentage of 81 percent emerges. In other words, the body we defined as formal operational achieved 81 percent on its evaluation. We felt we had tasks that would allow us to isolate the formal operational thinker.

B | Overview of Concepts Found in Science—A Process Approach

The primary objective of *Science—A Process Approach* is that the child acquire competence in the processes of science. Children develop this competence as they use the processes in science experiences, and as they behave as scientists, they learn science. This section reviews briefly the variety of science content of the program under the headings: physical sciences, biological sciences, and mathematics. The letters in parentheses indicate the Part in which an experience is encountered.

Physical Sciences

The physical science content is drawn from physics, chemistry, and earth sciences. Because simple physical systems are relatively easy to investigate, there is more physics than chemistry content in the early Parts. Chemistry and earth science content is found mainly in the last three Parts.

Solids and liquids and their properties

Pupils use all of their senses to observe and distinguish between various solid objects and liquids. Properties that can be observed directly are introduced first. The pupils observe color, shape, size, texture, odor, and taste (cautiously—when the teacher tells them they may) in identifying, describing, and classifying objects (A). The properties of luster and hardness are introduced later (E) and are used

Reproduced with permission from *Commentary for Teachers of Science—A Process Approach*, American Association for the Advancement of Science, Washington, D.C., 1971, pp. 179–187.

together with other properties, such as color, in identifying minerals.

The pupils further investigate the property of color when they construct a color wheel (C) and when they use a grating spectroscope (G) to observe the spectrum of white light and of light that is transmitted by filters of different colors.

One property that distinguishes solids and liquids from gases is called *compressibility*. The pupils investigate compressibility of solids and liquids at two levels. First (C), they put solids, such as sand or paper clips, and water into balloons and try to compress them in a cylinder fitted with a piston. At the higher level (F), they put water and other liquids into a graduated syringe and try to measure their compressibility by increasing the force on the plunger.

Magnetic properties of certain solids are introduced (B) to give the children an opportunity to observe a property that is not immediately obvious. Two bars may look alike, but to find the one that is a magnet the pupil must test both bars with paper clips, iron nails, or other iron objects. He learns that some objects are attracted by a magnet while others are not. Later (D), he observes the magnetic field around a magnet as it is revealed in a pattern of iron filings. In the same exercise, the child identifies the north-seeking and south-seeking poles of a magnet. He also learns to construct an electromagnet and compares its properties to those of a permanent magnet. Later (F), the children map the magnetic field around a magnet by constructing compass-direction lines. Interpreting these in relation to the geographic orientation of the magnet on the earth's surface, they discover that the earth itself behaves like a large magnet.

After working with properties such as physical state and magnetism, the child is ready to work with properties such as density (G). Density is calculated from measurements of two properties—mass and volume. The pupils determine density both graphically (by plotting the masses and volumes of objects) and arithmetically (by dividing the mass by the volume). Some children may independently discover Archimedes' principle in this exercise.

The pupils compare the viscosities of various liquids in two ways (G): by the rates at which similar objects fall through columns of the liquids and by the rates at which liquids flow through an orifice. In this exercise, the pupils investigate the effect of temperature on viscosity and experiment to determine whether or not there is a simple relationship between the densities and the viscosities of liquids.

In another exercise (D), the pupils investigate the effect of the size of an object on the rate at which it falls through water. They shake up a mixture of clay, sand, pebbles, and water, and note that the solids settle out with the pebbles mainly on the bottom, the sand in the middle, and the clay on top.

The most sophisticated property of solids considered in *Science—A Process Approach* is semipermeability (G). Children investigate various plastic membranes and measure qualitatively or semi-quantitatively whether various substances in aqueous solution will pass through them.

Gases and their properties

As one might expect, children have more difficulty with the idea of gases than with the concept of solids and liquids. There are probably two main reasons for this. First, there are not many gases that can be seen; second, most primary grade children think *gas* means gasoline. Gases are introduced early (B) and are used in ten exercises in the following five Parts. The pupils balance an inflated and an uninflated balloon and learn that air has mass (B). Later (C), they put an inflated balloon into a cylinder fitted with a plunger and observe the decrease in size of the balloon as air is forced into the cylinder. The compressibility of air and also carbon dioxide is investigated quantitatively (G) by measuring the volume of gas in a graduated syringe as increasing force is applied to the plunger. In this same exercise, the pupils investigate the effect of reducing the force on the plunger of a syringe partly filled with air, with the plunger down, by placing weights on a pan fastened to the plunger. With this apparatus, the pupils make a rough measurement of atmospheric pressure and come surprisingly close to the proper value of about 10 newtons per square centimeter.

The pupils collect and test for carbon dioxide and oxygen (G). They learn that carbon dioxide is a gas that turns limewater milky and that turns bromthymol blue solution from green to yellow; they learn that oxygen is a gas that makes a glowing splint burst into flame. Armed with these operational definitions, they test the gases produced by *Elodea* in light, by seltzer tablets in water, by hydrogen peroxide and manganese dioxide, by germinating seeds, by yeast fermenting sugar, and by a carbonated drink.

Changes in properties

Describing properties that change is a more difficult task for children than describing static properties. It is partly for this reason that that chemistry content is used more in the latter Parts of *Science—A*

Process Approach. Chemical properties of substances are observed only when their properties change. The first exercise involving change in properties requires children to observe and describe color changes (A), such as the change in color of pieces of cloth dyed with Congo red dye as the pieces are dipped into a solution of citric acid or sodium bicarbonate. A follow-up to this exercise is one with content from the biological sciences, observing color changes in plants (B).

In other exercises, children observe and describe solids changing to liquids (A). In an investigation of the rate at which water evaporates from different kinds of cloth, they are introduced to the fact that liquids evaporate (D). They determine the rate of evaporation by weighing each piece of cloth at intervals, and they investigate the effects of temperature and air movement on evaporation rate.

Several exercises with content from the earth sciences involve change. Children observe and record wind velocity, cloud cover, air temperature, and other aspects of the weather (B) and describe the changes in these characteristics from day to day. They construct a simple sundial (C) and observe changes in the direction and length of a shadow during the day. Later (F), they make similar observations of the shortest shadow. Combining this information with their investigation of the magnetic field of the earth, they identify and define magnetic declination.

The pupils investigate chemical reactions (E) as a means of identifying materials. They work with four white powders (baking soda, baking powder, corn starch, and talc) and three liquids (water, vinegar, and dilute iodine solution). They prepare liquid-solid pairs in all the possible combinations, observe any changes that occur, and record their data on punch cards. The recorded information is then used to identify an unknown powder which is one of the powders they have investigated previously. In another exercise on chemical change (F), the pupils study the variables that affect the development of the color of blueprint and Ozalid papers. In that same Part (F), they measure the time required for seltzer tablets to dissolve in water of different temperatures. They plot their data on a graph and learn that as temperature increases reaction time decreases, but that the relationship is not linear.

Rate of change of volume of an enclosed gas is used as a measure of the rate at which steel wool rusts under various conditions (G). The pupils learn that as steel wool rusts something disappears from the air. A related exercise is an investigation of the burning time of a candle covered by a glass jar (D). In that exercise, the children do not measure the change in volume of gas. Instead, they measure the burning time under jars of different volumes and find that the larger the jar the longer the candle burns. The jars must, of course, be approximately the same shape.

Temperature and heat

Pupils are introduced to temperature with comparative adjectives such as *warmer* and *cooler* (A). They order containers of water first by feeling them and then by using a color-coded thermometer. Next (B), they use a thermometer with a numbered scale and later (C), one with a numbered scale which includes negative numbers. The child is already familiar with the fact that an incandescent light gives off white light and that an electric toaster wire glows red. He learns (C) that the color of a glowing object can be used as a measure of the temperature of the object.

The term *heat* is first used in an exercise (E) in which the children compare the rates at which rods of different materials conduct heat from the flame of an alcohol lamp. The concept of heat is developed further and a technique for measuring heat is learned in an exercise (G) in which the pupils heat different (measured) volumes of water over similar candles. They learn that the calorie is the unit in which heat is measured. At the end of this exercise, they measure the rate at which heat is transferred from an immersion heater to a measured volume of water. A little later in the same year, the pupils use their knowledge of how to measure heat in an exercise (G) in which they measure roughly the amount of heat that is produced in a film cassette filled with water as the cassette is rubbed back and forth many times between two meter sticks fastened together with stout rubber bands.

Force and motion

The science content of almost one-tenth of the exercises in *Science —A Process Approach* involves force and motion. The first exercise (A) in the group emphasizes motion such as a fish swimming or a flag blowing in the wind; it also discusses direction of motion. Next, the children roll a ball down an inclined plane arranged so that the ball strikes a box at the bottom of the plane. By using balls of different weights, they learn that the heavier the ball is, the farther the box will move.

The children become acquainted with the concept of speed in an exercise (D) in which they use a stopwatch and metric tape to measure the speed at which various objects move. The idea of speed is used in several later exercises. In one of these (D), they are introduced to the notion of relative motion as they first describe the motion of a block in a wagon that is being pulled past them. Then they describe the lack of motion, relative to themselves, as they sit in the moving wagon, holding the block.

Circular motion is introduced in an exercise (D) in which the pupils describe the motion of an object placed in different positions on a phonograph turntable. Later (E), they measure the linear speed of different size wheels rotating at the same speed and learn that the larger wheels roll farther than the smaller ones in the same amount of time. They learn that the ratio of the circumference to the diameter of a circle is always the same, about 3.1, and use this knowledge to predict how far a wheel will roll when it makes one or several rotations.

The pupils use an equal-arm balance for the first time (B) and learn that it is in balance when the earth-pull on the two pans is equal; here they begin to become familiar with the concept of *force*. Later (C), the pupils use springs and a color-strip scale to measure not only earth-pull, but also the force required to move a box across the floor.

They use vectors to represent forces in Part D, using arrows to show direction and magnitude. They also learn that if all the forces acting on a movable object are balanced, the object will not move; if one of the forces is removed, the forces are unbalanced, and the object will move.

By attaching a rubber band to a four wheel cart, stretching the band and letting the cart go, the pupil learns that the farther the band is stretched the farther the cart will roll before it stops (E). In this exercise, the pupil learns to use the term *acceleration* to describe change in speed—either speeding up or slowing down. Pupils' abilities to use vectors are reinforced in this exercise. In the following exercise (E), *the newton* is introduced as the unit of force. Throughout the remaining parts of the program the pupils are expected to be able to measure and describe the magnitudes of forces in newtons. Forces are considered in several other exercises. For example, in Part F the pupils learn the law of the lever.

The terms *inertia* and *mass* are introduced in Part F, but in previous exercises the pupils investigate phenomena which lay the groundwork for a discussion of those terms. In one of these exercises (E), the pupil is given several cylinders all of the same diameter but of different lengths. Some of the cylinders are solid and some are hollow. Some are made of steel, some of aluminum, and some of plastic. The pupil rolls pairs of cylinders down an inclined plane and tries to determine what variable or variables account for the fact that some cylinders roll faster than others. He tries mass, length, and material from which the cylinder is made and finally reaches the conclusion that all of the solid cylinders roll faster than the hollow ones.

The idea of inertia becomes explicit in the exercise in which mass is introduced as the measure of inertia (F). In that exercise, the pupils use rubber bands to accelerate carts with different loads and a vibrator to compare the masses of various small objects.

Miscellaneous topics

In several exercises, the pupils investigate electric circuits. First (E), they use a simple dry-cell-and-bulb circuit to test the hidden connections of terminals on circuit boards. Next (E), they learn to identify and construct series and parallel circuits using several bulbs and dry cells. The pupils use a simple circuit to test a variety of substances to determine whether they will conduct electricity (E). In this exercise, they also test the hypothesis that good conductors of heat are also good conductors of electricity.

The pupils do some work with light and optics in the last three Parts of *Science—A Process Approach*. They reflect beams of light with mirrors and learn that the angle of reflection is equal to the angle of incidence (E). They use lenses and pin-hole cameras and investigate the relationship of the sizes of the object and the image and the distances of the object and image from the lens or pin hole (F).

Biological Sciences

Biological concepts form the bases of exercises throughout the entire span of *Science—A Process Approach*. The exercises are intertwined with those that describe and measure the physical universe, thus satisfying in major degree the specification that the child learn as much as he can about the interaction between living things and their environment.

Observing and describing living things

In their earliest school experiences, children are introduced to living things and things that have been living. The children learn to identify similarities and differences of living things and those that have been living. Using these similarities and differences, they classify them.

Then, using these classification schemes a child describe;
so that another child can readily identify it. These abilitie
solid basis for later and more detailed study of interaction
things with their environment. In *Science—A Process App*
B), children become acquainted with a multitude of living tr
as leaves, nuts, shells, animals, and plants in an aquarium,   ... animals and plants in their natural environment. They begin to see what
distinguishes living from nonliving objects around them. Living things
eat, grow, reproduce, and move about freely. The children describe
their color, their size, their shape, their symmetry or lack of it, their
odor, and their locomotion. Soon they are able to describe color
changes that occur in plant leaves and the movement of a potted plant
in response to sunlight or the response of a sensitive plant to touch
or heat (B).

Modes of living and behavior of animals

Soon after, the child starts his investigation of modes of living and
behavior of animals. He is ready to study how animals walk, run, or
fly and can investigate for himself their responses to stimuli. He
studies living things in an aquarium (C) in greater depth than he did
earlier (B); he walks through the woods observing animal tracks and
traces, inferring the existence and function of claws and beaks, and
inferring the strengths of other animal parts as, for example, legs for
digging (D). The children begin their study of life cycles early (C)
and then meet other examples as their study of animals is continued
in later grades. Use of living animals rather than pictures is emphasized, and field trips for collection of species are recommended. Young
children like to hear and read about dinosaurs. This interest is used
as a basis for study of scale drawings in pictures and maps (C).

Because children enjoy having live animals in the classroom and
can learn a great deal about their development and behavior from day
to day observations, several exercises are included to guide investigation of specific phenomena. Two of these are *Guinea Pigs in a Maze*
(E) and *Nutrition of a Small Warm-Blooded Animal* (F). The guinea
pigs are kept in the classroom two weeks or so before the children
place them in a maze they have constructed. The children record
running time in the maze over several trials. They then compare
changes in learning time in several trials of two or more guinea pigs.
The nutrition exercise provides for a number of variations in the study
of warm-blooded animals including the study of reproduction of
gerbils and perhaps an introduction to population problems. A further

illustration of the rapid multiplication of populations is provided by the study of imaginary animals called *glurks* (F). Glurks are small animals that separate into two parts, each a new glurk, at the end of each day.

The children study the responses of brine shrimp hatched in the classroom to changes in environmental factors (F). Will brine shrimp hatch in fresh water? Will they hatch faster in warm water than in cold water? Can brine shrimp live if given sugar for food instead of yeast? What is the effect of crowding on young shrimp? These and other questions lead to hypotheses the children test.

An introduction to genetics is provided in two exercises. One is concerned with tasters and nontasters using PTC papers (F). An experiment with reproduction of two generations of drosophila (G) enables the children to study the passing on of dominant and recessive characteristics through two generations.

Human behavior and physiology

While children recognize that humans are part of the family of animals, this content review treats human studies separately from animal studies. In the human category, there are a number of studies that ordinarily are classified as belonging to the social rather than the biological sciences.

First, the children learn to use all of their senses in making accurate observations. They see, listen, smell, taste (with caution), and examine a variety of objects for texture (smooth or rough), for weight, for hardness, for the presence of warmth, and for furriness. They experience what they can do with their bodies through their senses.

Later, when their interest in themselves and their bodies has increased, they are ready to investigate such body functions as the path by which stimuli pass through their central nervous system to produce responses (F), whether they are tasters or nontasters of PTC paper (F), and the variations in their perceptual judgment in viewing optical illusions (G). They count their own and their classmates' pulsebeats, as a doctor does. They also count the number of times they inhale (or exhale) in a minute, and measure the volume of the air they exhale, using a polyethylene tube to collect the air exhaled (F). Simple charts are provided for them in tracing a stimulus to the eye that may result in a response with hand or foot. That some can taste PTC paper and others not taste it (with little middle ground) comes as a revelation to them. Some parts of their experimenting with their own perceptual judgment may also be a surprise when they discover what factors may modify this judgment. They also find out about how they learn and why forgetting takes place; they investigate their reaction time to light, sound, or touch (F), and the resolving power of the eye (G). They learn codes for sending messages in order to study how interference may affect learning (G). For example, if a new code is to be learned after they already know one, what characteristics of the two codes will interfere with their new learning?

In the tryout classes, children often had great enthusiasm for these psychological topics that have rarely been introduced in elementary schools. Although an immediate reaction was often that these topics are "not science," the application of their competence in the processes of science soon convinced the children that the methods of the natural sciences are equally useful in social studies, which then become social sciences.

Microbiology

In *Science—A Process Approach* the child may first use a microscope in examining the surface of a leaf (D). He sees small openings (stomates) through which water can pass in transpiration. Then he becomes more proficient in the use of the microscope in the study of living cells (E) and in measuring small things by comparing them with the size of the field of the microscope (F).

He examines both living things (algae, elodea, insect wings, tissues of vegetables, yeast) and nonliving things (cork, grains of salt, sugar or sand) under the microscope, constructs drawings of what he sees and makes comparisons of cell structures. The children also examine more carefully the growth of mold colonies in investigation of factors in the environment that affect mold growth (E). Much earlier (B), they examine mold gardens and describe their appearance and growth changes. Finally (G), they meet living things that produce carbon dioxide in the process of fermentation—again investigating environmental factors that affect the rate of fermentation.

Seeds, seed germination, and plant growth

Most elementary school children have enjoyed the experience of planting seeds in the spring and watching them grow. In *Science—A Process Approach*, the children have this experience in each of at least three years in a new investigation each time. They see and measure how some seeds expand by soaking up water before planting (B). They cut open the seeds and examine the embryo plant with some care. They observe the growth of roots, stems and leaves of seedlings at regular intervals, watching the changes in a grid or series of markings they have put on the plant part (D).

Some of the other phenomena related to plant growth and development that the children investigate are growth from parts of plants (bulbs, leaves, or a section of a potato) (C), environmental factors affecting orientation of growth, such as sunlight and gravity (F), and how plants grow in various colors of light (G) and with different soil nutrients (G). They test for the presence of starch in the growing plants as they are introduced to photosynthesis.

The pupils investigate the transpiration of water from plants by measuring the amount of water used each hour by a plant during different parts of the day, and they predict the amount of water that will be used during other hours in other parts of the day. By wrapping the plants in a polyethylene bag, they find that moisture is lost from the leaves and stems. Then, they measure the amount of water lost (D). In Part E, they study the loss of moisture from potatoes by evaporation. Parts of plants (cotyledon, stem, leaf, petiole) are identified by operational definitions so that these terms become a part of the children's vocabulary (F). When they are studying sections of cut things, the children observe the growth rings in trees or pieces of wood and learn to determine whether a cut of a plant part is a transverse, longitudinal, or slant section (E), a skill that will become more useful as slides of plant sections are examined for cell structure in later study of biology.

Mathematical Topics

So that *Science—A Process Approach* will accurately reflect the spirit of modern science, the science experiences of the children are often quantitative. Traditional elementary school science has been almost exclusively descriptive. Important descriptive science concepts are not neglected here. They are strengthened by making them also quantitative. In *Science—A Process Approach*, science and mathematics are deliberately impossible to separate. The mathematical topics reviewed here comprise an important part of science—certainly graphs, measurement, and much of informal geometry are science topics. One day the distinction between science and mathematics in elementary school will no longer be recognized!

Five of the processes of science include many of the skills that should be developed in a school's mathematics program—*Using Numbers, Using Space/Time Relationships, Communicating* (with tables and graphs), *Measuring,* and *Interpreting Data.* These skills, needed for the study of quantitative science, are not taught in all elementary mathematics programs, and if they are included it is often after the time that the children need to use them in this program. The three topics for which supplementary work in science classes becomes most necessary are graphing, division, and decimals.

Numbers and number notation

First children learn about sets and their members, order properties of whole numbers, counting, and numerals (A). They are then introduced to the number line, including the negative integers —1, —2, —3, . . . , —9 (B). The number line is also used to introduce addition of positive integers less than 10. A little later they add positive and negative integers between —10 and 10 (B and C). An exercise in multiplication of positive integers less than 10 is provided for the purpose of enabling the children to divide in order to find rates (an exceedingly important topic in science) and means (D). Until the children need to divide, the work in numbers is not too far ahead of the treatment of these topics in a modern mathematics program.

The metric system of measurement is used from the first introduction of a standard unit of length (B). Later, the children use decimal notation to record tenths of a unit (D, E). Using the number line, decimal notation for tenths can be introduced and used before the children have acquired skills with common fractions. Most elementary school science experiences can be adequately taken care of by using decimals correct to the nearest tenth, at least until grades 5 and 6. Children are introduced to scientific notation for whole numbers more because of a need for knowledge about this notation in outside reading than for the science class (E, F).

Measurement

Children first learn to measure by using arbitrary units. Later, standard metric units are introduced and used. This procedure is followed in measuring lengths (B), temperature (B, C), weight, forces, and mass (B, C, F), and angles (E). Early in their experience they learn to compare areas and volumes using arbitrary units (B). Metric measures of volume in milliliters becomes a useful skill (C). Their attention is first called to comparisons of time intervals (A, B). Later, they learn to read time on the clock to the nearest minute (B) and to use a stopwatch to record intervals to the nearest tenth of a second (E). As a part of the study of measuring, the children learn not only to measure carefully, but they also acquire experience in estimating length, volumes, time, weight, and mass. They measure angles in order to specify direction (B). They learn about angles of incidence and reflection (E), and they study angular velocity (E). In measuring, they learn how scientists use the terms *precision* and *accuracy* (E). They also measure small things using a microscope (F).

Graphing

Scientists in all fields use graphs as one of their principal means of communication. Inferences, predictions, and hypotheses are often derived from graphs. A scientist uses graphs to point a direction for new experiments and new generalizations as well as to record and report what he has already found out. The children first construct bar graphs (B, C). The rectangular coordinate system is then introduced (C) and used throughout the remainder of the program. Three-dimensional coordinates are utilized in relation to describing position on contour maps (F). In the intermediate grades, the interpretation of data recorded in tables and graphs is an essential skill in experimenting.

The children learn to interpolate and extrapolate from graphs (C) and use these skills frequently thereafter. Their study of scales in pictures, maps, and charts is related to their work in choosing scales for coordinate axes (C, D). Two applications of graphs that provide experience with other mathematical concepts are the construction of graphs of data collected in a survey of opinion (C) and graphs of data obtained in determining a relationship between the distance of a viewer from an object and his field of vision (E).

Probability

There is one exercise on probability (F) which builds on the exercise that immediately precedes it in which the children study the human characteristics of being a taster or a nontaster. Later, in a supplementary exercise (G), the children explore probability further as they experiment with generations of drosophila with different characteristics. Probability has an exceedingly important place in modern science. Even though many scientific uses of probability are not appropriate for elementary school science, probability itself is so important to science and so appealing to children (and so often neglected in elementary school mathematics) that it deserves a place in modern elementary school science.

Other geometric topics

In acquiring competence in *Using Space/Time Relationships,* young children identify and name both plane and three-dimensional shapes (A). They use this skill in communicating about objects and phenomena in a variety of scientific experiences. Included in this study is symmetry with respect to a line and a plane (B). The pupils also become accurate in the use of the terms *straight* and *curved lines,* and *plane* and *curved surfaces.* (C). They learn, for example, that straight lines can be drawn on some surfaces and not on others and about great circles on a sphere. An important skill for them in later scientific work is the ability to see the relationships between two-dimensional and three-dimensional figures, such as the rectangular faces of a rectangular prism (A), the plane-figure shadows of three-dimensional objects (D), and the plane sections of three-dimensional objects (E). They learn to construct plane representations of three-dimensional figures (E) and to identify three-dimensional objects from their shadows or plane sections.

C | Selected Readings

Inquiry, Children, and Teachers
John W. Renner and Donald G. Stafford[1]

Is the use of inquiry in elementary school and college classrooms valuable as an experience for children and teachers? Are the behaviors of children and teachers changed by the inquiry experience? Let's begin by examining the impact of inquiry teaching and materials upon children, as revealed in several recent research studies.

In determining the effects of inquiry upon children, materials that permit inquiry to be utilized and a procedure for evaluating those effects must be selected. Stafford[2] selected the first-grade unit of the Science Curriculum Improvement Study entitled *Material Objects*[3] as the focus of attention in his research. This unit was selected because, to teach it, the teacher must employ inquiry techniques. The entire unit is built around a classroom procedure that follows the pattern of child exploration of materials and/or experiments, conceptual invention,[4] and discovery. For his evaluation tools, Stafford

Reprinted with permission from *The Science Teacher*, Vol. 37, No. 4, April 1970. Copyright © 1970 by the National Science Teacher's Association.

[1] Stafford, Donald G., Associate Professor of Science Education and Chemistry, East Central State College, Ada, Oklahoma, and Renner, John W., Professor of Science Education, University of Oklahoma, Norman, Oklahoma.

[2] Stafford, Donald G. *The Influence of the First Grade Program of the Science Curriculum Improvement Study on the Rate of Attainment of Conservation.* Unpublished doctoral dissertation, University of Oklahoma. 1969.

[3] Science Curriculum Improvement Study, *Material Objects.* D. C. Heath & Co., Boston, Massachusetts. 1966.

[4] For a discussion of conceptual invention see Myron Atkin and Robert Karplus, "Discovery or Invention?" *The Science Teacher* 29:45–51; September 1962.

turned to the work of Piaget whose theory states that children pass through four distinct stages[5] as their thinking develops. The thinking of most first-graders (the educational level with which Stafford concerned himself in his research) is typical of what Piaget calls the pre-operational level. Children at the pre-operational stage cannot use conservation reasoning, which means that a child cannot comprehend changes in an object that are the result of a physical transformation. If a child cannot comprehend such change, Piaget describes him as not being able to conserve.[6] The relationship of a child's being able to conserve to his success in school, for example, is illustrated by the following quotation:

> . . . the finding in our studies of a rather substantial correlation between performance in conservation tasks and progress in beginning reading suggests that, to some extent, similar abilities are involved. A program to nurture logical thinking should contribute positively to reading readiness.[7]

Stafford used the development of conservation reasoning in children as an evaluative tool to determine the success of inquiry-centered teaching with *Material Objects*. He found that those first-grade children who have experiences with the unit achieved the ability to conserve much more rapidly than did those children who did not have these experiences. Stafford utilized 120 first-grade children in his research. Sixty of the children were taught *Material Objects*[8] (the experimental group), and 60 were taught science from a textbook (the control group). Although the control group did have a slightly higher mean IQ than had the experimental group, that difference was not statistically significant at the 5 per cent level. In September and again in December, all the children were given the Piaget tasks for the ability to conserve number, liquid amount, solid amount, length, area, and weight.

In September the number of conservations of the control group equalled or excelled the experimental group on every test. After four months of experience with *Material Objects*, the experimental group excelled the control on all the conservation tasks except area. Even on

[5] Karplus, Robert, and Herbert D. Thier, *A New Look at Elementary School Science*. Rand McNally and Co., Chicago, Illinois. 1967. P. 21.

[6] *Ibid.*

[7] Almy, Millie. *Young Children's Thinking*. Teachers College Press, Columbia University, New York, 1966. Pp. 139–140.

[8] The educational laboratory in which the researches described in this manuscript were conducted is the Norman, Oklahoma, Public School System. Gratitude is expressed to the Board of Education of that system and its Superintendent, Lester M. Reed, for their cooperation.

the conservation-of-area task, the experimental group made greater numerical gains in the number of children achieving conservation than did the control group. The achievement of the ability to conserve is, according to Piaget, indicative that a child is moving from the intellectual level called pre-operational to the next higher intellectual level known as concrete operational. Since *Material Objects* is a science unit which is taught by inquiry, Stafford's research does indicate that children so taught do show more rapid intellectual development than do those children not having such experiences. If, however, children are going to have experiences which will influence their developmental level, as did *Material Objects* in Stafford's research, the teacher must provide such experiences for them and permit the interaction between the children and their environment to take place.

During the past few years, the Science Education Center in the College of Education at the University of Oklahoma has conducted several studies designed to determine the effectiveness of providing teachers with special educational experience in inquiry-centered science teaching. The teachers who participated in these experiences have been studied with regard to how they teach science before and after the experience and when matched with other teachers who have not had the experience. The participating teachers have also been studied to determine whether the special experience in science education affected the way they taught reading and social studies. The details of the individual research follow.

Wilson[9] made extensive observation of 30 classes of elementary children who were studying science in the first through the sixth grades. Fifteen of those classes were taught by teachers who had been educated in inquiry-centered methods and materials for science instruction; the other 15 teachers had no such educational experience. The teachers were matched by pairs on such criteria as education, age, years of experience, and type of teaching environment. The purposes of Wilson's study were to determine whether or not there were significant differences in (1) the number of essential science experiences[10] (observation, measurement, experimentation, data interpretation, and prediction) encouraged by teachers who had received instruction in the inquiry approach and teachers who had been educated in the traditional textbook-centered, expository approach to science teaching

---

[9] Wilson, John H. *Difference Between the Inquiry-Discovery and the Traditional Approaches to Teaching Science in Elementary Schools.* Unpublished doctoral dissertation, University of Oklahoma. 1967.

[10] Renner, John W., and William B. Ragan. *Teaching Science in the Elementary School.* Harper and Row, New York. 1968. Pp. 112–197.

and (2) in the number of questions asked while teaching science by the inquiry-educated teachers which required more analytical thinking than did the questions asked by the traditional teachers. Wilson found that:

1. The inquiry-educated teachers provided the children significantly more of the essential science experiences than did the traditional group.
2. Recognition and recall questions were recorded a significantly larger proportion of times for the traditional-teachers group than for the inquiry-educated teachers.
3. Analysis and synthesis-type questions were recorded a significantly larger proportion of times for the inquiry-educated teachers group than for the traditional group.
4. Comprehension-type questions were recorded a significantly larger proportion of times in favor of the traditional-teachers group, while demonstration of skill-type questions were higher in proportion of times in favor of the inquiry-educated teachers.

From these findings it seems that inquiry-educated teachers employ what they have learned about inquiry. They encourage pupils to become involved in experiences and find their own answers to problems. Pupils learn how to do this systematically and scientifically if they are given the chance. Inquiry-educated teachers question more and tell less.

A significant question arises as a result of this study: Could it be that the materials which the pupils have at hand, rather than an inquiry-educated teacher, make significant differences in the approaches to teaching science by the traditional teacher and the inquiry-educated teacher?

The modifications of teacher instructional patterns in science and social studies classes as a result of an educational experience in a summer workshop in "new science" were investigated by Schmidt.[11] In his investigation, 16 teachers of both elementary school science and social studies who had no previous formal exposure to the philosophy and objectives of inquiry were observed. The observer was searching for the different types of experiences these teachers provided their pupils, the use these teachers made of the experiences they provided their pupils, and how each of them used divergent and convergent questions. During the following summer, the 16 teachers participated in a summer workshop in "new science." Observations

[11] Schmidt, Frederick B. *The Influence of a Summer Institute in Inquiry-Centered Science Education Upon the Teaching Strategies of Elementary Teachers in Two Disciplines.* Unpublished doctoral dissertation, University of Oklahoma. 1969.

based on the same criteria were again conducted in the fall as the teachers worked in both science and social studies classes.

Schmidt compared the before and after (spring-fall) observations and found that four interrelated and significant modifications in teacher behavior followed the teacher's participation in the summer workshop in "new science." These modifications are:

1. Teachers asked fewer recall and convergent questions.
2. Teachers asked more questions that required pupils to operate on the higher levels of the rational powers.[12]
3. Teachers provided the pupils with a greater number of the essential learning experiences in science.
4. The foregoing modifications in teacher instructional patterns appeared in the teachers' social studies classes as well as in their science classes.

The teachers Schmidt observed were using inquiry-centered materials in science following their workshop experience, but they were using traditional materials in their social studies classes. These results seem to suggest that the deviation from the traditional mode of teacher education and not the materials is the significant factor in changing the teachers' instructional patterns.

Another area of investigation has been the approach of inquiry-centered science teachers to teaching reading. Porterfield[13] studied the effectiveness of providing teachers an educational experience in inquiry-centered science when he examined whether or not teachers so educated ask significantly different proportions of divergent questions while teaching reading than do elementary-school teachers who have not had such an experience. The teachers in Porterfield's sample were using the conventional elementary-school reading materials. Porterfield selected this research area because reading has long been thought to be an excellent medium for the development of the ability to think. The Educational Policies Commission has called the rational powers the " . . . essence of the ability to think." Porterfield, then, was essentially testing whether or not teachers who had an inquiry experience in science education were teaching reading in a manner which led to rational-power development.

---

[12] Educational Policies Commission, *The Central Purpose of American Education*, NEA, Washington, D.C., 1961. P. 5. This document describes the rational powers as ". . . the essence of the ability to think. . . ."

[13] Porterfield, Denzil. *The Influence of Preparation in the Science Curriculum Improvement Study on the Questioning Behavior of Selected Second and Fourth Grade Reading Teachers*. Unpublished doctoral dissertation, University of Oklahoma. 1969.

The results of Porterfield's research on teachers' questioning behavior can be summarized as follows:

1. Teachers not having had an educational experience in inquiry ask questions which dwell on recognition and recall. Since these questions require the use of memory exclusively, perhaps the acquisition and retention of information represents the instructional goal of these teachers.
2. Translational, interpretation analysis, and synthesis questions were used significantly more in reading by the inquiry-educated teachers than by those teachers not so educated.
3. Recall questions were used more than any other type of question by both groups, but the inquiry-educated teachers, taken as a group, tend to ask fewer recall-type questions.
4. The overall general pattern shows a definite trend toward questioning aimed at levels above recognition and recall for inquiry-educated teachers. There was substantial evidence to support the idea that the oral question was generally and more thoughtfully used by inquiry groups.
5. The inquiry-educated teachers underwent a period of instruction during which they were exposed to a variety of questioning techniques. Discussions were conducted on the kinds and purposes of questions classroom teachers may ask and the concomitant thinking skills that are motivated by these questions. One may assume that teachers transferred this theoretical and practical use of questions and questioning into the area of reading instruction. Inquiry-educated teachers asked questions aimed at levels above recognition and recall
6. The influence of materials is not a factor; both groups of teachers used the same types of material. The fact that the inquiry educated teachers asked questions which called for higher levels of thought than did teachers who had not been so instructed can be attributed to their inquiry-centered experience in science education.

Based upon the data from the research studies just described, we hypothesize that specialized educational experiences in inquiry-centered science teaching encourage a teacher to become sensitive to children, functionally aware of the purposes of education, and equipped to lead children to learn how to learn in all subject areas. In short, we are hypothesizing that an inquiry-centered experience in science education prepares a teacher to teach all subjects from an inquiry point of view. While the foregoing statement is a hypothesis, the data presented here suggest that the profession cannot afford to leave it untested.

Teaching and the Expanding Knowledge
Albert Szent-Györgyi[1]

The simplification that comes with expanding knowledge enables teaching to encompass this knowledge.

Our attempt to harmonize teaching with expanding—or rather exploding—knowledge would be hopeless should growth not entail simplification. I will dwell on this sunny side. Knowledge is a sacred cow, and my problem will be how we can milk her while keeping clear of her horns.

One of my reasons for being optimistic is that the foundations of nature are simple. This was brought home to me many years ago when I joined the Institute for Advanced Studies in Princeton. I did this in the hope that by rubbing elbows with those great atomic physicists and mathematicians I would learn something about living matters. But as soon as I revealed that in any living system there are more than two electrons, the physicists would not speak to me. With all their computers they could not say what the third electron might do. The remarkable thing is that it knows exactly what to do. So that little electron knows something that all the wise men of Princeton don't, and this can only be something very simple. Nature, basically, must be much simpler than she looks to us. She looks to us like a coded letter for which we have no code. To the degree to which our methods become less clumsy and more adequate and we find out nature's code, things must become not only clearer, but very much simpler, too.

Science tends to generalize, and generalization means simplification. My own science, biology, is today not only very much richer than it was in my student days, but is simpler, too. Then it was horribly complex, being fragmented into a great number of isolated principles. Today these are all fused into one single complex with the atomic

Reprinted with permission from *Science*, Vol. 146, December 4, 1964, pp. 1278–1279. Copyright 1964 by the American Association for the Advancement of Science. Also with permission of the author.

[1] Dr. A. Szent-Györgyi is director of research at the Institute for Muscle Research, Marine Biological Laboratory, Woods Hole, Mass. This article was originally presented as part of a panel discussion at the bicentennial celebration of Brown University, 28 September 1964.

model in its center. Cosmology, quantum mechanics, DNA and genetics, are all, more or less, parts of one and the same story—a most wonderful simplification. And generalizations are also more satisfying to the mind than details. We, in our teaching, should place more emphasis on generalizations than on details. Of course, details and generalizations must be in a proper balance: generalization can be reached only from details, while it is the generalization which gives value and interest to the detail.

After this preamble I would like to make a few general remarks, first, about the main instrument of teaching: books. There is a widely spread misconception about the nature of books which contain knowledge. It is thought that such books are something the contents of which have to be crammed into our heads. I think the opposite is closer to the truth. Books are there to keep the knowledge in while we use our heads for something better. Books may also be a better place for such knowledge. In my own head any book-knowledge has a half-life of a few weeks. So I leave knowledge, for safekeeping, to books and libraries and go fishing, sometimes for fish, sometimes for new knowledge.

I know that I am shockingly ignorant. I could take exams in college but could not pass any of them. Worse than that: I treasure my ignorance; I feel snug in it. It does not cloud my naiveté, my simplicity of mind, my ability to marvel childishly at nature and recognize a miracle even if I see it every day. If, with my 71 years, I am still digging on the fringes of knowledge, I owe it to this childish attitude. "Blessed are the pure in heart, for they shall see God," says the Bible. "For they can understand Nature," say I.

I do not want to be misunderstood —I do not depreciate knowledge, and I have worked long and hard to know something of all fields of science related to biology. Without this I could do no research. But I have retained only what I need for an understanding, an intuitive grasp, and in order to know in which book to find what. This was fun, and we must have fun, or else our work is no good.

My next remark is about time relations. The time spent in school is relatively short compared to the time thereafter. I am stressing this because it is widely thought that everything we have to know to do our job well we have to learn in school. This is wrong because, during the long time which follows school, we are apt to forget, anyway, what we have learned there, while we have ample time for study. In fact, most of us have to learn all our lives, and it was with gray hair that I took up the study of quantum mechanics, myself. So what the school has to do, in the first place, is to make us learn how to learn, to whet our appetites for knowledge, to teach us the delight of doing a job well and the excitement of creativity, to teach us to love what we do, and to help us to find what we love to do.

My friend Gerard quoted Fouchet as advising us to take from the altar of knowledge the fire, not the ashes. Being of more earthly disposition, I would advise you to take the meat, not the bones. Teachers, on the whole, have a remarkable preference for bones, especially dry ones. Of course, bones are important, and now and then we all like to suck a bit on them, but only after having eaten the meat. What I mean to say is that we must not *learn* things, we must *live* things. This is true for almost everything. Shakespeare and all of literature must be *lived*, music, paintings, and sculptures have to be *made*, drama has to be *acted*. This is even true for history: we should live through it, through the spirit of the various periods, instead of storing their data. I am glad to say that this trend—to live things—is becoming evident even in the teaching of science. The most recent trend is not to *teach* the simpler laws of nature, but to make our students *discover* them for themselves in simple experiments. Of course, I know data are important. They may be even interesting, but only after we have consumed the meat, the substance. After this we may even become curious about them and retain them. But taught before this they are just dull, and they dull, if not kill, the spirit.

It is a widely spread opinion that memorizing will not hurt, that knowledge does no harm. I am afraid it may. Dead knowledge dulls the spirit, fills the stomach without nourishing the body. The mind is not a bottomless pit, and if we put in one thing we might have to leave out another. By a more live teaching we can fill the soul and reserve the mind for the really important things. We may even spare time we need for expanding subjects.

Such live teaching, which fills both the soul and the mind, may help man to meet one of his most formidable problems, what to do with himself. The most advanced societies, like ours, can already produce more than they can consume, and with advancing automation the discrepancy is increasing rapidly. We try to meet the challenge by producing useless things, like armaments. But this is no final answer. In the end we will have to work less. But then, what will we do with ourselves? Lives cannot be left empty. Man needs excitement and challenge, and in an affluent society everything is within easy reach. And boredom is dangerous, for it can easily make a society seek excitement in political adventure and in brinkmanship, following irresponsible and ignorant leaders. Our own society has recently shown alarming signs of this trend. In a world where atomic bombs can fly from one end to the other in seconds, this is tantamount to suicide. By teaching live arts and science, the schools could open up the endless horizons and challenges of intellectual and artistic life and make whole life an exciting adventure. I believe that in our teaching not only must details and generalizations be in balance, but our whole teaching must be balanced with general human values.

I want to conclude with a few remarks on single subjects, first, science. Science has two aspects: it has to be part of any education, of humanistic culture. But we also have to teach science as preparation for jobs. If we distinguish sharply between these two aspects then the talk about the "two cultures" will lose its meaning.

A last remark I want to make is about the teaching of history, not only because it is the most important subject, but also because I still have in my nostrils the acid smell of my own sweat which I produced when learning its data. History has two chapters: National History and World History. National history is a kind of family affair and I will not speak about it. But what is world history? In its essence it is the story of man, how he rose from his animal status to his present elevation. This is a fascinating story and is linked to a limited number of creative men, its heroes, who created new knowledge, new moral or ethical values, or new beauty. Opposing this positive side of history there is a negative, destructive side linked to the names of kings, barons, generals, and dictators who, with their greed and lust for power, made wars, fought battles, and mostly created misery, destroying what other men had built. These are the heroes of the history we teach at present as world history. Not only is this history negative and lopsided, it is false, too, for it omits the lice, rats, malnutrition, and epidemics which had more to do with the course of things than generals and kings, as Zinsser ably pointed out. The world history we teach should also be more truthful and include the stench, dirt, callousness, and misery of past ages, to teach us to appreciate progress and what we have. We need not falsify history; history has a tendency to falsify itself, because only the living return from the battlefield to tell stories. If the dead could return but once and tell about their ignominious end, history and politics would be different today. A truer history would also be simpler.

As the barriers between the various sciences have disappeared, so the barriers between science and humanities may gradually melt away. Dating through physical methods has become a method of research in history, while x-ray spectra and microanalysis have become tools in the study of painting. I hope that the achievements of human psychology may help us, also, to rewrite human history in a more unified and translucent form.

The story of man's progress is not linked to any period, nation, creed, or color, and could teach to our youngsters a wider human solidarity. This they will badly need when rebuilding political and human relations, making them compatible with survival.

In spite of its many chapters, our teaching has, essentially, but one object, the production of men who can fill their shoes and stand erect with their eyes on the wider horizons. This makes the school, on any level, into the most important public institution and the teacher into the most important public figure. As we teach today, so the morrow will be.

The First-Grade Scientist
Don G. Stafford and John W. Renner[1]

Imagine yourself assigned the task of teaching science to a group of children after having been told that every child in the group believed that the simple act of pouring all the water from a glass into a taller, thinner glass changed the amount of water. Also, that each child believed that the simple act of stacking up a row of checkers changed the number of checkers; that bending a string of beads changed the length; and that flattening out a piece of clay changed the amount as well as the weight of the clay. Would it be possible to teach science, or anything else that required thinking, to this group?

The answer is "Yes, it certainly would be possible." As a matter of fact, this is the situation with which every first-grade teacher is faced throughout most, if not all, of the first year of school. Joachim Wohlwill of Clark University has described the first-grade child as ". . . living in a kind of Alice in Wonderland World."[2] It does not appear

Reprinted with permission from *Science and Children*, December 1969. Copyright 1971 by the National Science Teachers Association, 1201 Sixteenth Street, N.W., Washington, D.C. 20036.

[1] Don G. Stafford, Associate Professor of Chemistry and Science Education, East Central State College, Ada, Oklahoma, and John W. Renner, Professor of Science Education, University of Oklahoma, Norman, Oklahoma.

[2] Wohlwill, Joachim F. "The Case of the Prelogical Child." *Psychology Today*, July 1967. p. 25.

to bother the six-year-old at all that based on adult point of view, his conclusions are contradictory. *What he perceives, he believes.* In spite of the inability of the first-grade child to follow an object through the transformations described in the introductory paragraph, first-grade teachers do manage somehow to teach most of their pupils to read, write, work with numbers, and perform other equally complex tasks.

Science too can be taught to first-grade children if the limitations of the child's thinking ability are taken into account when selecting what is to be taught. Since the child believes what he perceives, the ideas he meets must be those that can be found and developed through observation and manipulation of actual objects from the child's environment. Areas of science which require the manipulation of abstract concepts would not be suitable areas of study. This would, of course, eliminate many of the areas which many adults think of as the significant ones of science—space travel, rockets and satellites, and the world of molecules and atoms and energy. Areas chosen for study should be geared to the children's intellectual abilities rather than adult appeal. This does not mean that the child will be limited to trivia. On the contrary, he can work with legitimate science that would be recognizable as such by a scientist and which will be exciting and meaningful to him.

Consider, for example, the following activities engaged in by the first-grade children at the University of Oklahoma Laboratory school. Six gallon-size aquaria (jars obtained from the school cafeteria) containing guppies, snails, water weed, and white sand were placed in locations in the classroom where they could be observed by the children. Periodically (weekly or as often as developments in the aquaria made it feasible), the teacher asked the children to report on their observations. Since the childern were not yet able to record their own observations, the teacher acted as recorder and wrote each different observation on a large class-size writing pad. These observations were referred to and compared with other observations later in the year. During one such class discussion of observations made by the children, one child stated that he thought that there were two different kinds of guppies in the aquaria. Most of the other children agreed. A suggestion from another child that perhaps one kind of guppy was a father and the other a mother set the stage for a simple investigation. When asked by the teacher how one might be able to determine which was the father and which was the mother, one child suggested that "we could watch them and see which one has babies." A large guppy of each type was placed in separate containers to be observed. Sure enough, to the delight of the children, one did have babies—21 of them. The other guppy although observed for many weeks never did. Of course, there were uncontrolled variables in this experiment that could affect the results, but if the teacher had attempted to require the children to consider all of them, they would have become confused. (Six-year-olds have difficulty in considering more than one variable at a time.) They were able to isolate a problem from their observations and imagine an experiment to solve it to their satisfaction.

When the guppies were born, another problem which the teacher had not anticipated arose. A child observed that every one of the 21 guppies looked alike. Were all of them either mother or father guppies? During a class discussion on the problem, the decision was made that the guppies might be like chickens, i.e., they change in looks as they grow older. Daily observations of the baby guppies were made until two different kinds of guppies could be distinguished.

Another first-grade class worked with seeds and plants. Beans, mustard, rye grass, and pumpkin seeds were examined and compared for size, shape, color, texture, etc. These seeds were then planted in separate containers (half-gallon milk cartons cut in half) by the children. A record of the growth of plants placed in various locations in the room was made in the following way. Each child made twice weekly measurements of the same four containers of plants by holding a strip of construction paper alongside the plant and cutting the strip of paper the same height as the plant. These strips of construction paper, a different color for each kind of plant, were pasted on a sheet of paper to form a simple growth chart or record. The different growth rates of plants could be observed.

There are many other areas that first-grade children can explore using observational and descriptive skills to isolate simple problems and concepts. Consider this classroom happening. As the children were observing their aquaria one day, the teacher asked them how the aquaria differed that day from the last time they had been examined. The class was in complete agreement that all the aquaria contained less water than when they had been previously examined. The teacher asked what happened to the water and got four responses.

1. The fish drank it.
2. It soaked into the sand at the bottom of the aquarium.
3. It went into the air.
4. Someone spilled it.

The six-year-old investigators were then asked how they could determine which of their reasons were correct. They decided that to investigate the four possible explanations, they needed seven identical aquaria used in the following way:

1. Two identical aquaria would be set up except one would not have fish in it; that procedure would let them test their first idea.
2. Two of the aquaria would be identical except one would not have any sand on the bottom.
3. Two more identical aquaria would be assembled, and one of them would be covered. This procedure would test the third idea.
4. The children decided they only needed one aquarium to test idea four. They would assemble it and give it to the teacher; he would not spill it.

This problem (Where did the water from the aquaria go?) could now be solved by direct observation and comparisons of the aquaria involved in the experiment. First graders can observe and compare. A fair amount of teacher guidance was needed, especially in setting up a controlled experiment, but the suggestions were the children's *not* the teacher's.

One might ask at this point, "Since a teacher using this method to a great extent follows the lead of the class, would he not have to possess a broad knowledge of science?" A teacher "might" do a better job if he had a broad scientific background. But on the other hand, he might do a poorer job if his foreknowledge of the outcome of each experiment tempted him to "tell" the answer; or look for the expected solution. The exact answer to the posed question depends on how the teacher uses his knowledge. It is far more important than an elementary teacher, especially a first-grade teacher, know children than it is that he know a great collection of information about science.

The teacher must be careful that the investigations and problems are an outgrowth of the children's own explorations and observations rather than attempting to pull them in the direction he would like to go. The foregoing example demonstrates this point adequately. This, of course, is not intended to suggest that the teacher should offer no guidance. *The fact that he selects the materials to explore establishes definite guidelines and direction for the class.* He may even by questions or suggestions focus the attention of the children on certain aspects of the objects being explored, but he should not dictate the direction of the investigations or synthesize problems according to his own preconceived notion of how the investigation should proceed. It should be the children's problems and ideas which are explored and at the children's own rate rather than following a timetable. To do otherwise is to thwart the accomplishment of the very goals he is trying to achieve.

Allowing a child time to think and an opportunity to express his ideas is of utmost importance in accomplishing the goals of education. If a child is to develop his "ability to think," the central purpose of American education, and of course, a goal of science, it must be in an atmosphere conducive to thinking and where thought is respected.[3] One does not ponder the solution of difficult problems hurriedly. And if you expect rapid fire answers to questions, you are not establishing an atmosphere conducive to thinking.

When should a teacher begin science experiences such as the ones described? How long after the start of school will the children be ready? There are no hard and fast answers to these questions. The teacher *must* make that professional judgment since each group of children is unique. There are, however, certain activities which should precede activities such as those described above and should be initiated immediately. These are activities designed to enhance the child's observational and descriptive skills.

Children tend to view an object in terms of what can be done with it—a pencil is to write with; a balloon is to blow up; a piece of clay is to squeeze—rather than the more fundamental characteristics or properties of shape, color, size, texture, and weight. Therefore, several class periods should be devoted to allowing children to describe objects in the classroom, or objects brought from home using property words. It is also a good idea to take the class outside on the playground to describe objects that cannot be brought inside such as houses, clouds, trees, airplanes, and insects. A trip to the zoo or a farm during which the children describe the various animals is great fun and very productive. (These provide not only good science experiences but can be used in story writing, drawing, vocabulary development, etc.)

From these activities, children reap a threefold reward. They are becoming acquainted with their environment; they are developing observational and descriptive skills; they are using and developing their rational powers or "ability to think."[4]

These then are not prescience activities, they are basic or beginning science activities. These observational and descriptive skills are utilized and further enhanced during activities such as those described

[3] Educational Policies Commission. *The Central Purpose of American Education.* National Education Association, 1961.

[4] Renner, John W. and Ragan, W. B., *Teaching Science in the Elementary School.* Harper and Row, New York City. 1968. pp. 54–55.

with the guppies and plants. These simple experiments will allow the children to use and develop other rational powers such as imagining, classifying, generalizing, comparing, and evaluating. As one can readily see, these kinds of activities are not only legitimate science, they are good sound education!

Can primary school children actually do science? The answer is *emphatically YES! They can and they should!*

The Central Purpose of American Education
Educational Policies Commission (NEA)

Part I   Education in the American Society

In any democracy education is closely bound to the wishes of the people, but the strength of this bond in America has been unique. The American people have traditionally regarded education as a means for improving themselves and their society. Whenever an objective has been judged desirable for the individual or the society, it has tended to be accepted as a valid concern of the school. The American commitment to the free society—to individual dignity, to personal liberty, to equality of opportunity—has set the frame in which the American school grew. The basic American value, respect for the individual, has led to one of the major charges which the American people have placed on their schools: to foster that development of individual capacities which will enable each human being to become the best person he is capable of becoming.

The schools have been designed also to serve society's needs. The political order depends on responsible participation of individual citizens; hence the schools have been concerned with good citizenship. The economic order depends on ability and willingness to work; hence the schools have taught vocational skills. The general morality depends on choices made by individuals; hence the schools have cultivated moral habits and upright character.

Educational authorities have tended to share and support these broad concepts of educational purposes. Two of the best-known definitions of purposes were formulated by educators in 1918 and

1938. The first definition, by the Commission on the Reorganization of Secondary Education, proposed for the school a set of seven cardinal objectives: health, command of functional processes, worthy home membership, vocational competence, effective citizenship, worthy use of leisure, and ethical character. The second definition, by the Educational Policies Commission, developed a number of objectives under four headings: self-realization, human relationship, economic efficiency, and civic responsibility.

The American school must be concerned with all these objectives if it is to serve all of American life. That these are desirable objectives is clear. Yet they place before the school a problem of immense scope, for neither the schools nor the pupils have the time or energy to engage in all the activities which will fully achieve all these goals. Choices among possible activities are inevitable and are constantly being made in and for every school. But there is no consensus regarding a basis for making these choices. The need, therefore, is for a principle which will enable the school to identify its necessary and appropriate contributions to individual development and the needs of society.

Furthermore, education does not cease when the pupil leaves the school. No school fully achieves any pupil's goals in the relatively short time he spends in the classroom. The school seeks rather to equip the pupil to achieve them for himself. Thus the search for a definition of the school's necessary contribution entails an understanding of the ways individuals and societies choose and achieve their goals. Because the school must serve both individuals and the society at large in achieving their goals, and because the principal goal of the American society remains freedom, the requirements of freedom set the frame within which the school can discover the central focus of its own efforts.

The freedom which exalts the individual, and by which the worth of the society is judged, has many dimensions. It means freedom from undue governmental restraints; it means equality in political participation. It means the right to earn and own property and decide its disposition. It means equal access to just processes of law. It means the right to worship according to one's conscience.

Institutional safeguards are a necessary condition for freedom. They are not, however, sufficient to make men free. Freedom requires that citizens act responsibly in all ways. It cannot be preserved in a society whose citizens do not value freedom. Thus belief in freedom is essential to maintenance of freedom. The basis of this belief cannot be laid by mere indoctrination in principles of freedom. The ability to recite the values of a free society does not guarantee commitment to those values. Active belief in those values depends on awareness of them and of their role in life. The person who best supports these values is one who has examined them, who understands their function in his life and in the society at large, and who accepts them as worthy of his own support. For such a person these values are consciously held and consciously approved.

The conditions necessary for freedom include the social institutions which protect freedom and the personal commitment which gives it force. Both of these conditions rest on one condition within the individuals who compose a free society. This is freedom of the mind.

Freedom of the mind is a condition which each individual must develop for himself. In this sense, no man is born free. A free society has the obligation to create circumstances in which all individuals may have opportunity and encouragement to attain freedom of the mind. If this goal is to be achieved, its requirements must be specified.

To be free, a man must be capable of basing his choices and actions on understandings which he himself achieves and on values which he examines for himself. He must be aware of the bases on which he accepts propositions as true. He must understand the values by which he lives, the assumptions on which they rest, and the consequences to which they lead. He must recognize that others may have different values. He must be capable of analyzing the situation in which he finds himself and of developing solutions to the problems before him. He must be able to perceive and understand the events of his life and time and the forces that influence and shape those events. He must recognize and accept the practical limitations which time and circumstance place on his choices. The free man, in short, has a rational grasp of himself, his surroundings, and the relation between them.

He has the freedom to think and choose, and that freedom must have its roots in conditions both within and around the individual. Society's dual role is to guarantee the necessary environment and to develop the necessary individual strength. That individual strength springs from a thinking, aware mind, a mind that possesses the capacity to achieve aesthetic sensitivity and moral responsibility, an enlightened mind. These qualities occur in a wide diversity of patterns in different individuals. It is the contention of this essay that central to all of them, nurturing them and being nurtured by them, are the rational powers of man.

The central role of the rational powers

The cultivated powers of the free mind have always been basic in achieving freedom. The powers of the free mind are many. In addition to the rational powers, there are those which relate to the aesthetic, the moral, and the religious. There is a unique, central role for the rational powers of an individual, however, for upon them depends his ability to achieve his personal goals and to fulfill his obligations to society.

These powers involve the processes of recalling and imagining, classifying and generalizing, comparing and evaluating, analyzing and synthesizing, and deducing and inferring. These processes enable one to apply logic and the available evidence to his ideas, attitudes, and actions, and to pursue better whatever goals he may have.

This is not to say that the rational powers are all of life or all of the mind, but they are the essence of the ability to think. A thinking person is aware that all persons, himself included, are both rational and nonrational, that each person perceives events through the screen of his own personality, and that he must take account of his personality in evaluating his perceptions. The rational processes, moreover, make intelligent choices possible. Through them a person can become aware of the bases of choice in his values and of the circumstances of choice in his environment. Thus they are broadly applicable in life, and they provide a solid basis for competence in all the areas with which the school has traditionally been concerned.

The traditionally accepted obligation of the school to teach the *fundamental processes*—an obligation stressed in the 1918 and 1938 statements of educational purposes—is obviously directed toward the development of the ability to think. Each of the school's other traditional objectives can be better achieved as pupils develop this ability and learn to apply it to all the problems that face them.

Health, for example, depends upon a reasoned awareness of the value of mental and physical fitness and of the means by which it may be developed and maintained. Fitness is not merely a function of living and acting; it requires that the individual understand the connection among health, nutrition, activity, and environment, and that he take action to improve his mental and physical condition.

Worthy home membership in the modern age demands substantial knowledge of the role that the home and community play in human development. The person who understands the bases of his own judgments recognizes the home as the source from which most individuals develop most of the standards and values they apply in their lives. He is intelligently aware of the role of emotion in his own life and in the lives of others. His knowledge of the importance of the home environment in the formation of personality enables him to make reasoned judgments about his domestic behavior.

More than ever before, and for an ever-increasing proportion of the population, *vocational competence* requires developed rational capacities. The march of technology and science in the modern society progressively eliminates the positions open to low-level talents. The man able to use only his hands is at a growing disadvantage as compared with the man who can also use his head. Today even the simplest use of hands is coming to require the simultaneous employment of the mind.

Effective citizenship is impossible without the ability to think. The good citizen, the one who contributes effectively and responsibly to the management of the public business in a free society, can fill his role only if he is aware of the values of his society. Moreover, the course of events in modern life is such that many of the factors which influence an individual's civic life are increasingly remote from him. His own firsthand experience is no longer an adequate basis for judgment. He must have in addition the intellectual means to study events, to relate his values to them, and to make wise decisions as to his own actions. He must also be skilled in the processes of communication and must understand both the potentialities and the limitations of communication among individuals and groups.

The *worthy use of leisure* is related to the individual's knowledge, understanding, and capacity to choose, from among all the activities to which his time can be devoted, those which contribute to the achievement of his purposes and to the satisfaction of his needs. On these bases, the individual can become aware of the external pressures which compete for his attention, moderate the influence of these pressures, and make wise choices for himself. His recreation, ranging from hobbies to sports to intellectual activity pursued for its own sake, can conform to his own concepts of constructive use of time.

The development of *ethical character* depends upon commitment to values; it depends also upon the ability to reason sensitively and responsibly with respect to those values in specific situations. Character is misunderstood if thought of as mere conformity to standards imposed by external authority. In a free society, ethics, morality, and character have meaning to the extent that they represent affirmative, thoughtful choices by individuals. The ability to make these choices depends on awareness of values and of their role in life. The home and the church begin to shape the child's values long before he goes to school. And a person who grows up in the American society inevitably acquires many values from his daily pattern of living.

American children at the age of six, for example, usually have a firm commitment to the concept of fair play. This is a value which relates directly to such broad democratic concepts as justice and human worth and dignity. But the extension of this commitment to these broader democratic values will not occur unless the child becomes aware of its implications for his own behavior, and this awareness demands the ability to think.

A person who understands and appreciates his own values is most likely to act on them. He learns that his values are of great moment for himself, and he can look objectively and sympathetically at the values held by others. Thus, by critical thinking, he can deepen his respect for the importance of values and strengthen his sense of responsibility.

The man who seeks to understand himself understands also that other human beings have much in common with him. His understanding of the possibilities which exist within a human being strengthens his concept of the respect due every man. He recognizes the web which relates him to other men and perceives the necessity for responsible behavior. The person whose rational powers are not well developed can, at best, learn habitual responses and ways of conforming which may insure that he is not a detriment to his society. But, lacking the insight that he might have achieved, his capacity to contribute will inevitably be less than it might have become.

Development of the ability to reason can lead also to dedication to the values which inhere in rationality: commitment to honesty, accuracy, and personal reliability; respect for the intellect and for the intellectual life; devotion to the expansion of knowledge. A man who thinks can understand the importance of this ability. He is likely to value the rational potentials of mankind as essential to a worthy life.

Thus the rational powers are central to all the other qualities of the human spirit. These powers flourish in a humane and morally responsible context and contribute to the entire personality. The rational powers are to the entire human spirit as the hub is to the wheel.

These powers are indispensable to a full and worthy life. The person in whom—for whatever reason—they are not well developed is increasingly handicapped in modern society. He may be able to satisfy social standards, but he will inevitably lack his full measure of dignity because his incapacity limits his stature to less than he might otherwise attain. Only to the extent that an individual can realize his potentials, especially the development of his ability to think, can he fully achieve for himself the dignity that goes with freedom.

A person with developed rational powers has the means to be aware of all facets of his existence. In this sense he can live to the fullest. He can escape captivity to his emotions and irrational states. He can enrich his emotional life and direct it toward ever higher standards of taste and enjoyment. He can enjoy the political and economic freedoms of the democratic society. He can free himself from the bondage of ignorance and unawareness. He can make of himself a free man.

The changes in man's understanding and power

The foregoing analysis of human freedom and review of the central role of the rational powers in enabling a person to achieve his own goals demonstrate the critical importance of developing those powers. Their importance is also demonstrated by an analysis of the great changes in the world.

Many profound changes are occurring in the world today, but there is a fundamental force contributing to all of them. That force is the expanding role accorded in modern life to the rational powers of man. By using these powers to increase his knowledge, man is attempting to solve the riddles of life, space, and time which have long intrigued him. By using these powers to develop sources of new energy and means of communication, he is moving into interplanetary space. By using these powers to make a smaller world and larger weapons, he is creating new needs for international organization and understanding. By using these powers to alleviate disease and poverty, he is lowering death rates and expanding populations. By using these powers to create and use a new technology, he is achieving un-dreamed affluence, so that in some societies distribution has become a greater problem than production.

While man is using the powers of his mind to solve old riddles, he is creating new ones. Basic assumptions upon which mankind has long operated are being challenged or demolished. The age-old resignation to poverty and inferior status for the masses of humanity is being replaced by a drive for a life of dignity for all. Yet, just as man achieves a higher hope for all mankind, he sees also the opening of a grim age in which expansion of the power to create is matched by a perhaps greater enlargement of the power to destroy.

As man sees his power expand, he is coming to realize that the common sense which he accumulates from his own experience is not a sufficient guide to the understanding of the events in his own life or of the nature of the physical world. And, with combined uneasiness and exultation, he senses that his whole way of looking at life may be challenged in a time when men are returning from space.

Through the ages, man has accepted many kinds of propositions as truth, or at least as bases sufficient for action. Some propositions have been accepted on grounds of superstition; some on grounds of decree, dogma, or custom; some on humanistic, aesthetic, or religious grounds; some on common sense. Today, the role of knowledge derived from rational inquiry is growing. For this there are several reasons.

In the first place, knowledge so derived has proved to be man's most efficient weapon for achieving power over his environment. It prevails because it works.

More than effectiveness, however, is involved. There is high credibility in a proposition which can be arrived at or tested by persons other than those who advance it. Modesty, too, is inherent in rational inquiry, for it is an attempt to free explanations of phenomena and events from subjective preference and human authority, and to subject such explanations to validation through experience. Einstein's concept of the curvature of space cannot be demonstrated to the naked eye and may offend common sense; but persons who cannot apply the mathematics necessary to comprehend the concept can still accept it. They do this, not on Einstein's authority, but on their awareness that he used rational methods to achieve it and that those who possess the ability and facilities have tested its rational consistency and empirical validity.

In recent decades, man has greatly accelerated his systematic efforts to gain insight through rational inquiry. In the physical and biological sciences and in mathematics, where he has most successfully applied these methods, he has in a short time accumulated a vast fund of knowledge so reliable as to give him power he has never before had to understand, to predict, and to act. That is why attempts are constantly being made to apply these methods to additional areas of learning and human behavior.

The rapid increase in man's ability to understand and change the world and himself has resulted from increased application of his powers of thought. These powers have proved to be his most potent resource, and, as such, the likely key to his future.

The central purpose of the school

The rational powers of the human mind have always been basic in establishing and preserving freedom. In furthering personal and social effectiveness they are becoming more important than ever. They are central to individual dignity, human progress, and national survival.

The individual with developed rational powers can share deeply in the freedoms his society offers and can contribute most to the preservation of those freedoms. At the same time, he will have the best chance of understanding and contributing to the great events of his time. And the society which best develops the rational potentials of its people, along with their intuitive and aesthetic capabilities, will have the best chance of flourishing in the future. To help every person develop those powers is therefore a profoundly important objective and one which increases in importance with the passage of time. By pursuing this objective, the school can enhance spiritual and aesthetic values and the other cardinal purposes which it has traditionally served and must continue to serve.

The purpose which runs through and strengthens all other educational purposes—the common thread of education—is the development of the ability to think. This is the central purpose to which the school must be oriented if it is to accomplish either its traditional tasks or those newly accentuated by recent changes in the world. To say that it is central is not to say that it is the sole purpose or in all circumstances the most important purpose, but that it must be a pervasive concern in the work of the school. Many agencies contribute to achieving educational objectives, but this particular objective will not be generally attained unless the school focuses on it. In this context, therefore, the development of every student's rational powers must be recognized as centrally important.

Part II   Achieving the Central Purpose

It is no easy matter to adopt school programs to this central purpose. To make an enduring change in a mind which has already had some years of experience is among the most complex of all human enterprises. Although the school's obligation to develop the ability to think is widely accepted, there is much uncertainty as to the procedures most likely to achieve that objective. There is a great need to learn more than is now known about how men think, what rationality and creativity are, how they can be strengthened, and how the opportunities of the school can best be employed to develop whatever rational potential a child may have.

The need for further research

Development of rational powers is unfortunately an area of relative neglect in research. The emphasis of recent research has been on the conditions under which learning occurs and on the pathological aspects of learning in specific situations. The psychology of thinking itself is not well understood. The process of inference, for example, can be described as a leap from a given body of data to a conclusion suggested but not guaranteed by the data, and therefore in need of validation. Although the logic of this process may be thus stated, its psychology remains little known. Considerable research would need to be done before one could, with reasonable assurance, design a program of study that would develop the ability to make valid inferences.

Research by Thorndike, Woodworth, Cattell, James, and others disproved early theories of faculty psychology and mental discipline. But these psychologists did not fully develop a theory on the processes by which knowledge and skills are transferred to new situations and reorganized in new generalizations. Yet such transfer and reorganization obviously occur.

Another gap in research on learning relates to apparent inability, or very low ability, to deal with high-level abstractions. Some pupils appear to lack potential for significant development of the rational powers. Yet, except perhaps in cases of physical damage to the brain, the reasons for this apparent lack are not understood. Psychological studies increasingly reveal unsuspected potential for growth in the development of human beings. Abilities sometimes appear to vary with environment. What is needed is an understanding of the influence of early environment on the susceptibility of the rational powers to development. Ways might then be found to overcome the effects of inadequate early environment.

There is no known upper limit to human ability, and much of what people are capable of doing with their minds is probably unknown today. In this sense, it can hardly be said that any person has ever done the best he can. Research might make possible for all people constantly higher levels of aspiration and attainment.

Thus, in the general area of the development of the ability to think, there is a field for new research of the greatest importance. It is essential that those who have responsibility for management and policy determination in education commit themselves to expansion of such research and to the application of the fruits of this research. This is the context in which the significant answers to such issues as educational technology, length of school year, and content of teacher education must be sought and given. A new emphasis on this field by educational research may be expected to yield great dividends to the individual citizen and to the nation as a whole. And it would endow with greater substance America's belief in freedom and equal opportunity.

Prerequisites of rationality

The school must be guided, in pursuing its central purpose or any other purposes, by certain conditions which are known to be basic to significant mental development. The school has responsibility to establish and maintain these conditions.

One of them is physical health. The sick or poorly nourished pupil, the pupil suffering from poor hearing or vision, is hampered in learning. An adequate physical basis for intellectual life must be assured.

Mental health is also of profound importance. With it, the pupil can have that desire and respect for learning which promote the satisfactory development of his capacity for effective mental performance. Without it, the likelihood of such development is drastically reduced, if not rendered impossible. The pupil who is in rebellion against authority, who feels inadequate, insecure, or unduly apprehensive, is hampered in his learning; and he frequently hampers the learning of others. As the child is helped to view himself and the society in a healthy way, to develop self-discipline, and to feel secure in his relationships, he becomes better able to respond positively to the school.

It is a responsibility of the society to identify and combat the forces which militate against healthy growth, but the school must also deal with the pupil as he is. Rapport must be established with every pupil, and when emotional maladjustment impedes progress or when motivation is lacking, the school must help him cope with his personal difficulties. It must create the conditions in which the school experience can mean something to him. This may require starting from programs with limited use of the higher intellectual processes and planning for him a sequence of stimulating activities to engage and expand his interests and progressively to raise the level at which he is able to attack problems.

The school must be guided in all things by a recognition of human individuality. Each pupil is unique. He is different in background, in interests, moods, and tastes. This uniqueness deeply affects his learning, for he can react to the school only in terms of the person he is. No two pupils necessarily learn the same thing from a common learning experience. The school must not only recognize differences among pupils; it must deal with each pupil as an individual.

While the development of rational powers is central among the several important purposes of the schools provided for all youth, the ability to utilize such opportunity varies considerably. The schools must meet the needs of those who are handicapped in their rational powers by cultural deprivation, low levels of family aspiration, or severely limited endowment. Hence, to take account of these and other individual needs and differences, the schools must and should vary the relative emphasis they place on the development of rational powers among their other important purposes.

Developing rational powers

Although research has not yet yielded a firm base for planning programs to develop intellectual power, the research which has been done, combined with the experience of teachers, does provide some guidance.

The school which develops the ability to think is itself a place where thought is respected and where the humane values implicit in rationality are honored. It has an atmosphere conducive to thinking, and it rewards its pupils for progress toward the goals that it values. Such a school consciously strives to develop its pupils' rational powers. It achieves its goals because it aims directly at them.

The rational powers of any person are developed gradually and continuously as and when he uses them successfully. There is no evidence that they can be developed in any other way. They do not emerge quickly or without effort. The learner of any age, therefore, must have the desire to develop his ability to think. Motivation of this sort rests on feelings of personal adequacy and is reinforced by successful experience. Thus the learner must be encouraged in his early efforts to grapple with problems that engage his rational abilities at their current level of development, and he must experience success in these efforts.

The teacher has the critical role in enabling the student to achieve these successes, selecting problems which are within his grasp, providing clues and cues to their solution, suggesting alternative ways to think about them and assessing continuously the progress of the pupil and the degree of difficulty of the problems before him. Good teaching can help students to learn to think clearly. But this can be done only by careful selection of teaching procedures deliberately adapted to each learner.

Choice as to methods and means of developing the ability to think is necessarily in the hands of the individual teacher. Professional and lay assistance may be brought into the classroom but the intimate awareness of changes in pupils which permits evaluation of progress cannot be possessed by persons who have only limited or irregular contact with the pupils. It is therefore crucial that the teacher possess a thorough knowledge of the material to be taught, a mature mastery of a variety of teaching procedures, an understanding of his pupils, and the quality of judgment that will enable him to blend all in making decisions.

Study of an abstract subject like mathematics or philosophy, in and of itself, does not necessarily enhance rational powers, and it is possible that experiences in areas which appear to have little connection may in fact make a substantial contribution to rational development. As a case in point, the abilities involved in perceiving and recognizing pattern in a mass of abstract data are of considerable importance in learning to analyze, deduce, or infer. These abilities may be developed in the course of mathematical study; but they may be developed as well through experiences in aesthetic, humanistic, and practical fields, which also involve perception of form and design. Music, for example, challenges the listener to perceive elements of form within the abstract. Similarly, vocational subjects may engage the rational powers of pupils.

Also, there is a highly creative aspect in the processes of thought. All the higher mental processes involve more than simple awareness of facts; they depend also on the ability to conceive what might be as well as what is, to construct mental images in new and original ways. Experiences in literature and the arts may well make a larger contribution to these abilities than studies usually assumed to develop abstract thinking.

Further, the processes of thought demand the ability to integrate perceptions of objective phenomena with judgments of value in which subjective emotional commitments are important elements. Perceptions of the feelings of individuals—one's own and those of others— also provide data for the processes of thought. There is no assurance that the ability to perceive or to integrate these varied elements is acquired by abstract study alone.

No particular body of knowledge will of itself develop the ability to think clearly. The development of this ability depends instead on methods that encourage the transfer of learning from one context to another and the reorganization of things learned. The child can transfer learning when he is challenged to give thought to the solution of new problems, problems in which he becomes interested because they are within his range of comprehension, problems that make him strive to use fully his developed and developing abilities.

Although the substance of knowledge does not of itself convey intellectual power, it is the raw material of thought. The ability to think cannot be developed or applied without subject matter. There are two bases for choosing the substantive knowledge which pupils should learn. One is the potential of the knowledge for development of rational powers; the other is the relative importance of the knowledge in the life of the pupil and of society.

The social sciences, for example, provide an excellent opportunity to acquire knowledge which is of considerable importance in daily living and simultaneously to improve the ability to analyze, compare, generalize, and evaluate information. Individual and social interests alike require that the citizen understand the nature and traditions of the free society and that he have skill and insight in studying the issues which his society faces. This requires the tools of the historian, economist, political scientist, sociologist, geographer, and anthropologist. The pupil who learns to use these tools and to integrate the insights to which they lead will improve his ability to think wisely about social problems and to acquire information of significance to himself and his society. He will also develop a sense of the complexity of society and the difficulties which lie in the path of those who would understand it and meet its problems.

The school must foster not only desire and respect for knowledge but also the inquiring spirit. It must encourage the pupil to ask: "How do I know?" as well as "What do I know?" Consequently, the school must help the pupil grasp some of the main methods—the strategies of inquiry—by which man has sought to extend his knowledge and understanding of the world. This requires emphasis on the strategies that have proved most successful. The students should, for example, develop some understanding of the methods of inquiry characteristic of the natural and social sciences. Educators, working with experts in the various disciplines, should choose content on the basis of its appropriateness for developing in pupils of various ages understanding of the various strategies of inquiry.

Application of these strategies of inquiry has led not only to substantive knowledge of the objective world, but also to insights into the nature of reality and of the place of man in the general scheme of things. The free mind is aware of these insights: the astronomer's view of the vastness of space, the physicist's view of the almost infinitesimal, the biologist's view of endless change, the geologist's view of the infinity of time, the historian's view of continuity, the anthropologist's view of human variation.

In acquainting students with the strategies of inquiry, the teacher can further their ability to identify and qualify generalizations, to recognize statements which are not and perhaps cannot be supported by data, to move from data to appropriate generalizations, and to project new hypotheses.

Emphasis on the strategies of inquiry can have the additional effects of arousing appreciation of the competence and work of the masters of these fields of learning and of contributing to the ability to reach the decisions required by responsible citizenship today.

In addition to seeking development of the specific rational powers, the school must help the student extend the areas of his life to which he applies them. Thus the school goes beyond the experiences which develop thinking to encourage the student to think about his environment and himself, to use his mind to make of himself a good citizen and contributing person. Through his ability to perceive form and design he can appreciate the role of beauty in his life. His awareness of his values and his reasoned commitment to them provide him with a basis for looking objectively at his own values and those of others and thus for achieving a moral life. The school should encourage the student to live the life of dignity which rationality fosters.

Part III Conclusion

Individual freedom and effectiveness and the progress of the society require the development of every citizen's rational powers. Among the many important purposes of American schools the fostering of that development must be central.

Man has already transformed his world by using his mind. As he expands the application of rational methods to problems old and new, and as people in growing numbers are enabled to contribute to such endeavors, man will increase his ability to understand, to act, and to alter his environment. Where these developments will lead cannot be foretold.

Man has before him the possibility of a new level of greatness, a new realization of human dignity and effectiveness. The instrument which will realize this possibility is that kind of education which frees the mind and enables it to contribute to a full and worthy life. To achieve this goal is the high hope of the nation and the central challenge to its schools.

Piaget Is Practical

John W. Renner, Judith Brock, Sue Heath, Mildred Laughlin, and Jo Stevens[1]

Piaget's theory of developmental stages has been outlined by E. A. Chittenden in his article, "Piaget and Elementary Science" in *Science and Children*, December 1970, on pages 9–15. In his article, Chittenden discusses factors necessary for cognitive growth which we shall identify in the following text as (1) maturation, (2) experience, (3) disequilibration, and (4) social transmission. Social transmission occurs when children interact with other children and their teacher, but until you provoke a child's mind into a state of doubt there is no disequilibration.

We were interested in employing Piaget's theory in a practical way in our elementary classrooms. In order to do that, however, we needed information about where in Piaget's model, children in the elementary school really are operating. We began our inquiry concerning its usefulness by administering six conservation tasks[2] to 252 children in the Norman, Oklahoma Public Schools with the results shown in Table C–1.

The data shown in Table C–1 demonstrate that all children do not become concrete thinkers on all tasks at the same time. Piaget has said:

> We have followed the accepted custom of considering a test successfully passed when at least 75% of the children of the same age have answered correctly.[3]

If Piaget's procedure is followed, the children in the sample all conserved number by the age of 84 months (seven years). We believe

Reprinted with permission from *Science and Children*, October 1971. Copyright 1971 by the National Science Teachers Association, 1201 Sixteenth Street, N.W., Washington, D.C. 20036.

[1] Renner, John W., Professor of Science Education, University of Oklahoma, and Brock, Judith; Heath, Sue; Laughlin, Mildred; and Stevens, Jo, John F. Kennedy Elementary School, Norman, Oklahoma.

The authors express their gratitude to Leticia Bautista, Norris Grant, James Nickel, Mary Smith, Shirley Stone, and Alta Watson, Science Education Center, College of Education, University of Oklahoma for their valuable assistance.

[2] For a description of the tasks used, see the explanation at the end of this article.

[3] Piaget, Jean. *Judgment and Reasoning in the Child*. Littlefield, Adams and Company, Totowa, New Jersey. 1966. P. 100.

Table C–1

Age—months	Sample size	Conservation of					
		Number	Solid amount	Liquid amount	Length	Area	Weight
60–64	12	3	2	2		1	1
65–68	12	7	2		2	2	3
69–72	12	6	3	4	1	2	1
73–76	12	8	7	7	3	6	3
77–80	12	8	5	5	3	2	6
81–84	12	9	5	5		3	5
85–88	12	11	11	9	6	9	10
89–92	12	11	9	11	9	8	11
93–96	12	9	9	8	7	6	8
97–100	12	12	12	11	9	8	11
101–104	12	12	11	8	5	7	8
105–108	12	11	9	9	7	8	10
109–112	12	11	10	10	7	7	6
113–116	12	11	11	10	7	7	7
117–120	12	12	12	10	7	6	9
121–124	12	9	12	11	7	8	9
125–128	12	11	11	10	9	7	11
129–132	12	12	11	11	12	10	10
133–136	12	12	12	12	8	7	12
137–140	12	12	10	10	10	10	12
141–144	12	12	12	12	12	12	12

NOTE: The number shown in each cell is the number of children at that particular age who demonstrated conservation reasoning on a particular task. The total number of children in the sample was 252.

that to thoroughly understand the concept of number, as opposed to memorizing the digits or how to count, a child must conserve number. Perhaps this will help to explain why some children have trouble with mathematics in the primary grades.

The children in the sample exercised conservation reasoning on solid amount and liquid amount by the age of 88 months (7 years, 4 months). Those two tasks require that a child hold the image of an object in his mind while it is distorted and then be able to recognize that the distorted object still has many of the same properties as the nondistorted one.

These conservation tasks also are excellent indications of the child's ability to reverse his thinking; i.e., to start at one point (equal amounts of liquid), think ahead to another point (same amounts in different sized vessels), do a thinking reversal, and see that the two amounts are still the same. Perhaps that characteristic sheds some light on why some children have difficulty with subtraction. Piaget has stated that not being able to reverse one's thinking is a characteristic of a pre-operational thinker.

The data in Table C–1 show that the children in the sample were not consistent (even using Piaget's 75 percent rule) in their development of the ability to conserve length until 128 months (10 years, 8 months) of age, area until 132 months (11 years), and weight until 120 months (10 years). These data might indicate why elementary school mathematics teachers become frustrated in trying to teach that area = length × width, why trying to teach the use of a ruler to young children is difficult, and why some children seem unable to master a system of weights and measures. Studying when children conserve can influence one's expectations in the classroom; it influenced ours.

The age at which children begin to use conservation reasoning, which means that they are understanding thoroughly any concepts the tasks include, makes a teacher question our present curricula. This teacher might even become thoroughly discouraged and say, "Why do anything if the children are not capable?" Such reasoning is fallacious under our present instructional scheme. The responsibility still lies with the teacher to provide growth experiences for each child. As the data in Table C–1 show, the preoperational child will eventually become concrete in his thinking, but what can his teacher do presently?

The data clearly show that just because a child is seven years old, he has not necessarily left the preoperational stage. Let us consider the following five characteristics of thinking which are characteristics of the preoperational child; i.e., centering irreversibility, egocentrism, inability to see states in a transformation, and transductive reasoning. There are many activities during the course of a normal day which can encourage a child to lose his preoperational characteristics and pass into the state of concrete thinking. A few such experiences which have been successful for us are these:

Treating all points on a continuum equally encourages divergent thinking and thus releases the child from centering.

1. Play "Simon says." This will give the child an opportunity to respond to another point of view.

2. Draw a heavy dot on a sheet of paper. Lightly sketch a familiar object such as a Christmas tree around the dot. Ask the child what he sees. Observe how many children center on the dot. These children need further experiences.

3. Make a ball out of clay or play dough. Flatten it. Give the children an opportunity to make different objects out of the same amount of clay. Discuss which object has the most clay. Children who still have the tendency to center may think that a tall thin or short flat shape have different amounts of clay.

4. Serve the children equal amounts of Kool-Aid in glasses of different sizes and shapes. Have each child choose a glass of Kool-Aid. The children will discuss the reasons for the choice of a particular glass. Have measuring cups available so that the children can measure their Kool-Aid before drinking it. You may be surprised at the number of children who center on the shape of the glass.

5. Have the children classify different colored objects of the same size and shape; i.e., jaw breakers or wooden cubes. This gives them an opportunity to consider more properties than merely size and shape.

A child who cannot continually transpose as he moves forward in his thinking exhibits irreversibility.

1. This activity can be done with a seesaw or a smaller balance device inside the school. Begin with the equipment in balance. Add a child to the seesaw or an object to the balancing device. Ask the child to put it in balance again. If the child can make it even again, he is reversing his thinking.

2. Arrange a group of children in different positions so that one has his hand raised; another has his foot extended. Have a child observe the positions and then leave the area. Another child then changes the positions. The first child comes back and tries to return the children to their original positions. His ability to do this shows a reversal in his thinking.

3. Plant seeds and watch the growth. Later, have the children draw what was planted. Children who cannot reverse their thinking will not picture the original seed.

4. Observing a whole pumpkin, have the children make a jack-o-lantern. Ask one of the children to make the pumpkin look like it did before.

5. Allow the group to observe a container of water. Pour the water into an ice tray and freeze it. A child who is reversing will be able to describe the original state of the water.

Egocentric children need experience in observing from different frames of reference.

1. Place a box somewhere in the classroom. After the children have drawn the box as they observe it from their position, they will move to a new location and draw the box again. By performing this task, the child will be observing an object from a different frame of reference.

2. Have a child stand facing an object in the center of the room. Ask him to stand as he would if he were on the opposite side of the room without actually changing his location. Unless the child is now standing with his back to the object he is not able to observe from a different frame of reference.

3. Give the following directions for a relay game. Place your left arm in the proper sleeve of a coat. Run to the opposite end of the area and return to face the next player. Continue facing the next player until you have removed the coat and he has placed his arm in the proper sleeve. Children who have right and left confusion because they are facing a partner cannot cope with a change in reference frame, but such experiences will help them to develop reversibility in their thinking.

4. Ask the child to record his views on a pertinent problem. Have him interview five people and record their views. It's obvious in this case that the child will be exposed to other points of view.

States in a transformation involve a continuum of thinking in which motion and stages are realized as well as the beginning and ending.

1. Let the children build towers with clay and push them over. Ask them to draw what happened. If the child draws only the beginning and the end and shows no intermediate stages, he does not see states in a transformation.

2. Show a candle to your class. Light it and let it burn. Give the children an opportunity to describe what they saw.

3. Give a child a set of dominoes. Suggest that he stand them on end. Push them over. The child may draw what happened.

4. Mix batter from a cake mix and bake it. As a follow up the children may record data of what happened through sequential pictures.

5. Place a stick of celery in water to which red food coloring has been added. Ask the children to record what they saw.

A child who practices transductive reasoning cannot equate seemingly unrelated parts of a continuum. For example:

Teacher: I wear many green clothes. My car is green. Much of my furniture in my home is green. Keeping this in mind, what do you know about me?

Pupil: You wear glasses.

Some children need activities involving pure logic. You might say or do the following:

1. Encyclopedias are stored in alphabetical order. You are returning Volume C. Where does it go?

2. People wear special clothes for certain activities. As the teacher shows pictures of a football player, nurse, etc., she asks, "What does each person do?"

3. Litmus paper turns red when dipped into an acid. Vinegar is an acid. If I dip litmus paper into vinegar, what color will it be?

4. A quart holds two pints of water. I poured three pints of water into a quart jar. Draw what happened.

5. Select a reel full of tape. Place it on a tape recorder. Have a child choose a take-up reel of the appropriate size from a group of 3–, 5–, and 7–inch black reels.

6. Abe Lincoln and Robert E. Lee lived in the same century. Lee lived in the 1800's. When did Abe Lincoln live?

With statistical data in mind, and activities such as these as a beginning, the practicality of Piaget's ideas is limited only by imagination.

Description of
Conservation Tasks Used

1. Conservation of number.

Six black checkers in one row and six red checkers in another row were arranged for the child.

The child was asked if he agreed that there was the same number of red checkers as there were black checkers. After he agreed to this fact, the red checkers were stacked, one on top of the other, and the black checkers were left as they were:

The child was then asked if there was still the same number of black checkers as there were red checkers and why.

2. Conservation of solid amount.

See Rodger Bybee and Alan McCormack, "Applying Piaget's Theory." **Science and Children** 8: 14-17; December 1970. Task 1, Conservation of Matter.

3. Conservation of liquid amount.

See Bybee and McCormack, Ibid., Task 2, Conservation of Volume. We agree with this test and its use as explained by Bybee and McCormack but believe it reflects conservation of amount rather than volume. There is a specific test designed by Piaget for the conservation of volume.

Figure A–1.

4. Conservation of length.

Place a rod 12 inches long and three other pieces each 4 inches long next to each other. These rods represent two roads. Next, place a toy car at the beginning of each road:

Ask the child if he agrees that both roads are the same length. After he agrees to this fact, pose the problem: "If the cars travel the same speed, which car, the red one or the black one, will reach the end of the road first? Or will they reach the end of the road at the same time?" Record the child's answers. Then move one piece of the three-piece road ahead of the other two pieces, ask the same question, and why.

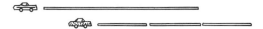

5. Conservation of area.

See Bybee and McCormack, Ibid., Task 7, Conservation of Area.

6. Conservation of weight.

Form two balls of clay equal in size and let the child experience that they weigh exactly the same:

Deform one of the balls of clay to make a pancake and do not let the child handle the clay.

Ask the child which would weigh more, the ball or the pancake, or would they both weigh the same and why.

Index

Achievement tests, standardized, 316
Action(s)
  and logico-mathematical experi-
    ence, 64
  vs. operation, 71
Airplane, paper, lesson plan, 167–168
"Airs" and gases, 274
Animal Activity, 272
Animals
  investigating, 124–129
  modes of living and behavior, 357–
    358
Area, conservation of, 81–82
Astronomy, daytime, 273
Atom, model of, 183
Atomic field, model of, 183
Attitude areas, in pupil evaluation,
  296–297
Attribute games, 286
Authoritarianism vs. inquiry, 106–107

Background and future learning, 242–
  245
Balloons and Gases, 272–273
Batteries and Bulbs, 273
Beans
  and peas, life of, 274–275
  seeds, investigations, 130 131, 132
Becquerel, Henri, case study, 19–22
Beetle environment lesson plan, 180–
  182
Behavior and physiology, human,
  358–359
Berzelius, J. J., 11
Biological sciences, 356–360

Biotic potential, investigating, 135
Bohr, Niels, 2, 183
Bruner, Jerome S., 44, 94, 107, 114,
  156, 200, 219, 348
Bulbs and batteries, 273
Bush, Vannevar, 29
Butler, Nancy Baldwin, 216
Button box lesson plan, 138–139

Centering, 75–76
Changes, 273
Chlamydomonas investigation, 130
Chamberlin, T. C., 21, 171, 228
Charting the Universe, 106, 107
Charts and rocks, 276–277
Children. *See also* Learners; Pupils
  inquiry, teachers, and, 364–369
  ways of involving with science,
    239–241
Classifying, evaluation of, 304–306
Classroom
  flexible inquiry, 245–250
  inquiry-centered, 235–239
Clover seed investigation, 131–132
Cognition and learning, 58–60
Cognitive structure
  factors affecting changes in, 62–67
  learning and, 66
Communities, 264
Conservation, 78–79
  of area, 81–82
  of length, 82
  of liquid, 80
  of number, 79–80
  reasoning, 395–396

Conservation (*continued*)
  of solid amounts, 80–81, 342
  tasks, 400–401
  of volume, 343
  of weight, 82–83, 342
Contradictions, elimination of,
  343–344
Crystal structure, Pasteur study of,
  5–9
Curie, Marie, case study, 22–30
Curie, Pierre, 22–29 *passim*
Curriculum
  facts and, 289–291
  responsibility for, 218–219

Daphnia investigation, 126–127
Data interpretation, 121, 123, 174–182
Daytime Astronomy, 273
Detritus, 260
Development. *See* Intellectual de-
  velopment; Mental development;
  Preoperational development
Dewey, John, 43, 45, 105, 234–235
Discovery, 208–211
  in inquiry teaching, 112
  and intellectual development, 66
Dumas, Jean Baptiste André, 27

Ecosystem, 256
Ecosystems, 265
Education
  achieving central purpose of,
    387–393
  in American society, 379–387
  commonality in, 37–38
  freedom of mind in, 46–50
  information acquisition, 44–46
  mental development, 38–44
  "Old Deluder, Satan" law, 36
Educational Policies Commission,
  32, 33, 173, 177, 211, 221, 230,
  268, 368, 379
Egocentrism, 72–73
Ehrlich, Paul, 333
Einstein, Albert, 2
Elementary schools
  evaluating science curricula,
    316–320
  placing essential experiences in,
    197–202

Elementary Science Study (ESS), 253,
  269–278, 283–284, 285
  activities, 286–288
Energy, 255
Energy Sources, 264
Environments, 263
Equilibrium and learning, 60–62
Evaluation
  of elementary school science cur-
    ricula, 316–320
  of experimenting, 307–310
  of pupils, 293–316
  of teachers, 320–322
  testing techniques of, 348–349
Exclusion, operation of, 99–100
Experience(s)
  essential, placing in elementary
    schools, 197–202
  and intellectual development,
    63–64
  logico-mathematical, 64
  physical, 63–64
Experimenting, 157–172
  evaluation of, 307–310
Exploration, 205–206
  in inquiry teaching, 112
  and intellectual development, 65

Facts and curriculum, 289–291
Fermentation, Pasteur study of, 9–18
Feynman, Richard P., 2
Force and motion, 354–356
Formal operations in intellectual
  development, 93
Formal operational thinker. *See*
  Operational thinker
Friot, Faith Elizabeth, 91, 101
Fruit flies investigation, 125–126

Gardner, John W., 36
Gases
  and balloons, 272–273
  properties of, 352
Gases and "Airs," 274
Geo-blocks, 286
Geometry, 363
Germination of seeds, 359–360
Graphing, 362
Growing Seeds, 274
Guppies, experiments with, 375–376

Hawkins, David, 285
Heat and temperature, 354
Holt, John, 247, 284
Human behavior and physiology,
   358–359
Hutchins, Robert M., 290
Hypothesis
   formation of, 30–31, 169–172
   vs. prediction, 192
   verification of, 31–32

Information, acquisition of, 44–46
Inhelder, Barbel, 58, 100, 342
Inquiry
   vs. authoritarianism, 106–107
   children, teachers, and, 364–369
   defined, 59–60
   in elementary school science,
      114–117
   flexible, 245–250
   and learning, 59–60
   and science teaching, 107–114
   and teaching methods, 326–328
Intellectual development. *See also*
      Mental development; Preopera-
      tional development
   experience and, 63–64
   exploration and, 65
   language and, 62–63
   maturation and, 62
   Piaget's stages-of-development
      model, 67–96
   social transmission and, 63
Interaction and Systems, 260–261
Interaction concept, lesson plan on
   inventing, 206–208
Interpretation of data, 121, 123,
   174–182
Interpreting, evaluation of, 310–312
Interview, semiformal, in pupil
   evaluation, 301–314
Invention, 206–208
   in inquiry teaching, 112
   of scientific models, lesson plan,
      184–186
Investigation
   criteria for selecting topics, 217
   life science, 125–135
   physical science, 117–125
   responsibility for continuing,
      221–233

responsibility for selecting topics,
   216–221
Irreversibility, 74–75
Isopods
   environment lesson plan, 162–166
   investigations, 128–129

Jacobson, Willard, 2

Karplus, Elizabeth F., 91, 101, 102
Karplus, Robert, 53, 96, 101, 102, 223,
   224, 239, 244, 249, 324, 326
Kitchen Physics, 274

Lake measurement lesson plans,
   148–155
Language and intellectual development, 62–63
Learners. *See also* Children; Pupils
   correcting wrong concepts of,
      176–177
   functions in inquiry-centered
      classroom, 113
Learning
   and cognition, 58–60
   and cognitive structure, 66
   environment, 211–216
   equilibrium and, 60–62
   future, background and, 242–245
   and inquiry, 59–60
   interaction and structure, 56–58
   Piaget's model of, 56–67
Length, conservation of, 82
Lenses investigation, 118–119
Lesson plan
   aluminum and copper chloride
      solution, 208–210
   beetles environment, 180–182
   experimenting with common
      objects, 205–206
   first-grade science, 86–87
   Grandma's button box, 138–139
   inventing the interaction concept,
      206–208
   inventing scientific models, 184–186
   inventing water cycle, 187–189
   isopods environment, 162–166
   measurement of lakes, 148–155
   object hunt, 140–141
   paper airplane making, 167–168

Lesson plan (*continued*)
  predicting angle of stopper popper,
    193–196
  predicting variation in raisin bread,
    190–191
  rock candy and sugar cubes,
    161–162
Levers investigation, 119–121
Life Cycles, 260, 261
Life of Beans and Peas, 274–275
Life science investigations, 125–135
Liquids
  conservation of, 80
  and their properties, 350–352
Listening, 212
Living things, observing and
    describing, 356–357
Locke, John, 41
Logico-mathematical experience, 64

Manolakes, George, 294
Material Objects, 88–90, 140, 169, 258,
    288–289, 364, 365, 366
Materials, importance in investiga-
    tion, 222–223
Mathematics, 360–363
Matter, 255
Maturation and intellectual develop-
    ment, 62
McElroy, William, 36
McKinnon, Joe W., 91, 95, 101
Mealworms
  behavior of, 273
  experiments with, 169, 219, 246–247
  interpretation of data on, 178–179
  investigations, 127–128
Measurement, 142–157, 361–362
  investigations, 117–118
  variation and, 149, 190
Measuring, evaluation of, 306–307
Mental development, *See also*
    Intellectual development
  classical view, 38–42
  modern view, 42–44
Microbiology, 359
Microgardening, 275
Mirror Cards, 286
Model(s)
  atom, 183
  atomic field, 183
  building, 182–189

learning, 56–67
lesson plan for "inventing,"
    184–186
scientific, 257–258
stages of development, 67–96
*Models: Electric and Magnetic Inter-
    action*, 265–266
Motion
  and force, 354–356
  and relative position, 262–263
Musical Instruments Recipe Book,
    275
Mystery Powders, 275–276

National Education Association, 35
Noise and productivity in classroom,
    237–238
Notation and numbers, 361
Number(s)
  conservation of, 79–80
  and notation, 361

Object hunt lesson plan, 140–141
Observation, 137–142
  evaluation of, 303–304
Observing an Animal, 287–288
Operation vs. action, 71
Operational thinkers, 90–100
  research in identifying, 100–104
Operation of exclusion, 99–100
Operations and logico-mathematical
    experience, 64
Orderliness and productivity in
    classroom, 235–237
Organism, living, 255–256
Organisms, 259–260

Paper airplane lesson plan, 167–168
Particles and peas, 276
Pasteur, Louis, case study, 4–19
Pasteurization, 9–18
Pattern Blocks, 286–287
Peas and beans, life of, 274–275
Peas and Particles, 276
Pendulum investigation, 118
Peterson, Rita, 102, 324, 326
Phenix, Phil H., 243
Phillips, John L., Jr., 60, 61, 67, 72, 93
Physical sciences, 350–356
  investigations, 117–125
Physics, kitchen, 274

Physiology and human behavior, 358–539

Piaget, Jean, 43, 85, 91, 93, 100, 169, 198, 201, 341, 342, 348, 365, 366, 394, 396, 399
  learning model, 56–67
  and science teaching, 323–326
  stages-of-development model, 67–96

Plant growth, 359–360
  measuring, 143–145

Plants, investigations of, 129–135

Platt, John R., 17, 18, 21

Poincaré, J. H., 3

Polonium, Curie discovery of, 25

Pond Water, 276

Populations, 262

Porterfield, Denzil, 368–639

Position, relative motion and, 262–263

Powders, mystery, 275–276

Prediction, 189–197
  evaluation of, 312–314

Preoperational development, 70–77

Preoperational thinker, identifying, 77–90

Probability, 362

Problem identification and hypothesis formation, 30–31

Productivity in classroom
  and noise, 237–238
  and orderliness, 235–237

Properties, 256
  changes in, 352–354
  gases, 352
  solids and liquids, 350–352

Pupils. *See also* Children; Learners
  evaluation of, 293–316
  involvement of, 239–241
  out-of-doors activities, 247–249

Questions, importance in investigation, 223–230

Radiation, Curie experiments, 22–29

Radium, Curie discovery of, 26–27

Raisin bread, lesson plan on predicting variation in, 190–191

Rationality, prerequisites of, 389–390

Rational powers
  developing, 48–50, 390–392
  role of, 382–385

science and, 50–52

Reciprocal implication task, 98–99

Relative Position and Motion, 262–263

Renner, John W., 91, 95, 101

Rock candy and sugar cubes experiment lesson plan, 161–162

Rocks and Charts, 276–277

Roller, Duane, 2

Röntgen, Wilhelm, 19

Rye grass investigation, 133

Schmidt, Frederick B., 367–368

School, purpose of, 386–387

Science
  biological, 356–360
  curricula evaluation, 316–320
  curriculum of the future, 334–337
  defined, 1–30
  inquiry and teaching of, 107–114
  inquiry in, 114–117
  investigations, 117–135
  lesson plan for first-grade, 86–87
  life, 125–135
  nature of, 3–4
  objectives, 52–54
  physical, 117–125, 350–356
  Piaget on teaching of, 323–326
  processes of, 30–34
  and rational powers, 50–52
  spirit of, 328
  teaching and research results, 346–348
  teaching structure of, 329–332
  ways of involving children with, 239–241

Science—A Process Approach (SAPA), 253, 278–283
  concepts in, 350–363

Science Curriculum Improvement Study (SCIS), 141, 253, 254–268, 283–84, 288, 294, 364. *See also* *Material Objects*

Science teaching. *See* Teaching

Scientific literacy, need for 332–334

Scientist, first-grade, 374–379

Seeds
  bean, 130–131, 132
  clover, 131–132
  germination, 359–360
  growing, 274

Self-regulation and logico-mathematical experience, 64
Sensory-motor development, 68–70
Small Things, 277
Smedslund, Jan, 96
Social transmission and intellectual development, 63
Solid amounts, conservation of, 80–81, 342
Solids and their properties, 350–352
Solubility investigation, 123–124
Stafford, Donald G., 364, 366
Stages-of-development model, Piaget's, 67–96
States in a transformation, 76–77
Stendler, Celia B., 198
Stimulus-response learning model, 59
Stopper popper angle, lesson plan on "predicting," 193–196
Structures, 277–278
Students. *See* Children; Learners; Pupils
Subsystem, 257
Subsystems and Variables, 261–262
System(s), 257
    and interaction, 260–261
Szent-Györgyi, Albert, 243, 244, 370

Tangrams, 286
Teacher(s)
    evaluation of, 320–322
    functions in inquiry-centered classroom, 113
    inquiry, children, and, 364–369

Teaching
    evaluation in, 293
    and expanding knowledge, 370–374
    and inquiry, 107–114, 326–328
    and research results, 346–348
    of science, Piaget and, 323–326
    structure of science, 329–332
Temperature and heat, 354
Thier, Herbert D., 239, 244, 249
Thompson, Sir. J. J., 183
Transduction, 77

Uranium, Becquerel experiments with, 19-22

Variables
    exclusion of irrelevant, 344
    and subsystems, 261–262
Variation and Measurement, 149, 190
Volume, conservation of, 343
von Liebig, Justus, 11

Water cycle, lesson plan for inventing, 187–189
Water investigation, 124–125
Weight, conservation of, 82–83, 342
Whistles and Strings, 278
Whitehead, Alfred N., 45
Wilson, John H., 366–367
Wohler, Friedrick, 12
Wohlwill, Joachim, 374
Written work in pupil evaluation, 297–301

72 73 74 75 76   9 8 7 6 5 4 3 2 1